Political Islam from
Muhammad to Ahmadinejad

Political Islam from Muhammad to Ahmadinejad

Defenders, Detractors, and Definitions

JOSEPH MORRISON SKELLY, EDITOR

Foreword by Bernard Lewis

PRAEGER SECURITY INTERNATIONAL
An Imprint of ABC-CLIO, LLC

A B C CLIO

Santa Barbara, California • Denver, Colorado • Oxford, England

Copyright 2010 by Joseph Morrison Skelly

All rights reserved. No part of this publication may be reproduced, stored in
a retrieval system, or transmitted, in any form or by any means, electronic,
mechanical, photocopying, recording, or otherwise, except for the inclusion of brief
quotations in a review, without prior permission in writing from the publisher.

Library of Congress Cataloging-in-Publication Data

Political Islam from Muhammad to Ahmadinejad : defenders, detractors, and definitions /
Joseph Morrison Skelly, editor ; foreword by Bernard Lewis.
    p. cm.
    Includes bibliographical references and index.
    ISBN 978-0-313-37223-0 (hardcover : alk. paper) — ISBN 978-0-313-37224-7 (ebook)
  1. Islam and politics—History. I. Skelly, Joseph Morrison.
    BP173.7.P653 2010
    320.5′57—dc22   2009031610

ISBN: 978-0-313-37223-0
EISBN: 978-0-313-37224-7

14 13 12 11 10   1 2 3 4 5

This book is also available on the World Wide Web as an eBook.
Visit www.abc-clio.com for details.

Praeger Security International
An Imprint of ABC-CLIO, LLC

ABC-CLIO, LLC
130 Cremona Drive, P.O. Box 1911
Santa Barbara, California 93116–1911

This book is printed on acid-free paper ∞

Manufactured in the United States of America

Copyright Acknowledgments
The editor and publisher gratefully acknowledge permission for use of the following
material:
    Philip Carl Salzman, "Balanced Opposition: The Tribal Foundations of Arab Middle East-
ern Islamic Culture," reprinted from Philip Carl Salzman, *Culture and Conflict in the Middle
East* (Amherst, NY: Humanity Books, 2008), 9–16, 137–48, 159–60. Copyright 2008 by Philip
Carl Salzman. All rights reserved. Adapted and reprinted with permission of the author and
publisher.
    Robert P. Barnidge, Jr., "War and Peace: Negotiating Meaning in Islam," reprinted with
permission. Originally published as "War and Peace: Negotiating Meaning in Islam," *Critical
Studies on Terrorism* 1, no. 2 (2008): 263–78, http://www.informaworld.com.
    Joseph C. Myers, "The Quranic Concept of War," reprinted with permission. Originally
published as Joseph C. Myers, "The Quranic Concept of War," *Parameters: U.S. Army War
College Quarterly* 36, no. 4 (Winter 2006–07): 108–21.

Contents

Acknowledgments

I wish to thank the staff of the Association for the Study of the Middle East and Africa for their tireless assistance, especially David Silverstein, Patrick Creamer, Kaitlyn Reif, and Caitlyn Walters. I am deeply grateful to the founders of the Association, Professor Bernard Lewis and Professor Fouad Ajami, for their sustained guidance and unremitting support. I wish to express my gratitude to the following ASMEA officials for their leadership and counsel: Mark T. Clark, President; J. Peter Pham, Vice President; and the members of the Academic Council: Leslie H. Gelb, Victor Davis Hanson, David S. Landes, Robert J. Lieber, Fedwa Malti-Douglas, Gerard Prunier, Secretary George P. Shultz, Kenneth Stein, and Bassam Tibi. Several scholars contributed to the success of the Association's inaugural conference in Washington, DC, in April 2008, including Donovan Chau, James Mabry, Richard Saccone, Kim Shienbaum, Kemal Silay, and Norman Stillman.

At Praeger Security International, the editorial, production, design, and marketing teams have lent inspired support to this project from inception to completion, especially Anthony Chiffolo, Steve Catalano, Elizabeth Potenza, Nicole Azze, Valentina Tursini, Nancy Cambareri, and Devon Hay.

I greatly appreciate the efforts of Dr. Timothy R. Furnish, who assisted with the early stages of the publication of this book. I value the insights of my academic colleagues, including David Gordon of the City University of New York, David Gregory of Saint John's University School of Law, William Cobert of Manhattan, Richard English of Queen's University Belfast, Iain Atack of Trinity College Dublin, and, at the College of

Mount Saint Vincent, Brother Daniel Adams, Kathleen Bonner, Mayra Figueroa, Mary Fuller, Dianne Hopkins, Evelyn Lopez, Cathryn McCarthy, Edward Meyer, Jeanne Papazian, Lillian Ruane-Kiely, Ron Scapp, and Odalia Taveras.

Abbreviations

DC	District Commissioner
EAP	East African Protectorate
IAEA	International Atomic Energy Agency
ILSA	Iran-Libya Sanctions Act
IRGC	Iranian Revolutionary Guards Corps
ISA	Iran Sanctions Act
ISG	Iraq Study Group
KAR	King's African Rifles
MOIS	Ministry of Intelligence and Security (Iran)
NFD	Northern Frontier District
NIAC	National Iranian-American Council
PBO	Plan and Budget Organization (Iran)
PIJ	Palestinian Islamic Jihad
PRISM	Project for the Research of Islamist Movements

Foreword

I welcome the opportunity to reflect on this new and important collection of essays exploring the theme of political Islam. The authors in this volume are members of the Association for the Study of the Middle East and Africa (ASMEA). Their chapters are based on papers presented to the organization's inaugural conference in Washington, DC, in April 2008. Its mission is to promote the highest standards of academic research and teaching in the fields of Middle Eastern and African studies. It is a response to the growing interest in these interrelated subjects and the absence of any single group addressing them in a comprehensive, multidisciplinary fashion. In its short life, it has already had a salutary effect on scholarship and public debate vis-à-vis Africa and the Middle East.

ASMEA is located squarely within the Western intellectual tradition. As chairman of its academic council, I highlighted this feature in my keynote address to the inaugural conference by drawing upon the insights of one of eighteenth-century England's finest writers, Samuel Johnson. I said, on that occasion:

> I wish to situate our profession, the academic study of the Middle East, in a historical context. And I would like to begin with a quotation from the famous Dr. Johnson, from one of his conversations recorded by Boswell. He says, "A generous and elevated mind is distinguished by nothing more certainly than an eminent degree of curiosity. Nor is that curiosity ever more agreeably or usefully employed than in examining the laws and customs of foreign nations." A very interesting statement, I feel, and as I shall try to demonstrate, one uniquely Western, uniquely distinctive of this Western Civilization of which we are the heirs at the present time. And I use the word "we" in the widest sense.

The members of ASMEA share Dr. Johnson's "eminent degree of curiosity" and endorse the idea of a liberal academic community dedicated to the study of the Middle East and Africa. Due to their efforts, these two fields are being reformed, renewed, and infused by a new spirit of free academic inquiry.

This volume, the first of what promises to be a steady stream of scholarly publications from ASMEA and its members, epitomizes the intellectual curiosity that Dr. Johnson considered essential to "a generous and elevated mind." Its concentration on the evolution of political Islam, or Islamism, is timely. In it, academic experts explore various dimensions of this ideology. The manner in which they do so is significant, for they successfully overcome obstacles to the study of the Islamic world that I identified in my address to the ASMEA conference. These hurdles include a combination of political correctness and multiculturalism that has established orthodoxies in the academy and a degree of thought control, or limitations on freedom of expression, without parallel in the democratic West since the eighteenth century. The deadly hand of political correctness, in other words, has asphyxiated the rational discussion of Islam, which is harmful not only to the West, but to the Islamic world as well.

The contributors to this volume, however, are not dissuaded from grappling with some of the most vexing questions posed by the phenomenon of political Islam. That they do so in a professional manner, in a spirit of tolerant, open-minded scholarly inquiry, is to their credit. It is also one of the many reasons why I recommend this collection. In it readers will discover not only some of the detours down which Islamism has taken one of the world's great religions, but also signs pointing toward the renaissance of an enlightened Islamic civilization.

Bernard Lewis
Princeton, NJ
April 2009

PART I

Introduction

CHAPTER 1

Political Islam from Muhammad to Ahmadinejad

Joseph Morrison Skelly

Eight years after the terrorist attacks of September 11, 2001, the propensity of radical adherents of Islam to transform their religion into a political ideology continues unabated. The outcome of this convergence is known as political Islam. Today, people throughout the world seek a fuller comprehension of this synthesis, which is also called Islamism. This collection of essays responds to that imperative. The fusion of Islam and politics is its central theme. It examines a series of chapters in the evolution of political Islam from the era of the Prophet Muhammad to the presidency of Mahmoud Ahmadinejad. An accomplished array of international scholars carry out this task from the interdisciplinary perspectives of anthropology, philosophy, theology, history, economics, political science, and international relations. They illuminate various stages in the politicization of Islam. They also articulate viable reform models that may assist an enlightened Islam to navigate through the many challenges it confronts at the outset of the twenty-first century.

The features of this volume enable it to elucidate several interrelated dimensions of Islamism. Its historical framework, which encompasses events from the lifetime of Muhammad to the Umayyad and Abbasid dynasties to jihad in colonial Africa to the emergence of militant Islam today, addresses the fact that while a politicized Islam is generally understood as a reaction to the trauma of modernity in the Middle East,[1] some of its roots can be traced to earlier stages of the religion. This book's geographical scope comprises case studies in Somalia, Egypt, Ghana, Iran, Iraq, Palestine, and Pakistan. It assesses important Islamist theorists, early writers like Ibn Taymiyya and Ibn Khaldun and contemporary defenders such as Abul A'ala Mawdudi, Sayyid Qutb, Sayyid Imam, and Ayman al-Zawahiri. It examines Sunni Salafism, Saudi Wahhabism, and Shi'a Mahdism. It considers the nature of the theocratic regimes in medieval Arabia and modern Iran. It interrogates extremist doctrines like jihad, *istishhad* (deliberate martyrdom), and *takfir*, and investigates terrorist groups such as al-Qaeda, Palestinian Islamic Jihad, Hamas, Hezbollah, and the Iranian Revolutionary Guards Corps.

Against this background, the contributors to this collection engage in the robust scholarly debate regarding political Islam that has been underway since well before 9/11. Their essays are best read in this academic context, that is, the work of experts such as Bernard Lewis, Daniel Pipes, Walid Phares, Bassam Tibi, John L. Esposito, Graham Fuller, and their many colleagues.[2] These specialists have distilled a range of conclusions. Some, such as Olivier Roy, Ray Takeyh, and Nikolas K. Gvosdev, have argued that Islamism has been overestimated.[3] Others, like Samuel Huntington, insisted long before September 11, 2001, that it was not being taken seriously enough.[4] Fawaz A. Gerges has evaluated political Islam's relationship with the United States.[5] Beverley Milton-Edwards and Peter Mandaville have analyzed its impact on international affairs.[6] Mohammed Ayoob has explored its variations in the Muslim world.[7] Bernard Lewis has assessed its political terminology.[8] Gilles Kepel, David Cook, and Laurent Murawiec have contested the meaning of jihad.[9] Daniel Pipes has properly emphasized the imperative of supporting moderate Muslims.[10] Numerous scholars have explored paths that may reconcile Islam with democracy—and thus the modern age.[11] The authors in this volume participate in all of these discussions and, at the same time, add to the corpus of scholarly literature in meaningful ways.

Before turning to the specific contents of this book, a word about definitions will be helpful. Islamism, according to Daniel Pipes, "has three main features: a devotion to sacred law, a rejection of Western influences, and a turning of faith into ideology."[12] It signifies a belief in the inseparability of Islam and politics. In its approach to government, it advocates the establishment of an Islamic state ruled by Shari'a law. Adherents of Islamism are called Islamists. Some are willing to work patiently, if not relentlessly, for the establishment of an Islamic theocracy, like the followers of Fethullah Gülen in the Republic of Turkey, who threaten the secular government in that country.[13] But many Islamists, as we know, endorse the use of violence and terror to achieve their goal of an Islamic state, such as the members of al-Qaeda and the Taliban. Thus Islamism is also equated with militant Islam, radical Islam, or jihadism.

Islamism, however, should not be confused with Islam, per se, one of the world's great religions. Daniel Pipes draws a distinction between radical and traditional Islam. "Although militant Islam is often seen as a form of traditional Islam," he notes, "it is something profoundly different—and far more dangerous. Traditional Islam seeks to teach human beings how to live in accord with God's will; militant Islam aspires to create a new order."[14] Islamists, therefore, should not be confused with devout mainstream Muslims who eschew violence and the merging of mosque and state. While there is no such thing as a moderate Islamist, there are moderate Muslims. Jihadists, in fact, often target their orthodox co-religionists. "As an ideology," Pipes concludes, "militant Islam can claim none of the sanctity that Islam the religion enjoys."[15]

FROM MUHAMMAD TO AHMADINEJAD

This collection is divided into several parts. Following this introductory section, the essays in Part II address the early origins of politicized Islam. In chapter 2, "Balanced Opposition: The Tribal Foundations of Arab Middle Eastern Islamic Culture," the acclaimed anthropologist Philip Carl Salzman demonstrates how the tribal form of social control known as balanced opposition was an important driving force in the early expansion of Islam and, since then, has been "a dominant theme in Arab culture, a central structure in Arab society, and a fundamental principle of political Islam." How does it work? "If there is a confrontation, everyone unites with closer kin against more distant kin, so that small groups unite to face opposing small groups, middle-sized groups unite to face opposing middle-sized groups, or large groups unite to face opposing large groups: family versus family, lineage versus lineage, clan versus clan, tribe versus tribe, confederacy versus confederacy, sect versus sect, and the Islamic community, *umma*, versus the infidels." Applied to historical events, balanced opposition helps to account, in part, for the early expansion of Islam, about which Salzman is quite forthright. By opposing "the Muslim to the infidel, and the *Dar al-Islam*, the land of Islam and peace, to the *Dar al-Harb*, the land of the infidels and conflict," Muhammad offered the tribes on the Arabian Peninsula a "common interest and common project," thus ensuring unity and rapid growth.

The next two essays build on these themes. David Cook analyzes one of Islam's initial conquests through a religious prism in chapter 3, "Why Did Muhammad Attack the Byzantines? A Re-examination of Quran *Sura* 30:1–2." He first discerns Muslim empathy for the Byzantines in these two verses, but then cuts to "the heart of the problem," namely, "why is it that with this strong sympathy for the Christian Byzantines inside the Quran that the Byzantines were the first targets for the early Muslim polity to attack in 629–32 and later? One must ask the reason for this sudden change in policy." His conclusion is quite compelling. "I would propose that the background for this sudden change should be seen in the triumphal return of the True Cross by the Byzantine Emperor Heraclius in 629 [or 630] and the identification of the Christians as polytheists as opposed to some previous perception of them as fellow monotheists." In other words, the first "Muslim attacks were actually theological in nature." "This view," Cook acknowledges, "is not a common one among the standard histories of the early conquests," but it is an interpretation, he persuasively argues, that properly understands how "[t]hese invasions complete a logical process during which, according to the Muslim perception of events, Christians deliberately provoked retribution by their obscene veneration of the True Cross in the holy city of Jerusalem." In chapter 4, "Challenging the Islamist Politicization of Islam: The Non-Islamic Origins of Muslim Political Concepts," Sherko Kirmanj interrogates Islamists, both medieval and modern, who "sanctify their message with a religious gloss," especially by claiming that their political doctrines such as *shura* (consultation), *hilf* (pact), *anfal* (war-booty), and the caliphate "are derived from Islamic scriptural sources, primarily the Quran." On the contrary, Kirmanj argues, "a close scrutiny of the historical roots and cultural origins of these Muslim political practices shows that they are based on pre-Islamic Arab tribal traditions as well as Iranian and Byzantine political concepts; they are not exclusively Islamic, in other words." Like Salzman, Kirmanj uncovers some of the tribal impulses that permeate political Islam; he goes on to identify policies inherited from foreign empires; he then links both to contemporary Islamist political principles.

In Part III, two scholars offer new ways to interpret Islamism in an era of persistent hostilities. In chapter 5, "War and Peace: Negotiating Meaning in Islam," Robert P. Barnidge, Jr. highlights how in the recent past "a passionate politics has played out in attempts to understand Islam, particularly as relates to espousals of radical, Islamically articulated challenges to the status quo and prevailing institutional structures." Rather than relying on the simplified dichotomy of whether the religion is one of peace or one of war, Barnidge's chapter advocates on behalf of a new paradigm. "It argues that the varied experiences of those who act in the name of Islam and justify their actions according to the life of Mohammad and devotion to Allah require a new and radical framework, a framework that prioritizes diversity and a decentralized ethic of understanding over homogenization and hegemonization and avoids postcolonial constructions of inevitable inferiority and weakness." This conceptual apparatus "has the advantage of being more methodologically satisfying because it can better account for and deal with the diverse perspectives and complexities in the debate and better appreciate the political implications and undertones inherent in the practice of interpretation."

In the following chapter, "The Quranic Concept of War," Joseph C. Myers analyzes a contemporary theory of conflict relevant to the main themes of this book. The starting points for his assessment are two crucial questions about Islamists: "Is there a philosophy or treatise such as

Clausewitz's *On War* that attempts to form their thinking about war? Is there a document that can be reviewed and understood in such a manner that we may begin to think strategically about our opponent?" His reply: "There is one work that stands out from the many," that is, *The Quranic Concept of War* by Brigadier S. K. Malik of the Pakistani Army. This Islamist text is important to consider, Myers reminds us, for the source of Malik's ideas, the Quran, "places warfighting doctrine and its theory in a much different category than Western thinkers are accustomed to, because it is not a theory of war derived from man, but from God."

Part IV focuses on manifestations of Islamism in Africa, past and present, with special attention paid to jihad, the operative form of the Quranic theory of war, which has had a long presence on the continent. In chapter 7, "Mad Mullahs and the Pax Britannica: Islam as a Factor in Somali Resistance to British Colonial Rule," George L. Simpson, Jr., examines the role of jihad, as spearheaded by Maxamed Cabdulle Xasan and his Dervishes, in resistance to colonial rule in British Somaliland from 1899 to 1920. His "central thesis is that the centripetal potential of political Islam as an integrating, proto-nationalist force as well as a means of primary resistance to colonialism proved incapable of overcoming centrifugal, particularistic Somali institutions such as clan and kinship bonds and *xeer*, or customary law." In the past, while "scholars have emphasized the difficulty Islamism has faced overcoming ethnic barriers in an acephalous society composed of segmentary lineage groups, they have failed to emphasize fully the degree to which militant Islamism historically has proved a procrustean fit to other traditional Somali institutions." At the same time, Simpson deflates the nationalist myth that envelops Maxamed Cabdulle Xasan, or "the Sayyid," noting that the jihad he instigated resulted in the deaths of more than one-third of the male population of Somaliland.

Daniel Lav, in chapter 8, "Jihadists and Jurisprudents: The 'Revisions' Literature of Sayyid Imam and Al-Gama'a Al-Islamiyya," studies "the writings and polemics associated with two Egyptian groups that have now officially called off their war on the Egyptian regime and have expressed criticism of other jihad groups such as al-Qaeda," for they are "a particularly fertile and promising area of study in that they themselves explicitly raise the issue of what constitutes normative Islam and whether the jihadist movement has deviated from it." His main argument is that while the latter organization, al-Gama'a al-Islamiyya, "has ceased to view the Egyptian government as apostate, and thus the issue of jihad against it does not even arise," the Jihad group under the leadership of Sayyid Imam "seems to still hold that the government is apostate. Thus for him the obligation to wage jihad against the regime remains in force" in principle. At the same time, certain "suspension mechanisms" have come into play in the light of current conditions in Egypt, so jihadists are temporarily "exempt from their obligation to fight . . . jihad at the present time is judged to do more harm than good." Still, future circumstances might once again make jihad compulsory. In the next chapter, "*Takfir* as a Tool for Instigating Jihad Among Muslims: The Ghanaian Example," Mohammed Hafiz laments how discord has split the Islamic community in that country over the past three decades. While recent studies have addressed elements of this unsettled era, such as latent tribal tensions, the author posits that "another force was also responsible for dividing Muslims in Ghana. An ideological fissure opened up between the Ahlus Sunnah and the Tijaniyya sects when Islamic revivalists in the former camp, in a bid to revive what they deemed true Islam, transgressed acceptable limits by implicitly pronouncing *takfir* on their co-religionists." He therefore examines "the role that *takfir* played in fomenting strife" and "the peril that it poses to Muslim harmony" in Ghana today.

Part V assesses contemporary dimensions of politicized Islam in three countries in the Middle East. Ofira Seliktar, in chapter 10, "Reading Tehran in Washington: The Problems of Defining the Fundamentalist Regime in Iran and Assessing the Prospects for Political Change," sheds light on the inscrutable nature of the Iranian government. "From its inception," she notes, it "has defied classification, triggering a fierce debate among observers. This lack of consensus stems from the difficulty of Western analysts to comprehend key features of the Islamic Republic, aggravated by the limits of Western political vocabulary." Is it an Islamic theocracy, an Islamic police state, an Islamofascist regime, a clerical oligarchy, or even a theodemocracy? An alternative framework is better. "Using Max Weber's analysis of political authority," Seliktar argues, "the Iranian clerics have evolved a unique hybrid political system that reflects Islamist and European elements. The sheer intricacy, confusion, and unpredictability of this system have repeatedly confounded Iran watchers and made assessment of political change difficult."

In the next chapter, "The Modern Impact of Mahdism and the Case of Iraq," Timothy R. Furnish explores the effect of recent events such as the election of Mahmoud Ahmadinejad as president of Iran, the terrorist attacks of 9/11, and the subsequent wars in Iraq and Afghanistan on the status of Mahdism in the Middle East. He believes that they have "revivified Twelver Shi'a Mahdism in Iraq and Iran . . . while at the same time heightening Sunni Mahdist fervor around the globe." He asks two central questions about Mahdist organizations in Iraq and the region at large—that is, will the Mahdism of the Ansar al-Mahdi, Jund al-Sama', and Jaysh al-Mahdi "switch from defensive to offensive jihad? And, will Mahdism spread from Shi'a Iraq to the larger Sunni world?" His answers are significant. For example, while Mahdists may conclude that "it might be permissible soon to move from defensive to offensive jihad . . . even if that official step is not taken, several aspects of Twelver defensive jihad . . .

should give us pause," not least its approach to treaties and the treatment of Muslims who "aid the unbelievers." In chapter 12, "Palestinian Precedents: The Origins of Al-Qaeda's Use of Suicide Terrorism and *Istishhad,*" Benjamin T. Acosta analyzes how a Sunni terrorist organization came to utilize in Iraq a tactic "with operational roots in Shi'a Iran and southern Lebanon." The link is found in Palestine. The use of large-scale homicide bombings "required significant preparation before its exportation to Iraq and elsewhere by Sunni jihadis. Indeed, the Palestinian *shahid* (martyr) has paved the way." Palestinian terrorist groups "refined the *modus operandi* of suicide-homicide bombers" and established "important precedents that precipitated waves of Sunni suicide terrorists, such as those employed in al-Qaeda's post-9/11 strategy."

This book's final section, Part VI, is very important. It looks to the past, present, and future to develop a series of reform principles that may encourage Muslim societies to move beyond the constraints of Islamism to a new understanding of economics, philosophy, and politics. In chapter 13, "Economic Justice in the Middle East: A Bad Idea, Badly Done," Patrick Clawson of the Washington Institute for Near East Policy focuses on the subject of political economy. He laments how in the region "ideology has often impeded sensible economic policymaking; leaders have been unwilling to challenge long-held shibboleths, afraid that the short-term political risks would outweigh the long-term economic advantage." This prioritization of "politics over economics has become a self-reinforcing cycle in which poor economic performance creates discontent off of which radical ideologues can feed. Prosperity could facilitate solution of the region's political problems: people who are more satisfied are more likely to consider difficult political compromises." Clawson, as a result, refutes the notion of "economic justice" imposed by government intervention as a template for growth and contends instead that the most promising program for development in the Middle East has been designed not by Islamists, Third World socialists, or pan-Arabists, but by international experts committed to "globalization and Western-style economic reform."

In chapter 14, "'For Truth Does Not Oppose Truth': The Agreement of Divine Law and Philosophy in Averroës' *The Book of the Decisive Treatise (Kitab Fal al-Maqal),*" Terence J. Kleven finds in the enlightened thought of the great medieval Islamic philosopher a viable source for intellectual revival and political progress in the Muslim world. What is more, Kleven argues, Averroës demonstrates how "the harmonization of religion and philosophy" can accelerate this process. A "proper account of Averroës' enlightenment," he asserts, "may still offer modern states, whether they be Eastern, Middle Eastern, or Western, a true enlightenment that will lead to an ennobling of the political order and of the place of religion in that order." Kleven thus challenges the assumptions of Western academics and Islamists alike. Scholars "who suggest that Averroës can be commandeered into the service of secularism do not seem to have absorbed the import of his argument in the *Decisive Treatise*. The Islamists who argue that he is too secular seem to have accepted a reading of the book that denies its endeavor to show that the truth of philosophy, rightly understood, confirms and elucidates the truth of religion, rightly understood."

Edward T. Barrett takes this reform paradigm one step further in chapter 15, "Hermeneutics and Human Rights: Liberal Democracy, Catholicism, and Islam." His objective is "to refine the ideological component of an adequate strategy to counter Salafism, arguing that the primary goal should be neither public diplomacy nor secularization, but instead theological and philosophical reform in support of an Islamic theory of human rights." He thus sketches out Roman Catholicism's reconciliation with liberal democracy and human rights in the modern era in order to trace a similar course for Islam. Following a rigorous analysis of several major liberal Islamic philosophers, he determines that this path ultimately passes through the ethical philosophy of George Hourani, whose "primary goal is to validate, on Islamic theological grounds, the ontological and epistemological preconditions for an Islamic theory of natural law."

INSIGHTS INTO ISLAMISM

As the foregoing essays demonstrate, the contributors to this collection participate in the serious discourse vis-à-vis political Islam that is now taking place. Their work deepens our comprehension, extends our intellectual horizons, and opens a window onto this ideology. Its relationship to tribal culture, for instance, emerges as a theme that dilutes Islamism's assertion of divine sanction and, at the same time, situates its confrontational nature within the context of balanced opposition. Paradoxically, balanced opposition can sometimes circumscribe the boundaries of jihad when tribes disavow an Islamist agenda, which is partially what transpired in Somaliland in the early twentieth century and, more recently, in al-Anbar province in Iraq when the Sunni Awakening rejected al-Qaeda.[16] Still, Timothy Furnish's chapter on modern Mahdism reminds us that tribal divisions are sometimes superseded by a shared commitment to holy war, while David Cook's essay highlights the religious dimension of the first Muslim conquests. Competing forces like these merit further study. So, too, do the other significant themes explored here, including the early history of political Islam, definitions of Islamic jurisprudents versus Islamist jihadists, methodologies for interpreting Islamism, jihad in Africa, the deleterious effects of doctrines like *takfir* and *istishhad*, the influence of Mahdism in the Middle East, strategies for enhancing the region's economic performance, and the potential of enlightened Islamic—as opposed to Islamist—political philosophy.

This volume has policy implications in several areas. One of the reasons this is the case is that its contributors take the role of religion in society seriously, in contrast to broad swaths of the academic and diplomatic elite in the United States. "Ignorance of religion," writes Angelo Codevilla, "is perhaps the defining cultural characteristic of America's foreign policy establishment."[17] It is not a trait shared by the authors in this collection. This book is therefore relevant to international diplomacy, international terrorism, national security, and economic development. "The quest to understand the Islamic Republic has vital policy applications," writes Ofira Seliktar about Iran, whose essay helps us to do just that, especially in the wake of the disputed reelection of Mahmoud Ahmadinejad in June, 2009. Events unfolding in Pakistan, where elements of an official government agency, the Directorate of Inter-Services Intelligence, are backing the Taliban,[18] mean that Joseph C. Myers' exposition of the Quranic theory of war, as articulated by a former Pakistani general, is timely. Both of these chapters, and others, are relevant to the War on Islamic Terrorism. All of them demonstrate that the scholars in this volume, far from avoiding controversial subjects, tackle them head on, in a rigorous and disciplined manner.

This book also points us in positive new directions. By proposing ways to resolve Islam's conflict with modernity, the essays in the last section highlight ideas that may help to marginalize extremism—one of the default options for thousands of young men and women in the Middle East who are frustrated by social stagnation. The authors of these three chapters join a committed community of scholars investigating substantive means of reform. Their aim is to lead Islam out of the labyrinth of Islamism. This collection not only presents a sophisticated dissertation on political Islam, but also illuminates a viable path to progress and renewal in the Muslim world.

NOTES

1. Daniel Pipes, *Militant Islam Reaches America* (New York: W.W. Norton and Company, 2002), 5–11. For a historical perspective on the effect of modernity on the Islamic world, see Bernard Lewis, *What Went Wrong? Western Impact and Middle Eastern Response* (Oxford: Oxford University Press, 2002).

2. John L. Esposito, ed., *Political Islam: Revolution, Radicalism, or Reform* (Boulder: Lynne Rienner Publishers, 1997); Bassam Tibbi, *The Challenge of Fundamentalism: Political Islam and the New World Disorder* (Berkley: University of California Press, 1998); Pipes, *Militant Islam Reaches America*; Bernard Lewis, *The Crisis of Islam: Holy War and Unholy Terror* (New York: The Modern Library, 2003); Graham E. Fuller, *The Future of Political Islam* (New York: Palgrave

Macmillan, 2003); Walid Phares, *The Confrontation: Winning the War Against Future Jihad* (New York: Palgrave Macmillan, 2008).

3. Olivier Roy, *The Failure of Political Islam* (Cambridge: Harvard University Press, 1994); Ray Takeyh and Nikolas K. Gvosdev, *The Receding Shadow of the Prophet: The Rise and Fall of Political Islam* (Westport: Praeger Publishers, 2004).

4. Samuel P. Huntington, *The Clash of Civilizations and the Remaking of World Order* (New York: Simon and Schuster, 1998).

5. Fawaz A. Gerges, *America and Political Islam: Clash of Cultures or Clash of Interests?* (Cambridge: Cambridge University Press, 1999). See, also, Walid Phares, *Future Jihad: Terrorist Strategies Against America* (New York: Palgrave Macmillan, 2005).

6. Beverley Milton-Edwards, *Islam and Politics in the Contemporary World* (Cambridge: Polity Press, 2004); Peter Mandaville, *Global Political Islam* (London: Routledge, 2007).

7. Mohammed Ayoob, *The Many Faces of Political Islam: Religion and Politics in the Muslim World* (Ann Arbor: University of Michigan Press, 2008).

8. Bernard Lewis, *The Political Language of Islam* (Chicago: University of Chicago Press, 1988).

9. Gilles Kepel, *Jihad: The Trail of Political Islam*, trans. Anthony F. Roberts (Cambridge: Harvard University Press, 2002); David Cook, *Understanding Jihad* (Berkeley: University of California Press, 2005); Laurent Murawiec, *The Mind of Jihad* (Cambridge: Cambridge University Press, 2008).

10. Pipes, *Militant Islam Reaches America*, 251–57; Daniel Pipes, *Miniatures: Views of Islamic and Middle Eastern Politics* (New Brunswick: Transaction Publishers, 2004), 45–47.

11. See, for example, John L. Esposito and John O. Voll, *Islam and Democracy* (New York: Oxford University Press, 1996); Richard K. Khuri, *Freedom, Modernity, and Islam: Towards a Creative Synthesis* (Syracuse: Syracuse University Press, 1998); Khaled Abou El Fadl, *Islam and the Challenge of Democracy* (Princeton: Princeton University Press, 2004); M.A. Muqtedar Khan, *Islamic Democratic Discourse: Theory, Debates and Philosophical Perspectives* (Lanham: Rowman and Littlefield, 2006); Bassam Tibi, *Political Islam, World Politics and Europe: Democratic Peace and Euro-Islam Versus Global Jihad* (London: Routledge, 2008). For a skeptical view of Western-oriented approaches to the reform of political Islam, see Amr G. E. Sabet, *Islam and the Political: Theory, Governance and International Relations* (London: Pluto Press, 2008).

12. Pipes, *Militant Islam Reaches America*, 7.

13. Rachel Sharon-Krespin, "Fethullah Gülen's Grand Ambition," *Middle East Quarterly* 16, no. 1 (Winter 2009): 55–66.

14. Pipes, *Militant Islam Reaches America*, 10. See, also, Tibi, *Political Islam, World Politics and Europe*, xii–xxii.

15. Pipes, *Militant Islam Reaches America*, 12.

16. Bing West, *The Strongest Tribe: War, Politics, and the Endgame in Iraq* (New York: Random House, 2008), 211–15.

17. Angelo Codevilla, *Advice to War Presidents: A Remedial Course in Statecraft* (New York: Basic Books, 2009), 56.

18. Fisnik Abrashi, "Afghan Intel Chief: Pakistan Spies Support Taliban," *Washington Times*, March 26, 2009.

PART II

The Origins of Political Islam

CHAPTER 2

Balanced Opposition: The Tribal Foundations of Arab Middle Eastern Islamic Culture

Philip Carl Salzman

Arab culture, the dominant culture of the central Middle East and the founding culture of Islam, is both a brilliant construction of human creativity and a practical response to many human problems. Like all cultures, it opens some paths and closes others. In other words, Arab culture, like every other culture, solves some problems and opens some possibilities, while presenting problems of its own and limiting other possibilities. This chapter touches upon the contours and consequences, both liberating and restricting, of Arab culture and of other similar Middle Eastern cultures as an approach to understanding Middle Eastern life as well as some of the political elements of Islam.

Arab culture, like all cultures, is a way of construing the world, the universe, society, and men and women. It is a matrix of meaning, a framework for understanding, and a plan for action. It defines desirable goals, appropriate means, and the broader values to be honored in human action. By so doing, Arab culture is a force in human action, a sculptor of society, and a major influence on human events. Arab Middle Eastern culture is a potent force, but not the only one, for human life is shaped by multiple influences: internal ones such as biology and psychology, parallel ones such as the laws of sociology and economics, and external ones such as contact with other cultures and societies. However, understanding these other influences without taking into account Arab culture would be insufficient for appreciating the realities of the central Middle East and neighboring areas with similar cultures.

Arab culture addresses the universal problem of order and security in an ingenious and time-tested fashion. Every human society must find a way to establish a substantial degree of order and security if it is going to survive and prosper. By order I mean a predictable repetitiveness of behavior, such that members of the society can count on a reliable result for any of their acts. Order is absolutely critical. Without it, people do not know the results of their actions, and so either do not act, or act arbitrarily, and thus chaos ensues.

For example, if it is not known whether a cultivated crop will be burned, trampled under hoof, or stolen, or if people do not know there is a good chance they will benefit from the fruits of their labor, they will not bother to plant, and so there will be no cultivation of food or medicinal and raw material crops. If people do not know whether their children will respect them and support them in old age, or will usurp and destroy them at the first opportunity, they will be reluctant to nurture them and keep them close. If people do not know whether strangers coming to their community will respect their lives and property, or whether they will attack and loot them, they will be loath to welcome strangers at all, and strive to drive away anyone who approaches.

Security is confidence that persons, rights, and property—however defined in a particular culture—will be respected. Every culture defines norms, or rules of correct behavior, about persons, rights, and property, and validates a set of social arrangements to guarantee that these are respected. Social arrangements to guarantee security can be referred to as the organization of social control. Arab culture in the central Middle East and similar cultures elsewhere in the Middle East are characterized by a particular form of social control that has a major impact on human experience and social life. This form, or structure, is what I will call "balanced opposition."[1]

BALANCED OPPOSITION

Balanced opposition is an ingenious way to organize security. It is decentralized, in that no central officials or organizers are required. It is democratic, in that decision making is collective and everyone has a say. It is egalitarian, in that there is no ascribed status, rank, or hierarchy into which people are born, and all groups and individuals are equal in principle. It is also to a substantial degree effective, in that balanced opposition often successfully deters attack by threatening reprisal.

This is how balanced opposition in the Middle East works: each person is a member of a nested set of kin groups defined by patrilineal descent, from very small to very large. These groups are vested with responsibility for the defense of each and every one of its members and responsibility for harm each and every one of its members does to outsiders. This is called by anthropologists "collective responsibility," and the actions taken by a group on its own behalf are called "self-help." If there is a confrontation, everyone unites with closer kin against more distant kin, so that small groups unite to face opposing small groups, middle size groups unite to face opposing middle size groups, and large groups unite to face opposing large groups: family versus family; lineage versus lineage; clan versus clan; tribe versus tribe; confederacy versus confederacy; sect versus sect; the Islamic community, *umma*, versus the infidels. This is where the deterrence lies, in the balance between opponents; individuals do not face groups, and small groups do not face large groups. Any potential aggressor knows that his target is neither solitary nor meager, but is always, in principle, a formidable formation much the same size as his.

There is also an internal group aspect to this deterrence. Because of the collective responsibility, in which all members of a group are responsible for each and every member, each member of the group is implicated in the actions of every other member. This means that all group members may be called to fight in order to defend a member in a conflict, or to seek vengeance in the case of loss of property, injury, or death, or to pay compensation in the case of a group member causing injury to another, or would be a legitimate target for a member of the opposing group. Of course, many individual group members would much rather avoid being dragged into fights or payments by the arrogant assertions, irrational passions, or rash adventures of their fellow group members. So these group members put pressure on other group members to behave cautiously and prudently, and to avoid pursuing opportunities to enter into conflict. Here is the internal deterrence: in the pressure and even threat of withdrawal of support of fellow group members. It is common, for example, for older men to urge caution upon young men who tend to have quicker tempers, and for those group members somewhat more distant in kinship from those directly involved in the conflict to urge prudence upon the close kin, who would feel the insult, injury, or loss more strongly.

Balanced opposition works to the extent that it does because individual members of groups come to the aid of their fellow group members, even at serious risk of injury or loss of life, or with serious material cost. Why do they do this? For two main reasons: one pragmatic, the other cultural. The pragmatic reason is the strong belief that the only ones that can be counted on for help are members of one's kinship group. You act to support your fellow members, on the understanding that they will come to your aid when you are in need. This is what anthropologists call "generalized reciprocity," in which you act now to support group members with the expectation that sometime later, they will support you when needed. This is sensible self-interest. The cultural reason is that your honor depends upon your living up to your commitments, in this case as a member of the group. If you are not willing to set aside your short-term personal interest, your comfort and safety, to come to the aid of your fellow members, you lose your honor and standing, get a bad reputation, are not respected by others, and are avoided as a partner in any enterprise.

Balanced opposition, a decentralized system of defense and social control characterized by self-help, is a "tribal" form of organization, a tribe being a regional organization of defense based on decentralization and self-help. Tribes operate quite differently from states, which are centralized, have political hierarchies, and have specialized institutions—such as courts, police, and an army, with tax collectors providing the means for support—to maintain social control and defense. While tribes tend to operate democratically, states in the Middle East, and elsewhere until modern times, have tended to rule tyrannically. Those who governed did so in their own interest, and usually at the expense of the general populace. Thus states expanded whenever possible, bringing in more loot for the rulers and their followers, more bodies for their armies, and more peasants to tax. Members of tribal societies understandably resisted being incorporated into states, preferring their independent and egalitarian communal lives to exploitation by an arrogant and brutal elite. "Tribal" is thus used here primarily in a descriptive sense. If any evaluation were intended, it would not be disparaging, for it is not difficult to prefer independence to oppression, equality to hierarchy, and self-help to suppression.

One important consequence of reliance on balanced opposition is an emphasis on individual independence, freedom, and responsibility, and also on equality and democracy. At the same time, the military virtues of prowess and courage and the goal of domination are highly valued. The reasons for this are clear. A decentralized system of defense based upon self-help, such as balanced opposition, relies on each individual to make judgments and act on his own and freely in collaboration with his fellow group members. Acting in defense and retaliation means engaging in violence, for which skill and courage are desirable.

In tribal societies based on balanced opposition, male children are raised to be independent, to take responsibility for themselves, and to be ready and able to engage in sanctioned violence against designated enemies. Collective decisions about action are made democratically, in councils in which all group members are free to speak. No mechanisms of coercion are available to force group members to act. Collective agreement on decisions puts moral pressure on each individual to fulfill his duty, and his reputation and honor are at stake. But ultimately it is up to each individual to decide and act. The honorable man has no ruler and bows to no man, but stands on his own feet and his own reputation as an equal to all others.

Thus adherence to balanced opposition results in individual and group independence, freedom, responsibility, equality, bellicosity, and courage. At the same time, however, balanced opposition is a frame that limits alternatives, some of which might prove useful. Balanced opposition emphasizes particular loyalties: my lineage against the other lineage; my tribal section against the other tribal section; my tribe against the other tribe; my sect versus the other sect; or Muslims against infidels.

The remarkable development of Islam in the seventh century CE must be understood, to a degree, within the context of Arabian balanced opposition. Islam provided in the *umma*, the community of Muslims, a more inclusive level of integration than tribal organization. But at the same time, it also provided an opponent to the *umma*, the world of infidels, which had to be confronted for the glory of God and for the profit of loot (which was deemed already to belong to Muslims as representatives of God). Islam, whatever its many dimensions and complexities, incorporated the balanced opposition structure of the tribal society that it overlay. Perhaps it could hardly have done otherwise and been accepted by the Bedouin tribes that were its primary adherents and its military arm. As a result, balanced opposition is a dominant theme in Arab culture, a central structure in Arab society, and a fundamental principle of political Islam. It shapes other aspects of social life and, like all structures, limits the possibilities.[2]

THE RISE OF ISLAM

What was extraordinary in Middle Eastern history was the unification of the Arabian tribes under the banner of Islam and their conquest of much of the known world. Prior to Muhammad, the tribes of northern Arabia engaged in ongoing raiding and feuding, fighting among themselves for the spoils of livestock, territory, and honor. Muhammad's genius was in finding a way to unite the myriad of fissiparous, feuding Bedouin tribes of northern Arabia into a cohesive polity. Just as he had provided a constitution of rules under which the people of Medina could live together, so did he provide a constitution for all Arabs; but this one had the imprimatur not just of Muhammad, but also of God. Submission—*islam*—to God and His rules was spelled out in the Quran and bound into solidarity Arabian tribesmen, who collectively became the *umma*, the community of believers.

Building on the tribal system of balanced opposition, Muhammad was able to frame an inclusive structure within which the tribes had a common, God-given identity as Muslim. Their common identity gave the tribes a common interest and common project. But unification was only possible by extending the basic tribal principle of balanced opposition. This Muhammad did by opposing the Muslim to the infidel, and the *Dar al-Islam*, the land of Islam and peace, to the *Dar al-Harb*, the land of the infidels and conflict. Balanced opposition was raised to a higher structural level, and the newly Muslim tribes were unified in the face of the infidel enemy. Bedouin raiding was thus sanctified as an act of religious duty.

With every successful battle against unbelievers, especially after the critical early battle against the Meccans, more Bedouin joined the *umma*. Once united, the Bedouin warriors of the *umma* turned outward, teaching the world the meaning of jihad, holy war. The rest, as they say, is history.

In lightning thrusts, the Arabs challenged and beat the Byzantines to the north and the Persians to the east, both weakened by their continuous wars with one another, thus imposing control over the Christian majority in the Levant and the Zoroastrian majority in Persia, and therefore over the entire Middle East. These stunning successes were rapidly followed by conquests of Christian and Jewish populations in Egypt, Libya, and the Maghreb (Arabic for "the West"), and, in the east, Central Asia and the Hindu population in northern India. Not content with these triumphs, Arab armies invaded and subdued much of Christian Spain and Portugal, and all of Sicily. Since the Roman Empire, the world had not seen such power and reach. Almost all fell before the Saracen blades.

Conquest of vast lands, large populations, and advanced civilizations is bound to be a bloody and brutal task. This is true of all great invasions, including those of the Greek, Roman, Arab, Mongol, Russian, British, Dutch, French, and Zulu empires and, more recently, the short-lived invasions by the German and Japanese empires, as well as the campaigns to defeat those empires. Of course, some campaigns and occupations are known to have been particularly and gratuitously savage and cruel.

We must touch on the nature of the Islamic conquests, not from prurience for violence, or a desire to condemn Arabs or Muslims, but to clarify an obscure and obfuscated history that demonstrates and illuminates attitudes and relations. This is necessary because it is common for university students and non-specialists, well indoctrinated with the mantra "Islam is the religion of peace," to ask whether—and these are quotes from advanced students—"anything bad really happened" or "anyone got hurt" during the Islamic conquests of most of the civilized world. Most accounts of Islamic history glide over the conquests, as if they were friendly takeovers, really to everyone's satisfaction. This includes Charles Lindholm's esteemed work, *The Islamic Middle East:*

> After the death of Muhammad in 632 expansion was rapid; in 638 Jerusalem fell, and in the next thirty years all of ancient Mesopotamia, Egypt and most of Iran were conquered, while other Muslim armies pressed northwest into Byzantine territory . . . [This] miraculously solved the old regional problem of economic and political impasse by forcibly dissolving the two competing deadlocked opponents [Byzantium and Persia] into Islamdom, abruptly uniting the Middle East into one open trade area and paving the way for the rapid creation of a new prosperity. At the same time, the Muslim message of the equality of all believers struck a chord with the common people of the empires, who, theoretically at least, were liberated from their inferior status by the simple act of conversion. The rise of Islam was both

an economic and social revolution, offering new wealth and freedom to the domin-
ions it assimilated under the banner of a universal brotherhood guided by the message of the Prophet of Allah.[3]

Yes, no doubt it was the best of all possible worlds; that is, if one had not
been one of the multitude slain, the myriads enslaved, or the remainder
expropriated, suppressed, and degraded.

Fortunately, there are some accounts we can turn to for franker
accounts of the Islamic conquests. *The Legacy of Jihad: Islamic Holy War and
the Fate of Non-Muslims*, a collection of essays edited by Andrew G.
Bostom and published in 2005, provides lengthy quotes from major Islamic
authorities, ancient and modern, verifying the obligation of jihad, or holy
war against infidels, for every Muslim. Accurate historical accounts of
jihad campaigns in all parts of the world are provided by David Cook in
Understanding Jihad (2005), by Efraim Karsh in *Islamic Imperialism* (2006),
and, earlier, by P.M. Holt, Ann Lambton, and Bernard Lewis in *The
Cambridge History of Islam* (1970). A few illustrations will suffice.

An article on Greek Christian accounts of jihad, by Demetrios Constantelos in the Bostom volume, reports the following:

> John of Nikiu speaks of the early invasion of the Arabs in Egypt as merciless and
> brutal. Not only did the invaders slay the commander of the Byzantine troops and
> all his companions when they captured the city of Bahnasa, but "they put to the
> sword all that surrendered, and they spared none, whether old men, babes, or
> women." They perpetrated innumerable acts of violence and spread panic
> everywhere.[4]

Religious institutions were a favored target, according to Constantelos:
"Greek sources of the eighth century speak also of the savagery of Saracen robbers who raided various monasteries, killing and plundering. For
example, during the caliphate of Harun al-Rashid (786–809), the monasteries of Palestine suffered from numerous raids. Many monks were put
to death."[5]

About the Armenian rebellion of 703, the Arab historian Yaqubi (died
897) wrote, "[General Muhammad-ibn-Marwan] invaded Armenia
whose population had rebelled. He massacred, enslaved and wrote a letter to the nobility who are called freemen, gave guarantees and promised
to give honors. Hence they gathered in their churches, in the province of
Khlat (Khram) and he ordered to encircle the churches with fire-wood,
closed the doors on them and burnt all of them."[6] Here was a foresha-
dowing of the Turkish and Kurdish jihad genocide of the Armenians in
the second decade of the twentieth century.

Muslim occupiers of southern Spain, the allegedly "tolerant" civilization of al-Andalus, are advised in the late fourteenth century by the
Grenadan Ibn Hudayl that:

> [i]t is permissible to set fire to the lands of the enemy, his stores of grain, his beasts
> of burden—if it is not possible for the Muslims to take possession of them—as well

as to cut down his trees, to raze his cities, in a word, to do everything that might ruin and discourage him . . . suited to hastening the Islamization of that enemy or to weakening him. Indeed, all this contributes to a military triumph over him or to forcing him to capitulate.[7]

In fact, only Muslim dominance is tolerated, and any means of extending it to new lands is sanctioned and sanctified. Documentation challenging any notion of internal "tolerance" in Islamic Spain is presented in research by David G. Littman and Bat Ye'or.[8]

One of the main characteristics of the Arab Empire was the enslavement of conquered peoples.[9] During conquest, men were commonly slaughtered, while women and children were taken in slavery. Men who willingly converted were spared, but their wives and children were taken as slaves. In conquered regions, children were regularly taken from parents, while on the borders—especially in Central and Eastern Europe, Central Asia, and Africa south of the Sahara—raiding for slaves was normal practice. Of the male slaves, a substantial number were made eunuchs by the removal of sex organs, in order to serve in harems. The women and children were used as domestics and sex slaves.

The Arab campaign in northern India, recounted by K.S. Lal, illustrates the usual procedures:

During the Arab invasion of Sindh (in 712), Muhammad bin Qasim first attacked Debal, a word derived from *Deval*, meaning temple. It was situated on the seacoast not far from modern Karachi. It was garrisoned by four thousand Kshatriya soldiers and served by three thousand Brahmans. All males of the age of seventeen and upwards were put to the sword and their women and children were enslaved. "[Seven hundred] beautiful females, who were under the protection of Budh (that is, had taken shelter in the temple), were all captured with their valuable ornaments, and clothes adorned with jewels." Muhammad dispatched one-fifth of the legal spoil to Hajjaj which included seventy-five damsels, the other four-fifths were distributed among soldiers. Thereafter whichever places he attacked like Rawar, Sehwan, Dhalila, Brahmanabad, and Multan, Hindu soldiers and men with arms were slain, the common people fled, or, if flight was not possible, accepted Islam, or paid the poll tax, or died with their religion.[10]

The multitude of reports from Muslim, indigenous, and other sources of the Islamic conquests are equally detailed and equally daunting to a modern reader. The reports provided above are sufficient to remind us of their true nature.

MUSLIMS VERSUS INFIDELS

How did the Arabs conceive and perceive other peoples, cultures, and societies? What was their understanding of other lives? For the newly minted Muslims, Islam was God's word and God's way, and any other religion or belief was regarded as false. Judaism and Christianity were seen as superseded by Islam, and inferior and degraded remnants. All non-Muslims were infidels, and should be subject to Islam, God's way.

Jews and Christians were to be allowed to live as inferiors and subordinates, dhimmi, under Muslim domination, but with obligatory, legally mandated humiliation; other infidels, such as Zoroastrians, Hindus, and pagans, were given the choice between conversion to Islam and death. In practice, however, slavery of infidels was often more attractive to the Muslim conquerors, so some infidels were allowed to live enslaved lives of degradation and service to Muslims.

The reader may find this characterization of relations between Muslims and infidels harsh and uncongenial. We have repeatedly been told of the tolerance that existed in the Muslim world, and of the flourishing of minorities under the enlightened guidance of Islamic law and Muslim rulers. But the historical evidence for a darker picture is overwhelming and irrefutable. It is true that, throughout history, intergroup relations in most of the world were exploitative and repressive, and not infrequently brutal and bloodthirsty. The world of Islam was not so much an exception to this, as exemplary of it.

ISLAM MUST DOMINATE

The theological foundation of the Arab empire was the supremacy of Islam and the obligation of each Muslim to advance its domination. Bat Ye'or sums up this point:

> The general basic principles according to the Quran are as follows: the pre-eminence of Islam over all other religions (9:33); Islam is the true religion of Allah (3:17) and it should reign over all mankind (34:27); the *umma* forms the party of Allah and is perfect (3:106), having been chosen above all peoples on earth it alone is qualified to rule, and thus elected by Allah to guide the world (35:37). The pursuit of *jihad*, until this goal will be achieved, is an obligation (8:40). [Citations in the text refer to the Quran.][11]

The relationship between Muslims and non-Muslims is thus defined by Islamic doctrine as one of superiority-inferiority, and of endless conflict until the successful conquest of the non-Muslims. As Ye'or explains:

> *Jihad* divides the peoples of the world into two irreconcilable groups: the Muslims—inhabitants of the *Dar al-Islam*, regions subject to Islamic law; and infidels [*kafir*]—inhabitants of the *Dar al-Harb* (*harbis*), the territory of war, destined to come under Islamic jurisdiction, either by the conversion of its inhabitants or by armed conflict. *Jihad* is the Muslim's permanent state of war or hostility by the *Dar al-Islam* against the *Dar al-Harb*, until the infidels' conclusive submission and the absolute world supremacy of Islam.[12]

Ye'or substantiates this generalization with quotes from Muslim sources. I include one here, from Ibn Taymiyya, a famous Hanbali jurist of the fourteenth century:

> In ordering *jihad* Allah has said: "Fight them until there is no persecution and religion becomes Allah's." [2:189]

> Allah has, in fact, repeated this obligation [to fight] and has glorified *jihad* in most of the Medina *suras:* he has stigmatized those who neglected to do so, and treated them as hypocrites and cowards.
>
> . . . *Jihad* is the best form of voluntary service that man consecrates to Allah.
>
> Therefore, since *jihad* is divinely instituted, and its goal is that religion reverts in its entirety to Allah and to make Allah's word triumph, whoever opposes the realization of this goal will be fought, according to the unanimous opinion of Muslims.[13]

Any male infidel who resists Islamic domination may be killed or enslaved; women and children must be taken into slavery.[14]

We may ask whether the doctrinal views of the fourteenth century are outdated, or whether they have been carried down to the present day. Here anthropologists have a contribution to the discussion. E.E. Evans-Pritchard, late professor of social anthropology at Oxford University, had close contact with the Bedouin of Libya during World War II; as reported in his brilliant account, *The Sanusi of Cyrenaica*, the Bedouin saw it as their special religious responsibility to carry out holy war, jihad, leaving others to pray and study the Quran.[15] When Libya was invaded by the Italians early in the twentieth century, the Bedouin of Cyrenaica (the eastern half of Libya) were unwilling to accept the Italians as rulers under any terms, no matter how generous. Although the Bedouin were heavily outgunned, they chose to fight and continued to fight courageously for decades until they were virtually exterminated.

While jihad must never be terminated until Islam is universal and all follow Allah's way, a break in military hostilities is lawful. An-Nawawi, Shafi'i jurisconsul of the thirteenth century, said:

> An armistice is only allowed when some advantage to Muslims ensures: for example, if we are weak in numbers, or if we lack money or ammunition, or even if there is hope that the infidels may convert or offer to surrender and pay the capitation tax . . . On the other hand, it is perfectly lawful for the sovereign, when he agrees to an armistice, to reserve the right to commence hostilities when it seems good to him.[16]

Strategic pauses are thus sanctioned, as long as the obligation to continue the jihad is honored.

BALANCED OPPOSITION VERSUS A UNIVERSALISTIC CONSTITUTION OF RULES

From a political point of view, Islam raised tribal society to a higher, more inclusive level of integration. But it was not able to replace the central principle of tribal political organization, balanced opposition, which was honored in the framing of the Muslim-versus-infidel opposition. Thus, as with tribal lineage organization, affiliation and loyalty are defined by opposition, and, notwithstanding the common requirements of Islam, the ultimate importance of group membership is not superseded by a universalistic constitution of rules.

The basic tribal framework of "us versus them" remains and, in Islam, is validated by God. In the tribal framework, the conception "my group right or wrong" does not exist, because the question of whether "my group" is right or wrong does not come up. Allegiance is to "my group," period, full stop. Most importantly, "my group" is defined by and always stands against "the other." An overarching, universalistic, inclusive constitution is not possible. Islam is not a constant referent, but rather, like every level of tribal political organization, is contingent. That is, people act politically as Muslims only when in opposition to infidels. Among Muslims, people will mobilize on a sectarian basis, as Sunni versus Shi'a. Among Sunni, people will mobilize as the Karim tribe versus the Mahmud tribe; within the Karim tribe, people will mobilize according to whom they find themselves in opposition to: tribal section versus tribal section; major lineage versus major lineage; and so on.

The structural fissiparousness of the tribal order makes very difficult societal cohesion in the Middle East. The particularism of affiliation constantly places people and groups in opposition to one another. There is no universal referent that can include all parties. Oppositionalism is the cultural imperative. Thus the ingenious tribal system, based on balanced opposition, so effectual in supporting decentralized nomads, tends to inhibit societal integration at a more inclusive level, and to preclude civil peace, based on settlement of disputes through legal judgment, at the local level. As is often the case, a structure suitable for one way of life is not readily adaptable to another.

NOTES

1. In this usage, I follow the brilliant work of E. E. Evans-Pritchard, *The Sanusi of Cyrenaica* (Oxford: The Clarendon Press, 1949). For further elaboration, see Philip Carl Salzman, *Black Tents of Baluchistan* (Washington, DC: Smithsonian Institution Press, 2000), and Philip Carl Salzman, *Pastoralists: Equality, Hierarchy, and the State* (Boulder: Westview, 2004). For a longer discussion of my treatment of balanced opposition in the Middle East, see Philip Carl Salzman, *Culture and Conflict in the Middle East* (Amherst: Humanity Books, 2008).

2. Perhaps at this point we should ask whether this thesis is open to the criticism widespread in postmodern and postcolonial theory that characterizing societies is a form of essentializing distortion, assuming uniformity, and denying the humanity of the members of the society. The postcolonial argument (see Edward Said, *Orientalism* and elsewhere, and a host of followers) that people around the world are really more or less the same, and that any distinctions between cultures impose a false essentialism aimed at defining certain populations as "other," primarily to demean them and justify imperial and colonial oppression, rashly dismisses culture as of nugatory significance. The assumption that all people are just like "us" is a kind of ethnocentrism that projects our values, our ways of thinking, and our goals onto other peoples. The

anthropological study of culture around the world is based on a recognition of cultural differences, on an appreciation of the importance of culture in people's lives, and on respect for other people's cultures.

The postcolonial argument that knowledge of other cultures is impossible, because people and cultures do not exhibit uniformity, jumps from a known fact to a false inference. All knowledge is based on abstraction, and abstraction draws commonalities and averages that exist beyond the acknowledged variation of the particulars. For example, there are different species and varieties of camel, but we would not therefore conclude that we cannot validly distinguish camels from horses. Tents, too, are different from one another, in materials used and in structure; yet tents are not houses, and the differences are fairly obvious. As regards cultures, there are variations both between and within Arab societies and cultures, but anyone who argues on that basis that it is impossible to distinguish Arab culture from Hindu culture would not be being frank. It is clear to me, and I believe any serious anthropologist would agree, that we can successfully study Arab and Middle Eastern society and establish sound knowledge of it (see, for example, Charles Lindholm, *The Islamic Middle East*, revised ed. [Oxford: Blackwell Publishing, 2002], 6). In that knowledge, an understanding of balanced opposition would play a major role.

3. Lindholm, *The Islamic Middle East*, 79.

4. Demetrios Constantelos, "Greek Christian and Other Accounts of the Muslim Conquest of the Near East," in *The Legacy of Jihad: Islamic Holy War and the Fate of Non-Muslims*, ed. Andrew Bostom (Amherst: Prometheus Books, 2005), 390.

5. Ibid, 393.

6. Quoted in Aram Ter-Ghevondian, "The Aremenian Rebellion of 703 Against the Caliphate," in Bostom, *The Legacy of Jihad*, 412.

7. C.E. Dufourcq, "The Days of *Razzia* and Invasion," in Bostom, *The Legacy of Jihad*, 419–20.

8. David G. Littman and Bat Ye'or, "Protected Peoples Under Islam," in *The Myth of Islamic Tolerance*, ed. Robert Spencer (Amherst: Prometheus Books, 2005), 93.

9. See, for example, Andrew G. Bostom, "*Jihad* Conquests and the Imposition of *Dhimmitude*—A Survey," in Bostom, *The Legacy of Jihad*, 86–93.

10. K.S. Lal, "Enslavement of Hindus by Arab and Turkish Invaders," in Bostom, *The Legacy of Jihad*, 549–50.

11. Bat Ye'or, *Islam and Dhimmitude: Where Civilizations Collide* (Madison: Fairleigh Dickinson University Press, 2002), 40–41.

12. Ibid., 43.

13. Quoted in Ibid., 44.

14. Ibid., 44–45.

15. E. E. Evans-Pritchard, *The Sanusi of Cyrenaica*, 63.

16. Quoted in Ye'or, *Islam and Dhimmitude*, 46.

CHAPTER 3

Why Did Muhammad Attack the Byzantines? A Re-examination of Quran *Sura* 30:1–2

David Cook

THE PROBLEM

According to the classical Muslim sources, the early Muslims (or *mu'minun*, "believers") were those who not only held to an absolute monotheism in opposition to the pantheistic belief systems of Arabia, but also supported other monotheistic systems such as Judaism, Christianity, and the mysterious Sabeans, among others. Support for Christianity in this time period was not necessarily politically beneficial for the believers. Starting from 602, the Zoroastrian Sasanian Persians, led by Chosroes II Perviz (591–628), invaded the Christian Byzantine Empire. For a number of years, as Islam was developing in distant Mecca and was facing the persecution of the Meccan pagans, the Byzantines lost battle after battle. By 614 the city of Jerusalem was lost, and the True Cross located within the Church of the Holy Sepulcher was taken by the Sasanians. Syria, Egypt, and Anatolia were all lost to the Byzantines, and finally Constantinople itself was under attack for a decade. In essence, during the birth pangs of Islam, Christianity, from an Arabian point of view, was both physically distant and looked to be defeated, with its holiest cities torched and its sanctities desecrated.

Into this context we must consider Quran *sura* 30:1–2, which uniquely within the Quran contains a prophecy and also refers to political events that can be verified in history: "The Greeks [or Byzantines] have been vanquished in the nearest part of the land; but after being vanquished, they shall vanquish, in a few years. Allah's is the command before and after; and on that day the believers shall rejoice."[1]

The significance of this pair of verses for the history of Islam and Christianity is huge and can hardly be overestimated. First, there is some identification between the Byzantines and the believers, a feeling of shared loss. Second, there is a confidence in the ultimate triumph of the Byzantines after their apparent loss. Again, one must stress the fact that during the years 614–28, while Islam was developing, this ultimate victory must have seemed highly unlikely. Third, the location of the place in which the Byzantines were defeated—the "nearest part of the land" that is most probably a reference to Palestine—allows us to date this verse sequence to the immediate aftermath of the conquest of Jerusalem in 614.

In summary, one can say from the one document that is reasonably certain to date from the time of Muhammad—the Quran—that there was a strong feeling of sympathy and even religious support for the Christian Byzantines *at this time*, when politically the believers had nothing to gain from manifesting such sympathy. Moreover, these verses were never modified or changed, *apparently*, despite the bitter wars that were to divide the Christian Byzantines from the Muslims for the next seven centuries. This is the heart of the problem: why is it that with this strong sympathy for the Christian Byzantines inside the Quran that the Byzantines were the first targets for the early Muslim polity to attack in 629–32 and later? One must ask the reason for this sudden change in policy. I propose that the background for this sudden change should be seen in the triumphal return of the True Cross by the Byzantine Emperor Heraclius in 629 (or 630, see below) and the identification of the Christians as polytheists, as opposed to some previous perception of them as fellow monotheists.[2]

QURAN *SURA* 30:1–2 AND BEYOND

Quran 30:1–2 cannot be read without its context. Although frequently the context, according to the *tafsir* literature, is some type of bet made between the Muslims and the pagans of Mecca,[3] the identification of the believers with the Christian Byzantines in the passage is strong. According to the early account of Muqatil (died 767), the Muslims learned that the Byzantines had defeated the Persians finally at the time of the Truce of Hudaybiyya (628) and rejoiced at that time.[4] If this is indeed the case, then it would mean that a scant year prior to the time when the Muslims began to attack the Byzantines formally, they had been spiritually allied to them and had rejoiced at their victory over the Persians. Once again this raises the question: what changed the Muslims' positive attitude toward the Byzantines to a willingness to attack them? Almost immediately after the description of the future victory of the Byzantines over their enemies, and the fact that the believers will rejoice on that day, verse 4 states: "It is Allah's promise. Allah does not break His promise . . ." It is unclear from the sequence whether this promise is being accorded to the Byzantines or is implied to the believers themselves. Probably the safest way to read the verses would be to see them as a unity in this particular case.

Continuing to read through this chapter of the Quran, *surat al-Rum*, reveals reasons why the change in attitudes would occur. Further historical sense for the defeat of the Byzantines appears in verse 7, which reads: "Have they not traveled in the land to see what was the fate of those who preceded them? They were stauncher than them in strength, and they ploughed the earth and built it up better than they themselves built it up, and their messengers came to them with clear proofs. Allah would never wrong them, but they wronged themselves." This verse is obviously designed to highlight the difference between those who are apparently strong during the present (such as the Persians) and those who were equally strong but had collapsed very suddenly as a result of their own misdeeds. This critique, however, could equally apply to the Christian Byzantines if they rejected messengers such as Muhammad or demonstrated arrogance against the revelations of God.

This type of idea is best revealed in verse 31: "When people are visited by some adversity, they call upon their Lord, turning to Him; but when He lets them taste a mercy from Him, behold, a group of them associate [other gods] with their Lord, so as to be ungrateful for what We have given them. Indulge yourselves, then. For you shall certainly know." If Muhammad and the Muslims understood the tenets of Orthodox Christianity and the importance of the doctrine of the True Cross for it, they may have viewed the sufferings of the Byzantines as a point where there should be repentance from their sins. If this was not forthcoming, then it is easy to see the veiled threat implied in this verse for the Christians, as the rest of the *sura* speaks about God taking revenge against unbelievers and those who do not repent. The entire *sura* can be seen both as a prophecy of the future Byzantine triumph as well as a prelude to the future Muslim attack upon the Byzantines.

HERACLIUS, THE BYZANTINES, AND THE TRUE CROSS

One cannot doubt that while the twenty-six-year war between the Byzantines and the Sasanians was primarily political, it did have religious ramifications.[5] And when the war was concluded one of the major issues for the treaty was the return of the True Cross, held by the Sasanians. Heraclius' triumphal return of the True Cross to Jerusalem is commemorated by a number of different historical accounts. In the spring of 629 the Byzantine historian Theophanes records:

> In this year at spring the Emperor [Heraclius] left the imperial city to travel to Jerusalem, bringing back the precious and lifegiving wood to restore it as a thanksgiving to God . . . Herakleios entered Jerusalem. He restored Zacheriah the patriarch

and the precious and lifegiving wood to their own place, and gave thanks to God. He expelled the Hebrews from the holy city, ordering that they should not be allowed to come within three miles of it.[6]

Similarly, Nikephorus records in his *Short History*:

Taking the life-giving [True] Cross (which had remained under seal as it was when it was removed), he [Heraclius] came to Jerusalem and exhibited it to the archpriest Modestos and his clergy, who acknowledged the seal to be intact. Seeing that (the Cross) had been preserved untouched by the profane and murderous hands of the barbarians and unseen by them, they offered to God a hymn of thanksgiving. The bishop produced the appropriate key which had remained in his possession and, when the Cross was opened, everyone worshipped it. And after it had been elevated there, the emperor immediately sent it to Byzantium [Constantinople].[7]

Other Christian sources such as Sebeos mention the return of the True Cross as well:

When the blessed, pious and late-lamented king Heraclius had received the Lord's holy Cross, he gathered his army with ardent and happy heart. He set out with all the royal retinue . . . there was no little joy on that day as they entered Jerusalem. [There was] the sound of weeping and wailing; their tears flowed from the awesome fervor of the emotion of their hearts and from the rending of the entrails of the king, the princes, all the troops and the inhabitants of the city. No one was able to sing the Lord's chants from the fearful and agonizing emotion of the king and the whole multitude. He set it back up in its place . . .[8]

Interestingly enough, other contemporary sources, such as those West Syriac sources,[9] or the almost contemporary Coptic source of John of Nikiu, either do not mention the return of the True Cross or give it low prominence.[10] All of these sources, however, were written under Muslim rule, or preserved by communities who would have been all too aware of how offensive the spectacle of the cross was to Muslims, whether the True Cross or the veneration of the cross in general.

It is easy to see how offensive these spectacles would be to the believers. The Quranic presentation of Christians is one more of humility and acceptance of the message, such as in 5:82–3:

You shall find the most hostile people to the believers to be the Jews and the poly-theists; and you shall find the closest in affection to the believers those who say: "We are Christians." For among them are priests and monks, and they are not arrogant. And when they hear what was revealed to the Apostle, you see their eyes overflow with tears on account of the truth they recognize.

The context associated with these verses is usually that of a group of Christians who joined the Muslims returning from Ethiopia (approximately 628, just prior to the return of the True Cross).[11] Although the commentary of Tabari and others associates these Christians solely with the Ethiopians—who always had a better image in the Muslim world as a result of their hosting the first two *hijras*—it is significant that the much earlier commentary of Muqatil states that eight Syrian Christians were among this group.[12] Whether this is actually the case, it is clear from the series of attacks that Muhammad mounted toward the north during this period that Christians would have been more and more on his mind.

The Quranic selection represents a spirituality that is a world away from the type of imperial pomp that characterized Heraclius' triumphal entry into Jerusalem in which, according to the account of Nikephorus above, "everyone worshipped" the True Cross. It may have been this disconfirmation of what constituted the essential characteristics of Christianity known to Muhammad and the believers that led to the first attacks upon the Byzantines. Whereas the Christians who are described in the Quran would have been Monophysite monks and anchorites, located in various desert retreats throughout northern Arabia, the cult of the cross promoted by the Empire would have seemed alien and, in truth, polytheist in itself. Imagine the horror that a Muslim would have felt seeing the Christians return to Jerusalem, only to worship Jesus.

Attacking Christians after an initially conciliatory number of verses concerning them also would follow the pattern Muhammad and the Muslims displayed toward the Jews. Initially there was a period of conciliation and theological disputation in which the Muslims were worsted. As a result, after the first year and a half in Medina, Muhammad turned against the Jews, exiling some and massacring others (Quran 59:1–9).[13]

TWO PROBLEMS

There are several problems with interpreting the Muslim attacks upon the Byzantines as a response to the return of the True Cross to Jerusalem. The first is chronological. When, precisely, did Heraclius visit Jerusalem? The account of Theophanes cited above says during the spring of 629, which would accord well with the interpretation given above, as the Battle of Mu'ta, according to the traditional accounts, occurred in August of 629. But the Theophanes date is not generally accepted by Byzantinists, who believe that it would be unlikely that Heraclius would have come to Jerusalem at that time, but went to Constantinople, and then appeared in Jerusalem the following spring (of 630).

I would not want to gloss over this chronological issue. Obviously, it would be easier just to accept the date of Theophanes, because it would accord so nicely with my own interpretation, and follow Donner in throwing up his hands at the sometimes insurmountable problems with reconciling early Muslim chronologies (or occasionally Byzantine ones, for that matter). However, even if one does hold to the later chronology, there is another major attack, that of Tabuk in the summer of 631, that also could be seen as a response to the return of the True Cross. Personally, I would prefer to have Mu'ta be the response, because of the obvious religious significance that is accorded to it by the Muslim sources—especially given the important personalities who were killed during it. But it is impossible to come to a final conclusion concerning this matter.

An additional problem is the obvious question: If the return of the True Cross was indeed the catalyst for the change in Muslims' attitudes, then how were they not already aware of the Christian veneration of it, which has always been a major theme in Christianity? Would they have not already been aware of it and, by extension, the Trinitarian conception of the function of Jesus (opposed in Quran 4:157, 171, 5:116)? I think the answer to this question lies in the type of Christianity with which Muhammad was familiar. First, his familiarity would have been progressive and incomplete. Just as with Judaism, he would have gradually become familiar with the major tenets of Christianity. His primary knowledge of Christianity would have come from wandering and mendicant monks or second-hand from Ethiopian Christians. These types of Christianity could very well have downplayed the importance of the True Cross, whereas the imperial pomp of Heraclius' return to Jerusalem emphasized it. Although one cannot be absolutely certain when Muslims fixated upon the cross as a symbol of their differences with Christianity, one can note that Muslim attacks upon the cross as the symbol of Christianity are documented from an early period in Egypt and in Syria.[14]

MUSLIM ATTACKS: POLITICAL OR THEOLOGICAL OR BOTH?

I would propose that the initial Muslim attacks were actually theological in nature. This view is not a common one among the standard histories of the early conquests, which usually portray them as resulting from the aspirations of Muhammad to dominate the region of Syria-Transjordan or at least the desert areas bordering these provinces.[15]

Although one could say that later attacks carried out by the early Muslim community against the Byzantine and Sasanian empires were often driven by the desire for loot or by their own success on the battlefield, one cannot say that about the three raids Muhammad sent against the Byzantines. In actuality, each was a failure, and a large number of early Muslims died (especially at Mu'ta in Jumada al-Ula in August 629).[16] They served no strategic purpose, despite what Donner says about their function to increase Muhammad's control over northern Arabia. If that had been the case, then why go into Transjordan or Palestine at all? The region of northern Arabia contained many other areas not subdued by the Muslims. In fact, what would be the point of attacking the Byzantines at all, considering they were at their weakest after experiencing twenty-six years of warfare?

One cannot just dismiss this as some type of historical mistake or miscalculation. On the contrary, the sources say specifically that the target of the Muslim attacks was the Byzantines (although most probably the battles were fought with their Arab *foederati*).[17] Nor can one downplay the importance of these attacks from the point of view of Muhammad and the Muslims. For the Battle of Mu'ta, for example, Muhammad sent a number of his most trusted followers, such as Zayd bin Haritha, Ja'far bin Abi Talib, and 'Abdallah bin al-Rawaha, who all perished in the battle. On his deathbed he was sending out a similar column of troops under Usama bin Zayd (son of his former adopted son, Zayd, killed at Mu'ta). No fewer than three major attacks by the Muslims against the Byzantines occurred during this critical penultimate period of the Prophet's life. It is no wonder, then, that Muslims took the hint and began the great Islamic conquests, first against the Byzantine Christians in Syria-Palestine rather than the Sasanian Persians in Iraq.

These invasions complete a logical process during which, according to the Muslim perception of events, Christians deliberately provoked retribution by their obscene veneration of the True Cross in the holy city of Jerusalem. This type of desecration is one in which it is easier to understand the fury that Muslims brought to bear against Christian Byzantium, and the persistence with which they attacked it over the following 750 years. Consistently, despite periods of truce or weakness on the Muslim side, Byzantium was the principal foe of the Muslim world, as can be seen from discussions on this subject in the jihad literature. Given the fact of the Quranic verse prophesying the return of the Byzantines as an event at which "the believers shall rejoice" (and understanding the immutable aspect of the eternal Word of God in the Quran), there must have been some type of fundamental betrayal or heresy that caused such a radical change in the Muslims' attitude. The Muslims' abhorrence of the cross could be the catalyst for such a change.

NOTES

1. *The Qur'an: A Modern English Version*, trans. Majid Fakhry (London: Garnet, 1997).

2. For extensive discussion, see Suliman Bashear, "The Mission of Dihya al-Kalbi and the Situation in Syria," in *Studies in Early Islamic Tradition* (Jerusalem: Max Schloessinger Memorial Foundation, 2004), originally appearing in *Jerusalem Studies in Arabic and Islam* 14 (1991): 84–114.

3. See, for example, Abd al-Razzaq, *Tafsir*, ed. Mahmud Muhammad 'Abdu (Beirut: Dar al-Kutub al-'Ilmiyya, 1999), 3: 15; for other traditional *asbab al-nuzul*, see al-Wahidi, *Asbab al-nuzul* (Beirut: Dar al-Fikr, 1988), 231–32.

4. Muqatil b. Sulayman, *Tafsir Muqatil b. Sulayman*, ed. Mahmud Shihata (Cairo: al-Ha'iya al-Misriyya, 1983; repr., Beirut: Dar Ihya al-Turath al-'Arabi, 2003), 3: 407.

5. For details, see Walter Kaegi, *Heraclius* (Cambridge: Cambridge University Press, 2003), 78, 80, 175–79, 205–07, and passim.

6. *The Chronicle of Theophanes anni mundi 6095–6305 (A.D. 602–813)*, ed. and trans. Harry Turtledove (Philadelphia: University of Pennsylvania Press, 1982), 30. Walter Kaegi, in *Byzantium and the Early Islamic Conquests* (Cambridge: Cambridge University Press, 1993), 74–75, note 20, rejects this date (629), and states that he did not visit Jerusalem until March 630, but does not seem to confront this reference in Theophanes. See below.

7. *Nikephoros Patriarch of Constantinople, Short History*, trans. Cyril Mango (Washington, DC: Dumbarton Oaks, 1990), 67.

8. *The Armenian History Attributed to Sebeos*, trans. R.W. Thomson (Liverpool: Liverpool University Press, 1999), 1: 90.

9. *The Seventh Century in the West Syrian Chronicles*, trans. Andrew Palmer (Liverpool: Liverpool University Press, 1993).

10. Ibid., 142–43 (citing Dionysius of Tell-Mahre) has the reception of the True Cross from the Persians, but not its reinstallation in Jerusalem.

11. Tabari, *Jami' al-bayan fi ta'wil ay al-Qur'an* (Beirut: Dar al-Fikr, n.d.), 7: 1–4.

12. Muqatil, 1: 497–98.

13. M.J. Kister, "The Massacre of the Banu Qurayza," *Jerusalem Studies in Arabic and Islam*, 8 (1986): 61–96.

14. Robert Hoyland, *Seeing Islam as Others Saw It* (Princeton: Darwin, 1997), 151 (from 685), 462–63 (approximately the 630s), 549, 596–97.

15. Walter Kaegi, *Byzantium and the Early Islamic Conquests*, 71–74; Fred M. Donner, *The Early Islamic Conquests* (Princeton: Princeton University Press, 1981), 105–11; Hugh Kennedy, *The Great Arab Conquests* (London: Weidenfeld and Nicolson, 2007), 71.

16. See, for example, al-Bukhari, *Sahih* (Beirut: Dar al-Fikr, 1991), 3: 268 (no. 2798), where the four commanders are listed; for the date see Marsden Jones, "The Chronology of the *Maghazi*," *Bulletin of the School of Oriental and African Studies* 17 (1957): 245–80, at 255.

17. Muhammad bin Jarir Tabari, *Ta'rikh al-rusul wa-l-muluk* (Beirut: Rawa'i' al-Turath al-'Arabi, n.d.), 2: 36–42.

CHAPTER 4

Challenging the Islamist Politicization of Islam: The Non-Islamic Origins of Muslim Political Concepts

Sherko Kirmanj

One of the means used by Islamists to justify their ideology is to sanctify their message with a religious gloss. Islamists claim that most Muslim manners, values, rules, and regulations are derived from Islamic scriptural sources, primarily the Quran. They use this assertion as the basis for politicizing their faith. This chapter examines this Islamist claim. In particular, it investigates the origins of traditional Muslim political concepts, including *shura* (consultation), caliphate, *hilf* (pact), *dhimmis* (non-Muslims), jihad, *anfal* (war-booty), *din* (religion), and *dawla* (state), all of which constitute the basic building blocks of Islamist political theory.[1] It is argued here that a close scrutiny of the historical roots and cultural origins of these Muslim political practices shows that they are based on pre-Islamic Arab tribal traditions as well as Iranian and Byzantine political concepts; in other words, they are not exclusively Islamic.

Most Islamists avow that the core values and principles of their religion were divinely revealed to the Prophet Muhammad by Allah in order to dispel pre-Islamic beliefs.[2] The assertion that the priorities and practices of newly converted Arab tribes were radically altered by Islam lacks historical evidence.[3] Original Islamic documents do not provide guidelines for governance, and they rarely mention political issues.[4] Islamists, however, claim that several Islamic political concepts were employed for the first time by the Prophet Muhammad and by the Muslim rulers who succeeded him. Generally speaking, religions, including Islam, have no inherent political principles; however, religions sometimes favor the political values of the community in which they were formed. In the case of Islam, these initially were the traditions of the pre-Islamic Arab tribes and, later, practices imported from the Iranian and Byzantine Empires as Islam expanded beyond the Arabian Peninsula.

To consider this subject in depth, it is helpful to divide Islamists (those who argue for the inseparability of Islam and politics) into two groups. First, there are early Islamists, who include Muslim *'ulama* (learned people) and Muslim *fuqaha* (jurists) living between the seventh and fourteenth centuries, such as Abu Hamid al-Ghazali, Ibn Taymiyya, and Ibn Khaldun. Second, there are contemporary Islamists, those who emerged after the collapse of the Ottoman Empire in the early twentieth century and their intellectual heirs today, including Hasan al-Banna, Abul A'ala Mawdudi, Sayyid Qutb, and Yousuf al-Qaradawi. The term "Islamism" will be employed to refer to the political ideology of early and contemporary Islamists, which is based upon Islam's main sources, namely, the Quran and the Sunna (the sayings and practices of the Prophet Muhammad).[5] As mentioned above, the concepts used by Islamists to politicize Islam can be classified as pre-Islamic and non-Islamic (i.e., deriving from the Iranian and Byzantine empires). In the following pages their origins will be explored.

PRE-ISLAMIC POLITICAL CONCEPTS: *SHURA* AND CALIPHATE

A claim of discontinuity between pre- and post-Islamic practices is artificial, because Islam was born within the framework of Arab tribal culture, and that culture became the foundation of Muslim civilization.[6] Indeed, most early Muslim practices stemmed from Arabic tribal traditions. This is evident in three periods: the early years of Islam, that is, during the lifetime of the Prophet; the era of the four "rightly guided" caliphs following his death; and in the succeeding Umayyad and Abbasid dynasties. The practices and concepts that emerged during these early phases of the religion will now be considered.

In Islamic history *shura* has usually been associated with discussions and consultations among Muslim community leaders (who are often referred to as *ahl al-Hal wa al-'Aqd*—those who are qualified to unbind and bind). One of the main tasks of *ahl al-Hal wa al-'Aqd* was to select a caliph and give *bay'ah* (promise) to it. Thus *shura* is closely linked to a second concept, the caliphate, an Islamic institution whereby the caliph, the successor to Muhammad, is both spiritual leader and temporal ruler of the Islamic state. Both terms—*shura* and caliphate—need to be considered together.

Shura is an Arabic term meaning consultation, and is mentioned twice in the Quran. The first verse (3:159) reads: "thus it is due to mercy from Allah that you deal with them gently, and had you been rough, hard hearted, they would certainly have dispersed from around you; pardon them therefore and ask pardon for them, and take counsel (*shura*) with them in the affair." The second passage (42:37–8) states: "and those who respond to their Lord and keep up prayer, and their rule is to take counsel (*shura*) among themselves." For Islamists, the concept of *shura* is the basis for establishing Islamic government. Yousuf al-Qaradawi (born 1926), a contemporary Islamist, says Islam considers *shura* the foundation of the Islamic lifestyle and Shari'a.[7] In addition, according to Ibn Khaldun (1332–1406), an early Islamist, the appointment of a caliph is recognized as part of Shari'a through the *ijma'* (consensus, i.e., agreement of Islamic judges on legal matters, one of the sources of the Islamic legal tradition). He states that Abu Bakr al-Sidiq, the first caliph (ruled 632–634), appointed Umar bin Khatab, the second caliph (ruled 634–644) as his successor in the presence of the Prophet's companion.[8] Also, Abul A'ala Mawdudi (1903–1979), a leading Islamist figure, believes that the Islamic political system is based on three principles: *tawhid* (unity of Allah), *risalat* (the message), and the caliphate.[9]

Considered within its historical context, however, the practice of *shura* formed part of the pre-Islamic system of intertribal consultation among community leaders.[10] It represented an Arabian "nomadic egalitarian ethos."[11] But why did this tradition pass from pre-Islamic Arabs to Muslims? The explanation for the continuation of *shura* and other practices seems to lie in the deep-rooted Arab conviction that their safety could only be ensured by following exactly the ways of their ancestors.[12] Traditions can provide feelings of certainty and security, and also foster notions of community identity. The stories, narrations, and debates of people in Arab-Islamic culture are normally centered on their history, and they draw lessons from proverbs and historical events.

Returning to the main theme of this section, the selection of a successor following the death of a sheikh (tribal chief) was an important process in Arab tribes. The elders of a tribe were responsible for this choice, and the decision was made at a meeting of the adult males of the group. This process occurred after the death of the Prophet Muhammad; however, the main difference between the pre-Islamic and Islamic eras in the nomination of a successor is that the selecting group in the latter period was named *ahl al-Hal wa al-'Aqd*, and the new leader became the caliph of Muslims instead of the sheikh. These adaptations occurred for two reasons. First, since the Prophet's authority extended over more than one tribe, to call the successor a sheikh was no longer appropriate; and, second, the term "caliph" was adopted because it was more appealing due to being mentioned in the Quran several times. It was then used to silence opponents from tribes other than the Quraysh (the Prophet's tribe). After the death of the Prophet, the Muslims of Medina selected Sa'd bin Ubaida as head of the community, but Abu Bakr and Umar rejected this proposal and argued that the unity of the community could be preserved only if a man from the Quraysh was selected. They stressed that the Muslims from Mecca (emigrants) would not accept any leader outside the Quraysh.[13]

Regarding the title "caliph," it should be noted that when used in the Quran the term has no particular religious significance. The word appears in many places with different meanings. Generally, it signifies vicegerent, i.e., deputy or successor.[14] It also refers to people who occupy lands formerly held by other tribes who have been destroyed by God in punishment for disobedience. It means king, as in "O, David We have made you a caliph in the earth" (38:26). The term was used by the first four caliphs to indicate the successor of the Prophet and then by some Umayyad and Abbasid caliphs to mean "caliph of God" or "shadow of God on earth." It is also important to note that the theory of the caliphate was first formalized during the Abbasid era, not by the early Muslims of Mecca or Medina (see below).

The men selected as caliphs to succeed the Prophet were not chosen because of their religious affiliation, but because they were well-known Quraysh leaders. This is evident from the debate that took place on the day of the death of the Prophet, with the Quraysh leaders being represented by Abu Bakr and Umar and the Muslims of Medina by Sa'd bin Ubaida. Their lines of disagreement were based on tribal and regional affiliations rather than on religion. Each group wanted one of its own to be selected.[15] Abu Bakr, Umar, Othman bin Afan (the third caliph, ruled 644–656), Ali bin Abi Talib (the fourth caliph, ruled 656–661), all Umayyad caliphs, and most Abbasid caliphs were descended from the Quraysh. The process of selecting a leader was not mentioned in the Quran. It is recorded that on one occasion the Prophet Muhammad asked Abu Bakr to lead a public prayer in his stead, but this should be seen as a religious activity not as a political appointment to leadership of the community.

Another method of selecting a caliph among early Muslims entailed a reigning caliph appointing a suitable successor. Early Islamists, such as al-Mawardi (974–1058) and al-Baghdadi (980–1037), endorsed this method.[16] The appointee usually was a son or relative of the reigning caliph. The line of succession was not always clearly defined and not always confined to family members, because the tribe needed the best man available for the job, regardless of parentage or privilege.[17]

THE CONCEPT OF *HILF* (ALLIANCE)

It was a common practice among Arab tribes in pre-Islamic times to unite in the face of challenges or danger. This was usually between equals or between several individuals or groups, and it was common to pledge support against rivals in the event of conflict.[18] Sometimes the alliance was between unequal parties, and in such cases the strongest tribe usually agreed to aid the weaker. Both the Pact of Medina (in which the

Prophet Muhammad participated as leader of the community of believers) and the pre-Islamic *Hilf al-Fudul* (Alliance of the Virtuous, defined below) were conducted in conformity with traditional Arab practices.[19] The importance of these events to this study is that Islamists have inappropriately used the Medina Pact as justification for, and evidence of, religious involvement in government and politics.

Hilf al-Fudul was an agreement among several pre-Islamic Arab tribes in the seventh century to prevent injustice and to aid those who had been wronged. The immediate reason for forming this alliance was an insult suffered by a merchant from Yemen. A clan from the Quraysh tribe had stolen his goods, and in vain the Yemeni sought help from the Quraysh leaders. When the Banu Hashim (the clan of the Prophet) heard of this incident they called a meeting that resulted in the formation of the *Hilf al-Fudul*. Muhammad was present at the meeting, though this was prior to his prophethood. Afterward he is recorded to have said that if he were to be invited to a similar alliance in Islam he would accept without reservation. He further stressed that any good and noble contract made in *jahiliya* (i.e., the period of ignorance preceding the arrival of Islam) is automatically endorsed by Islam.[20] The Medina Pact was a similar agreement between several tribes in the region. Both alliances were in the Arab tribal tradition and neither was concerned with religion, contrary to the claims of Islamists.[21] It is misleading to suggest that the Medina Pact in any way constituted the formation of an Islamic state.[22] It is also relevant to note that despite the similarity of these traditional pacts, no Islamist has ever suggested that the *Hilf al-Fudul* should be considered as the first constitution of Mecca.

In the light of the above discussion, it can be seen that the Medina Pact was a simple tribal way of organizing local community affairs in the historical framework of its time. Such alliances were used before Islam and continued to be practiced after the emergence of Islam, and it is an exaggerated distortion of history to accord it a meaning or a significance that did not exist. The Medina Pact as a concept for organizing the affairs of the various communities in Medina was a pre-Islamic model subsequently adopted by Muslims and other sects. Consequently, instead of referring to this pact as the "Constitution of Medina" (as Islamists claim), it would be more accurate to describe it as the Alliance of Medina.

DHIMMIS (NON-MUSLIMS)

In evaluating the origins of political concepts in Islam, it is relevant to consider the notion of *dhimmis*, a term that Islamists use to regulate the relationship between Muslims and non-Muslims and also between Islamic and non-Islamic states. The word *dhimmi* comes from the Arabic root *dhim*, where *dhimma* means "being in the care of somebody." Muslims have used the term *dhimmi* to describe non-Muslims who are living among Muslims and are provided with security and freedom in return for a payment called *jizya* (poll tax). This arrangement was prescribed in the Quran (9:29): "fight those who do not believe in Allah, nor in the latter day, nor do they prohibit what Allah and His Messenger have prohibited, nor follow the religion of truth, out of those who have been given the Book, until they pay the tax in acknowledgment of superiority and they are in a state of subjection." Originally, *dhimmi* applied to Christians and Jews, but with the later expansion of Islam it was applied to other religions. The Islamic meaning of the term has developed from the Arab practice whereby a strong tribe protects weaker tribes or clans. For a powerful Arab tribe it was a matter of honor to demonstrate its ability and intention to protect smaller tribes; the protector tribe prohibited raiding against the tribes or clans under its custodianship—in other words, the latter had become clients of the former.[23]

During the early years of Islam this practice continued to be implemented by Muslims, though with a few slight changes. It was transformed from protecting others with a tribal allegiance to protection based on religious affiliation. Christians of Egypt and Mesopotamia were better-protected minorities under Arab-Muslim rulers than under Byzantine Greeks[24] because, as mentioned above, for pre-Islamic Arabs it was a matter of honor to see that their protection was effective, and this attitude passed on to Muslim rulers.

The principle of *dhimma* was a socio-tribal concept of pre-Islamic Arabs and was adopted as part of Islamic culture, though with the passing of years it became sanctified in religious terms. Although *dhimmis* is mentioned in the Quran, because it asserts the superiority of Muslims and endorses the subjugation of non-Muslims, *dhimma* (as stated in the above Quranic verse) is an inappropriate principle for determining the relationship between Muslims and non-Muslims.

JIHAD AND *ANFAL*

For Arabs living in the Arabian Peninsula, herding, agriculture, trading, and, more importantly, *ghazu* (raiding) were traditionally the principle sources of livelihood. Raiding was part of intertribal warfare, though it was practiced within strict guidelines. Its main objective was to capture livestock (camels, cattle, and sheep) from an enemy, though with a minimum of casualties.[25] After the Prophet's migration from Mecca to Medina, the Muslims in Medina (especially the emigrants from Mecca) could not afford to live without a source of income, so they resorted to raiding. Moreover, in the desert environment raiding was a ready way of redistributing resources. Raiding groups took all necessary measures to avoid casualties, but they missed no opportunity to attack caravans or contingents of their rival tribes to carry off booty and livestock.[26]

The Arabian concepts of raiding and *anfal* (war-booty) were integral to the first great expansion of Islam. Most of the participants in the expeditions probably fought for booty rather than for religion.[27] This is evident from the first clashes between Muslims and pagans of Mecca at the battles of Badr (624) and Uhud (625). The reason for the Battle of Badr was that emigrants fleeing persecution by the Quraysh in Mecca had escaped to Medina and started to conduct raids against the rich Meccan caravans, which became a source of income. These small raids continued until March 624, at which time the Prophet Muhammad led a large group of emigrants against a Meccan caravan laden with goods. The Muslims inflicted a stunning defeat on the Meccans at the Well of Badr and, as a result, acquired considerable treasure.

Regarding disputes about the distribution of the booty, the *sura* (chapter) of *al-Anfal* was revealed, and the relevant verse (8:1) reads as follows: "They ask you about the windfalls [spoils of war]. Say: The windfalls are for Allah and the Messenger."[28] The *sura* takes its name *al-Anfal* from the first verse. It was revealed after the Battle of Badr, the first major clash between Muslims and pagans. More importantly, in the Battle of Uhud (the second major skirmish) the situation was described in the Quran (3:152–3) this way: "And certainly Allah made good to you His promise when you slew them by His permission, until when you became weak-hearted and disputed about the affair [the booty] and disobeyed after He had shown you that which you loved . . . When you ran off precipitately and did not wait for any one." It appears from these verses that the main reason for losing the battle was that Muslim fighters ignored orders to maintain their position; the greed of the archers who left in search of spoils was the principal factor contributing to the defeat of the Muslim army.[29] This should not be understood as saying that Muslims were fighting only for booty and materialistic benefits. Indeed, there were many who thought that if they were killed on a battleground they would be martyrs and so would rest in heaven.

It is historically apparent that raiding was commonplace among Arabs in the pre-Islamic era. Also, raiding was not considered immoral unless it entailed stealing from kinsmen.[30] This became an integral part of the Muslim community in its search for resources and income, as raids ensured a substantial turnover of goods and wealth. Thus jihad, in the context of raiding, was the continuation of a pre-Islamic Arab practice later adopted by Muslims. Having said that, jihad has a religious context and was described by the Prophet as "the struggle against one's self."[31] This means, in strictly religious terms, making the maximum effort to keep control over one's own negative feelings, such as arrogance, jealousy, greed, revenge, and anger. It also means bringing oneself closer to God through self-denial, charity, and a moral life.[32]

In addition to jihad and *anfal*, another element of the Islamic faith is *khums* (fifth), which is prescribed in the Quran (8:41) as "whatever thing you gain [war-booty], a fifth of it is for Allah and for the Messenger and for the near of kin and the orphans and the needy and the wayfarer." The Prophet Muhammad's share of the war-booty was determined by a customary rule for distributing the plunder among the people in pre-Islamic Arabia. According to Arabic tribal traditions, the sheikh was entitled to one quarter or one-fifth of the booty.[33] Hence, the Islamic rule was only a slight alteration of an old practice.

Islamists use the historical example of the Prophet's role in fighting in the Medina period to conclude that jihad (fighting in the way of Allah) is an integral part of Islam's involvement in political affairs. It is argued here that the Prophet's involvement in raiding and fighting can only be understood in the context of the socioeconomic and cultural framework of Arabs of the day and in his role as a community leader, not in the context of his role as a religious leader. Therefore, the concept of jihad should not be used as a political principle and as a justification to politicize Islam, as alleged by Islamists. Additionally, it is clear from the Quranic verse about war-booty (cited above) that it is false and misleading to interpret it outside of its historical and cultural frameworks.

RELIGION AND STATE: A NON-ISLAMIC POLITICAL CONCEPT

The previous sections dealt with the political models used by Islamists to politicize Islam that actually have their origins in pre-Islamic Arab culture. It is appropriate now to examine the relationship between religion and state, a concept that has roots in the Iranian and Byzantine Empires. Before identifying the sources of the association of state and religion, it is necessary to look at how early and contemporary Islamists describe this relationship and how it has been Islamized. Abu Hamid al-Ghazali (1058–1111), an early Islamist, says that "Kingship and religion are twins, religion is the root and sultan (worldly authority) is the protector."[34] Ibn Taymiyya (1263–1328) also believes that state and religion are inseparable. He maintains that "the sultan is the shadow of God on earth," and if "religion and state are separated discord and disorder prevail."[35]

Basically, early Islamists argue that religion and state are indivisible, this belief being based on the traditional ways in which Muslim rulers applied their authority and how they related to the people. Both Muslim rulers and Islamists, however, were influenced by Iranian political thought, tradition, and practice, especially during the Abbasid era. The Iranian view of monarchy was transmitted in the *Testament of Ardashir* (an Iranian king, ruled 224–241). This document contained the famous statement that "Kingship and religion are twins . . . religion is the foundation of kingship and kingship the protector of religion . . . for whatever lacks a foundation must perish, and whatever lacks a protector disappears."[36] This Iranian concept echoes almost word-for-word al-Ghazali's statement cited above. It is now clear where both al-Ghazali and Ibn Taymiyya acquired the concept of an indivisible religion and state, and it is useful to consider how it was absorbed into Islamist ideology.

An early Muslim scholar, Abdullah Ibn Muqaffa' (720–759), strongly contributed to the incorporation of Iranian traditions into Islam by translating many books into Arabic. His most influential and best-known translation was *Kilila wa-Dumna*, a work comprising much traditional wisdom, some of a political character. Ibn Muqaffa' also translated two Iranian political treatises on kingship, *The Testament of Aradashir* (mentioned above) and *The Letter of Tansar*.[37] It seems that Ibn Muqaffa' was keen to extol Iranian royal achievement and the virtues of Persian monarchical statecraft.[38]

The influence of Iranian tradition is evident in the later Islamist theoreticians, especially those who had access to the Persian language. For example, al-Ghazali says, "if the king is just, the world will be prosperous and the subjects secure, as it was in the time of Ardashir, Afaridun, Bahram Gur and Anushirawan [Iranian monarchs]. But if the king is tyrannical, the world will be depopulated as it was in the time of Zahhak, Afrasiyab and Yazdigird." On the basis of these lines al-Ghazali reaches the conclusion that "the wise men of the world had spoken rightly when they said 'religion depends on kingship.'"[39] It is evident that al-Ghazali's writings were influenced in two ways by the Persian example. First, when he talks about noble and good rulers he mostly mentions the "just" Iranian kings. Second, the basis of his conclusion is the wisdom derived from Iranian traditions, and his statement that "religion depends on kingship" is said to be part of King Ardashir's testament.

The reason for intermingling religion with politics can be found in one of Ibn Muqaffa''s books, *Risala*. In that work he argues that "power based on a religion which prescribes the same duties for ruler and subjects is going to be more stable than power on subordination or arbitrary force."[40] Thus Ibn Muqaffa' and al-Ghazali's writings suggest that the symbiosis of religion and state in Islam was developed by early Islamists who were, in turn, influenced by Iranian ideas of the link between religion and kingship. This connection was founded on the assumption that religion was a means of ensuring stability within Muslim communities. Historically, the link seems to have been justified because, with the expansion of Islam and subsequent conversion of other communities (Persians, Kurds, Turks, Urdus, Indians, etc.), whether willingly or by force, religion was the only common element able to provide a sense of unity. The other explanation for the adoption of Iranian traditions into Islam is that the system of Arab-Islamic tribal rule was inadequate for administering an empire that extended from Central Asia to North Africa. Such a task required new concepts and ideas of government, and because Arabs had no experience of any form of government other than the tribe it was necessary for Islamist theoreticians to develop new approaches. The new notions of religion and government came from both Iran and the Byzantine Empire.

THE POLITICIZATION AND EXPANSION OF ISLAM: THE NECESSITY OF A STATE

As noted above, most political concepts in Islamic ideology originated from either pre-Islamic (Arabic) or non-Islamic (Iranian and Byzantine) sources. It is now appropriate to discuss the reasons for the politicization of Islam in its early stages and to consider why such a process was almost inevitable.

The rapid expansion of Islamic territory throughout non-Arab lands during and after the reign of Umar (ruled 634–644), and the ever-increasing numbers of Arabic-speaking Muslim converts, confronted rulers with problems of security and order, as well as with a financial crisis.[41] The massive gains by Muslim military leaders and caliphs obliged them to find ways to manage their new wealth. A distinctive characteristic of Arabs at the time was illiteracy,[42] so they needed the help of non-Arabs to manage their fledgling financial institutions.

In the formative years of Islam the system of administration was relatively simple. Regarding taxation and correspondence, there were no specific ranks, and there were no political matters that would have required the use of secretaries or written records because the caliphate was a religious function and had little to do with politics.[43] Moreover, it is apparent that during the years of the first four caliphs and the first Umayyad caliphs the continued use of pre-Islamic political practices was reasonably adequate. However, with the expansion of the faith these tactics proved inadequate for the administration of a great empire; thus, the development of more sophisticated ways of governance was needed. As a consequence, *diwan* (the office of tax collection) was established. *Diwan* is not an Arabic word but of Near East origin, and originally it meant "register" or "finance." The first caliph to establish a *diwan* was Umar, on the advice of Khalid bin al-Walid (a military leader), who is reported to have told him, "I have seen the rulers of Syria [Byzantines] keeping *diwan*." The official languages used in *diwan* until the time of Abdul Malik bin Marwan (an Umayyad caliph, ruled 685–705) were Persian in Iraq and Greek in Syria. Meanwhile, the office of *vizier* (executive officer) was incorporated into the Islamic state in the early Abbasid era; it was inherited from the Sassanian (Iranian) Empire.[44] In fact, even the word *vizier* came from the old Iranian word *vcir* (judge).[45]

Regarding the judicial institution known as *al-qada* (court of arbitration), again Umar was the first to appoint a *qadi* (judge) to avoid the need to adjudicate personally every dispute that arose in the community.[46]

However, the first official office of *qadi* developed during the Umayyad period. Each *qadi* made decisions as he thought fit because there were no fixed laws. A body of law was developed by four jurists, the founders of the four Sunni Islamic schools of law: Hanafi (699–767), Maliki (716–795), Shafi'i (767–820), and Hanbali (780–855). These men, and other *'ulama*, adopted the methodology of analogy to interpret Quranic texts, and their interpretations led to the formation of Shari'a.

From this account it can be seen that there were no state institutions in the early Islamic period; the need for such institutions arose as Islamic territory expanded by conquest, and administrative offices like *vizier* and *diwan* were adopted from neighboring empires. Furthermore, the transfer of the Islamic capital from Medina to Kufa to Damascus and, later, to Baghdad, and the development of the offices of *vizier*, *diwan*, and *qadi*, all facilitated the acceptance of Iranian and Byzantine traditions by Muslims.

POWER STRUGGLE: POLITICAL-RELIGIOUS ARGUMENTS

In addition to the expansion of the faith, internal power struggles and political arguments were key factors that contributed to the politicization of Islam during the first centuries of Muslim history. The first political issue concerned the claims and counter-claims of opposing groups, in particular Sunnis, Shi'as and Khawarijis.[47] After the murder of the third caliph, Othman, in 661 and the accession of Ali as the fourth caliph, Mu'awiyah bin Abi Sufyan (then governor of Syria) sought to avenge the murder of Othman, who was a member of his clan. During the course of a battle with the followers of Ali, Mu'awiyah called for negotiations while ordering his warriors to raise the Quran on the tips of their swords.[48] At first Ali did not trust Mu'awiyah's intentions; however, after an indecisive struggle (the Battle of Siffin, 657) he was forced to agree to arbitration by referees. This concession aroused the anger of a large group of Ali's followers (the Khawarijis), who protested that according to the Holy Book (6:57), "judgment belongs to God alone." They believed that arbitration would be a refutation of another Quranic verse (49:9): "If one party rebels against the other, fight against that which rebels." This historical example illustrates the socio-political conflicts about power between Sunnis, Shi'as, and Khawarijis and the ways in which the Quran was used to justify each party's cause. Such conflicts have been transformed into ideological arguments, and Islamic texts used (and abused) as tools.[49]

In later years, a lack of legitimacy forced the Umayyads and Abbasids to adopt the practice of using Islam as an ideological weapon to justify their rule. For example, al-Ghazali wrote the book *al-Mustazhir* to emphasize the legitimacy of the Abbasid Caliph al-Mustazhir (ruled 1094–1118). The purpose of the book was to argue against the *Batiniya*, a sect that recognized the Fatimid (a branch of Shi'ism), rivals to the Sunni Abbasid caliphate. A similar polemic was penned by Ibn Taymiyya, *Minhaj al-Sunna*, which was a repudiation of Shi'ism.[50] At about the same time, the Saljuk (Turkish) Sunni rulers initiated the establishment of *madrasas* (Islamic teaching schools). Nizam al-Mulik (1018–1092), a powerful Saljuk sultan, was the first to fund a madrasa, its purpose being to train students capable of countering the propaganda then being promoted by the rival Isma'ilis (Shi'as).[51]

The Islamist method of using religious texts as political tools has continued from the earliest years to the present. Sayyid Qutb, one of the most influential contemporary Islamists, stated that his religion had established the Islamic *umma* (nation), and that whenever the nation has to be revived it will be accomplished "only" by Islam.[52] In a similar vein, Fahmi Huwaidi, a contemporary Egyptian Islamist, asserts that in the past Muslim nations had a weapon in their hands they often used for victory (i.e., Islam), but when it was thrown away defeat and oblivion followed.[53] Islamists believe that Islam once brought into existence the best and most powerful of nations, and that the religion can be used again to reverse history. Hasan al-Banna suggests that "there is no reason why an accomplishment which was made by Islam in the past cannot be repeated today."[54]

It is clear that the main objective for contemporary Islamists is to gain power, and to do so they use religion as an ideological weapon, just as it had been used by their predecessors, the early Islamists. Basically, Islam is seen as a political ideology, not as a religion. It is argued here that if a religious text is placed at the mercy of the ideologues then the religion is open to ideological misappropriation.[55]

THE THEORY OF THE CALIPHATE

After the death of the Prophet Muhammad, the caliph headed the Islamic community. Nevertheless, the official theorization about the caliphate started during the Abbasid era. With the expansion of Islam, the main bond between the caliph and his subjects was religion, and so Ibn Muqaffa' made this the centerpiece of his political theory.[56] The theory of the caliphate was a response to the growing power of the Turkish sultans, and it also emerged at a time of declining Abbasid power in the tenth century. Other factors were the rise to power of a mainly Turkish praetorian guard in Baghdad and the Shi'a threats represented by the Buydis (a Shi'a sultanate in the east) and the Fatimids in the west. All of these trends encouraged the Sunnis to develop a strategy of radical disengagement between religious authority and political authority. Al-Ghazali was one of the first to write about this process, suggesting that "the caliph (religious authority) is he to whom the sultan (military or political authority) professes his allegiance."[57] He wanted to preserve the religious life of the community and sought a workable compromise between caliph and sultan. Basically, the aims of early Islamists were to strengthen the position of the caliph against the usurpation of power by Turkish, Buyid, and Fatimid sultans and thereby "vindicate and uphold the Divine purpose of the Muslim state."[58]

It is relevant to mention that early Islamists were unable to formulate the theory of the caliphate from the main Islamic sources and, consequently, they sought to harmonize an existing historical situation with Shari'a. This is evident in each individual Islamist's theory of the caliphate, for each one reflects the historical circumstances in which it was formed and its effects on the respective Muslim communities and rulers. For example, at the time of Ibn Taymiyya the Abbasid caliphate had already collapsed, and so the center of gravity of his theory shifted from the caliphate to the community, whose life, according to Taymiyya, must be regulated by Shari'a.[59] Hence, the theory of the caliphate was a reactionary response to both domestic and external challenges that faced the Abbasid rulers.

It can be argued, then, that Islamic political thought is the outcome of the selective interpretation of the principles and values revealed in the Quran, those principles being used to deal with the historical and political realities faced by the Islamic empire during its early expansion. Also, those interpretations were used during internal power struggles and ideological conflicts within Muslim communities. The outcome of these clashes was a body of political doctrine comprising pre-Islamic Arabian concepts intertwined with Byzantine and Iranian political theories.

CONCLUSION

Islamist political theory is based on concepts such as *shura* (consultation), caliphate, *hilf* (alliance), *dhimmis* (non-Muslims), jihad, *anfal* (war-booty), and the principle of the inseparability of state and religion. This study has traced the origins of these concepts and concluded that they are either pre-Islamic or non-Islamic. It has established that *shura, hilf, dhimmis,* jihad, and *anfal* were all part of traditional Arabian tribal values or practices. The notion of inseparability of state and religion was an Iranian concept adopted by Muslims after the expansion of Islam into that country, and it was intermingled with Islam by early Islamists.

The process of the politicization of Islam emerged after the events of the first *fitna* (strife), that is, the conflict between Ali and Mu'awiyah. At the same time, the Khawarijis used Quranic verses to provide the illusion of divine authority for their political arguments against Ali. Versions of this particular historic incident shaped the identity and political thought of the first generation of Muslims, and this has continued through subsequent generations until today. This internal conflict divided the Muslim community; as a consequence, deep ideological lines emerged as each party used Islam as a political tool to undermine the arguments of its rivals. On the other hand, the expansion of Islam and its control over vast territories and people from diverse ethnic backgrounds made Muslim rulers confront a number of financial, administrative, and military issues. The fact that the great majority of Arabs at the time had no experience of any form of administration other than the tribe was another reason that they reached out to Iranian and Byzantine political practices. It was at this stage that Islamic political theory emerged. Islam became politicized because Arab leaders found religion to be a force for uniting the disparate people over whom they ruled. It was the one factor that they all had in common; moreover, it was a way of controlling people, for rebellion against rulers was claimed to be tantamount to defying God.

NOTES

1. These are certainly not all of the political concepts used by Islamists; however, this study covers the ones mentioned as it is believed they are the most critical.

2. Sayyid Qutb, *Milestones*, trans. Abdul Naeem (New Delhi: Noida Printing Press, 1998), 9.

3. Alfons Teipen, "*Jahilite* and Muslim Women: Questions of Continuity and Communal Identity," *Muslim World* 92, no. 3–4 (2002): 437–60.

4. For a detailed analysis of this argument, see Sherko Kirmanj, "Islam, Politics and Government," *Totalitarian Movements and Political Religions* 9, no. 1 (2008): 55–57.

5. Kirmanj, "Islam, Politics and Government," 44.

6. Bassam Tibi, *The Challenge of Fundamentalism: Political Islam and the New World Disorder* (Berkeley: University of California Press, 2002), 48.

7. Yousuf al-Qaradawi, *Min Fiqih al-Dawlah fi al-Islam* (Cairo: Dar al-Shruq, 1996), 134–36.

8. Ibn Khaldun, *The Muqaddimah: An Introduction to History*, trans. Franz Rosenthal (Princeton: Princeton University Press, 1989), 167. Ibn Khaldun was a famous Arab Muslim historian, philosopher, and sociologist born in present-day Tunisia. He is regarded as a forefather of sociology, best known for his *Muqaddimah (Prolegomenon)*.

9. Abul A'ala Mawdudi, *Essential Features of the Islamic Political System* (1948), http://www.islam101.com/politics/politicalsystem.htm.

10. Tibi, *The Challenge of Fundamentalism*, 30, 174.

11. Nazih Ayubi, *Political Islam: Religion and Politics in the Arab World* (London: Routledge, 1991), 32.

12. Montgomery Watt, *Islamic Political Thought: The Basic Concepts* (Edinburgh: Edinburgh University Press, 1968), 37.

13. Ibid., 31.

14. From the viewpoint of the Quran, vicegerency is a social relationship, the bond that binds man to the earth and to his fellow human beings. For details,

see Muhammad Baqir al-Sadr, *Trends of History in the Quran* (Karachi: Islamic Seminary Publications, n.d.), http://www.al-islam.org/trends/10.htm.

15. Abu Ja'far al-Tabari, *Tarikh al-Tabari*, ed. Sidqi Jamil al-Atar (Beirut: Dar al-Fikir lil-Nashir, 1998), 3: 255–69; Ibn Qutaybah al-Dinawari, *al-Imamah wa al-Siyasa* (Beirut: Manshurat al-Sharif al-Ridhi, 1990), 1: 17–27. Al-Tabari (839–923) was a Muslim historian, perhaps the most famous chronicler of early Islamic history. Ibn Qutayba al-Dinawari (828–89) was another well-known early Muslim theologian and historian.

16. Antony Black, *The History of Islamic Political Thought from the Prophet to the Present* (Edinburgh: Edinburgh University Press, 2001), 85.

17. Karen Armstrong, *Muhammad: A Western Attempt to Understand Islam* (London: Victor Gollancz, 1991), 60; Erwin I. J. Rosenthal, *Political Thought in Medieval Islam: An Introductory Outline* (Cambridge: Cambridge University Press, 1962), 33–34.

18. Watt, *Islamic Political Thought*, 8.

19. Bernard Lewis, et al., eds., *Encyclopaedia of Islam*, 2nd ed. (Leiden: E. J. Brill, 1960–2005), 2: 389.

20. Rachid Ghannouchi, "Participation in Non-Islamic Government," in *Liberal Islam: A Sourcebook*, ed. Charles Kurzman (Oxford: Oxford University Press, 1998), 93.

21. Muqtedar Khan, "The Compact of Medina: A Constitutional Theory of the Islamic State," *Mirror International*, May 30, 2001, http://www.ijtihad.org/compact.htm.

22. For details, see Kirmanj, "Islam, Politics and Government," 51.

23. Karen Armstrong, *Islam: A Short History* (London: Phoenix Press, 2003), 16.

24. Watt, *Islamic Political Thought*, 49–51.

25. John L. Esposito, *Islam: The Straight Path* (Oxford: Oxford University Press, 1998), 3.

26. Armstrong, *Islam*, 16.

27. Watt, *Islamic Political Thought*, 18.

28. See, also, introduction to the *sura* by Abul A'ala Mawdudi, http://www.islamonline.net/surah/english/viewSurah.asp?hSurahID=18.

29. See introduction to the *sura* by Abul A'ala Mawdudi, http://www.islamonline.net/surah/english/viewSurah.asp?hSurahID=1.

30. Armstrong, *Muhammad*, 60.

31. See Roxanne L. Euben, "Killing for Politics: Jihad, Martyrdom and Political Action," *Political Theory* 30, no. 1 (2002): 12.

32. Patrick Lang, "Wahhabism and Jihad," *America* 188, no. 8 (March 10, 2003): 11.

33. Ann K. S. Lambton, *State and Government in Medieval Islam* (New York: Oxford University Press, 1981), 215; Watt, *Islamic Political Thought*, 22.

34. Abu Hamid al-Ghazali, *Ihya Ulum al-Din* (n.d.), http://www.al-eman.com/IslamLib/viewtoc.asp?BID=383; Black, *The History of Islamic Political Thought*, 100; al-Qaradawi, *Min Fiqih*, 19.

35. Ibn Taymiyya, *Al-Siyasa al-Shar'iyya fi Islah al-Ra'i wa al-Ra'iya* (Dar al-Ma'rifa, 1961), 137.

36. See Black, *The History of Islamic Political Thought*, 21; Lambton, *State and Government*, 45.

37. Lambton, State and Government, 45.

38. Watt, *Islamic Political Thought*, 81–82.

39. Abu Hamid al-Ghazali, *al-Tabr al-Masbuk fi Nasihat al-Muluk*, http://www.al-eman.com/Islamlib/viewchp.asp?BID=167&CID=3#s16; see also Lambton, *State*, 122–23.

40. See Black, *The History of Islamic Political Thought*, 22.

41. Ayubi, *Political Islam*, 4.

42. Ibn Khaldun, *The Muqaddimah*, 162–63.

43. Ibid., 191–92.

44. Ibid., 191–99.

45. *Encyclopaedia Britannica*, 15th ed. (Chicago: Encyclopaedia Britannica, Inc., 1982), 10: 477.

46. *Encyclopaedia Britannica* (Chicago: Britannica 2002 Deluxe Edition CD-ROM, 1994–2002), *Qadi*.

47. Khawarijis is a term used to describe those Muslims who initially supported the caliphate of the fourth Caliph Ali, but later rejected him. They first emerged in the late seventh century.

48. Al-Tabari, *Tarikh*, 6: 3.

49. Nasr H. Abu Zaid, *Naqid al-Khitab al-Dini* (Cairo: Seena lil-Nashir, 1992), 60.

50. Lambton, *State and Government*, 110, 144.

51. Black, *The History of Islamic Political Thought*, 91.

52. Qutb, *Milestones*, 37–38.

53. Fahmi Huwaidi, *al-Quran wa al-Sultan* (Cairo: Dar al-Shuruq, 1982), 18–19.

54. Hasan al-Banna, *Selected Writings of Hasan al-Banna Shaheed*, trans. S. A. Qureshi (New Delhi: Millat Book Centre, 1999), 206.

55. Nasr. H. Abu Zaid, "The Modernization of Islam or the Islamization of Modernity," in *Cosmopolitanism, Identity and Authenticity in the Middle East*, ed. Roel Meijer (London: Routledge Curzon Press, 1999), 71–86.

56. Lambton, *State and Government*, 51.

57. Black, *The History of Islamic Political Thought*, 82, 104.

58. Rosenthal, *Political Thought in Medieval Islam*, 27.

59. Ibid., 52.

PART III

Interpreting Political Islam

CHAPTER 5

War and Peace: Negotiating Meaning in Islam

Robert P. Barnidge, Jr.

In his 1946 essay "Politics and the English Language," George Orwell lashes out at unscrupulous writing habits and the abuses to which the English language has been subjected. Given his orientation and the unique context in which he wrote, the particular relevance of Orwell's counsel to writings of a political nature is obvious. Indeed, Orwell himself recognized the imprecision of political language, which, he asserted, "and with variations this is true of all political parties, from Conservatives to Anarchists—is designed to make lies sound truthful and murder respectable, and to give an appearance of solidity to pure wind."[1]

In recent years a passionate politics has played out in attempts to understand Islam, particularly as relates to espousals of radical, Islamically articulated challenges to the status quo and prevailing institutional structures. While somewhat simplifying the state of affairs, the thrust of these debates lies in John L. Esposito's rhetorical question: "Have they [militant Islamists] hijacked Islam for their own unholy purposes, or do they, as they claim, represent a return to the authentic teachings of the faith?"[2] Put differently, the chasm in these discussions has been between those who confidently assert that Islam is a religion of peace and those who, conversely, contend with conviction that it is a religion of war. Most of these conversations have been uncompromising and combative in tone and share in common little other than the avoidance of nuance and subtlety.

This chapter provides a framework for negotiating meaning in Islam on questions of war and peace. It begins by presenting some representative and contrasting understandings of Islam, particularly as they relate to militant Islam, and then suggests some ways in which negotiations of meaning can take place in this context. It argues that the varied experiences of those who act in the name of Islam and justify their actions according to the life of Muhammad and devotion to Allah require a new and radical framework, a framework that prioritizes diversity and a decentralized ethic of understanding over homogenization and hegemonization and avoids post-colonial constructions of inevitable inferiority and weakness. Such a framework has the advantage of being more methodologically satisfying because it can better account for and deal with the diverse perspectives and complexities in the debate and better appreciate the political implications and undertones inherent in the practice of interpretation.

ISLAM AS A RELIGION OF PEACE

A major contention in these debates is that Islam is a religion of peace. Essentially, this argument involves a two-pronged approach: an assertion of what Islam is, coupled with an assertion of what it is not or what it opposes. These prongs flow into and support one another.

The United Nations-supported Alliance of Civilizations has played a prominent role in promoting the position of Islam as a religion of peace. In a November 2006 report, its High-Level Group argues that the religions of the world "[a]ll promote the ideals of compassion, justice and respect for the dignity of life"[3] and that as belief systems they embody the seminal possibilities of tolerance, harmony, and appreciation.[4] South African Anglican Archbishop emeritus Desmond Tutu, a member of the High-Level Group, similarly contends that "[e]ach religion, when at its best, promotes community, compassion, caring, gentleness, and sharing."[5]

Regional bodies and many scholars also support the idea of Islam as a religion of peace. At the May 2007 Islamic Conference of Foreign Ministers, for example, Secretary-General of the Organization of the Islamic Conference Ekmeleddin Ihsanoglu stated that he and others were "doing . . . [their] best to defend Islam as a revealed faith and as a radiant civilization, shedding light on its values, most prominent among them moderation, peace, tolerance and diversity."[6] Likewise, Bernard Lewis characterizes Islam as "one of the great religions of the world . . . [that] shares with its sister religions a commitment to moral values, moral standards, and moral laws."[7]

Assertions of what Islam is not or what it opposes also support the view of Islam as a religion of peace. In this context, Islam is typically contrasted with terrorism and war. In Resolution 61/164, for instance, the United Nations General Assembly "Expresses its deep concern that Islam is frequently and wrongly associated with human rights violations and terrorism."[8] The High-Level Group's report asserts that "none of the world religions condones or approves the killing of innocents,"[9] thus relating the belief that Islam does not justify the slaughtering of innocent human life and that it can be contrasted with such behavior. The report also takes to task those who would understand Islam as something other than a peaceful religion. Contrarians, according to the report, "advocate narrow, distorted interpretations of Islamic teachings [and] . . . misportray certain practices . . . as religious requirements [that] . . . in the eyes of respected Muslim scholars . . . have no religious foundation."[10] At the February 2005 International Conference on Combating Terrorism, Ihsanoglu echoed these sentiments, asserting that the "unequivocal case for Islam's stance against terrorism . . . needs no further elaboration on my part."[11]

As further examples of this thinking, consider former United States President George W. Bush's contention that militant Islam "distorts and exploits Islam to justify the murder of innocent people and defiles a proud religion"[12] and British Prime Minister Gordon Brown's view that militant Islamists engage in religious "perversion."[13] Tony Blair, Brown's predecessor, likewise argues that the "extremist view of Islam is not just theologically backward but completely contrary to the spirit and teaching of the Koran"[14] and expresses the position that terrorism driven by the religious ideology of militant Islam amounts to "an utter perversion of the proper faith of Islam."[15] Before the United States Congress in July 2006, Iraqi Prime Minister Nouri al-Maliki described a "battle between true Islam, for which a person's liberty and rights constitute essential cornerstones, and terrorism, which wraps itself in a fake Islamic cloak."[16]

Similarly, Nafaa, writing in Egypt's *Al-Ahram*, unequivocally asserts that "there is no relationship between Islam as a religion and such horrendous political and social ideologies that embrace racism, tyranny, terror and corruption."[17] Others, such as Lewis[18] and Esposito,[19] tend to agree. The September 11 terrorist attacks, according to Singer, embodied a "self-evident violation of all moral and religious codes of conduct."[20] Armstrong similarly contends that the Quran and Shari'a law simply cannot justify them.[21]

ISLAM AS A RELIGION OF WAR

A polar opposite view of Islam is the equally closely held understanding of it as a religion of war. Byzantine Emperor Manuel II Paleologus' (ruled 1391–1425) exasperated view of Islam as quoted by His Holiness Pope Benedict XVI in his September 2006 Regensburg lecture—"Show me just what Mohammed brought that was new, and there you will find things only evil and inhuman, such as his command to spread by the sword the faith he preached,"[22]—exemplifies this thinking. This position characterizes militant Islam not as a distraction from Islam's peaceful essence but rather as an aggressive and central component of the faith. A minority of scholars, it is contended, hold this conviction. Perhaps most importantly and revealingly, however, the foundational ideology and multimedia communications of militant Islamists themselves reject Islam as a religion of peace and support and glory in understanding it as a religion of war.

Samuel P. Huntington, author of the "clash of civilizations" thesis, is one of the most prominent apologists for this position. According to him, the "underlying problem for the West is not Islamic fundamentalism. It is Islam, a different civilization whose people are convinced of the superiority of their culture and are obsessed with the inferiority of their power."[23] Indian-born author Salman Rushdie, who has himself been condemned to death in the name of Islam by *fatwa* for his dissenting views,[24] refers to the "barbarism, the barbaric face of certain parts of Islam."[25] Others contend that those who read in Islam a liberal ethos are being dishonest[26] and emphatically assert without equivocation that militant Islamists act upon "bestial wild instincts aroused in them by religious teachings, which incite to rejection of the other, to the killing of the other, and to the denial of the other."[27]

Furthermore, in the first volume of his *History of the English-Speaking Peoples*, former British Prime Minister Winston S. Churchill briefly but clearly comments upon the birth and territorial growth of Islam, contending that "[i]n Arabia Mahomet unfurled the martial and sacred standards of Islam," leading to the conquests of Arabia, Persia, and much of Byzantium, North Africa, and Iberia, up to the Battle of Poitiers.[28] Former Chief Justice of Saudi Arabia Sheikh Abdullah bin Muhammad bin Humaid, in an article exploring jihad in the Quran and Sunna, makes the point bluntly:

> . . . you will not find any organization past or present, religious or non-religious as regards (*jihad* and military) (ordering) the whole nation to march forth and mobilize all of them into active military service as a single row for *Jihad* in Allah's Cause so as to make superior the Word of Allah (i.e., none has the right to be worshipped but Allah), as you will find in the Islamic Religion and its teachings.[29]

Thus, from a scholastic point of view, ample evidence exists to support the view of Islam as a religion of war.

In a similar vein, the convictions of militant Islamists themselves insist, often with deadly seriousness, that Islam requires violent jihad in a wide variety of circumstances. The statements of al-Qaeda's Osama bin Laden and Ayman al-Zawahiri and the writings of Egyptian militant Islamist Sayyid Qutb, which provide a helpful reference point for understanding this politics of militant Islam, further attest to this.

A striking factor when analyzing militant Islam's statements of religious ideology is the thorough referencing of specific verses in the Quran and generous allusions to events in Islamic history. For example,

consider a statement in which bin Laden clearly articulates what he expects from the United States based on his interpretation of Islam in his *Letter to America*.[30] Among other demands, this statement insists that the United States convert to Islam, implement Shari'a law and overturn its secular political traditions, ban gambling, homosexuality, extramarital sexual relations, and interest on investments, and end its support for Israel and other specified states. Bin Laden makes clear that this is an ultimatum to the United States: "If you fail to respond to all these conditions, then prepare for [a] fight with the Islamic Nation."[31]

In an earlier statement from 1996, bin Laden also approved terrorism as a modus operandi and sanctified it as a "legitimate and morally demanded duty":[32] "Not all terrorism is cursed; some terrorism is blessed."[33] According to a *fatwa* jointly issued by him in 1998, the "ruling to kill the Americans and their allies—civilians and military—is an individual duty for every Muslim who can do it in any country in which it is possible to do it."[34] For bin Laden, "Refraining from performing *jihad*, which is sanctioned by our religion, is an appalling sin. The best way of death for us is under the shadows of swords."[35] "For the new-style terrorists," Lewis notes, "the slaughter of innocent and uninvolved civilians is not 'collateral damage.' It is the prime objective."[36]

The statements of al-Zawahiri, who is generally regarded as al-Qaeda's second-in-command after bin Laden, provide further evidence that, through certain interpretations, Islam is a religion of war and emphatically not a religion of peace. In a piece of correspondence from July 2005 sent by al-Zawahiri to his comrade Abu Musab al-Zarqawi, the former asserted that the "victory of Islam will never take place until a Muslim state is established in the manner of the Prophet in the heart of the Islamic world, specifically in the Levant, Egypt, and the neighboring states of the Peninsula and Iraq."[37] Al-Zawahiri's four-pronged agenda requires driving United States forces from Iraq, creating an Islamic state in Iraq, destroying secular states in the region, and crushing Israel.[38]

For al-Zawahiri, the clash involves those whom he has anointed as true Muslims[39] and the chosen enemy, whether, variously, Jews, Americans, or the United Nations.[40] Criticizing "[t]his rotten play of democracy [in Iraq]" in a video from April 2006, the chosen enemy had become for al-Zarqawi "any government that is formed in Iraq now regardless of who its members are, whether they are from the malicious rejectionists, the secularist Kurdish Zionists, or the collaborators that are falsely considered Sunnis . . . [such a government being] an agent, collaborating, and allied with the crusaders."[41]

In Qutb's militant Islam, the dichotomy of friend and enemy advanced by German political philosopher Carl Schmitt on the eve of the Second World War—according to which "[e]very religious, moral, economic, ethical, or other antithesis transforms into a political one if it is sufficiently strong to group human beings effectively according to friend and enemy"[42]—plays out as Islamic and *jahili* societies.[43] This is a world in which "there is only one party of God; all others are parties of Satan and rebellion,"[44] an existence of *Dar al-Harb* and *Dar al-Islam*,[45] "of unbelief and belief, of associating others with God and the Oneness of God, and of *Jahiliyyah* and Islam."[46] According to Qutb:

> The reasons for *Jihaad* [sic] which have been described in the above verses are these: to establish God's authority in the earth; to arrange human affairs according to the true guidance provided by God; to abolish all the Satanic forces and Satanic systems of life; to end the lordship of one man over others, since all men are creatures of God and no one has the authority to make them his servants or to make arbitrary laws for them. These reasons are sufficient for proclaiming *Jihaad* [sic].[47]

Qutb's is truly a revolutionary vision: "not a temporary phase but an eternal state—an eternal state, as truth and falsehood cannot co-exist on this earth . . . The eternal struggle for the freedom of man will continue until the religion is purified for God,"[48] and it continues to inspire militant Islamists in the twenty-first century.

President Bush's *National Strategy for Combating Terrorism* characterized this understanding of Islam as a religion of war, this thinking that insists upon its authenticity and bellicose posture, as a "radical ideology of hatred, oppression, and murder . . . [a] perverse vision of oppression and totalitarian rule . . . [a] radical ideology that justifies the use of violence against innocents in the name of religion"; a "common vision, a common set of ideas about the nature and destiny of the world, and a common goal of ushering in totalitarian rule"; and an "ideology of terror . . . a form of totalitarianism following in the path of fascism and Nazism."[49] Writing in 2002, Fukuyama described it as "Islamo-fascism—that is, the radically intolerant and anti-modern doctrine that has recently arisen in many parts of the Muslim world."[50] For Rushdie, the goal amounts to a "new religious, fascist rule over the planet . . . the Caliphate, the Talibanization of the earth."[51] According to Wedgwood, this politics of militant Islam uses "mercenary propaganda that inclines young men to a madman's death,"[52] while Friedman refers to it as a "jihadist death cult."[53] This interpretation of Islam—this militant Islam—is, to quote Arendt on totalitarian terror, the "kind of philosophy through which to express frustration, resentment, and blind hatred, a kind of political expressionism which used bombs to express oneself, which watched delightedly the publicity given to resounding deeds and was absolutely willing to pay the price of life for [recognition]."[54]

NEGOTIATING MEANING IN ISLAM

How can Islam, the last of the three great monotheistic faiths, open itself to such diametrically distinct and conflicting understandings? How can it be said to embody, depending on whom one asks, either perpetual peace or perpetual war? How should one negotiate meaning in this context when commentators, Islam's adherents and detractors, and militant Islamists themselves cannot agree and, in fact, emphatically disagree on issues as core as war and peace? Who has the authority, and on what basis, to declare what Islam is and what it can be? How is this to be determined, justified, and legitimated? Is there anything distinct about Islam regarding this confusion, or are diverse understandings of Islamic meaning as normal, pedestrian, and foreseeable as the interpretative debates that abound in myriad constitutional contexts, religious and secular?

One can begin to approach some of these questions by acknowledging that, like other constitutional traditions, Islam is not inherently anything: the interpretative approaches that are brought to bear on the debate make it something, transform it into, at least potentially, anything.[55] Interpretative approaches can, though they need not necessarily, prefer a "framer's intent" point of view; emphasize and add or deemphasize and excise certain passages and traditions; see in the Quran an unchallengeable and mandated way of living that remains as valid in the largely secular twenty-first century as it was originally understood in seventh-century Arabia; or adopt a "living document" perspective.[56] "Religious traditions," Esposito contends, "are a combination of text and context— revelation and human interpretation within a specific socio-historical context . . . While using the same text and referring to a common history, people come out with different interpretations."[57] In other words, "competing textual sources can only be understood and reconciled with reference to a contextual framework for their meaning and practical application today."[58] For example, those who want to argue that Islam is a religion of peace can stress Muhammad's pacific pre-*hijrah* utterances at Mecca, while those of the persuasion that Islam is a religion of war can argue that his bellicose words once the nascent Muslim community had consolidated itself at Medina take precedence according to the abrogation principle.

Islam is an "ideal that has taken many forms historically and has been capable of multiple interpretations, conditioned by reason and social contexts."[59] Its traditions support the mystical practice of looking for hidden meaning in Quranic words, as well as various degrees of reasoning by analogy[60] and perspectives on abrogation.[61] A radically decentralized and non-hierarchical understanding of communion and submission to Allah further promotes diverse interpretative approaches.[62]

Scholars have extensively commented upon the contested nature of Quranic meaning. One Egyptian scholar, for instance, refers to the Quran as "a supermarket, where one takes what one wants and leaves what one doesn't want."[63] In a sense complementing this questioning of the Quran as a seamless and cohesive whole, Iranian scholars Ladan and Roya

Boroumand insist upon its contradictory nature.[64] Ramadan highlights contradiction and confusion in the context of *fatwas* and asserts that Islamic scholars disagree as to the interpretation and definition of key Islamic terms.[65] An-Na'im similarly argues that the "rich diversity of opinion among Muslim jurists over almost every significant legal principle or issue of public policy clearly indicates a dynamic relationship between the Qur'an and Sunna, on the one hand, and human comprehension, imagination and experience, on the other."[66] Religiously based justifications and denunciations of suicide bombings provide an example of this diversity within Islam.[67]

Other observers refer to jihad's "multitude of meanings,"[68] acknowledge that militant Islamists "lay claim to the breadth of Islamic teachings in their efforts to justify their actions,"[69] and assert the reality of a *"fatwa free-for-all."*[70] Al-Maliki stated in the General Assembly in September 2007 that he and others had "cautioned all countries in the region that the continued overflow of weapons, money, suicide bombers, and the spreading of *'fatwas'* inciting hatred and murder . . . [would] only result in disastrous consequences for peoples of [the] region and the world."[71] An increasingly fragmented sense of authority within Islam, furthermore, radically democratizes discussions and spurs on plural visions, a struggle that involves what Piscatori refers to as "direct competition for control of the symbolic discourse of Islam."[72]

Consider an analogy to an exchange between the protagonist Joseph and the Spirit of Alternatives in Nobel Laureate Saul Bellow's novel *Dangling Man*. It provides some insight into the modalities and possibilities of interpretative hodgepodge. Joseph, in his exchange, mentions the concept of:

> [a]n ideal construction, an obsessive device. There have been innumerable varieties: for study, for wisdom, bravery, war, the benefits of cruelty, for art; the God-man of the ancient cultures, the Humanistic full man, the courtly lover, the knight, the ecclesiastic, the despot, the ascetic, the millionaire, the manager. I could name hundreds of these ideal constructions, each with its assertions and symbols, each finding—in conduct, in God, in art, in money—its particular answer and each proclaiming: "This is the only possible way to meet chaos."[73]

The interpretative approaches that are brought to bear upon negotiations of meaning in Islam resemble these "ideal constructions," these "obsessive devices." Through the particular interpretative approach that one chooses, one can declare in categorical language that Islam is a religion of peace, or a religion of war, or assert that it obviously forbids, or obviously commands, this or that jihad on particular facts and circumstances; however, these are, at their core, mere declarations and assertions, mere "ideal constructions," or "obsessive devices." Esposito, for example, refers to the legitimacy of declarations of jihad as being "like beauty . . . determined by the eye of the beholder/believer."[74] These contentions can be contested and refuted within particular established hierarchies of

authority within Islam, hierarchies which, one should point out, are not inevitable and exist only because they are recognized as such, because particular constituencies, particular captivated and convinced audiences, support them.[75] New hierarchies of authority can be created, kinetically, proactively, and on an ongoing basis, that can act as vehicles for legitimizing novel interpretative approaches. Put differently, the constitutional fabric of Islam has been cleared of any inevitable interpretative approach: the "gates of *ijtihad*" are closed and inaccessible only if one acknowledges and accepts them as such.

In this regard, consider the interpretative approaches of Abdullahi Ahmed An-Na'im and Tariq Ramadan, two noted Islamic scholars. An-Na'im contends that "[f]or Muslims, a reinterpretation should be accepted or rejected in terms of its own foundation in Islamic sources, instead of being rejected simply because it is new or unorthodox."[76] By contrast, Ramadan's *ijtihad* suggests a "historically grounded approach to these sources [the Quran and Sunna], and at the same time employ[ment of] human creativity to respond to the particular problems of our age."[77] An-Na'im's and Ramadan's approaches, similar in the sense that they emanate from thinkers who attempt a progressive scholarship, permit a virtually unlimited number of distinct possibilities and potential endgames, both within and between one another. Even if one were to assume that agreement could be reached to channel debate through either of their two approaches, in no tangible sense could either of them cage in or exclude the reaching of diverse alternatives. One can compare this with Kennedy's conception of legal pluralism, an experience in which lacunae, ambiguities, and conflicts that cannot be reconciled and that require human choice riddle the terrain of debate.[78]

PRIORITIZING DIVERSITY AND A DECENTRALIZED ETHIC OF UNDERSTANDING OVER HOMOGENIZATION AND HEGEMONIZATION

A more helpful framework for negotiating meaning in Islam would recognize and not hide from the complexities and confusions that come with interpretation. It would prioritize diversity and a decentralized ethic of understanding over homogenization and hegemonization and avoid post-colonial constructions of inevitable inferiority and weakness.

In an essay on homogenization and hegemonization in the context of globalization and Islam, Mazrui provides some useful definitions of these two somewhat related concepts. For him, homogenization means greater similarity, while hegemonization refers to ever-increasing power at a particular source.[79] As he puts it, "While homogenization is the process of expanding homogeneity, hegemonization is the emergence and consolidation of a hegemonic center."[80] In the context of negotiating meaning in

Islam, homogenization refers to the existence of one, or at least a limited and similar few, understanding or understandings of Islam; hegemonization, on the other hand, means the institutionalization, asserted or actual, of authority at, and in deference to, a particular center or select centers of interpretation or interpretations of Islam.

As noted above, those who attempt to negotiate meaning in Islam confront varied historical accounts and precedents and must wade through slews of plausible interpretations. In principle, this suggests the appropriateness of a heterogeneous, as opposed to homogenous, experience. The chasm in contentions in the Islam as a religion of peace or a religion of war debate supports a framework that appreciates and recognizes as legitimate and plausible myriad interpretative approaches. Diversity, of necessity, trumps homogenization. The discourse is democratized.

At the same time that diversity should be preferred to homogenization by virtue of the myriad sources and permutations of plausible interpretations of Islam, one must guard against the increasing tendency of actors to hegemonize the discourse—to, of course, their own particular advantage—to convince others of the righteousness of their cause, to insist, in Bellow's language, that theirs is the "only possible way to meet chaos." This hegemonic tendency, which must be struggled against and replaced with a decentralized ethic of understanding, effectively denies the legitimacy of diverse interpretations and seeks to elevate and privilege one interpretation at the expense of others.

To illustrate these points, consider how counterterrorism policies that ignore, whether willfully or not, the existence of diverse understandings of Islam both homogenize and hegemonize. For the United States and the United Kingdom, for example, Islam is, in a very assertedly unequivocal way, a religion of peace, and this is so precisely because they want it to be, precisely because they insist that it should be, for ideological reasons. Islam can be a religion of peace, of course, but one should recognize that when constructed as reasonable, perhaps even as quaint, it loses much of its political purchase and clout as a radical, oppositional, and alternative politics. State promotion of a "moderate" Islam through "hearts and minds" campaigns or the rejection of Islam as a lion in favor of conceptualizing it as a lamb constitutes a deliberate ideological maneuver. It homogenizes meaning and hegemonizes in favor of the state and against more militant Islamic interpretation. This thinking disenfranchises dissenting interpretations at the same time that it seeks to assimilate and integrate Muslims according to the state's preferred interpretation of Islam.

"EXPERTS" AND "EXPERTISE"

In creating a new and radical framework for negotiating meaning in Islam, one should avoid the frequent knee-jerk resort in these discussions to, among others, "experts" and the cautioning in these debates on Islam of religious defamation. Said defines an expert as one who can, almost in rote fashion, cite the accepted and anticipated authorities, fluently converse with her colleagues in the correct manner, and defend the right positions, as one who contributes to and reinforces the "cult of the certified expert."[81] Kennedy refers to this idea in the not unrelated context of legal pluralism as the "rulership of experts . . . [the] rulership of expertise."[82] Experts, with their "expertise," drive the debate.

In wielding their expertise, experts seek to privilege and hegemonize their voice and argument at the expense of alternative perspectives. In making their case that Islam is or is not a religion of peace, they depend on particular facts and circumstances to create a distinguished and privileged message. Acknowledged expertise amplifies one's influence and, in so doing, contributes to a process that both delegitimizes one's non-expert opposition and plays a part in the hegemonization of expertise. Indeed, the mere act of communicating and critiquing embodies both a yearning and a demand to be heard, a desire to have one's view digested because of its asserted uniqueness and originality.

This hegemonization of expertise, this impulse to dominate based on pedigree, artificially stunts the debate on Islam by seeking to unequivocally convince without recognizing the fallibility and limitations of one's own interpretative approach. This thinking, similar to what Koskenniemi refers to as the "mindset of well-placed, powerful actors, confident in their possessing the 'right' purpose,"[83] should be rejected. As Rushdie asserts, "You don't get a kind of get out of jail card if you happen to belong to a particular religion or club or cult."[84] A decentralized ethic of understanding challenges and rebels against this hegemonization of expertise. It radically empowers the individual.

RELIGIOUS DEFAMATION

While one should avoid undue deference to experts and posited expertise when negotiating meaning in Islam, one should equally exert caution when facing attempts to hem in and demonize good faith interpretations of Islam through charges of religious defamation. Such charges both mistake Islam for a static religious ideology, something that can be easily and uncontroversially grasped at, and seek to homogenize permissible interpretation and, a priori, hegemonize the debate toward what are asserted to be inoffensive interpretative conclusions. Invariably, this thinking divests dissident interpretations of their political legitimacy and demonizes radical, Islamically articulated challenges to the status quo and prevailing institutional structures.

Although not alone in stunting the debate on the nature of Islam, the United Nations has of late played an unfortunate role in using a defamation of religions charge to silence dissident interpretations of Islamic religious ideology. In Resolution 61/164, for instance, the General Assembly privileges its own interpretation of Islam, an Islam that it implies is inherently peaceful, and ignores the creative possibilities of interpreting Islam differently. Effectively, Resolution 61/146 broadly stigmatizes alternative interpretations of Islam as defamatory. To give an example, it "[s]tresses the need to effectively combat defamation of all religions, Islam and Muslims in particular, especially in human rights forums,"[85] and decries the dissemination of contrary interpretations, which it refers to as the "use of the print, audio-visual and electronic media, including the Internet, and any other means to incite acts of violence, xenophobia or related intolerance and discrimination against Islam or any other religion."[86] Furthermore, according to the General Assembly, negotiations of meaning in Islam must appreciate that state authorities can limit free expression, the freedom to understand and think differently, according to what is put forward in broadly articulated language as "limitations as provided by law . . . [that are] necessary for respect of the rights or reputations of others, protection of national security or of public order, public health or morals and respect for religions and beliefs."[87] The Human Rights Council has adopted a similar position on the defamation of religions issue in Resolution 4/9.[88]

The danger of privileging certain interpretations of Islam and stifling others lies in the fact that such thinking, by its very nature, circumscribes the acceptable parameters of the marketplace of ideas. Rather than appreciating the rich possibilities of diverse interpretations of Islam, this cautioning of religious defamation places particular interpretations on a pedestal. In doing so, it eliminates competing narratives, both horizontally because meaning becomes homogenized and artificially skewed and vertically because the asserted hierarchy of privilege effectively ensures the primacy of inoffensive interpretative conclusions. As Rushdie insists, "It becomes impossible to have any kind of interchange of thought in a society if you're told that there are ideas which are off-limits. Nothing is off-limits."[89] "[W]ith authorities who claim the secular right to defend divine decree," to quote Said, "there can be no debate no matter where they are, whereas for the intellectual, tough searching debate is the core of activity, the very stage and setting of what intellectuals without revelation really do."[90]

AVOIDING POST-COLONIAL CONSTRUCTIONS OF INEVITABLE INFERIORITY AND WEAKNESS

A framework for negotiating meaning in Islam should also avoid post-colonial constructions of inevitable inferiority and weakness. Broadly speaking, this idea refers to the tendency to unquestionably promote

Islam as a religion of peace, to demonize those who dispute this dominant view, and to dismiss those who dissent, those who understand and interpret Islam as commanding a bellicose posture. As discussed above, and as encapsulated in Hamas' call in its 1988 Charter of Allah: The Platform of the Islamic Resistance Movement that "Allah is its goal, the Prophet its model, the Qur'an its Constitution, *Jihad* its path and death for the case [sic] of Allah its most sublime belief,"[91] it is exactly this discourse of jihad that militant Islamists themselves affirmatively embrace. For them, the life of Muhammad and devotion to Allah demand it.

As an example of this tendency to patronize those who embrace a bellicose interpretation of Islam, consider the *European Union Counter-Terrorism Strategy's* insistence that the prevention of terrorism requires discussions that only acknowledge a "non-emotive lexicon."[92] Brown also maintains as unjustifiable the connoting of Islam and the Muslims who act in its name and terrorism.[93] For Archbishop of Canterbury Rowan Williams, Qutb can be dismissed as a mere "committed Islamic primitivist . . . [and] polemicist."[94] This thinking accords with the Alliance of Civilization's report, which recommends that public figures have a "duty to avoid using violent or provocative language about other people's beliefs or sacred symbols,"[95] presumably even when relating to their constituencies the substance of militant Islamists' raison d'être, programs of action, convictions, and closely held interpretations of Islam.

Part of this tendency to patronize those who interpret Islam differently involves an almost allergic reaction to the considered contention that Islam can be interpreted to support a fascist religious ideology. Certainly, if one uses Paxton's definition of fascism, "a form of political behavior marked by obsessive preoccupation with community decline, humiliation, or victimhood and by compensatory cults of unity, energy, and purity, in which a mass-based party of committed nationalist militants, working in uneasy but effective collaboration with traditional elites, abandons democratic liberties and pursues with redemptive violence and without ethical or legal restraints goals of internal cleansing and external expansion,"[96] the similarities between militant Islamic interpretation and fascism, while not exact, are striking. Paxton himself admits that religious devotion may be able to trump national devotion in a fascist politics.[97] For militant Islam, the transnational *umma* replaces the devoted Blackshirts; the caliphate re-emerges to demolish the Westphalian nation-state system.[98] To quote Rushdie, "If there is a fascistic politics which uses Islamic theology as a justification, I see no reason not to put those words together."[99]

The prevailing dismissive posture toward the religious ideology of militant Islam reveals a rather unsettling picture. It perpetuates the myth that, as Said notes in his critique of Orientalism in his book of the same name, "An Arab Oriental is that impossible creature whose libidinal energy drives him to paroxysms of overstimulation—and yet, he is a puppet in the eyes of the world, staring vacantly out at a modern land-scape he can neither understand nor cope with."[100] This condescending mentality toward those who support and glory in understanding Islam as a religion of war engages in what Rushdie describes in a similar con-text as a "kind of infantilization of people to say that they don't know any better, which would not happen if you were dealing with anyone else who was not brown of skin."[101] Hirsi Ali makes an excellent point in noting that "[w]ithholding criticism and ignoring differences are racism in its purest form" and that cultural elites who frame the terms of debate according to an eggshell sensitivity "feel superior and do not regard Muslims as equal discussion partners, but as the 'others' who should be shielded. And they think that criticism of Islam should be avoided because they are afraid that Muslims can only respond to criticism with anger and violence."[102] By ignoring the viability of alternative interpreta-tions of Islam, this thinking perpetuates an inevitably "controllable, toothless Islam that will defer to American power rather than resist it"[103] and obfuscates the existence of "revolutionary possibilities within a con-servative framework."[104] In so doing, it engages in what Kramer would describe as the "ultimate ethnocentrism."[105]

CONCLUSION

In our complex world, characterized as it is "more by instability than sta-bility, by flux and not stasis, by boundaries that are ambiguous and shift-ing rather than distinct and static, by multiple identities and fluid loyalties,"[106] interpretation requires recognition of one's own fallibility and courage to persevere. Real people, with real axes to grind and in pur-suit of real causes célèbres, not automata operating in a vacuum, engage in interpretation. Interpretation is the quintessential act of partisan con-viction and political critique, and negotiating meaning in Islam repre-sents but one specialized example of this. To quote Said, "Politics is everywhere; there can be no escape into the realms of pure art and thought or, for that matter, into the realm of disinterested objectivity or transcendental theory."[107]

Space constraints preclude a more detailed program of action than the framework briefly sketched above. In this regard, this chapter shares in common with Jeremy Bentham's "A Fragment on Government" a similar iconoclastic, deconstructive purpose—namely, to quote Bentham, "*to overthrow*. In the little, therefore, which has been done by it in the way of *setting up*, my view has been not so much to think for the Reader, as to put him upon thinking for himself."[108]

I wish to thank Jean Allain, Richard Jackson, Martha-Marie Kleinhans, Nikolai Kovalev, Phil Larkin, Mehdi Mokhtari, Phil Scraton, Niaz Shah, and two anonymous reviewers for comments on an earlier draft of this chapter.

NOTES

1. George Orwell, "Politics and the English Language," in *Why I Write* (London: Penguin, 2004), 120.

2. John L. Esposito, *Unholy War: Terror in the Name of Islam* (Oxford: Oxford University Press, 2002), x.

3. Alliance of Civilizations, *Report of the High-Level Group* (2006), 10, http://www.unaoc.org/repository/HLG_Report.pdf.

4. Ibid., 6, 26.

5. Alliance of Civilizations, *Summary Notes: Meeting of the High Level Group of the Alliance of Civilizations*, November 27–29, 2005, 2, http://www.unaoc.org/repository/9067First%20Meeting%20of%20High-level%20Group%20Summary%20Notes.doc.pdf.

6. Ekmeleddin Ihsanoglu, "Speech at the Thirty-Fourth Session of the Islamic Conference of Foreign Ministers," Islamabad, May 15–17, 2007, http://www.oic-oci.org/34icfm/english/Speeches/speeches-sg.htm.

7. Bernard Lewis, "Islamic Terrorism?" in *Terrorism: How the West Can Win*, ed. Benjamin Netanyahu (New York: Avon, 1987), 65.

8. United Nations General Assembly, Resolution 61/164, A/RES/61/164 (2006), para. 4.

9. Alliance of Civilizations, *Report*, 10.

10. Ibid., 14.

11. Ekmeleddin Ihsanoglu, "Speech at the International Conference on Combating Terrorism," Riyadh, February 5–8, 2005, http://www.oic-oci.org/press/English/2005/feb%202005/SG-terrrorism.htm.

12. White House, *National Strategy for Combating Terrorism* (2006), 11.

13. BBC News, "Terror Alert," *BBC Sunday AM*, July 1, 2007, http://news.bbc.co.uk/2/hi/programmes/sunday_am/6258416.stm.

14. Tony Blair, "Foreign Policy Speech I," London, March 21, 2006, http://www.pm.gov.uk/output/Page9224.asp.

15. Tony Blair, "What I've Learned," *Economist*, June 2–8, 2007, 27.

16. "Iraqi PM Addresses Congress," *Washington Post*, July 26, 2006.

17. Hassan Nafaa, "The Universality of Intolerance," *Al-Ahram*, June 14–20, 2007, http://weekly.ahram.org.eg/2007/849/op1.htm.

18. Lewis, "Islamic Terrorism?" 65.

19. Esposito, *Unholy War*, xi.

20. Peter Warren Singer, "America, Islam, and the 9–11 War," *Current History* 105, no. 695 (December 2006): 416.

21. Karen Armstrong, *Islam: A Short History* (London: Phoenix, 2002), 159–60.

22. His Holiness Pope Benedict XVI, "Lecture of the Holy Father: Faith, Reason and the University: Memories and Reflections," Aula Magna of the University of Regensburg, September 12, 2006, http://www.vatican.va/holy_father/benedict_xvi/speeches/2006/september/documents/hf_ben-xvi_spe_20060912_university-regensburg_en.html.

23. Samuel P. Huntington, *The Clash of Civilizations and the Remaking of World Order* (London: Free Press, 2002), 217.

24. Islamic Republic News Agency, "British Knighthood for Rushdie, Clear Sign of Islamophobia," June 17, 2007, http://www2.irna.com/index2.php?option=com_news&task=print&code=0706177335144730&Itemid=&lang=en.

25. Salman Rushdie, "Secular Values, Human Rights, and Islamism," New York, 9, October 11, 2006, http://www.centerforinquiry.net/uploads/attachments/Salman_Rushdie_Transcript.pdf.

26. Irshad Manji, "Irshad Manji Interview with Taslima Nasrin," October 28, 2002, http://www.muslim-refusenik.com/news/Taslima_Interview.html.

27. Middle East Media Research Institute, *LA Psychologist Wafa Sultan Clashes with Algerian Islamist Ahmad Bin Muhammad over Islamic Teachings and Terrorism,* July 26, 2005, http://www.memritv.org/clip_transcript/en/783.htm.

28. Winston S. Churchill, *A History of the English-Speaking Peoples: The Birth of Britain* (New York: Bantam, 1974), 66.

29. Abdullah bin Muhammad bin Humaid, *Jihad in the Qur'ân & Sunnah* (Riyadh: Darussalam, 1995), 29.

30. "Full Text: Bin Laden's 'Letter to America,'" *The Observer*, November 24, 2002, http://observer.guardian.co.uk/worldview/story/0,11581,845725,00.html.

31. Ibid., (Q2)(1)–(7).

32. "Ladenese Epistle: Declaration of War," *Washington Post,* September 21, 2001, trans. Committee for the Defense of Legitimate Rights, 2001, originally published in *Al Quds Al Arabi* in 1996.

33. "Transcript of Bin Laden's October Interview," *CNN,* February 5, 2002, http://archives.cnn.com/2002/WORLD/asiapcf/south/02/05/binladen.transcript/index.html.

34. World Islamic Front, "*Jihad* Against Jews and Crusaders: World Islamic Front Statement," *Washington Post,* September 21, 2001, originally published on February 23, 1998.

35. "Text: 'Bin-Laden Tape,'" *BBC News,* January 19, 2006, http://news.bbc.co.uk/1/hi/world/middle_east/4628932.stm.

36. Bernard Lewis, *The Crisis of Islam: Holy War and Unholy Terror* (New York: Modern Library, 2003), 147.

37. Ayman al-Zawahiri to Abu Musab al-Zarqawi, *Letter from Al-Zawahiri to Al-Zarqawi,* July 9, 2005, 2, http://www.dni.gov/press_releases/20051011_release.htm.

38. Ibid., 3.

39. Ayman al-Zawahiri, "Video: Excerpts," *BBC News,* April 29, 2006, http://news.bbc.co.uk/go/pr/fr/-/1/hi/world/middle_east/4957292.stm.

40. Al-Zawahiri to al-Zarqawi, *Letter*, 4–5.

41. "Excerpts: Zarqawi Message," *BBC News,* April 26, 2006, http://news.bbc.co.uk/go/pr/fr/-/1/hi/world/middle_east/4945878.stm.

42. Carl Schmitt, "The Concept of the Political," in *The Concept of the Political,* trans. George Schwab (Chicago: University of Chicago Press, 1996), 37.

43. Sayyid Qutb, *Milestones* (New Delhi: Islamic Book Service, 2005), 93.

44. Ibid., 117.

45. Ibid., 123–24.

46. Ibid., 137.

47. Ibid., 70.

48. Ibid., 65.

49. White House, *National Strategy*, 1, 5, 11.

50. Francis Fukuyama, "History and September 11," in *Worlds in Collision: Terror and the Future of Global Order*, eds. Ken Booth and Tim Dunne (New York: Palgrave Macmillan, 2002), 32.

51. Salman Rushdie, "Secular Values," 6.

52. Ruth Wedgwood, "Countering Catastrophic Terrorism: An American View," in *Enforcing International Law Norms Against Terrorism*, ed. Andrea Bianchi (Oxford: Hart, 2004), 105.

53. Thomas L. Friedman, "Muslims in Danger," *New York Times*, July 9, 2005.

54. Hannah Arendt, *The Origins of Totalitarianism* (New York: Harcourt, Brace, & World, 1966), 332.

55. Compare this argument with Anthony Chase, "Liberal Islam and 'Islam and Human Rights': A Sceptic's View," *Religion and Human Rights* 1, no. 2 (2006): 145–63.

56. Esposito, *Unholy War*, 159.

57. Ibid.

58. Abdullah Ahmed An-Na'im, "Upholding International Legality Against Islamic and American *Jihad*," in Booth and Dunne, *Worlds in Collision*, 165.

59. Esposito, *Unholy War*, 159–60.

60. Armstrong, *Islam*, 48, 50–51.

61. David Bukay, "Peace or *Jihad*?: Abrogation in Islam," *Middle East Quarterly* 14, no. 4 (2007), http://www.meforum.org/article/1754.

62. Armstrong, *Islam*, 52.

63. Alain Navarro, "Egypt Professor Compares Koran to Supermarket: Hanafi's Remarks About Islam's Holy Book Spark Fierce Demands from his Fellow Muslims. He Retracts Them," *Middle East Online*, October 2, 2006, http://www.middle-east-online.com/english/?id=17686.

64. Ladan and Roya Boroumand, "Terror, Islam, and Democracy," *Journal of Democracy* 13, no. 2 (2002): 12.

65. Tariq Ramadan, "A Case for Reform," *New Statesman*, April 10, 2006, 26.

66. Abdullah Ahmed An-Na'im, "Islam and Human Rights: Beyond the Universality Debate: Religion and the Universality of Human Rights," *American Society of International Law Proceedings* (2000), 98–99.

67. Shaul Mishal and Avraham Sela, *The Palestinian Hamas: Vision, Violence, and Coexistence* (New York: Columbia University Press, 2006), 76–77.

68. Esposito, *Unholy War*, 70.

69. Michael Moss and Souad Mekhennet, "Permission: The Guidebook for Taking a Life," *New York Times*, June 10, 2007.

70. Michael Slackman, "A *Fatwa* Free-For-All in the Islamic World," *International Herald Tribune*, June 11, 2007.

71. Nouri Kamel al-Maliki, "Statement Before the 62nd Session of the General Assembly," New York, 5, September 26, 2007, http://www.un.org/webcast/ga/62/2007/pdfs/iraq-en.pdf.

72. James Piscatori, "Order, Justice, and Global Islam," in *Order and Justice in International Relations,* eds. Rosemary Foot, John Lewis Gaddis, and Andrew Hurrell (Oxford: Oxford University Press, 2004), 283.

73. Saul Bellow, *Dangling Man* (New York: Penguin, 1996), 140.

74. Esposito, *Unholy War,* 41.

75. Compare this with Kennedy's focus in the context of international humanitarian law on the "persuasive[ness of rules] to relevant political constituencies." David Kennedy, *Of War and Law* (Princeton: Princeton University Press, 2006), 96.

76. An-Na'im, "Islam and Human Rights," 98.

77. Ramadan, "A Case for Reform."

78. David Kennedy, "Keynote Address, The TWAIL Conference," Albany, NY, April 2007, http://www.law.harvard.edu/faculty/dkennedy/speeches/TwailKeynote.htm.

79. Ali A. Mazrui, "Globalization, Islam, and the West: Between Homogenization and Hegemonization," *American Journal of Islamic Social Sciences* 15, no. 3 (1998): 2–3.

80. Ibid., 3.

81. Edward W. Said, *Representations of the Intellectual: The 1993 Reith Lectures* (London: Vintage, 1994), 58.

82. David Kennedy, "One, Two, Three, Many Legal Orders: Legal Pluralism and the Cosmopolitan Dream," London, 7, March 4, 2006, http://www.law.harvard.edu/faculty/dkennedy/speeches/LegalOrders.pdf.

83. Martti Koskenniemi, "What Is International Law For?" in *International Law,* ed. Malcolm D. Evans (Oxford: Oxford University Press, 2003), 98.

84. Rushdie, "Secular Values," 12.

85. United Nations General Assembly, Resolution A/RES/61/164 (2006), para. 8.

86. Ibid., para. 6.

87. Ibid., para. 9.

88. United Nations General Assembly, Resolution 4/9, A/HRC/4/123, in *Report to the General Assembly on the Fourth Session of the Human Rights Council* (2007), 19–21.

89. Rushdie, "Secular Values," 3.

90. Said, *Representations,* 66.

91. *Charter of Allah: The Platform of the Islamic Resistance Movement* (1988), art. 8, http://www.palestinecenter.org/cpap/documents/charter.html.

92. Council of the European Union, *European Union Counter-Terrorism Strategy* (2005), 7, http://ue.eu.int/uedocs/cms_Data/docs/pressdata/en/jha/87257.pdf.

93. Macer Hall, "Brown: Don't Say Terrorists Are Muslims," *Daily Express,* July 3, 2007, http://www.express.co.uk/posts/view/12172/Brown:-Don.

94. Rowan Williams, "Archbishop's Lecture—Civil and Religious Law in England: A Religious Perspective," February 7, 2008, http://www.archbishopofcanterbury.org/1575.

95. Alliance of Civilizations, *Report,* 20.

96. Robert O. Paxton, *The Anatomy of Fascism* (New York: Vintage, 2005), 218.

97. Ibid., 203–04.

98. In this regard, consider David A. Westbrook, "Strategic Consequences of Radical Islamic Neofundamentalism," *Orbis* 51, no. 3 (2007): 463–64.

99. Rushdie, "Secular Values," 16.

100. Edward W. Said, *Orientalism* (New York: Vintage, 2003), 312.

101. Rushdie, "Secular Values," 5.

102. Ayaan Hirsi Ali, *The Caged Virgin: An Emancipation Proclamation for Women and Islam* (New York: Free Press, 2006), xviii.

103. Piscatori, "Order," 272.

104. Ibid., 286.

105. Martin Kramer, "The Mismeasure of Political Islam," in *The Islamism Debate*, ed. Martin Kramer (Tel Aviv: Moshe Dayan Center for Middle Eastern and African Studies, 1997), 171.

106. Mishal and Sela, *Palestinian Hamas,* 12.

107. Said, *Representations,* 16.

108. Jeremy Bentham, "A Fragment on Government," in *A Fragment on Government and An Introduction to the Principles of Morals and Legislation,* ed. Wilfrid Harrison (Oxford: Basil Blackwell, 1948), 29 (emphasis in original).

CHAPTER 6

The Quranic Concept of War

Joseph C. Myers

The universalism of Islam, in its all-embracing creed, is imposed on the believers as a continuous process of warfare, psychological and political, if not strictly military . . . The Jihad, accordingly, may be stated as a doctrine of a permanent state of war, not continuous fighting.
—Majid Khadduri[1]

Political and military leaders are notoriously averse to theory, but if there is a theorist about war who matters, it remains Carl von Clausewitz, whose *Vom Kriege* (*On War*) "has shaped Western views about war since the middle of the nineteenth century."[2] Both points are likely true, and problematic, since we find ourselves engaged in war with people not solely imbued with Western ideas and values or followers of Western military theorists. The Hoover Institution's Paul Sperry warned in 2005, "Four years into the war on terror, U.S. intelligence officials tell me there are no baseline studies of the Muslim Prophet Muhammad or his ideological or military doctrine found at either the CIA or Defense Intelligence Agency, or even the war colleges."[3]

Would this be surprising? When it comes to warfighting, military audiences tend to focus on the military and power aspects of warfare: the tangibles of terrain, enemy, weather, leadership, and troops; quantifiables such as the number of tanks and artillery tubes; and the correlation of forces. Analysts steer toward the familiar rather than the unfamiliar; people tend to think in their comfort zones. The study of ideology or philosophy is often brushed aside, it is not the "stuff of muddy boots"; it is more cerebral than physical, and not action oriented. Planners do not assess the "correlation of ideas." The practitioners are too busy.

Dr. Antulio Echevarria recently argued that the U.S. military does not have a doctrine for war as much as it has a doctrine for operations and battles.[4] The military has a deficit of strategic and, one could add, philosophic thinking. In the war against Islamist terrorism, how many have heard of the Muslim Brotherhood's "Project"?[5] Is the political philosophy of Ayatollah Khomeini, who was in fact well versed in Western political theory and rigorously rejected it, studied in our military schools? Are there any implications to his statement in 1981 that "Iran . . . is determined to propagate Islam to the whole world"?[6]

To understand war, one has to study its philosophy, the grammar and logic of the opponent. Only then does one approach strategic comprehension. To understand the war against Islamist terrorism, one must begin to understand the Islamic way of war, its philosophy, its doctrine, and the meanings of jihad in Islam—and one needs to understand that those meanings are highly varied and utilitarian, depending on the source. With respect to the war against global jihad, its associated terror groups, individual terrorists, and clandestine adherents, one should ask if there is a unique method or attitude to their approach to war. Is there a philosophy or treatise, such as Clausewitz's *On War*, that attempts to form their thinking about war? Is there a document that can be reviewed and understood in such a manner that we may begin to think strategically about our opponent? There is one work that stands out from the many.

THE QURANIC CONCEPT OF WAR

The Quranic Concept of War, by Brigadier S. K. Malik of the Pakistani Army, provides readers with unequalled insight.[7] Originally published in Pakistan in 1979, most available copies are found in India or in small nondescript Muslim bookstores.[8] One major point to ponder when thinking about *The Quranic Concept of War* is the title itself. The Quran is presumed to be the revealed word of God as spoken through his chosen prophet, Muhammad. According to Malik, the Quran places warfighting doctrine and its theory in a much different category than Western thinkers are accustomed to, because it is a theory of war derived not from man, but from God. It is God's warfighting principles and commandments revealed. Malik attempts to distill God's doctrine for war through the examples of the Prophet. By contrast, the closest that Clausewitz comes to divine presentation is in his discussion of the trinity: the people, the state, and the military. In the Islamic context, the discussion of war is at the level of revealed truth and example, well above theory—God has no need to theorize. Malik notes, "As a complete Code of Life, the Holy Quran gives us a philosophy of war as well. This divine philosophy is an integral part of the total Quranic ideology."[9]

In *The Quranic Concept of War*, Malik seeks to instruct readers in the uniquely important doctrinal aspects of Quranic warfare. The Quranic approach to war is "infinitely supreme and effective . . . [and] points towards the realization of universal peace and justice . . . and makes maximum allowance to its adversaries to cooperate [with Islam] in a combined search for a just and peaceful order."[10] For purposes of this chapter, the term "doctrine" refers to both religious and broad strategic approaches, not methods and procedures. Malik's work is a treatise with historical, political, legal, and moral ramifications on Islamic warfare. It seemingly is without parallel in the Western sense of warfare since the "Quran is a source of eternal guidance for mankind."[11]

The approach is not new to Islamists and other jihad theorists fighting according to the "Method of Muhammad" or the Hadith. The lessons learned are recorded and form an important part of Quranic *sura* and jihadist scholarship.[12] Islamic scholars, both Muslim and non-Muslim, will find much to debate in terms of Malik's view of jihad doctrine and Quranic warfare. Malik's work is essentially modern scholarship, although he does acknowledge the classical views of jihad in many respects.[13] Malik's arguments are clearly parochial, often more editorial than scholarly, and his tone is decidedly confident and occasionally supremacist. The reach and influence of the author's work is not clear, although one might believe that given the idealism of his treatise, his approaches to warfare, and the role and ends of "terror," his text may resonate with extremists and radicals prone to using terroristic violence to accomplish their ends. For that reason alone, the book is worth studying.

Malik himself places Quranic warfare in an academic context relative to that used by Western theorists. He analyzes the causes and objects of war, as well as war's nature and dimensions. He then turns attention to the ethics and strategy of warfare. Toward the end of the book, he reviews the exercise of Quranic warfare based on the examples of the Prophet Muhammad's military campaigns and concludes with summary observations. There are important *jus en bellum* and *jus ad bellum* implications in the author's writings, as well as in his controversial ideas related to the means and objectives of war. It is these concepts that warrant the attention of planners and strategists.

INTRODUCTION

In his foreword, Muhammad Zia-Ul-Haq (1924–88), the former President of Pakistan and Pakistani Army Chief of Staff, opens the book by focusing on the concept of jihad within Islam and explaining that it is not simply the domain of the military:

Jehad fi sabilallah is not the exclusive domain of the professional soldier, nor is it restricted to the application of military force alone. This book brings out with

> simplicity, clarity and precision the Quranic philosophy on the application of military force within the context of the totality that is JEHAD [sic]. The professional soldier in a Muslim army, pursuing the goals of a Muslim state, cannot become "professional" if in all his activities he does not take the "color of Allah." The nonmilitary citizen of a Muslim state must, likewise, be aware of the kind of soldier that his country must produce and the only pattern of war that his country's armed forces may wage.[14]

General Zia states that all Muslims play a role in jihad, which is a mainstream concept of the Quran; that jihad in terms of warfare is a collective responsibility of the Muslim *umma;* and that it is not restricted to soldiers. General Zia emphasizes how the concept of Islamic military professionalism requires "godly character" in order to be fully achieved. Zia then endorses Malik's thesis as the "only pattern of war," or approach to war, that an Islamic state may wage.

BATTLING COUNTER-INITIATORY FORCES

In the preface, Allah B. K. Brohi, the former Pakistani ambassador to India, states that Malik has made "a valuable contribution to Islamic jurisprudence," or Islamic law, and has offered an "analytic restatement of the Quranic wisdom on the subject of war and peace."[15] He implies that Malik's discussion, though a valuable new version, is an approach to a theme already well developed. Brohi then defines jihad: "The most glorious word in the [v]ocabulary of Islam is *Jehad* [sic], a word which is untranslatable in English but, broadly speaking, means 'striving,' 'struggling,' 'trying to advance the Divine causes or purposes.'" He introduces a somewhat cryptic concept (defined below) when he explains man's role in a "Quranic setting" as energetically combating forces of evil or what may be called "counter-initiatory" forces that are at war with the harmony and the purpose of life on earth.[16] True Muslim harmony and purpose in life are only possible through man's ultimate submission to God's will, that all will come to know, recognize, and profess Muhammad as the Prophet of God. Man must recognize the last days and acknowledge *tawhid,* the oneness of God.[17]

Brohi recounts the classic dualisms of Islamic theology: that the world is a place of struggle between good and evil, between right and wrong, between *Haq* and *Na-Haq* (truth and untruth), and between *halal* and *haram* (legitimate and forbidden). It is the duty of man to opt for goodness and reject evil. He appeals to the "greater jihad," a post-classical jihad doctrine developed by the mystical Sufi order and other Shi'a scholars.[18]

Brohi places jihad in the context of communal, if not imperial, obligation–both are controversial formulations:

> When a believer sees that someone is trying to obstruct another believer from traveling the road that leads to God, [the] spirit of Jehad [sic] requires that such a man

who is imposing obstacles should be prevented from doing so. . . To do otherwise, by not striving to clear or straighten the path we [Muslims] become passive spectators of the counter-initiatory forces imposing a blockade in the way of those who mean to keep their faith with God.[19]

This viewpoint appears to reflect the classic, collective duty within jihad doctrine to defend the Islamic community from threats, that is, the concept of defensive jihad. Brohi is saying much more than that, however; he is attempting to delineate the duty—the proactive duty—to clear the path for Islam. It is necessary not only to defend the individual believer if he is being hindered in his faith, but also to remove the obstacles of those counter-initiatory forces hindering his Islamic development. This begs the question of what is actually meant by the initiatory forces. The answer is clear to Brohi: the force of initiative is Islam and its adherents. "It is the duty of a believer to carry forward the Message of God and to bring it to notice of his fellow men in handsome ways. But if someone attempts to obstruct him from doing so he is entitled, as a matter of defense, to retaliate."[20]

This formulation would appear to turn the concept of defense on its head. When Islam, as a faith, seeks to extend its invitation and reach—to initiate its advance—but is unable to do so, then that represents an overt threat justifying a defensive jihad. In other words, everywhere the message of God and Islam is hindered from expansion, resisted, or opposed by some "obstruction" (a term not clearly defined), Islam is intrinsically entitled to defend its manifest destiny.[21] While his logic is controversial, Brohi is not unique in his extrapolation. His theory, in fact, reflects the argument of Rashid Rida, a conservative disciple of the Egyptian Muhammad Abduh. In 1913 Abduh published an article evaluating Islam's early military campaigns and determined that Islam's early neighbors "prevented the proclamation of truth," thus engendering the defense of Islam. "Our religion is not like others that defend themselves . . . but our defense of our religion is the proclamation of truth and the removal of distortion and misrepresentation of it."[22]

NO NATION IS SOVEREIGN

The exegesis of the term *jihad* is often debated. Some apologists make clear that nowhere in the Quran does the term "Holy War" exist; that is true, but it is also irrelevant. War in Islam is either just or unjust, and that justness depends on the ends of war. Brohi, and later Malik, make clear that the ends of war in Islam, or jihad, are to fulfill God's divine purpose. Not only should that be a holy purpose, it must be a just war in order to be "Holy War."[23]

The next dualism Brohi presents is that of *Dar al-Islam* and *Dar al-Harb*, the house of submission and the house of war. To this end, Brohi quotes the Quranic manuscript *Sura al-Tawba:* "Fight those who believe not in Allah nor the Last Day, nor hold that forbidden which hath been forbidden by Allah and His Messenger, nor acknowledge the religion of Truth (even if they are) of the People of the Book, until they pay the *jizya* with willing submission, and feel themselves subdued."[24] Acknowledging Western critics who believe that Islam is in a state of perpetual struggle with the non-Islamic world, Brohi counters in a clearly dismissive tone by explaining that man is a slave to God, and defying God is treason under Islamic law. Obviously, much turns on how threats and aggression are characterized. It is difficult to understand, however, based on the structure of his argument, that Brohi views non-believers and their states as requiring conversion only over time by peaceful means, never without recourse to force. He echoes the doctrine of Abd al-Salam Faraj, author of *Al-Farida al-Ghaibah*, better known as *The Neglected Duty*, a work that is widely read throughout the Muslim world.[25]

Finally, Brohi examines the concepts of the *umma* and the international system: "The idea of *umma* of Mohammad, the Prophet of Islam, is incapable of being realized within the framework of territorial states." This is a consistent view that underpins many works on the concept of the Islamic state.[26] For Muslims, the *umma* is a transcendent religious and cultural society reflecting the unity (*tawhid*) of Islam and the idea of one God, indivisible, one community, one belief, and one duty to live and become godly. According to the Prophet, *"Umma* participates in this heritage by a set pattern of thought, belief and practice . . . and supplies the spiritual principle of integration of mankind—a principle which is supranational, supra-racial, supra-linguistic and supra-territorial."[27]

In his analysis of the law of nations and their international dealings, Brohi emphasizes that in "Islamic international law this conduct [war and peace] is, strictly speaking, regulated between Muslims and non-Muslims, there being, from [an] Islamic perspective, no other nation . . ." In other words, war is between Muslims and non-Muslims and not in actuality between states. It is transnational. He adds, "In Islam, of course, no nation is sovereign since Allah alone is the only sovereign in Whom all authority vests."[28] Here Brohi is echoing what Islamic scholars such as Majid Khadduri have described as the "dualism of the universal religion and universal state that is Islam."[29]

THE DIVINE PHILOSOPHY ON WAR

Brigadier Malik begins by categorizing human beings into three archetypes: those who fear Allah and profess the Faith; those who reject the Faith; and those who profess, but are treacherous in their hearts. Examples of the Prophet and the instructions to him by God in his early campaigns should be studied to fully understand these three examples in practice. The author highlights the fact that the "divine philosophy on war" was revealed gradually over a twelve-year period, its earliest guidance dealing with the causes and objects of war, while later guidance focused on Quranic strategy, the conduct of war, and the ethical dimensions of warfare.[30]

In chapter 3, Malik reviews several key thoughts espoused by Western scholars related to the causes of war. He examines the ideologies of Lenin, Geoffery Blainey, Quincy Wright, and Frederick H. Hartman, each of whom spoke about war in a historical or material context with respect to the nature of the state system. Malik finds these explanations wanting and turns to the Quran for explanation: "war could only be waged for the sake of justice, truth, law, and preservation of human society . . . The central theme behind the causes of war . . . [in] the Holy Quran, was the cause of Allah."[31] The author recounts the progression of revelations by God to the Prophet that "granted the Muslims the permission to fight . . ." Ultimately, God would compel and command Muslims to fight: "Fight in the cause of Allah." In his analysis of this *sura*, Malik highlights the fact that "new elements" were added to the causes of war: that in order to fight, Muslims must be "fought first"; Muslims are not to "transgress God's limits" in the conduct of war; and everyone should understand that God views "tumult and oppression" of Muslims as "worse than slaughter."[32] This oppression was exemplified by the denial of the right of Muslims to worship at the Sacred Mosque by the early Arab Quraysh, the people of Mecca, which Malik describes in detail.[33] He argues that the pagan Quraysh tribe had no reason to prohibit Muslim worship, since the Muslims did not impede their form of worship. He notes that the Quran distinguishes those who fight "in the cause of Allah and those who reject Faith and fight in the cause of evil."[34] In terms of Quranic just war theory, war must be waged "only to fight the forces of tyranny and oppression."[35]

Challenging Clausewitz's notion that "policy" provides the context and boundary of war, Malik says it is the reverse: war forces "policy to define and determine its own parameters," and since the policy discussion focuses on parochial issues such as national interests and the vagaries of state-to-state relations, it is a lesser perspective. In the divine context of the Quran, war is oriented toward the spread of "justice and faith in Allah altogether and everywhere." According to the author, war is to be fought aggressively; slaughter is not the worst evil. In the course of war, every opportunity for peace should be pursued and reciprocated, that is, every remonstrance of peace by the enemies of Islam, but only as prescribed by the Quran's "clear-cut philosophy and methodology" for preserving peace.[36]

Understanding the context in which the Quran describes and defines "justice and peace" is important. Malik refers the reader to the Battle of

Badr to elucidate these principles. There is peace with those pagans who cease hostilities, and war continues with those who refuse. He cites the following *sura:* "as long as these stand true to you, stand ye true to them, for Allah doth love the righteous."[37] Referring to the precedent-setting Hodaibayya Treaty in the ninth year of the *hijra*, or pilgrimages to Mecca, Malik outlines how Allah and the Prophet abrogated it and other treaties with the pagan Meccans.

Pagans who accepted terms voluntarily without a treaty were respected. Those who refused, the Quran directed, were to be slain wherever found. This precedent and divine "revelations commanded the Muslims to fulfill their treaty commitments for the contracted period but put them under no obligations to renew them."[38] It also established the precedent that Muslims may conclude treaties with non-believers, but only for a temporary period.[39] Commenting on Western approaches to peace, Malik views such approaches as not standing the "test of time," with no worthwhile role to play even in the future.[40] The author's point is that peace between states has only secular, not divine, ends; and peace in an Islamic context is achieved only for the promotion of Islam.

As the Prophet gained control of Mecca he decreed that non-believers could not assemble or watch over the Sacred Mosque. He later consolidated power over Arabia and many who had not yet accepted Islam. These non-believers were required to pay a poll-tax, or *jizya*, and accept the status of *dhimmitude* (servitude to Islam) in order to continue practicing their faith. According to Malik, the taxes were merely symbolic and insignificant. In summarizing this relationship the author states, "the object of war is to obtain conditions of peace, justice, and faith. To do so it is essential to destroy the forces of oppression and persecution."[41] This view is in keeping with that outlined by Khadduri: "The jihad, it will be recalled, regarded war as Islam's instrument to transform the *Dar al-Harb* into *Dar al-Islam* . . . in Islamic legal theory, the ultimate objective of Islam is not war, per se, but the ultimate establishment of peace."[42]

THE NATURE OF WAR

Malik argues that the "nature and dimension of war" is the greatest single characteristic of Quranic warfare and distinguishes it from all other doctrines. He acknowledges Clausewitz's contribution to the understanding of warfare in its moral and spiritual contexts. The moral forces of war, as Clausewitz declared, are perhaps the most important aspects in war. Reiterating that Muslims are required to wage war "with the spirit of religious duty and obligation," the author makes it clear that in return for fighting in the way of Allah, divine, angelic assistance will be rendered to jihad warriors and armies. At this point *The Quranic Concept of War* moves beyond the metaphysical to the supernatural element, unlike anything found in Western doctrine. Malik highlights the fact that divine assistance requires "divine standards" on the part of the warrior *mujahideen* for the promise of Allah's aid to be met.[43]

The author then builds upon the jihad warrior's role in the realms of divine cause, purpose, and support to argue that the Muslim warrior can be the bravest and the most fearless only through the correct spiritual preparation, beginning with total submission to God's will. The Quran reveals that moral forces are the "real issues involved in the planning and conduct of war."[44] The jihad warrior who dies in the way of Allah does not really die but lives on in heaven. Malik emphasizes this in several Quranic verses: "Think not of those who are slain in Allah's way as dead . . . Nay, they live finding their sustenance in the Presence of the Lord." Malik also notes that "[n]ot equal are those Believers . . . Allah has granted a higher grade to those who strive and fight . . ."[45]

The Quranic dimensions of war are "revolutionary," conferring on jihad warriors a "personality so strong and overbearing as to prove themselves equal to, indeed dominate over, every contingency in war."[46] This theme of spiritual preparation and pure belief has appeared in the prolific jihad writings of Usaman Dan Fodio in the early 1800s and was repeated by the Saudi writer Abdallah al-Qadiri in 1992, both emphasizing the role of the "greater jihad." Becoming a purer and more disciplined Muslim serves the cause of Islam better in peace and war.[47]

The author expands on the idea that moral and spiritual forces predominate in war. He contrasts Islamic strategic approaches with Western theories of warfare oriented toward the application of force, primarily in the military domain, as opposed to Islam, where the focus is on a broader application of power. Power in Malik's context is the power of jihad, which is total, both in the conduct of total war and in its supporting strategy, referred to as "total or grand strategy." Malik provides the following definition: "*Jehad* [sic] is a continuous and never-ending struggle waged on all fronts including political, economic, social, psychological, domestic, moral and spiritual to attain the objectives of policy."[48] The power of jihad brings with it the power of God.

The Quranic concept of strategy is therefore divine theory. The examples and lessons to be derived from it may be found in the study of the classics, inspired by such events as the battles of the Prophet, e.g., Badr, Khandaq, Tabuk, and Hudaibiyya. Malik again references the divine assistance of Allah and the aid of angelic hosts. He refers to the battles of Hunain and Ohad as instances where seeming defeat was reversed and Allah "sent down Tranquility into the hearts of believers, that they may add Faith to their Faith." Malik argues that divine providence steels the jihadi in war and "strengthens the hearts of [b]elievers." Calmness of faith, "assurance, hope, and tranquility" in the face of danger is the divine standard.[49]

STRIKE TERROR INTO THEIR HEARTS

Malik uses examples to demonstrate that Allah will strike "terror into the hearts of [u]nbelievers."[50] At this point he begins to develop his most controversial and conjectural Quranic theory related to warfare—the role of terror. Readers need to understand that the author is thinking and writing in strategic terms, not in the vernacular of battles or engagements. Malik continues, "when God wishes to impose His will on His enemies, He chooses to do so by casting terror into their hearts."[51] Malik's strategic synthesis is specific: "the Quranic military strategy thus enjoins us to prepare ourselves for war to the utmost in order to strike terror into the hearts of the enemies, known or hidden, while guarding ourselves from being terror-stricken by the enemy."[52] Terror is an effect, the end-state.

Malik identifies the center of gravity in war as the "human heart, [man's] soul, spirit, and Faith." Note that Faith is capitalized, meaning more than simple moral courage or fortitude. Faith in this sense is in the domain of religious and spiritual faith; this is the center of gravity in war. The weapon best deployed against this concept of the center of gravity is "the strength of our own souls . . . [keeping] terror away from our own hearts." In terms of achieving decisive and direct decisions, preparing for this type of battlefield first requires "creating a wholesome respect for our *Cause*"— the cause of Islam. This "respect" must be cultivated in advance of war and conflict in the mind of the enemy. Malik then introduces the informational, psychological, or perception management concepts of warfare. Echoing Sun Tzu, he states that if properly prepared, the "war of muscle," the physical war, will already be won by "the war of will."[53]

When examining the theme of the preparatory stage of war, Malik talks of the "war of preparation being waged . . . in peace," meaning that peacetime activities are, in fact, part of any war. This statement should not be taken lightly; it essentially means that Islam is in a perpetual state of war, while peace can only be defined as the absence of active war. Malik argues that peacetime training efforts should be oriented on the active wars to come, in order to develop the Quranic and divine "will" in the *mujahid*. When armies and soldiers find limited physical resources they should continue and emphasize the development of "spiritual resources," as these are complimentary factors and create synergy for future military action.

Malik's most controversial dictum is summarized in the following manner: in war, "the point where the means and the end meet" is in terror. He formulates terror as an objective principal of war; once terror is achieved the enemy reaches his culminating point. "Terror is not a means of imposing decision upon the enemy; it is the decision we wish to impose . . ." Malik's divine principal of Islamic warfare may be restated as "strike terror; never feel terror." As noted above, the ultimate objective of this form of warfare "revolves around the human heart, [man's] soul, spirit, and Faith."[54] Terror "can be instilled only if the opponent's Faith is destroyed . . . It is essential, in the ultimate analysis, to dislocate [the enemy's] Faith." Those who are firm in their religious conviction are immune to terror, for "a weak Faith offers inroads to terror." Therefore, as part of preparations for jihad, actions will be oriented on weakening the non-Islamic enemy's "Faith," while strengthening that of the Islamic warrior. What that weakening or "dislocation" entails in practice remains ambiguous. Malik concludes that "[p]sychological dislocation is temporary; spiritual dislocation is permanent." The soul of man can only be touched by terror.[55]

Malik then moves to a more academic discussion of ten general categories inherent in the conduct of Islamic warfare. These categories are easily translatable and recognizable to most Western theorists as the planning, organization, and conduct of military operations. In this regard, the author offers no unique insights. His last chapter is used to restate his major conclusions, stressing that "The Holy Quran lays the highest emphasis on the preparation for war. It wants us to prepare ourselves for war to the utmost. The test . . . lies in our capability to instill terror into the hearts of our enemies."[56]

EVALUATION OF *THE QURANIC CONCEPT OF WAR*

Malik's thesis cannot be discounted. Though controversial, his citations are accurately drawn from Islamic sources and consistent with classical Islamic jurisprudence.[57] As Malik notes, "Quranic military thought is an integral and inseparable part of the total Quranic message."[58] Policy planners and strategists striving to understand the nature of the "Long War" should consider Malik's writings in that light.

Malik makes clear that the Quran provides the doctrine, guidance, and examples for the conduct of Quranic or Islamic warfare. "It gives a strategy of war that penetrates deep down to destroy the opponents' faith and render his physical and mental faculties totally ineffective."[59] Malik's thesis focuses on the fact that the primary reason for studying the Quran is to gain a greater understanding of these concepts and insights. The Prophet Muhammad, as the Quran attests, changed the intent and objective of war, raising the sphere of war to a Godly plane and purpose: the global proclamation and spread of Islam. This obviously rejects the Clausewitizian politics and policy dyad: that war is simply policy of the state.

Quranic warfare is "just war." It is *jus en bellum* and *jus ad bellum* if fought "in the way of Allah" for divine purposes and the ends of Islam. This contradicts the Western philosophy of just war theory. Another important connotation is that jihad is a continuum, across peace and war.

It covers the spectrum from grand strategy to tactics, from the collective to the individual, from the preparatory to the execution phases of war.

Malik highlights the fact that the preservation of life is not the ultimate end or greatest good in Quranic warfare. Ending "tumult and oppression," achieving the war aims of Islam through jihad, are the desired ends. Dying in this cause brings direct reward in heaven for the *mujahid*; sacrifice is sacred. It naturally follows that death is not feared in Quranic warfare; indeed, "tranquility" invites God's divine aid and assistance. The "Base" of the Quranic military strategy is spiritual preparation and "guarding ourselves against terror."[60] Readers may surmise that the training camps of al-Qaeda (The Base) were designed as much for spiritual preparation as for military operations. One need only to recall the example of Mohammed Atta's "last night" preparations.[61]

The battleground of Quranic war is the human soul—it is religious warfare. The object of war is to dislocate and destroy the religious "Faith" of the enemy. These principals are consistent with the objectives of al-Qaeda and other radical Islamic organizations: "Wars in the theory of Islam are . . . to advance God's purposes on earth, and invariably they are defensive in character."[62] Peace treaties in theory are temporary, pragmatic protocols. This treatise acknowledges Islam's manifest destiny and the approach to achieving it.

Brigadier Malik's thesis in *The Quranic Concept of War* can be fundamentally described as "Islam is the answer." He makes a case for war and the revitalization of Islam. This is a martial exegesis of the Quran. Malik and other modern Islamists are, at root, romantics. They focus on the Quran for jihad, a doctrine that harkens back to the time of the Prophet and the classical-jihadist period, when Islam enjoyed its most successful military campaigns and rapid growth. The book's metaphysical content borders on the supernatural and renders "assured expectations" that cannot be evaluated or tested in the arena of military experience. Incorporating "divine intervention" into military campaigns, while possibly advantageous, cannot be calculated as an overt force multiplier. Critics may also point to the ahistorical aspect of Malik's thesis that Islam is in a state of constant struggle with the non-Islamic world, for there are numerous examples of Muslim armies serving side-by-side with Christian soldiers in combat, with Iraq being but a recent example.[63]

Malik's appraisal of the Quran as a source of divine revelation for victory in war can likewise be criticized by historical example. Were it fully true and operationalized, then the 1,400 years of Islamic military history might demonstrate something beyond its present state. War and peace in Islam have ebbed and flowed, as has the conduct of war across all civilizations, ancient and modern. Islam as an independent military force has been in recession since 1492, although the latest jihadist threat of terror against the international system is, at least in part, a possible reaction to this long recession. Malik's thesis essentially recognizes this historical pattern; indeed, Malik's book may be an attempt to reverse this trend. The events of 9/11 may be seen as a validation of Malik's thesis regarding spiritual preparation and the use of terror. The attacks on the World Trade Center and the Pentagon were intended to inculcate "respect" (fear) in the minds of Islam's enemies. These acts were not only directed at Western non-believers, but also the Muslim leaders who "profess the faith but are treacherous in their hearts" (i.e., allies and supporters of the United States). The barbarity of Abu Musab al-Zarqawi and others in Iraq reflects a focus on extreme terror designed to break the will of Islam's enemies.

Malik and Brohi both emphasize the defensive nature of jihad in Islam, but this position appears to be more a defense of a manifest destiny inevitably resulting in conflict. In their rendering of jihad, both, not surprisingly, owe an intellectual debt to the Pakistani Islamist theorist Abu A'ala Mawdudi. Mawdudi is an important intellectual precursor to the Muslim Brotherhood, to Sayyid Qutb, and to other modern Islamic revivalists. As Mawdudi notes, "Islamic jihad is both offensive and defensive," oriented toward liberating man from humanistic tyranny.[64]

The author's most controversial, and perhaps most noteworthy, assertion is the distinction of "terror" as an end rather than as a means to an end. The soul can only be touched by terror. Malik's divine principal of war may be summarized by the dictum "strike terror; never feel terror." Yet he does not describe any specific method of delivering terror into the heart of Islam's enemies. His view of terror seems to conflict with his earlier, limited discussion of the concept of restraint in warfare and what actually constitutes "excesses" on the part of an enemy. It also conflicts with the character and the nature of the response that the author says is demanded. Malik leaves many of these pertinent issues undefined under a veneer of legitimating theory.

In spite of certain ambiguities and theoretical weaknesses, this work should be studied and valued for its insight and analysis related to jihadist concepts and the asymmetric approach to war that radical Muslims have adapted and executed. With respect to global jihad terrorism, as the events of 9/11 so vividly demonstrated, there are those who believe, and will exercise, the tenets of *The Quranic Concept of War*.

NOTES

1. Majid Khadduri, *War and Peace in the Law of Islam* (Baltimore: John Hopkins Press, 1955), 64.

2. R. D. Hooker, "Beyond *Vom Kriege*: The Character and Conduct of Modern War," *Parameters* 35, no. 2 (Summer 2005): 4.

3. Paul Sperry, "The Pentagon Breaks the Islam Taboo," *FrontPage Magazine*, 14 December 2005, http://www.frontpagemag.com/Articles/ReadArticle.asp?ID=20539.

4. Antulio Echevarria, *Towards an American Way of War* (Carlisle: U.S. Army War College, Strategic Studies Institute, March 2004).

5. Patrick Poole, "The Muslim Brotherhood 'Project,'" *FrontPage Magazine*, 11 May 2006, http://www.frontpagemag.com/Articles/ReadArticle.asp?ID=22415.

6. Farhang Rajaee, *Islamic Values and World View: Khomeyni on Man, the State and International Politics* (Lanham: University Press of America, 1984), 71.

7. Brigadier S. K. Malik, *The Quranic Concept of War* (Lahore, Pakistan: Associated Printers, 1979). Quranic war or Quranic warfare refers to Malik's treatment in his book.

8. Irfan Yusuf, "Theories on Islamic Books You Wouldn't Read About," *Canberra Times*, 21 July 2005.

9. Brigadier S.K. Malik, "Author's Preface," in Malik, *The Quranic Concept of War*, i–ii.

10. Malik, *The Quranic Concept of War*, 1.

11. Malik, "Author's Preface," i.

12. See, for example, the discussion by Dr. Mary R. Habeck, "Jihadist Strategies in the War on Terrorism," *The Heritage Foundation*, 8 November 2004, http://www.heritage.org/Research/NationalSecurity/hl855.cfm.

13. David Cook, *Understanding Jihad* (Berkeley: University of California Press, 2005). There are 1,400 years of jihad scholarship beginning with Muhammad and his military campaigns, classical approaches to jihad as described by Muhammad's successors, the challenges presented by the struggles of succession to Muhammad, the *sufi* spiritual influences, the resistance to the Crusades and the Mongol invasion and rulership of Islamic lands, up through the period of European colonialism and the transformation of the Ottoman Empire and end of the Caliphate.

14. Muhammad Zia-Ul Haq, "Foreword," in Malik, *Quranic Concept of War*, i.

15. Allah Bukhsh K. Brohi, "Preface," in Malik, *Quranic Concept of War*, i.

16. Ibid., i. Note: the Christian concept of the Trinity contained in the Nicene Creed is considered polytheistic according to Islam. The Trinity is not *tawhid*.

17. John Esposito, *Islam: The Straight Path*, 3rd ed. (New York: Oxford University Press, 1998), 12–14, 89.

18. Bernard Lewis, *The Political Language of Islam* (Chicago: University of Chicago Press, 1988), 72; Khadduri, *War and Peace*, 65, 70–72; Cook, *Understanding Jihad*, 35–39.

19. Brohi, "Preface," ii.

20. Ibid., iii.

21. Ibid.

22. Cook, *Understanding Jihad*, 95–96. Cook places these concepts of jihad doctrine in the lineage of contemporary and radical theory.

23. The indexed term for "Holy War" is redirected to the term jihad in the classic book of Islamic law, or Shari'a, by Ahmad ibn Naqib al-Misri, *Reliance of the Traveller*, ed. and trans. Nuh Ha Mim Keller (Beltsville: Amana Publication, 1997).

24. Brohi, "Preface," vii.

25. Cook, *Understanding Jihad*, 107; Christoper Henzel, "The Origins of al-Qaeda's Ideology: Implications for U.S. Strategy," *Parameters* 35, no. 1 (Spring 2005): 69–80.

26. Ishtiaq Ahmed, *The Concept of an Islamic State: An Analysis of the Ideological Controversy in Pakistan* (New York: St. Martin's Press, 1987).

27. Brohi, "Preface," x. While in the Western tradition the state is viewed as a territorial and political body, based on "temporal elements such as shared memory, language, race, or the mere choice of its members," Khomeini rejected this view, seeing the secular, political state and nationalism as Western constructs of imperialistic design intended to damage the cohesion of the *umma* and impede the "advancement of Islam." Rajaee, *Islamic Values and World View*, 7, 67–71.

28. Brohi, "Preface," x.

29. Khadduri, *War and* Peace, 63.

30. Malik, *The Quranic Concept of War*, 6.

31. Ibid., 20.

32. Ibid., 20–21; Baqara: 190.

33. Malik, *The Quranic Concept of War*, 11.

34. Ibid., 22; Baqara: 217 and Nissaa: 76.

35. Malik, *The Quranic Concept of War*, 23.

36. Ibid., 29.

37. Ibid., 29; Tauba: 7.

38. Malik, *The Quranic Concept of War*, 31.

39. Khadduri, *War and Peace*, 212. Jurists disagree on the allowable duration of treaties; the operative concept is that the *Dar al-Harb* must be reduced to *Dar al-Islam* over time.

40. Malik, *The Quranic Concept of War*, 27.

41. Ibid., 33–4.

42. Khadduri, *War and Peace*, 141.

43. Malik, *The Quranic Concept of War*, 40.

44. Ibid., 37–38; Baqara: 216.

45. Malik, *The Quranic Concept of War*, 42–44; Al-I-Imran: 169–70 and Nissa: 95.

46. Malik, *The Quranic Concept of War*, 42–44.

47. Cook, *Understanding Jihad*, 77, 124.

48. Malik, *The Quranic Concept of War*, 54.

49. Ibid., 57.

50. Ibid., 57.

51. Ibid., 57.

52. Ibid., 58.

53. Ibid., 58.

54. Ibid., 58–59.

55. Ibid., 60.

56. Ibid., 144.

57. Rudolph Peters, *Jihad in Classical and Modern Islam* (Princeton: Markus Weiner Publishers, 1996), 44–51, 128.

58. Malik, *The Quranic Concept of War*, 3.

59. Ibid., 146.

60. Ibid., 58.

61. "In Hijacker's Bags, a Call to Planning, Prayer and Death," *Washington Post*, 28 September 2001.

62. Brohi, "Preface," iii.

63. Four notable examples are the Crimean War, where French, British, and Ottoman forces allied against the Russians; Fuad Pasha of the Ottoman Army served as a coalition partner with the French Army during the 1860 Rebellion in Syria; more recently Muslim Arab and Kabyle soldiers served in the Harkis of the French Army in the French-Algerian War; and, of course, today in Iraq. Malik would describe some of these events as alliances of convenience serving Islam's interests in accord with the Quran and Shari'a, others as *takfir* or treason.

64. Cook, *Understanding Jihad*, 99–103; Peters, *Jihad in Classical and Modern Islam*, 130.

PART IV

Jihad in Africa: Past and Present

CHAPTER 7

Mad Mullahs and the Pax Britannica: Islam as a Factor in Somali Resistance to British Colonial Rule

George L. Simpson, Jr.

He who does not harry the infidel belongs to the bowels of Hell.
— Maxamed Cabdulle Xasan[1]

This chapter examines Somali resistance to European colonialism that occurred at the close of the nineteenth century and during the first two decades of the twentieth century. It focuses on the jihad, or "holy war," conducted by the *Darwaawiish*, or Dervishes, in British Somaliland from 1899 to 1920 and led by Maxamed Cabdulle Xasan, who was known to his followers as "the Sayyid" and to the British as the "Mad Mullah" (*wadaad waalan* in Somali). Its central thesis is that the centripetal potential of political Islam as an integrating, proto-nationalist force as well as a means of primary resistance to colonialism proved incapable of overcoming centrifugal, particularistic Somali institutions such as clan and kinship bonds and *xeer*, or customary law. While scholars have emphasized the difficulty Islamism has faced overcoming ethnic barriers in an acephalous society composed of segmentary lineage groups, they have failed to emphasize fully the degree to which militant Islamism historically has proved a procrustean fit to other traditional Somali institutions. This chapter seeks to redress this important shortcoming while explaining why radical Islam failed to unite the Somalis in anti-colonial resistance.

Today, Maxamed Cabdulle Xasan occupies "a unique position as a national figure appealing to the patriotic sentiments of Somalis as Muslims irrespective of their clan or lineage allegiance," and has become "the embodiment of *Freedom* and *Liberty*" to many Somalis.[2] Curiously though, most of the victims of the two decades of upheavals were not foreigners but other Somalis. The best known biographer of the Sayyid, Douglas Jardine, poignantly observes that the "tears of Allah" fell upon the Somaliland in the "orgy of internecine warfare" that followed the British withdrawal from the Somali hinterland in 1909 as part of a feckless policy of "coastal concentration." Indeed, writing a decade before the Nazis came to power in Germany, Jardine estimates that "not less than one-third of the male population of Somaliland perished" in what he terms a "holocaust." In the famine that was part of this time of troubles, hundreds of *miskin*, or destitute people, desperately sought food, and there are eyewitness accounts of them "search[ing] through the dung of the Government ponies and camels in the hope of finding some undigested grain of corn." This "time of eating filth," as the Somalis themselves remember it, became so desperate that there were reports of women even resorting to cannibalism and eating their own children to stay alive.[3] Clearly, there is something in the myth of this nationalist hero that must be reconsidered.

SOMALI TRADITION

To appreciate the revolutionary nature of the events of the early twentieth century in Somaliland, one must first have some understanding of indigenous Somali institutions.[4] At the close of the nineteenth century, a small minority of Somalis were urban dwellers who thrived from trade in towns along the coast; growing numbers engaged in agro-pastoralism in the Webi Shabeelle ("Leopard River") region. Yet most Somalis were herders who engaged in dual pastoralism based upon the sexual division of labor. The men looked after camels and sometimes cattle in the pastoral economy, and the women and children tended small stock, which males claimed exclusively as their property. Somali clans claimed a common *tol*, or patrilineal descent.[5]

Somali political culture was patriarchal and egalitarian, and Somalis possessed a collectivist sense of identity. Traditional authority was dynamic and circumstantial among Somalis. To whit, men could achieve positions of preeminence and respect because they possessed such attributes as wisdom, piety, oratory, and negotiating or mediating skills that brought about consensus.[6] One's ability to exercise authority was transitory, however, as each Somali apparently had his own idea of the categorical imperative. An often quoted remark from the early twentieth century by a British officer who encountered a Somali caravan for the first time captures this anarchic tendency quite well. One of his African *askari*s, or soldiers, explained who the unfamiliar people were to him as follows: "Somalis, Bwana, they no good; each man his own Sultan."[7] That the Somali sense of identity was quintessentially linked to kinship also becomes clear as related in the following Somali proverb: "I and my clan against the world. I and my brother against the clan. I against my brother."[8]

The primary institution to which the individual held allegiance within Somali society was the *mag*-paying group, which was a small kinship network that collectively paid blood-wealth or compensation (*mag* in Somali or *diya* in Arabic) for *xaal*, or offenses, to stave off retaliation-in-kind and blood feuds. Above or acting as the *mag*-paying group were sub-clans and clans, with the next highest grouping in Somali society being the confederation, and with clan-families occupying the highest level.[9]

This practice of *mag*-paying was part of the indigenous institution of *xeer*, or customary law.[10] More precisely, *xeer* refers to the contracts that were negotiated between lineages of roughly equal power, which bound *mag*-paying groups together into a kind of collective security system. Under *xeer*, an individual or group of individuals who committed crimes such as homicide, rape, or theft could rely on the protection of the lineage group—without such an attachment, one would be essentially defenseless. Rather than face justice individually, it was through the clan system that Somalis redressed grievances. Negotiations conducted by elders and other men in a *shir*, or public assembly, determined the outcome of disputes. It was the collective entity that paid *mag* for the crimes and misdeeds of its members, and the amount of compensation was a function of the power of the clan.[11] When *mag*-paying groups or clans wielded roughly the same power, they could avoid conflict through compromise and both sides might gain something in a dispute. On the other hand, a powerful clan maintained an advantage over a weaker one, so that "justice" was not always impartial and the idea of "right and wrong" lost its absolute nature. Commenting on contemporary *xeer*, the German anthropologist Günther Schlee insightfully notes: "Force underlies the rules; the rules themselves provide the space in which force is exerted. If vengeance or acceptance of bloodwealth are equally legitimate options, it is always the party which is in a position to exert vengeance that can shape the outcome of the negotiations by an effective latent threat of violence. One can defend one's rights just as well as one's wrongs through this system."[12]

REALM OF ISLAM IN SOMALILAND

Xeer existed *pari passu* with a very different and competing Muslim conception of justice. Islam itself had come to Somaliland as early as the eighth century, yet the Islamization of Somali society was not accomplished overnight, and in reality had occurred over a millennium.[13] While the vast majority of Somalis became devout Muslims, the articulation of Islam was not equal among all the Somali lineages. That is to say that some clan-families, such as the Dir and Hawiye, had not accepted the religion as fully as did others. Moreover, as Somalis interpreted Islam through their indigenous belief systems, there were syncretic aspects to the Islam practiced among Somalis. Some rituals and institutions from the pre-Islamic, Eastern Cushitic past persisted among the Somalis as comparison with neighboring Oromoo-speakers demonstrates.[14] With respect to Shari'a, or Islamic law, there clearly was a "general disharmony" between it and Somali customary law.[15] As noted above, the Somali concept of *xeer* was more flexible than Shari'a and allowed for a wider variation in the adjudication of disputes. In addition, Islamic law held individuals rather than groups responsible for their acts, and was absolute in its conception of morality. Shari'a recognized *xeer*, but at a subordinate level and only as long as it did not conflict with it.[16] Given a choice between following customary law or its Islamic counterpart, Somalis usually gave precedence to the former.[17]

Along these lines, Somali society was a hybrid one that mixed kinship and contract and that melded traditional as well as Islamic concepts. The Somalis made a distinction between religious and political domains that would prove unacceptable to the religious revitalization movement led by Maxamed Cabdulle Xasan, and these contradictions were more than a militant Islamist reformer like the Sayyid could cope with.[18] While indigenous Somali institutions were in many ways conducive to the assimilation of Muslim ones, there were fundamental problems accepting the radical kind of political Islam that Maxamed Cabdulle Xasan sought to promote.[19]

The realm of Islam in Somaliland, in fact, was a contested one long before the arrival of Maxamed Cabdulle Xasan or the advent of European colonialism. Moreover, the Sufi *dariqat*, or orders, so prominent among the Somalis were in competition with both the clans and one another.[20] Thus, for example, although the Qaadiriyya *dariqa* managed to establish hegemony over the Rahanwiin clan-family in the Baardheere region in the early nineteenth century, it did not take long until a resurgent element of the clan-family, namely the Geledi clan, overthrew the *dariqa's* power.[21] The rival Sufi *dariqat* in Somaliland, the Qaadiriya and Axmadiya, likewise totally rejected the neo-Sufism of the Saalixiya and both Maxamed Cabdulle Xasan's claims and his methods. Thus, the irreconcilable contest between the Sayyid and the venerable Qaadiri sheikh, Sheikh Uways bin Maxamed al-Baraawa, led to the latter's assassination by Saalixi *Darwaawiish* in 1909.[22]

The *dariqat* occupied an interstitial place between secular and religious society in Somali society.[23] The *jamaac*, or religious center of a *dariqa*, served as a place of sanctuary for outcasts and from clan warfare. While a *wadaad*, or religious leader, could transcend lineage bounds in many ways, still there were limits on his authority, and he remained subordinate to his secular counterpart, the *warrenleh* (literally spear-bearer). The *dariqat* could be accepted as part of the Somali clientage system as *she-gaad*, or client, to a political leader. As the English explorer and Orientalist Sir Richard Burton observed in the mid-nineteenth century, "the religious code is ancillary and often opposed to . . . Civil Law." Or, as a Somali proverb has it, "God and the warrior chieftain (*'atoosh*) are fighting over us, and we are leaning towards *'atoosh!*"[24]

As the spheres of politics and religion overlap in Islam, it is not surprising that religious authorities also often became embroiled in clan disputes. As the nineteenth century had witnessed a host of dramatic changes, ranging from ecological devastation from rinderpest and drought to the rise of a long-distance trade in slaves and ivory to the advent of African and European colonialism and South Asian merchant capital, the power of Somali "holy men" concomitantly increased. Accordingly, more and more Somali males found solace in Islam by the beginning of the twentieth century by attaching themselves to a *dariqa* and performing the *hajj*, or pilgrimage to Mecca. The first two decades of the twentieth century have become known as the "era of the sheikhs," as a host of religious leaders immigrated to the region and established mosques and *madaris*, or Quranic schools, and became a powerful social and political force.[25] Not only did Maxamed Cabdulle Xasan get involved in clan disputes then, but he went far beyond and sought to reverse the roles of patron and client. His ambition was not to attain some kind of subordinate status, but to become the overlord of the Somali clan leaders who became associated with him, not to mention the entirety of Somaliland.[26]

Nonetheless, the Sayyid certainly was not the first Muslim leader to come into conflict with the prevailing Somali culture. An interesting historical example of the clash between *xeer* and Shari'a arose in the case of Nuurayn Axmed Sabr, an Axmadiya sheikh, or honored holy man. After Zanzibari Sultan Sayyid Barghash appointed the sheikh as *qadi*, or judge, in the Benaadir coastal town of Baraawa, he became involved in a dispute with urban notables and merchants. Following Shari'a, the *qadi* upheld the right of women to inherit property as opposed to the local customs, which excluded them and gave wealth to agnatic heirs. The town leaders managed temporarily to remove the sheikh, but he gained reinstatement after the *'ulama*, or religious authorities, in Zanzibar pronounced him a competent judge.[27]

THE PATH OF THE SAYYID

The Saalixiya neo-Sufism that Maxamed Cabdulle Xasan taught drew its doctrinal inspiration from the teachings of Sheikh Muhammad 'Abd al-Wahhab and the Wahhabi sect of Sunni Islam, which arose in mid-eighteenth-century Arabia. Wahhabism, in turn, is based on the strict

Hanbali school of *fiqh*, or legal interpretation, and seeks a return to the purified Shari'a, or Muslim law, and the piety of the time of the Salafi, or early generations of Islam. The literalist interpretation of Islam adopted by Sheikh Mohammed bin Salih Rashid, the Sayyid's mentor, was alien to the Somalis. As opposed to the classical Sufism long established in Somaliland as among the Qaadiriya, Maxamed Cabdulle Xasan, who became an adherent of the Saalixiya *dariqa*, rejected *tawassul*, or the inter-cession of deceased saints, which he considered *shirk*, or a form of poly-theism. The Sayyid was militant if not fanatical as he sought a rigorous submission to Shari'a and censured "the prevailing laxity in religious practice" among the Somalis.[28] For their part, Qaadiriya *muridun*, or fol-lowers, rejected the asceticism of the Saalixiya.[29]

From the point of view of a radical Islamist like Maxamed Cabdulle Xasan, *Dar al-Islam*, or the realm of the faithful, was under assault at the hands of Christians. Part of the threat came from the Somalis' long-standing rival, Ethiopia. Similarly pressed by ecological pressures, but also seeking expansion, the Ethiopians moved into the Ogaadeen and began raiding and looting the local population, as well as desecrating Muslim *jamaacat* and other holy places such as the tomb of the Qaadiriya saint, Cabd ar-Raxmaan az-Zeylici.[30] Maxamed Cabdulle Xasan also waged jihad against the Europeans, with his ultimate goals being to "drive the British infidel into the sea" and "to purge the country of Chris-tians."[31] As a devout Muslim, the Sayyid did give his British enemy the choice, however, of waging war or agreeing to pay the *jizya*, or tribute, required of Christian subjects.

The Sayyid forbade his followers, distinguished by the white turban (*duub caas*) they wore, to associate in any way with Christians and other non-believers or even to dress or walk like the *kuffir*, or infidels. Consist-ent with the teachings of the medieval Muslim scholar, Ibn Taymiyya, who had also influenced the Wahhabis, Maxamed Cabdulle Xasan declared *takfir*, or unbelievers, all Muslims who did so. Like the Wahha-bis, who staked their future on a merger with the politically powerful Saudi family, Maxamed Cabdulle Xasan hoped to merge religion with the sword (or *wadaad* and *waranleh*, in the Somali rendering) and to wage jihad as an individual obligation (*fard ayn*) since Christians had invaded the realm of Islam.[32]

With his pastoral origins in the rural hinterland and in a classically Khaldunian manner, the Sayyid likewise vehemently opposed the mate-rialism, consumerism, and corruption that he found among the urban dwellers who prospered from commerce at Berbera on the Somali coast. Some of these so-called "greedy" merchants were of South Asian origins, but others were Isxaaq Somalis who were charging interest in contraven-tion to the Quranic prohibition on *riba*, or usury. Maxamed Cabdulle Xasan further demanded abstinence from tobacco, coffee, and tea and proscribed the use of the mild stimulant *qaat*, or *Catha edulis*. The consumption of the latter was widespread at the time, as men often chewed it at *dhikr*, or Sufi meetings, to keep themselves awake. Dancing was also forbidden to his adherents. Elsewhere, on the Benaadir Coast in what became Italian Somaliland, the millenarian but more moderate Sheikh Uways bin Maxamed al- Baraawa, too, helped bring an end to the *hiikow*, a popular dance done by urban Somalis, which pious Muslims considered licentious.[33]

As a charismatic leader in the Weberian paradigm, Maxamed Cabdulle Xasan modified his version of traditional practices as well as Islam for his own opportunistic exigencies.[34] He brought in innovations not only to indigenous Somali customs, but also to Shari'a, even as he claimed to uphold the latter. The most notable example of this was the "you defied" (*waad xujowday*) penal provision that allowed him to punish not only other Muslims, but also those who rebelled against him from among his own *muridun*.[35] Thus armed, the Sayyid could liquidate his political rivals and his *Darwaawiish* could burn villages and seize the wives and property of other Muslims. They murdered devout Somalis and violated the sanctity of bodies by mutilating corpses. Disregarding the injunction that "there is no compulsion in Islam" (Quran, 2:256), the *muridun* compelled others to accept their version of the "true faith." When Maxamed Cabdulle Xasan suffered defeat, he blamed the reversal on the lack of piety of his followers. When *Darwaawiish* fled fortresses that came under British attack in 1914 without the permission of the Sayyid, he had them castrated. Maxamed Cabdulle Xasan treated deserters severely with "wholesale executions and mutilations." The Sayyid spared neither men, women, nor children, even among Muslims. Thus, during a feud with the Warsangali clan in May 1916, the *Darwaawiish* executed some 300 Warsangali women and children after capturing part of the town of Las Khorai. Maxamed Cabdulle Xasan similarly could not abide Dhulbahante neutrality and raided them. He did not do so officially, but let his followers act putatively as *buraad*, or roving robber bands.[36] In addition, *siyaaro*, or voluntary charity, became a compulsory tax to finance the Darwaawiish state.[37]

There are yet other examples of egregious conduct on the part of the Sayyid. Accordingly, he slit the throat of his new bride, the daughter of Cusman Maxamuud, after he and her father split diplomatically. Maxamed Cabdulle Xasan likewise violated *amaan*, or safe conduct, and murdered one of the envoys sent by Sir Reginald Wingate during the latter's mission to British Somaliland in 1909.[38] In August 1916, during the First World War, a German mechanic named Emil Kirsch joined the Sayyid to act as a gunsmith to the *Darwaawiish*. Maxamed Cabdulle Xasan imprisoned him as a "white infidel," impressed him for his services, and flogged him. The ill-starred Kirsch eventually died of thirst while trying to escape.[39]

Not only did the *kuffar* Europeans find the "Mad Mullah's" methods despicable, but so did other pious Muslims. For example, the Isxaaq poet and antagonist to the Sayyid, Cali Jaamac Haabiil, characterized Maxamed Cabdulle Xasan as "a crazed priest" who "slit the throats of a thousand pious men . . . [and who] enriched himself on the inheritance of the weak and the orphans." Cali Dhuux, another famous Somali poet who was the cousin of the Sayyid and an erstwhile follower, derisively called him a "lecherous infidel."[40] More significant still was the Sayyid's censure by his own mentor. This occurred when one of the Mullah's intimates, Cabdulla Shahari, became disillusioned with him over the *wadaad*'s disapproval of his marriage to a Majeerteen Somali woman and went to Mecca, where he denounced Maxamed Cabdulle Xasan to Sayyid Mohammed bin Salih Rashid. The sheikh excoriated Maxamed Cabdulle Xasan in a censorious letter, and wrote that the Sayyid "can be called now neither a Moslem nor a Christian; you have ceased to know your proper religion."[41] Moreover, when Maxamed Cabdulle Xasan's leading *qadi*, Cabdallah Koryo, upheld this *fatwa*, or religious ruling, the Sayyid had him killed. This event led to the desertion of his own brother-in-law, as well as four hundred *muridun*.[42]

It is also significant that the Sayyid himself never managed personally to abandon his own clan identity or to transcend ethnic politics. In a letter to Horace A. Byatt, the Commissioner of British Somaliland, he averred that "neither am I of the Dolbahanta, the Warsangli, the Mijjertein, nor the Ogaden . . . I am a Dervish, hoping for God's mercy and consent and forgiveness and guidance, and I desire that all the country and the Moslems may be victorious by God's grace."[43] From the start, Maxamed Cabdulle Xasan, the son of a Bah Geri Ogaadeen father and Dhulbahante Harti mother, nonetheless exploited kinship ties, especially among his own Darood clan-family, to establish a religious following.[44] Moreover, the Sayyid sought to use marriage to forge alliances with other clans. Thus, for example, Maxamed Cabdulle Xasan married the daughter of Maxmud bin Cali Shireh, *suldan* (sultan) of the Warsangali clan.[45] The use of marriage for diplomatic reasons also carried over to the Sayyid's *muridun*. For example, after Maxamed Cabdulle Xasan concluded the treaty of Ilig with the Italians in 1905 and put himself under an Italian protectorate, there were unions with the Somalis from the neighboring sultanates of Majeerteen and Hobya.[46]

LOST OPPORTUNITIES

Troubles brought on by the uprising of Maxamed Cabdulle Xasan had a multiplier effect that redounded to the south in the East Africa Protectorate (EAP) as well as Italian Somaliland. Nevertheless, the Sayyid never managed to exploit this to his advantage, mainly because of his failure to overcome clan politics. Much the same was true of those who might have become his allies. In Jubaland, there had been much British anxiety over wild rumors concerning the Sayyid's influence from the inception of the *Darwaawiish* jihad. There, a rebellion by the Awlyahan subclan (part of the Ogaadeen confederation) led by Cabdurraxman Mursaal resulted in the murder of the British Sub-Commissioner, Arthur Jenner, in late 1900. While word of events to the north in British Somaliland reached the Ogaadeen and seem to have inspired them, the two rebellions remained unconnected. Hence, the British were able to deal with Ogaadeen separately by dispatching a punitive expedition against them in 1901. It does appear that the Sayyid subsequently consulted with a would-be "Mullah" from the Harti confederation named Ashgar, but the British made short work of the latter, and killed him in a minor military clash.[47]

Maxamed Cabdulle Xasan missed another opportunity to expand his revolt with a union with the Biimaal clan who inhabited the area between Marka and the Webbi Shebelli in Italian Somaliland and who had risen in rebellion against the Italians between 1903 and 1908. The Sayyid had strong links with the Biimaal through a Saalixiya *jamaac* in their territory led by Sheikh Cabdi Gafle, and carried on a diplomatic correspondence with it. While he supported their jihad and might one day have combined with them, four British punitive expeditions in four years had exhausted the strength of the *Darwaawiish*, and a tactical alliance with the Italians after the treaty of Ilig in 1905 also prevented this until it was too late and the Biimaal had been suppressed.[48]

Ripples from the unrest in British Somaliland continued to reach the EAP. A couple of years later, Major Charles Gwynn, who demarcated the border between Ethiopia and the EAP in 1908–09, complained that elements of the Awlyahan had moved westward to lands south of the Dawa River in order to stay clear of the *Darwaawiish*. He added that whole "communities of brigands" had arisen, which were beyond the control of traditional authorities, and armed with the rifles that were being smuggled into the region. Fearing the "Mad Mullah's" influence in the protectorate, colonial officials were thus willing to allow frontier authorities remarkable latitude as they imposed a summary version of law and order in what they sometimes admitted in a "somewhat high handed" manner. With a flourishing illicit arms trade in the northeastern part of the EAP, colonial authorities also reluctantly moved in 1913–14 in a failed effort to disarm the Mareexaan, some of whom had fought with the Sayyid several years earlier. Finally, they were ever vigilant for some new poseur.[49]

A further chance that Maxamed Cabdulle Xasan let pass came with a second rebellion on the part of Cabdurraxman Mursaal in Jubaland during the First World War, between 1915 and 1918. So slight was the influence of the colonial authorities over the Somalis in the interior that they took help where they could get it—even from a former rebel whom at least one of their officials suspected of gun-running.[50] The Awlyahan leader had met with Sir Henry Belfield, the EAP governor, in 1915, and from this occasion he would later claim that Belfield "had given him all the territory between Serenli and Wajir."[51] His personal ambitions got the better of him in December of that year, when the Awlyahan raided a Samburu encampment in the EAP's Northern Frontier District (NFD), and followed this with the looting of Mareexaan Somalis. A demand by Lieutenant Francis Elliot, the District Commissioner (DC) at Serenli, that the Awlyahan pay *mag* to their victims resulted in tragedy for the British when Cabdurraxman Mursaal led a surprise attack against the frontier post, sacked it, and killed the DC along with many of the *askaris*. For the next eighteen months, the rebels held sway over Jubaland and threatened the neighboring NFD. Again, there were exaggerated reports that Maxamed Cabdulle Xasan was in touch with the Awlyahan, but the two never combined their forces. Thus, once the exigencies of fighting the Germans in East Africa made it possible, colonial authorities finally sent troops to suppress the rebellion and send the rebel leader to flee to parts unknown.[52]

Finally, there was the case of the King's African Rifles (KAR) patrol that in January 1920 mutinied and killed its commander, Lieutenant Frank Dawson-Smith. The men fled with the unit's machine gun across the Ethiopian frontier and ultimately toward the Sayyid's encampment in Somaliland. Although the KAR *askaris* established themselves not far from the person of Maxamed Cabdulle Xasan, he never got them to join him.[53] In summary, as E. Romily Turton has noted, a closer look at all these missed opportunities reveals that the religious appeal of the *Darwaawiish* was limited and tertiary in the EAP and Italian Somaliland, and that political aims in the form of lineage loyalties and personal self-interest superseded Muslim solidarity in each case.[54]

FINALE

Before concluding, it is worth noting that issues of class and age also likely influenced Somali attitudes toward resistance or collaboration, although it is difficult to understand this as fully as one would like because of the paucity of evidence. For example, in 1905, Captain Richard Salkeld, the Acting Sub-Commissioner of Jubaland, claimed that the local Ogaadeen "chiefs" were willing to allow the British to establish a post at Afmadow, which was a prerequisite for administering the district. The colonial official asserted that "the men of property" were prepared to accept British rule, but that "the feelings of the young men" had yet to be taken into account.[55]

Whatever their reasons for devotion, one should note that a loyal coterie of *muridun* stayed with the Sayyid until the bitter end. Among Maxamed Cabdulle Xasan's closest compatriots were Hajji Sudi, a former interpreter for the British navy, who died fighting in the final British expedition in 1920 against the "Mad Mullah." Far from being demoralized by the post-World War I version of "shock and awe" caused by the bombardment of British airplanes, the *Darwaawiish* sometimes fought to the last man. In fact, Jardine describes them as "firing and singing" as imperial forces breached the walls of their fortresses and snuffed out the last pockets of armed resistance.[56] While the Sayyid could arouse fear and hate for many, certainly for others he inspired a remarkable faithfulness even to death.

In retrospect, it is clear that Maxamed Cabdulle Xasan offered a return to a past that Muslim Somalis had never experienced. His militant brand of *takfiri* Islam was unlike the faith that Somalis had practiced since their conversion to the teachings of the Prophet. Moreover, its exclusiveness left little room for indigenous Somali institutions or syncretic beliefs. The Sayyid was ambitious and sought the routinization of power in his own hands by often brutal and un-Islamic means. His individualistic ethos envisioned a revolutionary transformation of Somaliland not in accord with the norms of his own people. While his call to arms against traditional Ethiopian enemies as well as the newly arrived Europeans engendered sympathy and perpetuates the myth of Maxamed Cabdulle Xasan to this day, it was not enough to overcome traditional obstacles to unity, whether in the guise of custom or kinship. Thus perished the rebellion of the Sayyid in the barren Somali hinterland.

NOTES

1. Quoted in Abdi Sheik-Abdi, *Divine Madness: Mohammed Abdulle Hassan (1856–1920)* (Atlantic Highlands: Zed, 1993), 70.

2. I. M. Lewis, *A Modern History of Somalia* (Boulder: Westview, 1988), 76; and Sheik-Abdi, *Divine Madness*, 54 (emphasis in original).

3. Douglas Jardine, *The Mad Mullah of Somaliland* (London: Herbert Jenkins, 1923), 196–98, 203, 256. The Somali characterization can be found in Lewis, *A Modern History of Somalia*, 77. See also B. G. Martin, *Muslim Brotherhoods in Nineteenth-Century Africa* (London: Cambridge University Press, 1976), 190.

4. The classic anthropological treatment of the Somalis is I. M. Lewis, *A Pastoral Democracy: A Study of Pastoralism and Politics among the Northern Somali of the Horn of Africa* (London: Oxford University Press, 1961).

5. Ibid., 56–58; and Walter Goldschmidt, "A General Model for Pastoral Social Systems," in *L'Équipe écologie et anthropologie des societés pastorales*, ed., *Pastoral Production and Society: Proceedings of the International Meeting on Nomadic Pastoralism* (Cambridge: Cambridge University Press, 1979), 16.

6. Ken Menkhaus, "Traditional Conflict Management in Contemporary Somalia," in *Traditional Cures for Modern Conflicts: African Conflict Medicine*, ed. I. William Zartman (Boulder: Lynne Rienner, 1999), 185–87.

7. Ralph E. Drake Brockman, *British Somaliland* (London: Hurst and Blackett, 1912), 102. Cf. Marcus V. Höhne, "Traditional Authorities in Northern Somalia: Transformation of Positions and Powers," Max Planck Institute for Social Anthropology, Working Paper no. 82 (Halle, 2006), 8.

8. Lee Cassanelli, *The Shaping of Somali Society: Reconstructing the History of a Pastoral People, 1600–1900* (Philadelphia: University of Pennsylvania Press, 1982), 21.

9. Ibid., 16–21.

10. This analysis follows Lewis, *A Pastoral Democracy*.

11. Michael Barry and Florian Bruyas, "Land Administration Strategy Formulation in Post Conflict Situations: The Case of Hargeisa, Somaliland," http:// 209.85.165.104/search?q=cache:Wal4aMViow4J:web.wits.ac.za/NR/rdonlyres/ 43461708-DDCD-40C3-BBC4-2ECA20AEE688/0/MikeBarry.doc+xeer+sharia& hl=en&ct=clnk&cd=5&gl=us&client=firefox-a.

12. Günther Schlee, "Regularity in Chaos: The Politics of Difference in the Recent History of Somalia," Max Planck Institute for Social Anthropology, Working Paper no. 18. (Halle, 2001), 10. Following Schlee, this writer bases this analysis of "transcontinuities," or persistent elements of indigenous practices, on modern anthropological sources yet notes their marked similarity with Sir Richard Burton's account from the 1850s as well as the absence of evidence to suggest any fundamental change in *xeer* since the early twentieth century. See Richard F. Burton, *First Footsteps in East Africa* (New York: Praeger, 1966); Menkhaus, "Traditional Conflict Management in Contemporary Somalia," 185–87; and "Human Rights and Security in Central and Southern Somalia," Joint Danish, Finnish, Norwegian, and British Fact-Finding Mission to Nairobi, Kenya (Copenagen, 2004), 30, http://209.85.165.104/search?q=cache:_cI6O0U5KQYJ:www.somali-jna.org/ downloads/HRandSecurity-CentralSouthSomalia2004.pdf+xeer+sharia+somali& hl=en&ct=clnk&cd=41&gl=us&client=firefox-a.

13. See Mohammed Haji Mukhtar, "Islam in Somali History: Fact and Fiction," in *The Invention of Somalia*, ed. Ali Jimale Ahmed (Lawrenceville, NJ: The Red Sea Press, 1995), 1. For the Islamization of the Somalis, see Cassanelli, *The Shaping of Somali Society*, 16–17.

14. Burton, *First Footsteps in East Africa*, 92; and I. M. Lewis, "Sufism in Somaliland: A Study in Tribal Islam in Islam," in *Tribal Societies: From the Atlas to the Indus*, eds. Akbar S. Ahmed and David M. Hart (London: Routledge and Kegan Paul, 1984), 127–28. For an extended, scholarly treatment of Oromoo religion, see Asmarom Legesse, *Gada: Three Approaches to the Study of African Society* (New York: The Free Press, 1973).

15. Lewis, "Sufism in Somaliland," 600.

16. Cassanelli, *The Shaping of Somali Society*, 19–21; and Schlee, "Regularity in Chaos," 10.

17. Michael van Notten, *The Law of the Somalis: A Stable Foundation for the Economic Development in the Horn of Africa*, ed. Spencer Heath MacCallum (Trenton: The Red Sea Press, 2005), xiii, 36–37.

18. Lewis, *A Pastoral Democracy*, 1–2; 213.

19. For example, the Sufi concept of the personal, genealogical transmission of *baaraka*, or divine grace, through sheikhs corresponds well with Somali custom of *abtirsiinyo*, or reckoning of lineage, and this made Sufism particularly congenial to the Somalis. Lewis, "Sufism in Somaliland," 127–28.

20. For a brief treatment of Sufi orders in Somalia, see Margaret Castagno, *Historical Dictionary of Somalia* (Metuchen: The Scarecrow Press, 1975), 8, 40, 128–29, 13, 135–36.

21. Lewis, "Sufism in Somaliland," 597; and Virginia Luling, "'The Law Then Was Not This Law': Past and Present in Extemporized Verse at a Southern Somali Festival," *African Languages and Cultures* 3 (1996): 223.

22. Sheik-Abdi, *Divine Madness*, 59.

23. Lewis, "Sufism in Somaliland," 599–600.

24. Burton, *First Footsteps in East Africa*, 97; and Said S. Samatar, *Oral Poetry and Somali Nationalism: The Case of Sayyid Mahammad 'Abdille Hasan* (New York: Cambridge University Press, 1982), 97.

25. Samatar, *Oral Poetry and Somali Nationalism*, 93; and Scott S. Reese, "Urban Woes and Pious Remedies: Sufism in Nineteenth-Century Benaadir (Somalia)," *Africa Today* 46, no. 3–4 (1999): 171–78.

26. Jardine, *The Mad Mullah of Somaliland*, 179–80.

27. Reese, "Urban Woes and Pious Remedies," 186.

28. It is noteworthy that Maxamed Cabdulle Xasan, like other Somalis, maintained his adherence to the Shafi'i *fiqh* rather than to the Hanbali school. Martin, *Muslim Brotherhoods in Nineteenth-Century Africa*, 197.

29. Robert L. Hess, *Italian Colonialism in Somalia* (Chicago: University of Chicago Press, 1966), 81.

30. Samatar, *Oral Poetry and Somali Nationalism*, 96.

31. Jardine, *The Mad Mullah of Somaliland*, 161, 192.

32. The quotes come from Sheik-Abdi, *Divine Madness*, 58, 86, n. 101. See also Abdul S. Bemath, "The Sayyid and Saalihiya Tariga: Reformist, Anticolonial Hero in Somalia," in *In the Shadow of Conquest: Islam in Colonial Northeast Africa*, ed. Said S. Samatar (Atlantic Highlands: Red Sea Press, 1992), 33–47; and Martin, *Muslim Brotherhoods in Nineteenth-Century Africa*, 195–201.

33. Reese, "Urban Woes and Pious Remedies," 176; and Mohamed M. Kassin and S. Scott Reese, "Arabic Writings of Somalia," in *Arabic Literature of Africa*, ed. R.S. O'Fahey (London: Brill, 2003), 79.

34. Max Weber, *Economy and Society: An Outline of Interpretive Sociology* (New York: Bedminster Press, 1968), 215.

35. Abdisalam M. Issa-Salwe, "The Failure of the Darwaawiish State: The Clash between Somali Clanship and State System," paper presented at the 5th International Congress of Somali Studies, December 1993, http://www.somalia-watch.org/archivemar03/040629602.htm.

36. Jardine, *The Mad Mullah of Somaliland*, 168–69, 241, 256, 261; Captain Malcolm McNeill, *In Pursuit of the "Mad Mullah": Service and Sport in the Somali Protectorate* (London: C. Arthur Pearson, Ltd., 1902), 6; and Sheik-Abdi, *Divine Madness*, 105.

37. Issa-Salwe, "The Failure of the Darwaawiish State."

38. Jardine, *The Mad Mullah of Somaliland*, 192.

39. Ibid., 247–48.

40. Sheik-Abdi, *Divine Madness*, 53. The Sayyid himself was, of course, one of the great Somali poets.

41. Jardine, *The Mad Mullah of Somaliland*, 185. See also Martin, *Muslim Brotherhoods in Nineteenth-Century Africa*, 188–89; and Lewis, *A Modern History of Somalia*, 75.

42. Jardine, *The Mad Mullah of Somaliland*, 186; Martin, *Muslim Brotherhoods in Nineteenth-Century Africa*, 189.

43. Ibid., 211.

44. Bemath, "The Sayyid and Saalihiya Tariga," 35.

45. Jardine, *The Mad Mullah of Somaliland*, 161, 256.

46. Martin, *Muslim Brotherhoods in Nineteenth-Century Africa*, 186–87.

47. E. R. Turton, "The Impact of Mohammad Abdille Hassan in the East Africa Protectorate," *Journal of African History* 10, no. 4 (1969): 643–47; George L. Simpson, Jr., "British Perspectives on Aulihan Somali Unrest in the East Africa Protectorate, 1916–1918," *Northeast African Studies* 6, no. 1–2 (New Series 1999): 14.

48. Martin, *Muslim Brotherhoods in Nineteenth-Century Africa*, 188.

49. See E.R. Turton, "The Impact of Mohammad Abdille Hassan in the East Africa Protectorate," 647–54; T.S. Thomas, *Jubaland and the Northern Frontier District* (Nairobi: Uganda Railway Press, 1917), 81; Precis for week ending Saturday, 30th September, T.S. Thomas, enclosure in Belfield to Law, 4 October 1916, Public Record Office [hereafter PRO], Kew, Colonial Office [hereafter CO], Kenya Official Correspondence, 1905–1935, 533/170/61876; Gwynn to Under-Secretary of State for the Colonies, 28 December 1908, CO 533/54/6399; and Minute by Read, 4 March 1909, on Ibid; Gwynn to Under-Secretary of State for the Colonies, 11 December 1908, CO 533/54/2875; Gwynn to Under-Secretary of State for the Colonies, 15 July 1909, CO 533/69/24365; and Intelligence Report by Barrett, Moyale, 29 January 1910, enclosure in Girouard to Crewe, confidential, 11 March 1910, CO 533/72/214.

50. Hope to [Chief Secretary, Nairobi, June 1910]; and Reddie to Hollis, 10 July 1911, Kenya National Archives [hereafter KNA], PC/NFD4/1/3.

51. Thomas H.R. Cashmore, "Studies in District Administration in the East African Protectorate" (unpublished Ph.D. diss., Cambridge University, 1966), 360.

52. For further information about the rebellion, see Simpson, "British Perspectives on Aulihan Somali Unrest," 7–43.

53. Northern Frontier District Annual Report, 1919–20, C.H.F. Plowman, KNA, PC/NFD1/1/2; and William Lloyd-Jones, *K.A.R.: Being an Unofficial Account of the Origin and Activities of the King's African Rifles* (London: Arrowsmith, 1926), 216–17.

54. Turton, "The Impact of Mohammad Abdille Hassan in the East Africa Protectorate," 654.

55. Salkeld to H. M. Deputy Commissioner, Mombasa, 15 November 1905, enclosure in Sadler to Lyttelton, 8 January 1906, PRO, Kew, CO 533/11/3250.

56. Jardine, *The Mad Mullah of Somaliland*, 269, 274, 278–79.

CHAPTER 8

Jihadists and Jurisprudents: The "Revisions" Literature of Sayyid Imam and Al-Gama'a Al-Islamiyya

Daniel J. Lav

A key issue in the study of contemporary jihadism is the problem of its relation to mainstream Islamic tradition. This chapter proposes to refine and elucidate this issue through an analysis of jihadist writings in the field of jurisprudence and a new corpus of "revisionist" jihadist texts. Of these latter, I have examined in particular the writings and polemics associated with two Egyptian groups that have now officially called off their war on the Egyptian regime and have expressed criticism of other jihad groups such as al-Qaeda. The first of these is al-Gama'a al-Islamiyya (sometimes referred to in the West as the Egyptian Islamic Group, or EIG), which declared a cease-fire in 1997 and further developed its new thinking in the first years of the new millennium. The second is the Jihad group (sometimes referred to as Egyptian Islamic Jihad, or EIJ) under the leadership of the influential jihadist jurisprudent Sayyid Imam (also known as 'Abd al-Qadir bin 'Abd al-'Aziz or Dr. Fadl). These writings and polemics are a particularly fertile and promising area of study in that they themselves explicitly raise the issue of what constitutes normative Islam and whether the jihadist movement has deviated from it. These texts are generally grouped under the single rubric of "revisions" (*muraja'at*); in what follows I will assess whether this terminology is truly appropriate for all the writings in question.

An understanding of these "revisionist" texts has required extended treatment of key issues in the standard jihadist works on jurisprudence, which to date have not received sufficient scholarly attention.[1] Those authored by Sayyid Imam had a seminal influence on the development of modern jihadism, and thus his pre-"revision" works will serve as the primary source for discussion of jihadist jurisprudence; his differences with other jihadist scholars will be noted as needed. Other jurisprudents whom jihadists consider authoritative include Abu Muhammad al-Maqdisi, who was Abu Mus'ab al-Zarqawi's mentor, but later expressed reservations about some of his disciple's practices; Abu Basir al-Tartusi, an unaffiliated Syrian scholar living in England; and Sheikh 'Umar 'Abd al-Rahman, who was the Emir of al-Gama'a al-Islamiyya in its heyday and is now serving a life sentence in a U.S. federal prison for conspiring to bomb several New York City landmarks in the early 1990s. Ayman al-Zawahiri's recently published polemical treatise against Sayyid Imam lists thirty-seven contemporaries, dead and living, whom he considers to be scholarly authorities.[2]

It would be fair to ask how seriously contemporary jihadists take Islamic jurisprudence. Indeed, it may well be that for al-Qaeda itself, political, ideological, or strategic considerations trump issues in jurisprudence—that, at least, is the criticism directed at it by some of the figures studied in this paper. Even so, such a contention can only be understood against the backdrop of the writings on which al-Qaeda's leaders and cadres were formed and in which they profess to believe.

Before engaging in these questions in detail, it is worth providing a brief characterization of what jihadist jurisprudence is. While mainstream Islamic scholars often accuse the jihadist jurisprudents of having deviated from classical norms,[3] the latter group certainly do not consider themselves to have done so. The modern jihad groups see themselves not only as normative Muslims, but also as loyal standard-bearers of the classical scholarly consensus. This is readily apparent in the pivotal issue of rebellion against the ruler. What jihadists have *not* done is to adopt a politically activist approach in conscious opposition to the medieval quietist consensus.[4] Jihadist jurisprudence is, or claims to be, as willing to tolerate profligate Muslim rulers as were mainstream classical jurisprudents; likewise, their contention that rebelling against an apostate ruler is a duty is so uncontroversial in classical jurisprudence as to be trivial. Thus the signal issue that distinguishes a jihadist jurisprudent from a mainstream one is that of how to determine whether a ruler is merely profligate or an outright apostate.

The issue of *takfir* of the ruler has wide-ranging implications beyond the obvious and immediate matter of jihad against the regime. In classical Islamic political theory, the ruler is the linchpin of the public order. In some matters he enjoys discretionary powers; others are not formally at his discretion, but their execution is nonetheless his exclusive prerogative. In the latter, the ruler's dereliction of his duty results in the suspension of the law *de facto*. For instance, offensive jihad is a collective duty whose performance is dependent on the ruler. He is obliged to wage offensive jihad, but if he does not, no one else may.

Thus as long as the ruler stays shy of outright apostasy, his rule is considered legitimate even when it differs significantly from the ideal outlined by the jurisprudents. The obverse of this position is that (in the jihadists' view, at least) the determination that the ruler is an apostate entails the devolution of his prerogatives onto the community at large[5] and, *ipso facto*, the elimination of the legitimate or tolerated margin of dereliction. This has important ramifications for issues such as jihad, application of Quranic punishments, and commanding right and forbidding wrong.

This brings us to the second major issue treated in this chapter. Alongside the elaboration of the law in the abstract, jurisprudents also deal with conditions under which the law is not to be implemented. An example of what we may term these "suspension mechanisms" is the following: if implementing a law can be expected to entail more harm than good, one is required to waive its implementation. This, of course, depends on how one weighs harms and goods—in other words, on one's wider value system. Another suspension mechanism, and one that proves particularly significant for the case of jihad, is the principle that a person unable to perform an obligation is not required to do so; the study of such cases is generally referred to as *fiqh al-istita'a* ("the jurisprudence of ability"). Here, as well, there is room for variation, depending on how widely or narrowly one wants to define "ability."

If we want to sum up in a single sentence the cases of the two Egyptian groups that have declared their desistance from jihad, we could say that al-Gama'a al-Islamiyya has exited jihadism through the window of *takfir* of the ruler, and that Sayyid Imam has exited (if at all) through the window of the "suspension mechanisms." In other words, al-Gama'a al-Islamiyya has ceased to view the Egyptian government as apostate, and thus the issue of jihad against it does not even arise; in consequence, it has also recognized the government's prerogatives and has left off a number of stock Islamist demands. Sayyid Imam, in contrast, still seems to hold that the government is apostate. Thus for him the obligation to wage jihad against the regime remains in force. However, he considers current conditions to be such that the "suspension mechanisms" come into play: the jihadists are judged to be in a state of inability, and are thus exempt from their obligation to fight; in addition, jihad at the present time is judged to do more harm than good. (Al-Gama'a has also used these arguments, but they are rendered redundant by its judgment that the regime is not apostate.)

The above must be taken with the following important caveat: this chapter deals primarily with scholarly discourse within the jihadist movement. While the rank and file will nearly always acknowledge this discourse as normative, their beliefs and actions often diverge from the jursiprudents' ideal formulations. A full and balanced understanding of jihadism requires not just a grasp of normative theoretical statements, but also an examination of the ways theory is transmitted and translated in the social context of the jihadist group and in its dealings with others (armies, civilians, rival jihad groups, etc.). While a detailed analysis of this issue lies beyond the purview of the present study, it will be addressed as far as it relates directly to the cases of al-Gama'a al-Islamiyya and Sayyid Imam.

THE STATUS OF JURISPRUDENCE IN EGYPTIAN JIHADISM

The sociological and intellectual profile of the members of Sayyid Imam's generation of radical Islamists has been treated in a number of studies.[6] Its most salient feature is the predominance of newly urban, university-educated youth, most of them from departments of science or engineering. Few if any of these youth received any kind of formal higher Islamic education. One member of al-Gama'a al-Islamiyya, Muhammad Shu'eib, described his recruitment to the group as resulting from his religious ignorance: "One reason for the spread of the Islamic [or "Islamist"] groups was that when we were young, the al-Azhar sheikhs were distant from us ... When I was in high school, I knew nothing about anything. At that time, I found no sheikh to advise me, take an interest in me, or teach me. In contrast, I suddenly found in the mosque an al-Gama'a member who took an interest in me, and even took an interest in my personal problems. So I became emotionally dependent on that man."[7]

This sociological profile has a clear corollary in the radical Islamists' intellectual preferences, namely, that the more accessible questions of 'aqida (creed) and social and political issues superseded fiqh (jurisprudence) in their thought and actions, notwithstanding their stated concern for implementing Shari'a law. This tendency may also be attributed to the fact that Islamism competed with the Left for the hearts and minds of students, and it may have absorbed or co-opted key left-wing concepts in the course of this struggle. For example, while the idea of a jihadist vanguard is ostensibly based on the Hadiths of "the sect made victorious" (al-ta'ifa al-mansura) and "the group of the saved" (al-firqa al-naji'a), it is hard not to hear in it echoes of Lenin as well. Thus for the Egyptian jihadists, modern ideologies likely influenced what elements in the repository of the Islamic tradition were to be brought to the fore and how they were to be interpreted. To continue with our example of the vanguard, the early glosses (Bukhari, Ibn Hanbal) on al-ta'ifa al-mansura held that this group was the 'ulama (Islamic scholars); in order to expand the definition to include the mujahideen, Sayyid Imam had to argue that the early gloss was because the primary problem facing the Muslim nation at that time was the creedal fight against schismatics, whereas today it is the jihad against infidels and apostates.[8]

Nowhere is this struggle with the modern more evident than in the writings of Sayyid Qutb, who exercised a tremendous influence on the Jihad group and on contemporary jihadism in general.[9] Even Sayyid Imam, despite his pronounced inclination to jurisprudence, says it was the 1965 Muslim Brotherhood trial that first sparked his interest in Islam as a socio-political doctrine,[10] and on occasion he adduces in his writings Qutb's commentary on the Quran.[11] Another factor mitigating the appeal of jurisprudence was the perceived supinity of the al-Azhar sheikhs and other establishment 'ulama; their willingness to legitimize any regime, whether monarchic or "progressive," lent to Islamic jurisprudence the odious taint of casuistry.[12]

Nonetheless, the science of jurisprudence retained its prestige; after all, a movement demanding an Islamic restoration and an implementation of Shari'a could hardly avoid developing its views in the language of jurisprudence. Thus from the very outset, a tension existed in the nascent jihad movement between a professed regard for jurisprudence and a deep-seated disdain for its practitioners. To put it quite simply, the jihad movement needed jurisprudents of its own. The political leadership—people like Ayman al-Zawahiri—was hardly up to the task; it had to locate scholars who could encapsulate the nascent jihadist *weltanschauung* and give it expression in the most classical and normative form possible.

Al-Gama'a al-Islamiyya and the Jihad group found different solutions to this problem. Al-Gama'a turned to a renegade scholar from within the establishment, the blind sheikh 'Umar 'Abd al-Rahman, who much later was convicted on terrorism charges and is currently in prison in the U.S. (His absence may well have been a key condition to the emergence of changes in al-Gama'a's thinking. His views on the group's revisions are not entirely known; it seems that he supported al-Gama'a's original ceasefire initiative, but did not agree with the later ideological revisions.[13])

The Jihad group employed a different strategy to overcome their jurisprudence deficit. They turned to Sayyid Imam, a precocious autodidact from within their own cohort, and elevated him to the status of Shari'a guide. In a 2007 interview with *al-Hayat*, Sayyid Imam relates the story of how al-Zawahiri first tried to recruit him to the Jihad group in 1977. Imam asked al-Zawahiri whether the group had religious authorities whom they followed, and the latter assured him that they did. Imam asked to meet with these authorities as a precondition for joining the organization. Al-Zawahiri told him that he would arrange the meeting, but never did, and he repeatedly put off Sayyid Imam whenever he raised the issue. This continued until Imam concluded that al-Zawahiri was lying and that the Jihad group did not in fact have any 'ulama in its ranks.[14] This episode speaks volumes of the ideological-political nature of the early Egyptian jihad groups and of their lack of—and need for—scholarly legitimization.

It was only years later, when the Jihad group was reconstituted in Pakistan, that Sayyid Imam agreed to join the organization. According to Imam's account, al-Zawahiri told him that al-Gama'a al-Islamiyya had been boasting of a first-rank scholar, 'Umar 'Abd al-Rahman, in the organization, whereas the Jihad group had no one of this stature. Thus al-Zawahiri once more asked Imam to join so as to lend the group scholarly legitimacy. The received wisdom said that he was al-Zawahiri's predecessor as Emir of the group, though Imam himself says that his position was rather that of Shari'a guide.[15]

Thus one major function of the jurisprudents is to lend legitimacy to the jihad groups. Yet to speak of the need for legitimization is to look at the issue in an instrumental manner and from the vantage point of the men of action. The jurisprudents themselves are independent actors with their own understanding of Islam and of the jihad movement, one that often leads them into conflict with the others. One could point to episodes such as Sayyid Imam's leaving the Jihad group and his public excoriation of al-Zawahiri;[16] Abu Muhammad al-Maqdisi's open letter to Abu Mus'ab al-Zarqawi;[17] or, in a rather different context, Abu Basir al-Tartusi's polemic against the reformed al-Gama'a al-Islamiyya.[18] These examples demonstrate the rallying of jurisprudents within the jihadist movement against the wayward tendencies of the political ideologues and field commanders, whether the latter be guilty of an excess of extremism or an excess of moderation. One cannot say that the jurisprudents form a cohesive faction; Sayyid Imam forbids jihad at present, whereas the others merely want it to be prosecuted within the boundaries of Shari'a law as they understand it. The jurisprudents may, however, be considered a cohesive class, sharing a common desire to assert scholarly authority over the jihadist movement.

OVERVIEW OF AL-GAMA'A AL-ISLAMIYYA'S REVISIONS AND SAYYID IMAM'S *TARSHID*

Al-Gama'a al-Islamiyya was one of the most prominent groups in modern jihadism. Together with the Jihad group, it was responsible for several waves of terrorism in Egypt in the 1980s and '90s, including attacks on high-ranking officials and foreign tourists, as well as acts of vigilantism against Copts and non-Islamist Muslims. On July 5, 1997, al-Gama'a al-Islamiyya announced that it was halting operations against the Egyptian regime. The regime at first approached the initiative with skepticism, especially as it was closely followed by the bloody attack on foreign tourists at Luxor, perhaps the work of rogue elements within al-Gama'a. After September 11, 2001, the regime changed its stance toward the initiative and began to engage with the group's leadership. Shortly thereafter the group's leadership, in prison at the time, began to publish a series of tracts called the Concepts Correction series (*Silsilat tashih al-mafahim*) and removed their earlier literature from circulation. These new writings contained far-reaching revisions; their publication was followed by a series of interviews in the Egyptian press, and eventually the release of the group's members from prison.

Al-Gama'a al-Islamiyya is a much simpler case than that of Sayyid Imam. The group's revisionist views are clear and leave no room for suspicion of ulterior motives; they depict the Egyptian regime as legitimate Muslim rule and even call Anwar al-Sadat a *shahid*.[19] For a jihad group to make such fundamental changes in its ideology was unprecedented, and to date the case of al-Gama'a remains something of an anomaly.

Sayyid Imam al-Sharif, a native of Egypt and a longtime associate of Ayman al-Zawahiri, was the author of two of the most influential works in jihadist jurisprudence, *al-'Umda fi i'dad al-'udda* ("The Essentials of Making Ready for Jihad," 1987) and *al-Jami' fi talab al-'ilm al-sharif* ("The Compendium on Religious Study," 1994). He was among the first Arabs to arrive in Pakistan with the aim of aiding the Afghan *mujahideen*, both in his professional capacity as a surgeon and as an informal Shari'a guide. It was there that he wrote the *'Umda*, a sort of textbook on the laws of jihad, specifically designed for use in the training camps of what would later become al-Qaeda.

When the Arabs were banished from Pakistan in the early 1990s, Imam left for Sudan before finally settling in Yemen. At this point he had already broken with the Jihad group, both over matters of doctrine and over a dispute concerning the publishing of his second book; this latter disagreement led him to issue a stinging public denunciation of Ayman al-Zawahiri. In Yemen, he devoted his time to his medical practice. In October 2001, he was arrested, ostensibly for charges brought against him in Egypt in the "Returnees from Albania" case, and he was later extradited to Egypt.[20]

In 2007, rumors began to circulate that Imam was writing a book in prison that would include significant revisions in his thinking; the precedent of al-Gama'a al-Islamiyya was inevitably invoked and likely colored the reception of the document when it came to light. The book was finally published in serial form in two newspapers, the Egyptian *al-Masri al-Yawm* and the Kuwaiti *al-Jarida*, under the title *Wathiqat tarshid al-'amal al-jihadi fi misr wa'l-'alam* (*The Document of Right Guidance for Jihad Activity in Egypt and the World*; hereafter referred to as *Tarshid*). It was hailed in much of the Egyptian and Arab media as a seminal event that could potentially lead al-Qaeda to moderate its positions or, alternatively, to break apart.[21] It should be noted that, while the book is Sayyid Imam's, it was also a kind of reconciliation initiative, with imprisoned members of the Jihad group signing on to the document as a formal statement that they were abandoning jihad against the regime.

The expectation that the book would have a great impact rested on Sayyid Imam's status as one of the most influential scholars of the jihad movement. Hani al-Siba'i, a well-known jihadist insider who today is a bitter opponent of Sayyid Imam's "revisions," had said of him before the publication of the document: "I say in all honesty that I have never in my life met a sheikh whose knowledge was like that of Sheikh Abu Yusuf (Sayyid Imam) . . . If he lived in an epoch that honored men of learning, he would be the *ka'ba* of the *'ulama* and their imam."[22]

Sayyid Imam's fellow jihadist jurisprudents also related to him as someone whose views had to be taken into account. When Abu Muhammad al-Maqdisi found matters in the *Jami'* with which he disagreed, he composed a short work enumerating these differences of opinion, though in a respectful tone and while still recommending that the book be studied.[23] When Abu Basir al-Tartusi wrote an evaluation of the *Tarshid*, the tone was far less respectful, but the fact that he wrote a response serves to show that Sayyid Imam is not a figure to be ignored.[24]

Ayman al-Zawahiri and other critics of Sayyid Imam dedicated great effort to countering the prospective influence of the *Tarshid* through videos, communiqués, and postings on the Internet. Hani al-Siba'i made frequent appearances on satellite TV talk shows from London, where he lives (on the dole) as a political refugee, and the screeds he posted on the Web site of his al-Maqreze Center for Historical Studies were reprinted in the mainstream Arab press.[25] An official spokesman for al-Qaeda's viewpoint was Muhammad Khalil Hakayma, an unreformed al-Gama'a al-Islamiyya member and head of al-Qaeda's Egyptian branch, Tanzim al-Qa'ida fi Ardh al-Kinana.[26] In the end, al-Zawahiri himself authored an entire book in refutation of Sayyid Imam's *Tarshid*; it was titled *Risala fi tabri'at ummat al-qalam wa'l-sayf min manqasat tuhmat al-khawar w'al-dha'f* (*A Treatise Exonerating the Nation of the Pen and the Sword from the Blemish of the Accusation of Weakness and Fatigue*).[27]

With the exception of al-Zawahiri's book, the jihadist reaction to the *Tarshid* focused largely on secondary issues: whether one is allowed to heed an imprisoned scholar, the possibility that the *Tarshid* was written under duress, whether jihadists were or were not killing people based on sectarian affiliation or skin color, and so on. The basic strategy was to concur with many of the principles behind Imam's specific criticisms, but to deny that the phenomena being criticized were occurring. At the same time, they rejected the *Tarshid's* central thesis: that the jihad groups were in a state of weakness and thus must forgo jihad for the time being.

While some of Imam's more canny critics pointed out that this latter dispute was in fact of old vintage, the common denominator among all the aforementioned responses was the premise that in the *Tarshid* Sayyid Imam had said something new and significant. This is certainly the first impression any reader would receive; the tone of the *Tarshid* could not be more different from that of his previous works. In the past Imam had seemed to go out of his way to emphasize his radicalism, even when this added nothing of substance; for instance, after clearly explaining the principles of offensive jihad (*jihad al-talab*) in the '*Umda*, he takes the trouble to point out that these principles contravene international law since they require the initiation of hostilities and the taking of others' land.[28] In marked contrast, the *Tarshid* consists largely of criticism of radical jihadist practices and explanations as to how these contradict Shari'a law. Topics covered include killing on the basis of nationality, sectarian affiliation, or skin or hair color; circulating videos of executions; stealing in order to finance jihad—all framed by repeated exhortations to adhere to the strictures of Shari'a law. In his polemic against the *Tarshid*, Abu Basir al-Tartusi writes that Imam's positions on issues such as these are (from his jihadist standpoint) the only positive aspect of the work; but he also points out, quite accurately, that the *Tarshid* does not say much on these matters that contradicts Imam's previous writings; the difference is in the tone and in the prominence given to these issues.[29]

Sayyid Imam himself goes much further than al-Tartusi and denies that there are any contradictions whatsoever between the *Tarshid* and his previous writings. He addressed this issue in his interview with *al-Hayat* shortly after the publication of the *Tarshid*:

> Where is the [alleged] change of mind in the *Document* [i.e., the *Tarshid*]? I forbade al-Zawahiri and his group [i.e., the Jihad] to fight against Egypt already in 1992 . . . the [only] thing I added in the *Document* is that I wrote what I have said time and again since 1992. So where is the change of mind and the alteration? Some of what is in the *Document* may be found in my book the *Jami'* . . . The jurisprudent is someone who chooses from the law what is appropriate to a [given] reality—war, peace, truce, and so on—and not someone who stays in a fixed mold, placing his friends in peril through his ignorance in the Shari'a.[30]

When asked what he had to say to "Islamists abroad" (a reference to Hani al-Siba'i) who had said they would refute the *Tarshid* using Imam's previous books, the '*Umda* and the *Jami'*, Imam responded: "I say to them that the one who wrote the '*Umda* and the *Jami'* is the one who wrote the *Document* [the *Tarshid*]. Do they know better than I do what is in my books, and what I meant by them?"[31]

A more explicit answer as to how he can claim that the *Tarshid* is entirely in harmony with his previous writings came in the following exchange. The interviewer, Muhammad Salah, asked: "Some ordinary people are wondering: how is it that you promoted a discourse that recognized [the legitimacy of] violence in two books, and then you went back after a few years and recognized that violence is wrong? [Their question] is the same as that of some Islamists who are opposed to the *Document* and think that there is a contradiction between it and your two books *al-'Umda fi i'dad al-'udda* and *al-Jami' fi talab al-'ilm al-rashid* [sic, *al-sharif*]?" Imam begins his answer by reiterating the point that he forbade the Jihad's armed activities already in 1992, and then continues as follows: "What *al-'Umda fi i'dad al-'udda* and the *Jami'* contain are abstract laws—pure [religious] knowledge—that may only be applied to reality, that is, be expressed as a *fatwa*, by someone who is competent to issue *fatwas*." He continues:

> I often use a metaphor from my own profession [i.e., medicine] to facilitate understanding [of this matter]: An expert surgeon teaches novice surgeons how to perform operations—this is pure knowledge. This is what is in the *'Umda* and the *Jami'*. Then perhaps one of the novice surgeons will come along and will want to perform the operation that he learned. This is application of the knowledge to reality. The expert surgeon forbids him from performing the operation, since it will fail, and the patient may die, [since] his condition does not permit this [i.e., carrying out the operation]. This is what is in the *Document* . . . So how can someone refute me from my own books, when he doesn't understand the principles of applying abstract laws to particulars and when he is not qualified to issue *fatwas*? All he can do is to bring things from one book and the opposite from another book, without understanding the reason for this, and in his ignorance he thinks it a contradiction . . .[32]

Thus Sayyid Imam, unlike al-Gama'a al-Islamiyya, does not express remorse or retract any of his previous views. He simply appeals to a distinction between jurisprudence in the abstract and its application to the real world.

What follows will address how this problem unfolds through an examination of specific doctrines as they are expressed in Imam's first two books and in the *Tarshid*. It should be noted parenthetically, however, that Imam's characterization of his own writings is not entirely in keeping with the facts. First of all, in the very first sentence of the *Tarshid* Imam writes, "I am not a scholar (*'alim*), a mufti, or a *mujtahid* in the Shari'a [one whose level of learning allows him to exercise independent judgment]; what my books contain are not *fatwas*, but simply the transmission of knowledge . . ."[33] This clearly contradicts the distinction Imam drew in the interview between the nature of his previous writings and the nature of the *Tarshid*. Al-Zawahiri puts his finger on this problem in his *Risala*: "[Imam's] statement on the impermissibility of applying what is in the scholars' books to reality, and that this is only permitted to one who is qualified, applies to him [as well]. Why does he apply laws from books of jurisprudence to reality, and says time and again 'don't wage jihad, don't command good, don't confront injustice or occupation'—when he himself asserted that he is not a *mujtahid* or a mufti or a scholar?"[34]

In addition, his previous books do contain judgments on contemporary reality; in particular, they clearly apply the principles of *takfir* to today's rulers. In the *'Umda* he describes the conditions under which the choice of an emir (in the sense of a field commander) devolves on the Muslims in general (instead of his being appointed by the *imam*); one of these conditions is "if the Muslims, or a group among them, undertake a collective task (in particular, training and jihad) at a time when the Muslims do not have an *imam, as is the case in our day*."[35] He is often explicit, or cites approvingly someone else who is explicit, on the subject of the apostasy of contemporary rulers; for instance, in the *'Umda* he cites the view of the former Mufti of Saudi Arabia, Sheikh Muhammad Bin Ibrahim Aal al-Sheikh (died 1969), that today's rulers who rule by man-made laws are apostates.[36]

GENERAL PRINCIPLES OF *TAKFIR*: THE DISPUTE OVER *JAHD* AND *ISTIHLAL*

We now turn to an exposition of classic jihadist doctrine on *takfir* of the ruler, which will serve as a point of reference against which the "revisions" writings may be compared. The issue of *takfir* of the ruler is a subset of the topic of *takfir* in general. The majority opinion in all the schools of classical jurisprudence is that there exists an obligation to kill an apostate.[37] The practical application of this principle is generally conditioned on a number of factors that are not of direct concern to us here; for now, we are interested in what constitutes apostasy.

Classical jurisprudents tended to give lists of offenses, rather than general rules, that make one an apostate. Nonetheless, it is possible to describe two basic schools of thought on apostasy, both more or less within the Sunni consensus. The one that is generally more lenient is that of Abu Hanifa and the theological tendency known as the *murji'a*. (This term can refer to a number of different views, some of which are considered heretical, and there is no consensus that it should be applied to Abu Hanifa. However, since our main interest here is analysis of the jihadist approach, I am following neo-Hanbalite usage, which characterizes Abu Hanifa as a moderate Murji'ite.)[38] It is the view of the *murji'a* that faith is a matter of the heart and the tongue, and not of works, and thus no act can cause one to lose one's status as a believer unless it is accompanied by a proof of intent.[39] This is phrased in a well-known Hanafi credo, *al-'Aqida al-Tahawiyya*, as follows: "We call believers all those who pray towards the same *qibla* as we do, so long as they acknowledge what the Prophet brought from Allah, and believe in all that he said and related . . . We do not declare the apostasy of anyone from *ahl al-qibla* [i.e., those who answer to the preceding criteria] for any sin, unless and until he declares what he has done to be permitted."[40]

The approach to *takfir* taken by non-Murji'ite Sunni scholars is that there are acts that make the one who performs them an apostate. There is no agreed-upon list as to what these acts of apostasy are, but they are generally considered to be words or acts that contradict basic matters of doctrine and worship;[41] failing to pray is a common example.[42] In addition, lesser sins may also entail apostasy, if they are accompanied by an explicit rejection of the commandment being violated (*jahd*) or an explicit assertion that the prohibition one is transgressing is permitted (*istihlal*). Abu Muhammad al-Maqdisi notes that even Hanafis who in principle hold the view characteristic of the *murji'a* may be largely in agreement with other Sunnis on what acts constitute apostasy; they will simply contend that such an act is an indication of unbelief in the heart, whereas other Sunnis contend that the act in itself is the cause of apostasy.[43] Certain Hanafis may actually declare apostasy for more sins than others do.[44]

A third school, which is firmly outside the Sunni consensus, is that of the Kharijites. They, like the non-Murji'ite Sunnis, considered both acts and belief, but they (or at least some of them) cast a wider net and held that all grave sins make one an apostate. While the jihadist movements are often labeled "the new Kharijites,"[45] jihadist jurisprudents consider themselves representatives of the second school—that of the Sunni mainstream. They certainly recognize the distinction between sins that cause apostasy and sins that do not, and Sayyid Imam naturally rejects the Kharijites as unorthodox,[46] as does Abu Muhammad al-Maqdisi.[47] On the other hand, they are adamantly opposed to the *murji'a*, who hold that *takfir* always requires *jahd* or *istihlal*, and the jihadists may in fact consider them even worse than the Kharijites.[48]

The elasticity of the category of sins that entail apostasy leaves room for expansive interpretations. One example of this is in Sayyid Imam's discussion, in the *'Umda*, of *jihad al-talab* (offensive jihad initiated by Muslims). He cites Quran 9:5 and 9:29 as mandating this offensive jihad ("Fight the idolators wherever you find them . . ." and "Fight those who do not believe in Allah . . ."), in addition to a number of Hadith. He then writes: "From the preceding you learn that one who denies that *jihad al-talab* is part of Islam—for instance, those who say that Islam only fights in [self-] defense and in order to repel aggression—is denying (*mukadhdhib*) the aforementioned verses and Hadith, and others like them. And Allah said (Quran 29:47): 'None deny (*yajhad*) my signs [or 'verses'—*ayatina*] but the unbelievers.'" Thus he who denies the verses mandating offensive jihad is an unbeliever, and if he was previously Muslim, then he is an apostate.[49]

Another tract published in Sayyid Imam's name (and is almost certainly his) states that one who condemns terrorism or says terrorism is un-Islamic is an apostate, since he has denied the verse (8:60): "Prepare for them what you can of force and steeds of war with which to terrorize Allah's enemy and yours." The logic here is similar to that in the previous example: Allah, in the Quran, commanded terrorism, and thus to deny that terrorism is part of Islam is to deny Allah's book and to commit apostasy.[50]

LEGISLATION AND FORSAKING RULE
BY WHAT ALLAH REVEALED

The preceding discussion dealt with the kind of *takfir* discussed in classical tracts of jurisprudence; let us call it private-sphere *takfir*. While the jihadists' approach to this issue does tend to be somewhat expansive, it is not here that they differ most from establishment jurisprudents. What accounts for the yawning gulf between these and jihadists is another category of *takfir*, that which could be termed public-sphere *takfir*, or *takfir* of the ruler.

It is generally accepted even among establishment Muslim scholars that government falls within the purview of religion; when, in 1925, 'Ali 'Abd al-Raziq published a work contending that Islam prescribes no particular form of government, he was promptly condemned by al-Azhar.[51] Yet there is no consensus on the meaning of governance in accordance with Islam. Sayyid Imam's view, and that of the jihadists in general, is that the following are all apostasy: forsaking rule by what Allah revealed; rule by other than what Allah revealed; and human legislation.

Following is a summary of Sayyid Imam's presentation of the issue in the *Jami'*:

1) *Forsaking rule by what Allah revealed.* The verse adduced to prove that this is apostasy is Quran 5:44: "Those who do not rule (*yahkum*) by what Allah revealed, they are the unbelievers."[52] The word *yahkum* here refers primarily to legal judgment (rather than executive decision-making); heads of state are guilty of this particular trespass because they sometimes ratify court decisions in order that they may be executed,[53] or order others to forsake rule by what Allah revealed.[54]

As in private-sphere *takfir*, Sayyid Imam vigorously rejects conditioning this act of apostasy on any form of intention or sign of volition; he holds that the act in itself is always apostasy. This leads him into a long polemic in the *Jami'* against those who do require the conditions of *jahd* (express rejection) or *istihlal* (an express statement that what Shari'a law forbade is permitted) in order to declare apostasy. In the course of this polemic, Imam criticizes the positions of writers from the Muslim Brotherhood, the Saudi Wahhabi establishment, and other jihad groups such as al-Gama'a al-Islamiyya.

When Sayyid Imam gave Ayman al-Zawahiri permission to publish the *Jami'*, the latter did so in an abridged form without first consulting Sayyid Imam, an action that led to the final rift between the two. While I have not seen this first edition, it appears from the preface to the second edition that it was primarily the polemic over *jahd* and *istihlal* that was omitted.[55] It does not seem that al-Zawahiri did so out of disagreement with Imam on the issue; al-Zawahiri's action in abridging the book was, rather, an excellent expression of the difference between a jihadist of jurisprudential temperament and one whose preoccupations are more political. The jurisprudent considers it a point of principle to thresh out differences of opinion, whereas the politically minded jihadist—like al-Zawahiri—is more open to a certain degree of ecumenism or obfuscation if it is judged to further the ultimate aims of the jihad movement.

We will see as well that al-Gama'a al-Islamiyya's change of heart was largely a matter of embracing the conditions of *jahd* and *istihlal* for *takfir* of the ruler. Al-Gama'a leaders portray their past disregard for these conditions as resulting from ignorance. In truth, given the great degree of attention paid to the issue in jihadist literature, it is hard to accept that their previous position resulted simply from a strict literalism that was innocent of the theoretical dispute; but if this is so, it is a testament to the chasm that exists between the world of the jurisprudents and that of other jihadists, like the al-Gama'a al-Islamiyya leadership. It would also suggest that while political jihadists may be more likely than jurisprudents to swing to the extreme of an al-Zawahiri or an al-Zarqawi, they are also more likely than jurisprudents to swing in the other direction and abandon jihadism altogether, since they are not as fully invested in particular positions on jurisprudential questions.

2) *Legislation.* A number of verses are adduced; what is common to all of them is the association of the language of legislation with terms relating to unbelief or idolatry. It must be said that in many of these verses the necessity of the relation between the two is not at all self-evident. In addition, the relation established is one between idolatry and specifically religious legislation; after reviewing a few examples, we will see how Imam generalizes this to all legislation as such. Take, for instance, Quran 42:21: "Or have they partners [in divinity, i.e., false gods] that have prescribed for them in religion that which Allah has not sanctioned?" In Sayyid Imam's reading, the prescription of law is not an incidental activity of the false gods, but a necessary and constitutive one; thus a human who prescribes religious law would necessarily also be called a false god (*sharik*).[56]

A more convincing case is made on the basis of a Hadith relating to Quran 9:31. The verse reads: "They have taken their priests and their monks as lords besides Allah, and so with Christ son of Maryam. They were only commanded to worship one God. There is no God but He, and His glory is far removed from their idolatry." An exegetical Hadith regarding this verse is cited in Ibn Kathir's commentary on the Quran: 'Adi bin Hatim, from the Tayy tribe, had already converted to Christianity in the pre-Islamic period. When Muhammad called him to Islam (before initiating hostilities), 'Adi fled to Syria; while there, his sister and some of his tribesmen were captured by the Muslims, but Muhammad had mercy on his sister and freed her. She then convinced 'Adi to go see Muhammad. When he went to greet Muhammad, he did so wearing a silver crucifix, and read out the first part of Quran 9:31, "They have taken their priests and their monks as lords besides Allah." He then objected to Muhammad that Christians do not worship their priests and monks as indicated in the verse. Muhammad answered: "Yes they do, for [the priests and monks] forbade them the licit and permitted them the illicit, and they [the Christians] obey them—that is their worship of them."[57]

These examples tie the concept of religious legislation to idolatry; but how does one generalize from religious legislation to what we would call secular legislation? It is precisely this question that led Sayyid Imam to include, as the first of 17 prefatory explanations to the issue of public-sphere *takfir*, a definition of the word *din*. *Din* is the normal Arabic word for "religion," but Sayyid Imam defines its primary meaning as "a way that is followed, whether right or wrong."[58] It is only under this expansive definition of "religion" that a verse like "Or have they partners [in divinity, i.e., false gods] that have prescribed for them in religion that which Allah has not sanctioned?" can be considered a proof that legislation of public affairs is apostasy. Thus the foundation of the jihadist conception of political rule is that politics is a matter of ritual and devotion (*'ibadat*), with the logical consequence being that exclusive adherence to Allah's law is monotheism, whereas condominium of Allah and man is polytheism.

This understanding of the public sphere as a matter of ritual and devotion is a sort of photo-negative of the concept of secularism (in the sense of *laïcité; 'almaniyya* in Arabic) that is such anathema to the jihadists. While all Islamists agitate for a greater role for religion in public life, they may do so out of different motives (e.g., a general concern for public morality) and not necessarily out of the jihadist rejection of human government as a form of idolatry. Saad Eddine El-Othmani, the former head of Morocco's Islamist Party of Justice and Development (PJD), has authored a tract attempting to prove, on the basis of Ibn Taymiyya's writings, that it is permitted (or perhaps obligatory) to participate in parliamentary elections. His principal line of argument draws a distinction between ritual and devotion (*'ibadat*) on one hand and matters of this world on the other, and claims that the holding of public office falls into the latter category, in which humans are given freedom to manage their own affairs as they think best, so long as they do not transgress what has been explicitly forbidden.[59]

It is precisely the applicability of this distinction to issues of government that Sayyid Imam rejects; for him, "legislating laws for created beings is among those activities of Allah that, if not attributed to Allah and Allah alone, one's belief in His unicity is deficient ... Thus one who, in Allah's stead, legislates to people, has made himself a partner to Allah in His Lordship and Divinity, and has set himself over the people as a lord, and in this he has committed apostasy."[60]

3) *Ruling by a law other than that which Allah revealed.* Some of the same verses used to prove that legislation is apostasy are employed here as well to show that one who rules by such legislation is an apostate. If the act of legislation is tantamount to claiming for oneself divinity, it follows that the act of following such legislation is tantamount to idolatry.[61]

There are several additional proofs as well. One is based on Quran 6:121: "Do not eat [meat] over which Allah's name has not been mentioned, for it is sinful. The devils inspire their friends to dispute you, and if you obey them, you are idolators." Ibn Kathir cites Ibn 'Abbas's explanation of what occasioned the revelation (*sabab al-nuzul*) of the second part of the verse. When the Persians heard "Do not eat [meat] over which Allah's name has not been mentioned," they sent a rider to the Quraysh tribe to say to them, "contest Muhammad and say to him: that which you slaughter by your own hand with a knife is permitted, and that which Allah kills by a golden sword (i.e., a natural death) is forbidden?" In response, the second part of the verse was revealed: "The devils inspire their friends to dispute you, and if you obey them, you are idolators." Sayyid Imam, drawing on Ibn Kathir and al-Shinqiti, writes that this is proof that anyone who accepts or obeys a law other than the Shari'a is an idolator.[62]

CONTEMPORARY APPLICATIONS: THE APOSTASY OF TODAY'S RULERS

We now turn from the abstract elaboration of these kinds of *takfir* to their application to today's rulers. Before doing so, it is worth briefly surveying the problem of the relation of theory and reality in the historical development of public-sphere jurisprudence.

Classical Muslim jurisprudence of government began to flourish just as the Islamic caliphate ceased to do so, and its emergence was largely a response to this decline. In the early centuries of Islam, when caliphal rule was a living reality, issues of political legitimacy centered on actual rulers and their legitimacy, or lack thereof. These disputes involved issues of lineage and personal merit, though such disputes often served as vehicles for deeper disagreements over the nature of Muslim rule. However, by the time Mawardi and Abu Ya'la wrote their identically titled works *al-Ahkam al-sultaniyya*, real power lay in the hands of the Persian Buwayhid dynasty; no jurisprudent would claim that that the Buwayhids answered to the criteria of the ideal ruler, but their legal status was legitimized through their formal subordination to the Abbasid caliph. From this point on, the mainstream of Muslim political thought moved from the personal to the systemic. It was concerned with providing theoretical constructs that sought to legitimize the contemporary political reality, while at the same time delineating an ideal of Muslim rule of normative value. In other words, the jurisprudence of government was an intellectual rearguard action that sought to salvage whatever could be salvaged of the united Muslim polity. As such, it was generally politically quietist, more interested in accommodation than confrontation. The jurisprudents were concerned with laying out a legally valid threshold that must be met for government to be considered religiously legitimate.[63]

While the jihadists often cite Ibn Taymiyya as their precedent for fighting against the rulers, Ibn Taymiyya was actually quite within the tradition of jurisprudence of government just described, and the jihadists are well aware of this. How, then, do they reconcile their activist approach with the classical tradition of jurisprudence they claim to uphold? In addressing this question, we will revisit some widely held assumptions about jihadist political theory as well.

The jihadists' revolt against the rulers of Muslim countries does not in fact place them on the "activist" side of the historical quietist/activist debate in Islamic jurisprudence. Sayyid Imam generally endorses the positions of the traditional quietist majority with regard to a profligate ruler; it is only due to his *takfir* of the rulers that jihad becomes possible (and mandatory). In his discussion of the profligate ruler in the *'Umda*, Imam cites Ibn Taymiyya's famous "Tatar" *fatwa*,[64] which serves as the primary precedent for the ruling of modern jihadists that present-day rulers of Muslim countries are apostates,[65] and he notes that in the very same *fatwa* Ibn Taymiyya discusses the obligation of following a profligate commander into war. This passage relates to a military commander, and not a head of state, but the principle is similar, as we will see further on:

> Ibn Taymiyya, in his *fatwa* on fighting the Tatars [i.e., the Mongols], mentioned raiding with a profligate Emir, and said: "If those who are fighting against them [against the apostate rulers] are all [fighting] with perfect intent, that is the most pleasing to Allah. If there is someone among them who is tainted with profligacy or corrupt intent, in that he fights in order to arrive at a position of leadership, or commits violations with regard to the others in some matters—if the damage caused to religion by abandoning the fight against them [i.e., the apostate rulers] is greater than the damage caused by fighting them in this manner [i.e., fighting together with the profligate], then the obligation here as well is to fight them so as to do away with the greater of the two damages through adhering to the lesser of them. This [the principle of choosing the lesser of two damages] is one of the fundamental principles of Islam that must be observed. And thus it is one of the fundamental principles of the Sunnis [*ahl al-sunna w'al-jama'a*] that one goes on raids with everyone, pious or profligate . . ."[66]

Thus Sayyid Imam is fully aware of Ibn Taymiyya's quietism, and he too embraces it. However, since he considers practically all Muslim rulers today to be apostates, they fall on the "Mongol" side of the equation, and the quietist approach that tolerates rulers who are merely profligate finds no practical expression.

When faced with problematic political realities, the classical jurisprudents had continually lowered the standard for legitimate Islamic government, since they considered the alternative to be a dystopia of legal,
moral, and political anarchy.[67] The jihadists' interpretation of reality does
not allow them to continue on this path; they posit a historical rupture,
roughly contemporaneous with the fall of the Ottoman Empire, on the far
side of which the rulers are no longer Muslim at all. They claim that their
legal rulings differ from those of the classical jurisprudents not because
of differences in principle, but because they are faced with a radical new
reality, i.e., precisely that dystopia that the classical jurisprudents feared.

Consider the following passage from Sayyid Imam's *Jami'*:

> The causes of apostasy we have mentioned in this chapter ["Review of the texts
> proving the apostasy of those who rule by other than that revealed by Allah"] are
> the following: abandoning rule by what Allah [revealed], legislation of that which
> contradicts it, and rule according to legislation that contradicts it. None of these
> had occurred in the time of Ibn 'Abbas (died 68h. [687–88]) or in the few centuries
> following his death. I examined the "books of firsts"—these are books whose
> authors record who was the first to do such-and-such or who was the first to say
> such-and-such—and I did not find in them the least indication of any of these
> causes of apostasy occurring in the first centuries [of Islam] . . . The worst thing
> the rulers and judges did was to rule unjustly in some matters through legal strata-
> gems or [spurious] interpretations. [These are cases where] it would be difficult to
> prove their legal culpability, though what they did was sinful from the religious
> perspective. An example of this is what Abu Hilal al-'Askari wrote in his *Book of
> Firsts*: "The first judge to rule unjustly was Bilal Ibn Abi Burda. Abu Ahmad relates
> an incident (with its chain of transmission): a creditor once brought his debtor
> before Bilal. The debtor admitted that he owed the debt, but Bilal had an interest in
> [taking] his [side]. The claimant said: let him pay the debt, or else we should
> imprison him on the basis of his admission. The judge said: he is bankrupt. [The
> claimant] said: he hasn't said he is bankrupt. [The judge] said: why need he say it
> when I already know it? If you want I will imprison him, and you will assume the
> upkeep of his dependents . . . The man [i.e., the creditor] went away and gave up
> on the defendant. Bilal was known for his injustice.[68]

Sayyid Imam then explains how this differs from the outright apostasy of
the governments in Muslim countries today:

> The Kharijites believe that injustice such as this makes one an apostate, as Ibn
> Hazm wrote in his discussion of the Kharijites' abominations: "The 'Ufiyya, who
> are a sect of the aforementioned Bayhasiyya, held that if the Imam made an unjust
> decision, [even if] he is in Khorasan, or any other [far-off] land, at that very time he
> and all of his subjects become apostates, wherever they may be, from the far east to
> the far west, even in Andalus, Yemen, and so forth." . . . This is [the sort of issue]
> that arose in those times. However, that a head of state, or a king, or a judge should
> assume his office on the basis of ruling by a man-made constitution and man-made
> laws to which he must unswervingly cleave—this absolutely never occurred, except
> among the Tatars [i.e., the Mongols] at the end of the seventh *hijri* century. These
> latter pronounced themselves Muslims, but ruled themselves by a man-made law
> that contradicted the Islamic Shari'a . . . Let no one think that the Companions and
> the generation that followed them would not have declared such people apostates,
> since to think thus is to belittle and show contempt for the righteous forefathers . . .

According to Sayyid Imam, the case of the Mongols was thus completely unprecedented, but when Ibn Taymiyya and Ibn Kathir ruled on the issue, they established a consensus (*ijma'*) that those who profess Islam but do not rule by Shari'a law are apostates.[69]

The subtext in the passage cited above is the uncomfortable fact that most classical jurisprudents were not in the habit of declaring Muslim governments apostate, a fact that presents a challenge to Imam's claim to represent the classical consensus. His answer is to point out that Ibn Taymiyya and Ibn Kathir were in the same situation when they ruled on the case of the Mongols, and nonetheless they did not hesitate to close the legal lacuna and declare the Mongols apostates. And since they established a scholarly consensus, it needs to be applied today as well to those who profess Islam but do not rule by Shari'a law; in fact, Imam writes that today's rulers are worse, since the Mongols only ruled by infidel law among themselves, whereas today's rulers impose infidel law on the entire country.[70] Thus his claim is that the jihadists have not diverged from the classical consensus in jurisprudence; they are merely applying the appropriate laws to a changed reality.

THE "DOMINO EFFECT" OF *TAKFIR* AND THE APOSTASY OF HASAN AL-BANNA

The determination that the ruler is an apostate has both direct and immediate implications for the *takfir* of large segments of society, in what could be called the "domino effect" of *takfir*. Following is Sayyid Imam's description of the implications of *takfir* of the ruler for the rest of society:

> Allah the Exalted obligates Muslims to obey the Muslim ruler and to extend him aid; likewise, he forbids them to obey the infidel ruler or succor him. [Thus] He obligates the Muslims to depose a ruler if he apostatizes . . . The importance of this is made clear by the fact that the [Shari'a] laws regarding lands ruled by man-made laws—as are various and sundry Muslim countries today—are very grave indeed . . .
>
> A. The rulers of such lands [i.e., those ruled by man-made laws] are apostates (*kuffar kufran akbar*), and they are outside of the Muslim community.
> B. The judges in such lands are apostates (*kuffar kufran akbar*); this means that [in such a country] it is forbidden to practice this profession [i.e., the judiciary]. The proof that the rulers and the judges are apostates is Allah's words (Quran 5:44), "Those who do not rule by what Allah revealed, they are the unbelievers" . . .
> C. It is forbidden to bring a case before the courts of such lands, or to act in accordance with them [i.e., their rulings]. Anyone who brings a case before the courts of his own consent is also an apostate.

D. The members of the legislative bodies in these lands—the parliament, national council, and so forth—are apostates (*kuffar kufran akbar*), since it is they who permit acting in accordance with these infidel laws, and it is they who legislate new ones.

E. Those who elect the members of these parliaments are apostates (*kuffar kuffran akbar*), since, through their act of voting, they have taken for themselves lawgiving gods other than Allah; [and while the voters do not refer to them as such,] it is the thing referred to that matters, [and not the name]. In addition, anyone who calls for such elections or encourages people to participate in them also apostatizes . . .

F. It is forbidden to pledge allegiance to these rulers when they take power in such a land or to affirm their remaining [in power], as occurs in the referenda dedicated to this purpose. This is because in this pledge there is [an expression of] desiring the persistence of unbelief, and one who desires such as a thing has apostatized . . .

G. The soldiers who defend this infidel situation are apostates (*kuffar kufran akbar*), since they fight for the sake of the *taghut*, and Allah said (Quran 4:76), "Those who disbelieve (*kafaru*) fight for the sake of the *taghut*." The *taghut* for whose sake [these soldiers] are fighting is that of rule by constitutions and man-made laws and the rulers who rule by them . . . This law applies to anyone who defends these apostate regimes by fighting for them, like soldiers, and those who defend them verbally, like some journalists, media figures, and sheikhs. Thus it is forbidden to serve in the armies of these infidel countries . . .

H. Obedience to the rulers of these countries is not incumbent on the Muslim, he need not abide by their laws, and he is at liberty to violate them in whatever way he wishes, pursuant to two conditions: that he not do that which the Shari'a forbids, and that he not harm Muslims or wrong them.

I. A land ruled by infidel laws is [in] the abode of unbelief, even if it was previously ruled by the Shari'a . . .[71]

Thus, for Sayyid Imam, the necessary consequence of *takfir* of the ruler is *takfir* of the courts, parliament, political parties, the army, and even voters. The lives of huge numbers of people in Muslim countries—perhaps even the majority—are considered forfeit. Imam's version of this domino effect is the most extreme, but all the jihadist jurisprudents agree on the principle. For example, al-Maqdisi objects to Imam's unqualified statement that voters are apostates, since some voters do not at all understand what a parliament does. Some voters simply vote for their relatives or for whoever says "Islam is the solution," and others think that the role of their parliamentary representatives is simply to bring public projects to their districts and their tribes, and not to legislate.[72] In principle, though, al-Maqdisi agrees that voting is apostasy; the disagreement is a secondary one over the threshold of knowledge required for the act to be considered intentional.

Sayyid Imam seems to consider even Hasan al-Banna, founder of the Muslim Brotherhood, an apostate, since the latter ran for parliament, saying that it was a pulpit from which the Brotherhood's message could reach the people. "Just as al-Banna called this [running for parliament] 'da'wah,' many contemporaries call it 'political activity.' But as you know, [giving it different] names does not at all change the true nature of a thing, and *kufr* is *kufr*."[73]

AL-GAMA'A AL-ISLAMIYYA: EXITING JIHADISM BY ABANDONING *TAKFIR* OF THE RULER

I have used Sayyid Imam as my principle source for the doctrine of *takfir* of the ruler, since he is the most systematic, and one of the most influential as well; thus, I will also use the preceding discussion as my base of comparison for al-Gama'a al-Islamiyya's revisions; the writings of 'Umar 'Abd al-Rahman, who was the Emir of al-Gama'a in the group's formative period, are generally very much in line with Imam's.[74]

Al-Gama'a al-Islamiyya can be said to have exited jihadism by the high road. They quite simply ceased considering the rulers of Egypt and other Muslim countries to be apostates. In consequence, the government, as legitimate Muslim rule, is held to possess fields of exclusive prerogative and discretion, and a margin of legitimate or tolerated dereliction of Shari'a duty, thus precluding vigilante "commanding of good," and so forth. In addition, there is no "domino effect" of *takfir*, since the first domino was not toppled; any fighting against the security forces is thereby considered religiously prohibited internecine warfare (*fitna*), and not religiously mandated jihad.

On takfir: A representative example of al-Gama'a al-Islamiyya's new position on *takfir* of the ruler is the following statement by Shura Council member Mamduh Yusuf, from a collective prison interview given by the members of the group's Shura Council to the *al-Musawwar* weekly magazine in 2002: "Regarding the ruler, we revised our position, and said that the [Quranic] verse that stipulates 'Those who do not rule by what Allah revealed, they are the unbelievers'—the intention of this verse is not that it applies to all rulers. It is only applied to the ruler who says that Allah's rule is not good (*la yasluh*)." The interviewer interjected that to the best of his knowledge the ruler of Egypt has not said that Allah's rule is not good, and Yusuf responded: "Indeed, he has not said this. This is what all of the brothers in al-Gama'a agreed on, and we [in the Shura Council] are together with them on this. The ruler who does not reject Allah's rule and does not say that Allah's rule is not good—he is a Muslim ruler, and it is forbidden to fight against him."[75] We see here that the al-Gama'a leaders quite simply "flipped" on the issue of the requirement of *jahd* for *takfir*, and adopted the position derided by the jihadists as that of the "modern-day Murji'a."[76]

The Muslim ruler's margin of discretion: Once the ruler is no longer an apostate, but a Muslim, the quietist doctrine that jihadists profess to hold with respect to legitimate Muslim rulers finally finds its expression. Consider the following statement by Hamdi 'Abd al-Rahman, one of the members of the group's Shura Council; after stating what the Shari'a mandates in principle, he continues:

> However, when the government refrains from implementing these laws, due to certain circumstances—for instance, that we [Egypt] are not alone in the world, or that there are other powers that are lying in wait [to attack us], or due to circumstances such as fear of internal *fitna* between Muslims and Christians—in this case we accept this excuse. We say: the ruler is a Muslim, and he is not denying the Islamic Shari'a or attacking it; there are [just] circumstances that prevent him from implementing these laws. He must absolutely not be declared an apostate.[77]

'Ali al-Sharif, who was accused Number Six in the Sadat assassination trial, emphasized the ruler's discretion regarding the formerly contentious issue of the government's encouragement of foreign tourism: "All that is needed here is for the brothers to cool their nerves and stay away from extremism and immoderation. This is because the state has its prerogatives, and we are forbidden to meddle in them."[78]

Abandoning jihad: Since the ruler is now considered a Muslim, the entire litany of classic quietist arguments may be taken from the shelf and marshaled to support the view that fighting is forbidden. Take, for instance, the following statement by Hamdi 'Abd al-Rahman:

> We emphasized in the studies we published, and in the historical examples we gave, that fighting against the ruler, throughout history, has caused the Islamic nation a great deal of harm. This is true not just of the case of President Sadat, but before that [as well], in all the episodes of fighting [against the rulers]—for instance, Husayn Bin 'Ali's rebellion against Yazid Bin Mu'awiya, the revolt of Ibn al-Ash'ath, and that of 'Abdallah Bin al-Zubayr . . .[79]

In his book criticizing what he terms al-Gama'a al-Islamiyya's "accursed initiative," the Syrian jihadist jurisprudent Abu Basir al-Tartusi calls the analogy between Mu'awiya and the *taghut* of Egypt "idle and false," since Mu'awiya was a Muslim ruler and Mubarak is an apostate.[80] But that is precisely the point: if someone could convince al-Tartusi that the current rulers were not apostates but rather something comparable to Mu'awiya, he too would forbid rebellion. That is exactly the transformation that al-Gama'a al-Islamiyya underwent. Everything hinges on the issue of *takfir* and, more specifically, on the issue of *jahd*.

I cited earlier a passage from Sayyid Imam's *Jami'* stating that the only time before the modern era that there was rule not according to Allah's law was among the Mongols; and since there exists a consensus (in his view) that they had to be fought, so too with the modern rulers. Al-Gama'a al-Islamiyya challenged this premise and cited other examples of non-application of Allah's law in the past. Muhammad Shu'eib cited the example of the second caliph, 'Umar Ibn al-Khattab, who refrained from cutting off the hands of thieves in the year 638, since it was a year of harsh drought when need drove many to steal. By analogy, he said that adulterers in our own day should not be stoned, since young people have to deal with many temptations that did not exist in the past.[81] Hamdi 'Abd al-Rahman cited the example of the Christian king of Abyssinia, al-Najashi, who converted to Islam but refrained from ruling by Islamic law; despite this, the prophet Muhammad told the Muslims to pray for him when he died.[82]

In other words, al-Gama'a al-Islamiyya abandoned the highly ideal-ized view of the Islamic past for a more nuanced one. When Sayyid Imam confronted the (implicit) question of why today's rulers should be fought when rulers in the past did not deserve to be fought, his answer was that the reality of government in Muslim countries had radically changed. Al-Gama'a al-Islamiyya, in contrast, decided that there was not in fact any great historical rupture.

This brings us to one final consideration in our analysis of al-Gama'a al-Islamiyya's revisions. There is a sense that the revisions came about due to a greater openness and a willingness to think outside the received jihadist constructs. While this may sound somewhat amorphous, it does come through clearly in the texts of the revisions, and even more so in the interviews. One expression of this new attitude is a greater empirical attention to reality. Consider the following example: in an anti-al-Qaeda pamphlet titled "Islam and the Laws of War" (al-Islam wa-tahdhib al-hurub), published in serial form in al-Sharq al-Awsat, 'Isam al-Din Dara-blah contested al-Qaeda's notion that the United States is waging a Cru-sader war against the Muslim world:

> The conception that America is waging a Crusade against Muslims is not true . . . in the worst of cases [one can say that] at times there have been American policies that have had a religious dimension in opposing some—but not all—of the Islamic world's causes. [The fact that this is not a Crusade] explains America's positive stand in supporting the Afghan *mujahideen* in their fight against the Soviet occupa-tion, and [America's] positive stand [against] the ethnic cleansing operation against the Muslims of Bosnia and Herzegovina and in the province of Kosovo.[83]

This observation testifies to a measure of openness, since it goes against a belief held not just by jihadists but by many in the Arab world on the whole. This could be contrasted with Sayyid Imam's statements on the U.S.'s intentions, in his interview with al-Hayat: "America always sup-ports Israel. Even [America's foreign] aid, the common people don't notice it, since it is either old weapons that America gets rid of to provide work for its factories, or old stocks of what it wants to get rid of, or birth control pills. This is American [foreign] aid—that is, America aids itself."[84] It may be that the fact that the members of al-Gama'a al-Islamiyya's Shura Council are not jurisprudents is what allowed them to think more openly and creatively about reality and to accept input from wher-ever it came. As Karam Zuhdi said when asked whether Muslims could accept democracy: "Wisdom is like the believer's lost animal—wherever it is found, he has the first right to it."[85]

This is in sharp contrast with Sayyid Imam's endless lists of prescribed reading materials in the *Jami'*, and his warnings against specific creedal mistakes even in those books he does recommend. At the end of his reading list for beginning students, he appends four books on non-religious subjects that comprise what the student needs to know about the contemporary world, Muslim and non-Muslim. The titles of these books are: *What the World Lost with the Decline of the Muslims, The Colonialist Plans to Fight Islam, The Attack on the Islamic World*, and *Western Leaders Say: Destroy Islam and Annihilate the Muslims*. Without having perused these books myself, it seems safe to assume that they are a poor introduction to world affairs. This is not the ignorance of the poor and the uneducated: Sayyid Imam is not just an Islamic scholar, but also a university graduate and a surgeon. For him, though, the enmity of non-Muslims for Muslims is a fixed template, and his "research" into the West flows accordingly. As he writes in the *Jami'*, "religious enmity is an inevitable reality, for Allah created the infidels such that they are hostile to the believers by nature . . . and likewise, Allah commanded the believers to be hostile to the infidels . . ."[86]

HAS SAYYID IMAM CHANGED HIS POSITION? *TAKFIR* OF THE RULERS IN THE *TARSHID*

As we have seen, the fulcrum of the change in al-Gama'a al-Islamiyya's ideology was the retraction of their *takfir* of the ruler, due to a revised position on the requirement of *jahd*. Anyone who looks for something similar in Sayyid Imam's *Tarshid* will be hard-pressed to find it. As Abu Basir al-Tartusi has noted, the *Tarshid* contains no clear statement as to whether the ruler is a Muslim or an apostate, but only vague hints at his perhaps being a Muslim—for instance, through the use of the word *sultan*. Al-Tartusi accuses Imam of intentional deception and concealing what he knows to be true (i.e., that the ruler is an apostate).[87]

In contrast with the prolix treatment of apostasy in the *Jami'*, the discussion of the issue in the *Tarshid* is relatively brief and abstract. It is prefaced by two general considerations: first, that *takfir* is part and parcel of Shari'a law; and second, the difference between *kufr akbar* ("greater apostasy") and *kufr asghar* ("lesser apostasy"), also known as *kufr bi-duni kufr* ("apostasy without apostasy"). The terminology of *kufr akbar* and *kufr asghar* is of early vintage, and exegetical rules for distinguishing between them were elaborated in works of classical jurisprudence. Of the various Quranic verses and Hadith that employ the root *k-f-r*, some are held to not designate outright apostasy (*kufr akbar*), but rather grave sin. In neo-Hanbalite literature, the determination of whether a given text refers to

true apostasy is made based on such considerations as whether the root
k-f-r appears as a verb or a noun, whether it is definite or indefinite, and
whether the text is from the Quran or from the Hadith.[88]

The *Tarshid's* presentation of the subject is meant to give the appearance of moderation; emphasis is placed on not assuming that all *kufr* is
kufr akbar, and Sayyid Imam provides a list of examples of sins that are
not apostasy. In truth there is no difference in substance between the *Tarshid* and Imam's earlier works, just one of emphasis; the issue of distinguishing between *kufr akbar* and *kufr asghar* was already treated in the
Jami'.[89]

As for the issue that concerns us here—public-sphere apostasy—the
Tarshid is silent as to whether it is *kufr akbar* or *kufr asghar*. This probably
should not be interpreted as a sign that Imam has changed his position,
but rather as a deliberate attempt at obfuscation. As we saw, Imam has
stated that there is no contradiction between the *Tarshid* and his previous
writings. In addition, Sayyid Imam writes in the *Tarshid*, in the course of
a discussion of an entirely different topic, that today there is no *Dar al-
Islam*.[90] Since the definition of *Dar al-Islam* traditionally hinges on the
issue of Muslim rule, this statement indicates that Imam does not think
there are any Muslim rulers. Thus it is nearly certain that he still holds to
what he wrote about the issue in the *Jami'*: "Anyone who divides [their
judgment on the issue of] ruling by laws other than those revealed by
Allah into two parts, namely, greater apostasy and lesser apostasy, is in
error. Ruling by laws other than those revealed by Allah is greater apostasy and nothing but . . ."[91] In sum, the chapter of the *Tarshid* on *takfir*
gives us little reason to believe that Sayyid Imam has changed his views
on the issue. Indeed, the book includes a warning against attaching too
little importance to *takfir*, and contains a number of Hadith to the effect
that being Muslim is not a fixed attribute, but rather one that can be easily lost.[92]

Elsewhere in the *Tarshid*, Imam explicitly addresses the issue of profligate and apostate rulers and whether one should fight them, and here
too he remains evasive on the status of present-day Muslim rulers. He
gives a survey of early Islamic revolts against rulers and their injustices
(the Medinans at al-Hara, Husayn Bin 'Ali, Ibn al-Ash'ath, and others)
and says that these did great damage. According to Imam, these rebels
believed they were performing the commandment of forbidding wrong
(*al-nahy 'an al-munkar*), but they were in error, since one is not permitted
to do this by force against the ruler, as stated in the Hadith: "Whoever
sees something in his Emir that he finds repugnant, he should bear this
steadfastly, and one who leaves off [obedience to] the ruler—even one
inch—dies a *jahili* death." Fighting the ruler is permitted only when he
commits apostasy, according to the Hadith related by 'Ubada Bin al-
Samit: "We should not contest the rule of the rulers; the Prophet said:

'unless you see among you open apostasy for which there is proof from Allah.'" Sayyid Imam then cites Ibn Taymiyya: "There was an old school among the Sunnis [that supported] fighting against profligate rulers (*a'immat al-jawr*), but then a consensus was formed that forbade this."

Thus, like al-Gama'a al-Islamiyya, Sayyid Imam discusses rebellions that occurred in early Islamic history and the damage they did. Unlike al-Gama'a, however, he does not use these examples to forbid rebellion today. He merely restates the classic position that fighting against profligate rulers is forbidden, and that fighting against apostate rulers is obligatory; he does not explicitly divulge his views as to which of these categories is relevant to today's rulers. He does give greater emphasis to the quietist side of the equation; this is in line with his overall attempt to appear more moderate without giving ground on issues of substance.

The passage continues:

> As for the case where the ruler has committed open apostasy: Ibn Hajar, in his commentary on the *al-fitan* and the *al-ahkam* chapters in Bukhari, brought the words of previous commentators: "Those who can, must fight him [i.e., the apostate ruler], and one who is in a state of inability (*'ajz*) is not required to do so." So there is a difference between the knowledge that the ruler has committed apostasy and the obligation to fight him, and it is not obligatory when one is in a state of inability or when the damage incurred by fighting him is greater [than the benefit].

He then segues from this principle into the question of jihad against the rulers today, a fact that could be taken as an indication that he does indeed see jihad against the rulers as an obligation that only due to contingencies must not be performed:

> Over the past few decades there have been many incidents of fighting the rulers in Muslim countries in the name of jihad in order to establish Shari'a rule, and these incidents have caused great damage both to the Islamist groups and to the countries. The jurisprudential principle [relevant here] is that "damage should not be stopped by another damage equal to it," and all the more so that "it should not be stopped by damage greater than it."

Further on, though, he remains careful to neither explicitly endorse nor reject the implication: "Whether abandoning Shari'a rule is apostasy, 'apostasy without apostasy' [i.e., *kufr asghar*], or [a lesser form of] sin, I don't believe that clashing with the rulers in Muslim countries in the name of jihad is the appropriate option for trying to implement the Shari'a . . ."[93] In the next section we will examine how he has come to this conclusion. As for the subject at hand: if we take the carefully parsed wording of the *Tarshid* together with the fact that Sayyid Imam has not retracted his previous writings, it remains more than probable that he still considers the rulers to be apostates and still holds to the 'domino effect' of apostasy this belief brings in its wake.

The opposing views of al-Gama'a al-Islamiyya and Sayyid Imam on the issue of *takfir* of the ruler may result from the fact that the former, not being jurisprudents, can more easily adopt a new position. For instance, when Hamdi 'Abd al-Rahman of al-Gama'a al-Islamiyya adduces the Hadith regarding the King of Abyssinia as a proof that not ruling by Allah's law is not in itself apostasy, he gives the impression that in the past he was simply unaware of the issue, and that when he approached the question with an open mind he found the proof convincing. It would be difficult for someone like Sayyid Imam to encounter such proofs that he had not already weighed in the formative stage of his intellectual development. Indeed, as regards the King of Abyssinia Hadith, the *Jami'* already contains a refutation of the use 'Abd al-Rahman makes of it: according to Imam, the fact that the king did not rule entirely in accordance with Islam was likely due to his simply being unaware of some of the religion's provisions, since he and the Companions who emigrated to Abyssinia were isolated and had not heard of all of the laws revealed in the Quran.[94]

ABILITY AS A PRECONDITION FOR JIHAD

The fact that Sayyid Imam still seems to consider the rulers apostates does not mean that he endorses jihad against them; the *Tarshid* forbids fighting against the Egyptian government in no uncertain terms. The rationale for this ruling is that the jihad groups are in a state of inability, and in such a state they may not undertake jihad. It is primarily due to the vigorous statement of this position that Imam has recently acquired a reputation for moderation.

As it happens, this position is not really new either. As mentioned previously, Imam had already stated his opposition to fighting against the Egyptian government to the leadership of the Jihad group in the early 1990s; in addition, its basic outlines are already present in the *Jami'*. This was, in fact, the crux of his dispute with Ayman al-Zawahiri and the Jihad group, just as it is his main bone of contention with al-Qaeda today. It is to Sayyid Imam's "inability" argument that al-Zawahiri referred when he titled his recent book *A Treatise Exonerating the Nation of the Pen and the Sword from the Blemish of the Accusation of Weakness and Fatigue*, and in the *Treatise* al-Zawahiri confirms that this is not a new dispute: "The author of the *Document* [the *Tarshid*] already announced his change of mind in his book the *Jami'* in 1994, and he turned to his private life, which he lived under his real name in Yemen, in a strange coexistence with the country's security apparatuses . . ."[95]

A normative statement of this principle is to be found even earlier, in Sayyid Imam's first work, *al-'Umda fi i'dad al-'udda*, directly following his introduction of the concepts of defensive and offensive jihad.[96] He writes there:

> The only thing that can keep Muslims from jihad is inability ('ajz), in which case they must make ready [for jihad, i.e., overcome their inability]. As Allah said

(Quran 47:35): "Do not be weary and call out for peace when you have the upper hand." As long as the Muslims have strength and have the upper hand over their enemies, there is no peace, no cease-fire, and no truce—just fighting until there is no more strife and religion will be entirely Allah's . . . This was the practice of the Prophet (peace be upon him) and the Caliphs after him in fighting the polytheists and the people of the book . . . The only thing that prevents this [i.e., the jihad] is inability . . . And I have already said and repeated in this treatise that if there is an inability that prevents jihad, it is obligatory to prepare [for jihad by overcoming the inability] . . .[97]

Thus "inability" as a legal impediment to jihad did receive mention in the *'Umda*, though the main emphasis was on the concomitant obligation of overcoming this state of inability, that is, the act of "*i'dad al-'udda*" that Imam chose as the title for the entire book.

In Sayyid Imam's discussion of the issue in the *Jami'*, the emphasis shifted to the state of inability itself and the impropriety of fighting jihad in such a state. This dovetails well with the fact that two years before the publishing of the *Jami'* he had tried to forbid the Jihad group from fighting in Egypt.[98] Imam opens his treatment of the issue in the *Jami'* with the observation that while many groups have risen to restore the caliphate and institute Islamic law, none have succeeded. He attributes this to a deficit in faith, which may express itself in one of two manifestations: either non-conformity to the Shari'a or impurity in the conception of Allah's unicity (*tawhid*). Under the first of these rubrics, he enumerates eight forms of overhastiness in various forms of "Islamic action"; the last and most fully elaborated of these is overhastiness in rushing to fight the government:

> Another form of overhastiness is that of being overly hasty in entering into armed conflict with apostate governments, before there has been sufficient preparation, as this at times leads to devastating consequences. The Shari'a obligation is not the mere inflicting of damage on the apostate governments, bravely undertaken by a few dozen Muslims. While inflicting such damage is in itself a righteous activity, as Allah said (Quran 9:120), "whenever they harm the enemy it is considered they have done a good deed," the obligation nonetheless is to replace these governments, depose them, and establish an Islamic government, and not just to inflict damage. This we learn from what Allah said (Quran 8:39): "Fight them until there will be no more discord and religion will be entirely Allah's."

Imam then lists a number of factors that lead to this overhastiness to fight the regime; the first and most important of these is the failure to understand that "ability" is a condition required for theoretical imperatives to become practical obligations:

> One is required to believe that jihad against these governments is obligatory as follows from the proofs I have presented; however, the performance of this obligation requires, in addition to the knowledge and the belief in it, the ability to perform it, just as is the case with the pilgrimage, the *zakat*, and other ritual obligations . . . The performance of them is conditional on ability. When one is in a state of inability there is no obligation, [as written in Quran 2:286] "Allah only imposes obligation on someone according to his ability."[99]

In essence, we have here two separate arguments. The first deals with the definition of the commandment of jihad, namely, that only fighting that may reasonably be expected to yield victory may be considered jihad. Anything short of that, while perhaps praiseworthy, is not obligatory. The second is a general principle that inability is an exemption from ritual obligations in general, with Imam stating that this applies to jihad as well.

Sayyid Imam also cites at length Ibn Taymiyya and Ibn Qayyim al-Jawziyya on the question of when to fight or desist from jihad. These passages seem to add two other reasons why fighting that is theoretically obligatory may not translate into an obligation in practice: 1) There exist contradictory verses on jihad, with some commanding fighting and others commanding (or permitting) desistance. The solution to this apparent contradiction is to say that different verses apply to different conditions, thereby preserving the legal validity of the earlier verses and applying them to conditions of weakness and inability.[100] 2) The Shari'a interest (maslaha) should determine whether one fights or not. Unlike the first argument, this is a general principle that is not specifically related to the commandment of jihad, though it would require investigation to determine whether Ibn Taymiyya (and Sayyid Imam) considers this a truly independent variable or whether it can only be taken into consideration due to the two options already having been determined to be legitimate.[101]

It should be noted that despite the increased emphasis on the issue of "inability" in the Jami', there is still no prohibition of fighting against the regime when one is in a state of inability and when there is no hope of victory. Indeed, Imam writes explicitly that inflicting damage on the regime is a good deed in and of itself. It is true that when he summarizes the various forms of overhastiness, including being overhasty to fight the regime, he calls them "not pious" (laysa min al-birr wa-laysa min al-taqwa), but there is still no prohibition.[102]

The new emphasis on "inability" and the negative aspects of fighting against the regime are further mitigated by the fact that the Jami' still contains a full elaboration of the concomitant obligation of "making ready": "But in the case of jihad in particular, one must make ready for it when one is in a state of inability, because of what Allah said in the Quran (8:59–60) 'The unbelievers should not think that they have outstripped [the believers], for they do not incapacitate the believers. Make ready for them what you can of force.'" The word translated here as "incapacitate" is yu'jizuna, i.e., to put the believers in a state of inability ('ajz). Imam understands these verses as a warning not to accept the permanence of the state of inability and as an exhortation to redress it through "making ready" for jihad.[103]

"INABILITY" IN THE *TARSHID*: PROHIBITING JIHAD IN THE HERE AND NOW

The issue of ability as a necessary condition for jihad makes up the heart of the *Tarshid*. The broad lines of the doctrine as presented in Sayyid Imam's latest book are quite similar to what I have just described, but the issue has been greatly elaborated and given far more prominence. The state of inability is held to give rise to a prohibition of jihad, and not just an absence of obligation, and Imam applies this prohibition explicitly to today's jihad groups.

These changes in emphasis, like Imam's obfuscation on the question of the apostasy of the rulers, partly result from a desire to downplay politically inconvenient aspects of his doctrine. Nonetheless, on the practical issue of forbidding jihad under present conditions, Imam is certainly stating a position in which he truly believes, and he decided to give it greater emphasis due to changing circumstances and not just out of a desire to appear moderate. This would be in accordance with his explanation in the *al-Hayat* interview for the apparent differences between the *Tarshid* and his other works, namely that one needs to determine what legal position applies to what reality.

The changed reality to which the *Tarshid* responds is simply the aftermath of 9/11. In the *al-Hayat* interview, Sayyid Imam expressed his views on the attack and its consequences:

[9/11] was a catastrophe for the Muslims. [Al-Qaeda] ignited strife that found its way into every home, and they were the cause of the imprisonment of thousands of Muslims in the prisons of various countries. They caused the death of tens of thousands of Muslims—Arabs, Afghans, Pakistanis, and others. The Taliban's Islamic Emirate was destroyed, and al-Qaeda was destroyed. They were the direct cause of the American occupation of Afghanistan and other heavy losses which there is not enough time to mention here. They bear the responsibility for all of this.[104]

The *Tarshid* is a response to these changing circumstances; Sayyid Imam has decided that what he said quietly in 1992 and wrote discreetly in 1994 needed to be stated emphatically in 2007. I will deal first with the definitions of ability and inability. In the *Tarshid*, as in Imam's earlier writings, Imam presents inability as a general principle exempting one from obligation. It is noteworthy, though, that when it comes to jihad, Imam chooses to set a higher threshold for "ability":

[Jihad] is like other matters in religion; ability to perform it is one of the conditions of its being incumbent. However, [the definition of] ability in jihad is not limited to the Muslim's person—such as his physical or financial ability—but rather it goes beyond this and [includes] the reality of the circumstances surrounding him, namely, who is with [him in religion] and who opposes [him in religion]. It is for this reason that Allah, may He be praised, lauded [all of the following]: those who wage jihad for His sake; those who took refuge in the cave when they separated themselves out from their people [see Quran *sura* 18]; and the believer from

Pharaoh's people who hid his faith [see Quran 40:28ff.]—this despite the fact that all three [of these groups and individuals] faced the same [general] reality, namely, the rallying of those who opposed them in religion. Each of their reactions ... was praiseworthy, since each one of them acted in accordance with what was legally incumbent on him at that place and time, and in accordance with the limits of his ability. Every Muslim must in this manner study his religion in order to choose the Shari'a obligation appropriate to the reality [he faces] and to his ability.[105]

He goes on to cite examples of this principle from the actions of the prophet Muhammad and the rightly guided caliphs; the prophet at first hid his faith, then separated out from his people; he and the Companions emigrated to Medina, and other Companions to Abyssinia; at times they were forbearing and bore the injury done them by the polytheists; at times they fought jihad against the polytheists, the apostates, and the Jews and Christians; and at times they concluded truces with the infidels. All of this is attested in the Quran and the Sunna, and none of these options has been abrogated. Rather, the choice of option depends on one's level of ability.

When he sets out to prove that these options were never abrogated, Sayyid Imam introduces two proofs that, as far as I am aware, he had never used before in his previous works. He starts with the observation that jihad was not commanded until after the *hijra* to Medina, when Muhammad acquired a base of operations. He then notes that even after jihad was commanded, it was not made incumbent on the Muslims who were unable to emigrate and remained behind in Mecca; thus, it is a lasting principle that when Muslims are in a state of inability similar to Muhammad's before the *hijra*, they are exempt from jihad.

The second proof is based on an eschatological Hadith taken from Muslim's *Sahih* (compendium of authoritative Hadith). This Hadith is set in the days after 'Isa (Jesus) returns to earth and defeats the Dajjal (the antichrist). Allah informs 'Isa that he has sent Ya'juj and Ma'juj (Gog and Magog), and no one (including 'Isa) will be able to fight them. Imam interprets this as Allah forbidding 'Isa to wage jihad due to the latter's inability when faced with a formidable enemy like Ya'juj and Ma'juj. (In the end they and their followers are killed miraculously by a plague of maggots.)[106]

Further on in the *Tarshid*, Imam turns to address the present-day situation in Egypt, and enumerates the reasons that led him, in 1992, to the conclusion that the Egyptian government should not be fought. This also serves as a recap of the discussion of the specific conditions needed for jihad, which are dealt with in detail after the general discussion of ability. Among these conditions are: an abode of emigration and support (like Medina was for Muhammad); parity in numbers and equipment (this is not actual parity; elsewhere he specifies that any disparity less than 2:1 is considered parity); the ability to safeguard the Muslims' women and children; having the ability to pay the expenses incurred for jihad; the existence of a group to whom one may turn in case of need; and a clear "differentiation of the ranks," i.e., that there be no intermixture of infidels with Muslims and others whose lives are inviolable during the fighting. Some of these seem to enter under the category of ability, while others, such as the differentiation of the ranks, are due to other concerns.[107]

The next element in the discussion of ability is a historical review of regime change in Egypt; while Imam calls this section "practical reasons" for not waging jihad against the government today, it may also enter into the category of ability, since he states that it is a Shari'a obligation to take history into account.[108] Sayyid Imam espouses the view that Egypt, as a hydraulic society centered on the Nile, is highly centralized; as such, regime change has only been possible in the past, and is only possible in the present in one of two ways: foreign conquest or palace revolt. Popular revolution, like that of the jihadist movements, has always failed. This leads to the final consideration, that jihad was decreed in order to put an end to harm to Islam and the Muslims. Thus if a given jihad does more harm than good, it is not obligatory. Imam seems to imply that this is an inherent consideration built into the commandment of jihad as well as a general principle that applies to all Shari'a obligations.[109]

What is most remarkable about the *Tarshid's* discussion of the condition of ability is not what it contains, but what it does not. The obligation of "making ready" for jihad, which was so central to Sayyid Imam's thought that it provided the title for his first work, *al-'Umda fi i'dad al-'udda* ("The Essentials of Making Ready for Jihad"), is given only perfunctory mention. In the last section of the book, Imam cites Quran 8:60, the verse on which the obligation is based. However, he uses it only to prove the general point that jihad remains an obligation in Islam;[110] if one were to read the *Tarshid* in isolation, one would not get the impression that "making ready" is a separate commandment requiring Muslims to remedy the condition of inability. Abu Basir al-Tartusi, for one, criticized Sayyid Imam on precisely this point, saying that Imam had described inability as though it were an inherent characteristic of the Muslim nation. He asked whether Hosni Mubarak is so terrifying that he should be considered a modern-day Ya'juj and Ma'juj that causes scholars to tell the people that 70 million Muslims are powerless to defeat him. Al-Tartusi writes that if there is a state of inability, it is rather the obligation of scholars to encourage the Muslims to overcome it; in other words, to "make ready."[111]

Nonetheless, and despite Sayyid Imam's changing emphases, there is no reason to believe that he no longer considers "making ready" an obligation. It has already been noted that throughout the *Tarshid* Imam attempts to emphasize aspects of his views that make him appear moderate and downplay others that make him appear radical. In addition, it is built into the nature of the commandment of "making ready" that it always applies; while inability can suspend other commandments, "making ready" is itself, by definition, a commandment that is in force even in a state of inability.

THE *TARSHID* AND THE JIHADIST MOVEMENT AFTER 9/11

The importance of this last point will be understood when we consider the following question: what would Sayyid Imam say if the Muslims (in essence, the jihadists) were not in a state of inability? There is every indication that he would exhort them to jihad against the apostate rulers and, if the balance of power were not too skewed, would fully endorse jihad against the West as well. (He already continues to support the jihad in Iraq and Palestine.)[112]

We saw how al-Gama'a al-Islamiyya's retraction of *takfir* of the rulers unraveled the entire jihadist doctrine; Sayyid Imam has not retracted *takfir* of the rulers, and for him nothing has unraveled. The prohibition of jihad that is the heart of the *Tarshid* instead relies on what we called a "suspension mechanism," but in principle the entire edifice of jihadist belief, which Imam himself did much to construct, remains in place. Thus if Sayyid Imam still considers "making ready" an obligation, the jihadists could arrive at a state of ability and the jihad would recommence. How likely this is depends on whether his threshold for "ability" is impossibly high, as his jihadist critics claim.

In any event, the arguments put forward by Sayyid Imam are not a renunciation of jihadist doctrine in any meaningful sense of the term. Al-Zawahiri, who claims that Imam wrote in the *Tarshid* more or less what the U.S. commanded him to write, offers the following surmise: "This method of trying to foil [the jihad] reveals the failure of the enemies of Islam to [successfully] confront the *mujahideen*'s proofs and Shari'a arguments. Since they were unable to refute them, they took a roundabout route and came through the issue of ability and inability . . ."[113] While I cannot concur with his ascription of the *Tarshid* to the CIA, his depiction of it as a poor refutation of jihadist doctrine is, in fact, fairly accurate. This is especially true since one can easily dispute who has the authority to determine whether a state of inability exists. For his part, al-Zawahiri writes in his habitual sardonic style: "What is remarkable is that the author [i.e., Imam] is trying to impose his own inability and his own weakness on the *mujahideen*, who don't feel themselves to be either unable or weak . . . The author writes that he is in a state of inability and weakness. That's his opinion, and that's his problem . . ." Al-Zawahiri continues, addressing Imam in the second person: "As for the *mujahideen*, they know better what they are doing than you do."[114]

If the *Tarshid* is not a renunciation of jihadism, like al-Gama'a al-Islam-iyya's revisionist writings were, what exactly is it? And why has it attracted so much attention, leading al-Zawahiri to write a nearly 200-page refutation and inspiring articles in the Western press asking whether this is the beginning of the end for al-Qaeda?[115] Part of the reason the *Tarshid* has had such an impact is that Sayyid Imam's effort at presenting himself as a moderate has, in large measure, succeeded. His searing criticism of al-Qaeda's lawless terrorism is impressive and easily understood, whereas his careful parsing of jurisprudential arguments is difficult and abstruse. He emphasizes at length the prohibition against fighting Muslim rulers, but does not bother divulging to the reader that he considers today's rulers apostates, to whom such a prohibition would not apply. He dwells on the distinction between "greater apostasy" and "lesser apostasy" without informing the reader that his domino effect of *takfir* makes much of society apostates in the full sense of the term. Anyone familiar with the fine points of Imam's jurisprudence could easily add further such examples.

Yet the *Tarshid* is not all smoke and mirrors; Imam's practical prohibi-tion of jihad is real enough, as is his insistence that jihad, when waged, must be governed by rules. In essence, the *Tarshid* is simply the most striking example of the fissure between the jihadist jurisprudents and others in the jihadist movement. This fissure has always existed, but in the past it remained more or less dormant; when Sayyid Imam decided to leave the Jihad group after they refused to heed his advice, he did so quietly and without fanfare.

In the aftermath of 9/11, however, these differences have come out into the open. Sayyid Imam now accuses the politically minded jihadists of employing a "jurisprudence of justification," i.e., doing whatever they think necessary to be victorious and then searching afterward for a Sha-ri'a justification for it, even if it comes from a pseudonymous sheikh on the Internet.[116] Sayyid Imam is an extreme case where these differences have burgeoned into outright schism, but Abu Basir al-Tartusi, Abu Muhammad al-Maqdisi, Salman al-'Awda, and others have all criticized various aspects of jihadist practice, such as suicide bombings, the killing of Shi'a, or simply the randomness of jihadist killing in general.[117]

For their part, the jurisprudents are not necessarily more moderate; the doctrine they espouse can still be quite extreme, as Sayyid Imam's seems to be, despite some attempts at obfuscation. The issue is simply whether control of the jihad movement should be in the hands of the scholars or in the hands of the *mujahideen*, with their more political and eclectic Qutb-derived worldview. It is this issue that Sayyid Imam was address-ing when, in the *al-Hayat* interview, he shot off a rebuke to Muhammad Khalil Hakayma, the head of al-Qaeda's Egyptian branch: "Hakayma, lay aside the sayings and positions of Sayyid Qutb, may Allah's mercy be upon him. There are differences of opinion among the *'ulama* as to whether the sayings and the actions of the Prophet's companions may be adduced as proofs, and thus this is all the more true with regard to Sayyid Qutb. Take Shari'a laws from their primary source . . ."[118]

CONCLUSION

The fundamental difference between jihadists and establishment jurisprudents is the issue of *takfir* of the rulers. The determination that the rulers are apostates brings in its wake the application of an entirely different set of Shari'a laws, while at the same time allowing the jihadist jurisprudents to claim that they speak in the name of the classical Sunni consensus. *Takfir* of the ruler also cancels out those prerogatives of the legitimate ruler that allow for some divergence from the jurisprudents' ideal, and sets off a domino effect of apostasy that engulfs much of society and sets the stage for widespread bloodshed.

The doctrine of *takfir* of the ruler rests on two legs; the first is the determination that the public sphere is a ritual space and that any condominium of man and Allah is apostasy. The second is the determination that modern forms of government, and legislative bodies in particular, are utterly unlike pre-modern Muslim government and are a clear example of such apostasy.

The centrality of *takfir* of the ruler was demonstrated in our analysis of al-Gama'a al-Islamiyya's ideological revisions; when they ceased to regard the rulers as apostates, other aspects of jihadist doctrine necessarily melted away. The ruler's prerogatives in place, a large degree of dereliction from Shari'a ideals and practice was tolerated. The reason for the group's abandonment of the *takfir* doctrine was, in technical terms, its adoption of a non-jihadist position on the issue of *jahd*—that is, the conditioning of *takfir* on a statement of explicit preference for man-made law over Shari'a law. More generally, the change was the result of the adoption of a more flexible and empirical worldview.

Sayyid Imam's *Document of Right Guidance for Jihad in Egypt and the World* does not renounce *takfir* of the rulers, and thus bears little resemblance to the revolution that occurred in al-Gama'a al-Islamiyya's thinking. The grounds on which the book calls for desistance from jihad relate rather to certain practical considerations and their Shari'a implications, and particularly the issue of ability as a condition for jihad. In a wider sense, the book is Sayyid Imam's way of throwing down the gauntlet between jihadist jurisprudents and more politically minded ideologues in the jihadist movement.

I would like to thank the Middle East Media Research Institute for their support while working on this chapter, and Professor Ella Landau-Tasseron of the Hebrew University of Jerusalem for her helpful comments.

NOTES

1. Most of the literature that is starting to emerge on jihadism focuses on strategy and ideology rather than jurisprudence or theology, e.g., Fawaz A. Gerges, *The Far Enemy: Why Jihad Went Global* (Cambridge: Cambridge University Press, 2005); Brynjar Lia, *Architect of Global Jihad: The Life of Al-Qaida Strategist Abu Mus'ab al-Suri* (New York: Columbia University Press, 2008). Quintan Wiktorowicz has written on the beliefs of the radical Saudi scholars Salman al-'Awdah and Safar al-Hawali, who are politically and intellectually close to the figures discussed in the present article. See Quintan Wiktorowicz, "The Anatomy of the Salafi Movement," *Studies in Conflict and Terrorism* 29, no. 3 (2006): 207–39.

2. Ayman al-Zawahiri, *Risala fi tabri'at ummat al-qalam wa'l-sayf min manqasat tuhmat al-khawar wa'l-dha'f* (2008), 21–47.

3. For one example from the Saudi religious establishment, see Muhammad bin Salih al-'Uthaymin, *Sharh kitab al-siyasa al-shar'iyya* (Beirut: Dar Ibn Hazm, 2004), 138–140.

4. Here I have adopted the terminology of Bernard Lewis in "On the Quietist and Activist Traditions in Islamic Political Writing," *Bulletin of the School of Oriental and African Studies* 49 (1986): 141–47.

5. Sayyid Imam al-Sharif, *al-'Umda fi i'dad al-'udda*, http://www.3llm.com/main/download.php?action=view&id=649, posted on http://www.alkashf.net/vb/showthread.php?t=1798; on jihad, 55–57, 75–87; on judicial matters, 102–03. For a classical precedent, see Abu al-Ma'ali 'Abd al-Malik bin 'Abdallah al-Juwayni, *Ghiyath al-umam fi iltiyath al-zulam* (Beirut: Dar al-Kutub al-'Ilmiyya, 2003), 172ff.

6. See Saad Eddin Ibrahim, "Islamic Militancy as a Social Movement: The Case of Two Groups in Egypt," in *Islamic Resurgence in the Arab World*, ed. Ali Dessouki (New York: Praeger, 1982); Gilles Kepel, *Muslim Extremism in Egypt: The Prophet and the Pharaoh* (Berkeley: University of California Press, 1985), 129ff.; Olivier Roy, "Les nouveaux intellectuels islamistes: essai d'approche philosophique," in *Intellectuels et militants de l'Islam contemporain*, eds. Gilles Kepel and Yann Richard (Paris: Seuil, 1990).

7. *Al-Musawwar* (Egypt), July 5, 2002; Yigal Carmon, Yotam Feldner, and Daniel Lav, "The Al-Gama'a Al-Islamiyya Cessation of Violence: An Ideological Reversal," Middle East Media Research Institute [hereafter MEMRI], Inquiry and Analysis, no. 309, December 22, 2006, http://memri.org/bin/articles.cgi?Page=archives&Area=ia&ID=IA30906#_edn94.

8. Imam, *al-'Umda*, 87.

9. See Adnan A. Musallam, *From Secularism to Jihad: Sayyid Qutb and the Foundations of Radical Islamism* (Westport: Praeger Security International, 2005), 105–07, 118–19, 161–62, inter alia.

10. *Al-Hayat* (London), December 8, 2007.

11. See, for example, Sayyid Imam al-Sharif, *al-Jami' fi talab al-'ilm al-sharif*, 2nd ed., http://www.almeshkat.net/books/open.php?cat=14&book=1222, 921, 1009.

12. Emmanuel Sivan, *Radical Islam: Medieval Theology and Modern Politics* (New Haven: Yale University Press, 1990), 50–56.

13. *Al-Sharq al-Awsat* (London), May 29, 2001; *al-Sharq al-Awsat* (London), December 10, 2002; Carmon, et al., "The Al-Gama'a Al-Islamiyya Cessation of Violence: An Ideological Reversal."

14. *Al-Hayat* (London), December 8, 2007; "Major Jihadi Cleric and Author of Al-Qaeda's Shari'a Guide to Jihad: 9/11 Was a Sin . . ." MEMRI, Special Dispatch, no. 1785, December 14, 2007, http://memri.org/bin/latestnews. cgi?ID=SD178507.

15. Ibid.

16. Sayyid Imam published a communiqué denouncing al-Zawahiri and the Jihad group in the harshest possible terms after they published a version of Imam's *al-Jami' fi talab al-'ilm al-sharif* in which changes were made without his permission. The communiqué is included in the preface to the second edition. Imam, *al-Jami'*, 8–13.

17. Abu Muhammad al-Maqdisi, "*al-Zarqawi: munasara wa-munasaha*," (2004), http://www.tawhed.ws/r?i=dtwiam56; Y. Yehoshua, "Dispute in Islamist Circles over the Legitimacy of Attacking Muslims, Shiites, and Non-Combatant Non-Muslims in Jihad Operations in Iraq: Al-Maqdisi vs. His Disciple Al-Zarqawi," MEMRI, Inquiry and Analysis, no. 239, September 11, 2005, http://memri.info/bin/articles.cgi?Page=subjects&Area=jihad&ID=IA23905.

18. 'Abd al-Mun'im Mustafa Halima (aka Abu Basir al-Tartusi), *Mubadarat al-jama'a al-islamiyya al-misriyya: i'tiraf bi'l-khat'a am inhiyar wa-suqut?*, February 1, 2003, http://www.abubaseer.bizland.com/books/read/b17.doc.

19. Carmon, et al., "The Al-Gama'a Al-Islamiyya Cessation of Violence: An Ideological Reversal."

20. "Major Jihadi Cleric," MEMRI.

21. See Muntasir al-Zayat's appraisal in *al-Misriyyun* (Egypt), November 19, 2007.

22. www.almaqreze.net/munawaat/hssba/ansr01.html.

23. Abu Muhammad al-Maqdisi, *al-Nukat al-lawami' fi malhuzat al-jami'* (1998); the book may be downloaded together with the *Jami'*: http://www. almeshkat. net/books/open.php?cat=14&book=1222.

24. 'Abd al-Mun'im Mustafa Halima (aka Abu Basir al-Tartusi), *Kalima hawla muraja'at al-sheikh Sayyid Imam*, November 29, 2007, http://www.abubaseer. bizland.com/refutation/read/f%2088.doc.

25. For instance, al-Siba'i's first written response to the *Tarshid*, titled simply "*Ta'liq awwali 'ala wathiqat tarshid al-'amal al-jihadi*," was posted on the Web site of the al-Maqreze Center on November 18, 2007: www.almaqreze.net/bayanat/artc1054.html [link no longer active]. Extracts were printed in the following day's edition of *al-Sharq al-Awsat*, and the text was reproduced in full in the November 23 edition of the Egyptian daily *al-Masri al-Yawm*.

26. Muhammad Khalil al-Hakayma, "*Bayan hawla ma nushira min wathiqat tarshid al-'amal al-jihadi*," November 29, 2007, http://www.shamikh.net/vb/showthread.php?p=65284.

27. See "Release of New Book by Ayman al-Zawahiri . . ." MEMRI, Special Dispatch, no. 1859, March 4, 2008, http://memri.org/bin/latestnews.cgi? ID=SD178507.

28. Imam, *al-'Umda*, 300.

29. Halima, *Kalima*, 2.

30. *Al-Hayat* (London), December 10, 2007.

31. Ibid., December 11, 2007.

32. Ibid., December 12, 2007.

33. Imam, *Tarshid* in *al-Jarida* (Kuwait), November 18, 2007.

34. Al-Zawahiri, *Risala*, 49.

35. Imam, *al-'Umda*, 54 (emphasis mine).

36. Muhammad Bin Ibrahim Aal al-Sheikh, *Risalat tahkim al-qawanin*; cited in Imam, *al-'Umda*, 90–91.

37. Yohanan Friedmann, *Tolerance and Coercion in Islam* (Cambridge: Cambridge University Press, 2003), 127.

38. See Ibn Taymiyya, *Majmu'at al-fatawa* (Al-Mansura: Dar al-Wafa', 2005), 7: 311–12.

39. See *Kitab al-'alim w'al-muta'allim*, article 5, cited in Joseph Schacht, "An Early Murci'ite Treatise: The Kitab al-'Alim w'al-Muta'allim," *Oriens* 17 (1964): 96–117, 106; *Risala ila 'Uthman al-Batti* (attributed to Abu Hanifa), cited in Wilferd Madelung, "Early Sunni Doctrine Concerning Faith as Reflected in the *Kitab al-iman* of Abu 'Ubaid b. Sallam (died 839)," *Studia Islamica* 32 (1970): 233–54; repr. in Wilfred Madelung, *Religious Schools and Sects in Medieval Islam* (London: Variorum Reprints, 1985); Wilfred Madelung, "Murdji'a," C.E. Bosworth, et al., eds., *Encyclopaedia of Islam*, 2nd ed. (Leiden, E. J. Brill, 1960–2005), 7: 605ff.

40. Abu Ja'far Ahmad Bin Muhammad Bin Salama al-Tahawi (died 933), *al-'Aqida al-Tahawiyya*, cited in Imam, *al-Jami'*, 503–04.

41. See Friedmann, 122–23; and Rudolph Peters and Gert J. J. De Vries, "Apostasy in Islam," *Die Welt des Islams* 17 (1976-7): 1–25.

42. See Ibn Qudama, *al-Mughni 'ala mukhtasar al-khiraqi* (Beirut: Dar al-kutub al-'ilmiyya, 1994), 2: 280–83.

43. Abu Muhammad al-Maqdisi, *Imta' al-nazar fi kashf shubuhat murji'at al-'asr* (1991–92), http://www.3llm.com/main/download.php?action=view&id=196, 11.

44. Ibid., 32.

45. The influential quietist Salafi scholar Muhammad Nasir al-Din al-Albani called Safar al-Hawali and those like him "the Khawarij of this era," in response to al-Hawali's accusation that al-Albani was a murji'ite. Wiktorowicz, "The Anatomy of the Salafi Movement," 231–32. The comparison of jihadists to Kharijites is ubiquitous in contemporary popular discourse as well. One recent example is from Algeria; according to a press report, armed jihadists entered a mosque in El-Oued after the evening prayer, dragged out two non-jihadist salafis, and killed them; before he was shot, one of them was reported to have shouted, "Oh Kharijites, you will yet be killed, Allah willing." *El-Khabar* (Algeria), March 18, 2008.

46. See *al-Jami'*, 547.

47. Al-Maqdisi, *Imta' al-nazar*, 19.

48. Ibid.

49. Imam, *al-'Umda*, 296–97.

50. Sayyid Imam (?), "*al-Irhab min al- islam wa-man ankara dhalika fa-qad kafara*," http://www.almaqreze.net/munawaat/artcl044.html. This document was distributed on the Internet by Hani al-Siba'i's al-Maqreze Center after Sayyid Imam was imprisoned in Yemen on October 11, 2001; the introduction states that it was incomplete and in manuscript form. See Muhammad al-Shafi'i, "Al-'Umda

al-marji' al-asasi li-tajnid 'anasir al-qa'ida," *al-Sharq al-Awsat* (London), May 19, 2006, who accepts it as authentic. There is also internal evidence attesting to Sayyid Imam's authorship; for instance, toward the end of *al-Irhab min al-islam* we find the following sentence: ". . . one of their philosophers, Mirabeau, said: 'Hang the last king with the entrails of the last priest.'" Imam clearly has in mind a saying commonly attributed to Diderot (and the misattribution is egregious, since Mirabeau was in fact a constitutional monarchist). We find this same misattribution in Imam's *al-Jami'*, 874. In the *al-Hayat* interview Imam seems to insinuate that Hani al-Siba'i did not understand the manuscript and that the form in which it was published did not accurately reflect his views. *Al-Hayat* (London), December 12, 2007. This claim is difficult to accept, since many of the arguments in *al-Irhab min al-islam* are in fact identical to arguments in Imam's other writings.

51. Albert Hourani, *Arabic Thought in the Liberal Age: 1798–1939* (Cambridge: Cambridge University Press, 1983), 188–89.

52. Imam, *al-Jami'*, 946.

53. Ibid., 945.

54. Ibid., 950.

55. Ibid., 8–13. Imam writes that the edition published by the Jihad group omitted his criticisms of Islamist groups and that what remained was only half as long as the manuscript; the only criticisms of such length in *al-Jami'* are those relating to *takfir*, *jahd*, and *istihlal*.

56. Ibid., 946.

57. Ibid., 948.

58. Ibid., 920–21.

59. Saad Eddine El-Othmani, *al-Musharaka al-siyasiyya fi fiqh sheikh al-islam Bin Taymiyya*, Silsilat al-hiwar 29, http://www.fassael.net/article.php3?id_article=82.

60. Imam, *al-Jami'*, 946.

61. Ibid., 950.

62. Ibid., 953–54.

63. See Patricia Crone, *Medieval Islamic Political Thought* (Edinburgh: Edinburgh University Press, 2004); Ann Lambton, *State and Government in Medieval Islam* (Oxford: Oxford University Press, 1981); and Erwin I. J. Rosenthal, *Political Thought in Medieval Islam: An Introductory Outline* (Cambridge: Cambridge University Press, 1958). On the predominance of political quietism, see Lewis, "On the Quietist and Activist Traditions in Islamic Political Writing;" and M. J. Kister, "Social and Religious Concepts of Authority in Islam," *Jerusalem Studies in Arabic and Islam* 18 (1994): 84–127, esp. 126–27. Some scholars have attempted to show that the classical works on jurisprudence were not just an intellectual rearguard action, but a political one as well; thus H.A.R. Gibb proposed that Mawardi's *al-Ahkam al-sultaniyya* was intended as a blueprint for an Abbasid revival. H. A. R. Gibb, "Al-Mawardi's Theory of the Caliphate," in his *Studies on the Civilization of Islam* (Boston: Beacon, 1962; repr. from *Islamic Culture* 11 (1937): 291–302). Henri Laoust, in his *La Pensée et l'action politique de al-Mawardi* (Paris: Librairie Orientaliste Paul Geuthner, 1968; repr. from *Revue des Études Islamiques* 36 [1968]), took up Gibb's theory with much gusto, seeing in Mawardi

a proponent of caliphal absolutism. In my view Gibb's theory is incorrect. Daniel Lav, "Revisiting Gibb's Theory on Mawardi's *al-Ahkam al-sultaniyya* and the Abbasid Revival," in preparation. Mawardi aside, Wael Hallaq has proposed an activist political reading of Juwayni's *Ghiyath al-umam.* Wael Hallaq, "Caliphs, Jurists, and the Saljuqs in the Political Thought of Juwayni," *The Muslim World* 74, no. 1 (January 1984): 26–41.

64. Ibn Taymiyya, *Majmu'at al-fatawa*, 28: 274–301.

65. This *fatwa* of Ibn Taymiyya's was popularized in particular through its adduction in 'Abd al-Salam Farag's tract *al-Farida al-gha'iba* ("The Neglected Duty"). See Sivan, *Radical Islam*, 103ff. Sivan translates the title more literally as "The Absent Precept."

66. Imam, *al-'Umda*, 70; and see 35, where he warns that one may not use the profligacy of the emir or of the other *mujahideen* as an excuse not to wage jihad. On 72 he adds that in addition to fighting together with a profligate emir, one is also required to pray behind him. Imam does introduce a distinction: he argues that one should go on raids only with an emir whose profligacy is merely in personal matters, but not if his profligacy is public and harms Islam and the Muslims. However, the example he gives of the latter are those who use Islam to urge Muslims to wage war in defense of secular regimes. Ibid., 73–74. As there is no doubt that Imam considers such people outright apostates, it is not clear that his second category of profligate Emirs is not an empty set.

67. See Crone, *Medieval Islamic Political Thought*, on al-Ghazali, 238ff; for earlier traditions, see Kister, "Social and Religious Concepts of Authority in Islam," 106–07.

68. Imam, *al-Jami'*, 990.

69. Ibid., 992.

70. Ibid., 993.

71. Ibid., 539–40; and see 879.

72. Al-Maqdisi, *al-Nukat*, 46–48.

73. Imam, *al-Jami'*, 878–79.

74. See 'Umar 'Abd al-Rahman, *Kalimat haqq: murafa'at al-sheikh 'Umar 'Abd al-Rahman fi qadiyat al-jihad*, http://www.tawhed.ws/dl?i=ord7bdij.

75. *Al-Musawwar* (Egypt), June 21, 2002, 9; Carmon, et al., "The Al-Gama'a Al-Islamiyya Cessation of Violence: An Ideological Reversal," note 23; Halima, *Mubadarat*, 13–14. For a similar statement from Karam Zuhdi, see *al-Sharq al-Awsat* (London), July 15, 2003; Carmon, et al., "The Al-Gama'a Al-Islamiyya Cessation of Violence: An Ideological Reversal," Part II.

76. See al-Maqdisi, *Imta'*; Wiktorowicz, "The Anatomy of the Salafi Movement," 228ff.; Muhammad Qasim Zaman, *The Ulama in Contemporary Islam: Custodians of Change* (Princeton: Princeton University Press, 2002), 156–57.

77. *Al-Musawwar* (Egypt), July 5, 2002, 15; cited in Halima, *Mubadarat*, 59.

78. *Al-Musawwar* (Egypt), June 28, 2002, 19; cited in Halima, *Mubadarat*, 17.

79. *Al-Musawwar* (Egypt), July 5, 2002, 11; cited in Halima, *Mubadarat*, 16–17.

80. Halima, *Mubadarat*, 27.

81. *Al-Musawwar* (Egypt), July 5, 2002; Carmon, et al., "The Al-Gama'a Al-Islamiyya Cessation of Violence: An Ideological Reversal," Part II.

82. *Akhir Sa'a* (Egypt), March 20, 2002; Carmon, et al., "The Al-Gama'a Al-Islamiyya Cessation of Violence: An Ideological Reversal," Part II.

83. *Al-Sharq al-Awsat* (London), August 28, 2006; "Al-Gama'a Al-Islamiyya vs. Al-Qaeda," MEMRI, Special Dispatch, no. 1301, September 27, 2006, http://memri.org/bin/articles.cgi?Page=archives&Area=sd&ID=SP130106#_edn5.

84. *Al-Hayat* (London), December 9, 2007; "Major Jihadi Cleric," MEMRI.

85. *Al-Musawwar* (Egypt), August 8, 2003; Carmon, et al., "The Al-Gama'a Al-Islamiyya Cessation of Violence: An Ideological Reversal," Part II.

86. Imam, *al-Jami'*, 896.

87. Halima, *Kalima*, 2–3.

88. Imam, *Tarshid* in *al-Jarida* (Kuwait), November 27, 2007. He writes that the second criterion was mentioned by Ibn Taymiyya in *Iqtida' sirat al-mustaqim*, and the third by Ibn Qayyim al-Jawziyya in *'Uddat al-sabirin*.

89. Imam, *al-Jami'*, 935–36.

90. Imam, *Tarshid* in *al-Jarida* (Kuwait), November 23, 2007.

91. Imam, *al-Jami'*, 877. Abu Muhammad al-Maqdisi took issue with this blanket statement. See *al-Nukat*, no. 13, 27. Al-Maqdisi's general tendency is to hold, as here, that Sayyid Imam is too quick to declare others apostates, though there are examples where he holds him to be too lenient, e.g., on the issue of joining an infidel army with the express aim of harming it. See *al-Nukat*, 40–44.

92. Imam, *Tarshid* in *al-Jarida* (Kuwait), November 27, 2007.

93. Imam, *Tarshid* in *al-Jarida* (Kuwait), November 22, 2007.

94. Imam, *al-Jami'*, 1035.

95. Al-Zawahiri, *Risala*, 4.

96. Imam, *al-'Umda*, 300.

97. Ibid., 303.

98. *Al-Hayat* (London), December 8, 2007; "Major Jihadi Cleric," MEMRI.

99. Imam, *al-Jami'*, 1018–20.

100. For a similar opinion, see Ibn Kathir's commentary to Quran 8:61, "If they turn to peace, turn you to it as well . . ."

101. Imam, *al-Jami'*, 1019.

102. Ibid., 1020.

103. Ibid., 1019.

104. *Al-Hayat* (London), December 9, 2007; "Major Jihadi Cleric," MEMRI.

105. Imam, *Tarshid* in *al-Jarida* (Kuwait), November 20, 2007.

106. Ibid.

107. Imam, *Tarshid* in *al-Jarida* (Kuwait), November 22, 2007; "Major Jihadi Cleric and Author of Al-Qaeda's Shari'a Guide to Jihad: 9/11 Was a Sin . . . (2)," MEMRI, Special Dispatch, no. 1826, January 25, 2008, http://www.memri.org/bin/articles.cgi?Page=archives&Area=sd&ID=SP182608.

108. This principle was already discussed at length in the final chapter of *al-Jami'*, 1096–1115.

109. Imam, *Tarshid* in *al-Jarida* (Kuwait), November 22, 2007; "Major Jihadi Cleric (2)," MEMRI.

110. Imam, *Tarshid* in *al-Jarida* (Kuwait), December 4, 2007.

111. Halima, *Kalima*, 6–8. The rhetorical question is designed to show that Imam's case is weak even if his assumptions are granted; al-Tartusi in fact rejects the proof from Ya'juj and Ma'juj.

112. Imam, *Tarshid* in *al-Jarida* (Kuwait), December 4, 2007.

113. Al-Zawahiri, *Risala*, 54.

114. Ibid., 53–54.

115. Bret Stephens, "How Al-Qaeda Will Perish," *Wall Street Journal*, March 25, 2008; Lawrence Wright, "The Rebellion Within: An Al-Qaeda Mastermind Questions Terrorism," *The New Yorker*, June 2, 2008; Peter Bergen and Paul Cruickshank, "The Unraveling: The Jihadist Revolt against Bin Laden," *The New Republic*, June 11, 2008.

116. Imam, *Tarshid* in *al-Jarida* (Kuwait), November 19, 2007.

117. "Expatriate Syrian Salafi Sheikh Al-Tartusi Comes Out Against Suicide Attacks," MEMRI, Special Report, no. 40, February 10, 2006, http://memri.org/bin/articles.cgi?Page=archives&Area=sr&ID=SR4006; (incidentally, al-Tartusi has posted these MEMRI translations on his own Web site: http://www.en.altartosi.com/suicide.htm#A); al-Maqdisi, *"al-Zarqawi: munasaha"*; Y. Yehoshua, "Dispute in Islamist Circles"; "Saudi Cleric Salman Al-Odeh," MEMRI TV Clip no. 1557, September 14, 2007, http://www.memritv.org/clip/en/1557.htm.

118. *Al-Hayat* (London), December 13, 2007.

CHAPTER 9

Takfir as a Tool for Instigating Jihad Among Muslims: The Ghanaian Example

Mohammed Hafiz

There has never been certitude regarding the exact genesis of Islam in Ghana. Historians estimate its arrival between the fourteenth and fifteenth centuries, with the north encountering Islam several decades before the south. Over time it expanded across the country, and by the close of the nineteenth century there was hardly any principal city, district capital, or town in Ghana that was devoid of Muslims. Still, it remains a minority religion. The 2000 census revealed that Christians constitute 69 percent of the Ghanaian population of 18.8 million, while Muslims make up 15.6 percent, with most living in the northern region (traditionalists constitute 8.5 percent, and 6.9 percent are listed as "other" religions).[1]

The history of Islam in Ghana since its inception has been characterized by deep tribal sentiments, which have sometimes provoked instability and, on occasion, rioting and the closing of mosques. The decades from the 1970s to the 1990s, alas, were especially divisive, with brutal clashes engulfing all of the regional capitals and leading to large-scale property damage, the loss of life, and the dislocation of the Muslim population. Two recent studies address this vexing era. With a focus on the apparent tribal cleavage, Nathan Samwini doubts whether the spirit of universal brotherhood that Islam emphasizes has been applied to Ghana or, for that matter, Africa at large, while Mbillah Johnson discusses the general causes of the conflict and its wider repercussions.[2]

In the view of this writer, however, another force was also responsible for dividing Muslims in Ghana. An ideological fissure opened up between the Ahlus Sunnah and the Tijaniyya sects when Islamic revivalists in the former camp, in a bid to promote what they deemed as true Islam, transgressed acceptable limits by implicitly pronouncing *takfir* on their co-religionists. Scholars, including Samwini and Johnson, have referred to this issue, but they have not examined in detail the role that *takfir* played in fomenting strife or the peril that it poses to Muslim harmony in the country.

This chapter carries out these tasks, which are essential to a fuller understanding of recent events in Ghana. It is divided into two sections. The first will discuss three concepts that Islamic revivalists have stressed—*jahiliya, takfir,* and jihad—and explore how they form the cornerstone of radicalized political Islam. In the second section, Ghana is used as a case study to establish the dangers that *takfir* presents to Muslim communities. This section emphasizes how *takfir* has instigated jihad among Muslims in Ghana and has caused them to oppose each other for three decades. Instead of pooling their resources to find solutions to common problems, Ghanaian Muslims have allowed these clashes to divide them. The nature of *takfir* in Ghana, the havoc it has caused, the intellectual debates it has generated, and the prospects for consolidating peace are among the topics treated in the second part of this chapter.

JAHILIYA, TAKFIR, JIHAD

Jahiliya is a term used to describe the miserable state of ignorance Arabs found themselves in prior to the arrival of Islam. Attempts to adequately translate the word into English have proven complicated. Notwithstanding the timeframe connotation that *jahiliya* is generally assigned in Arabic literature, there are eminent classical and contemporary scholars who strongly contest this popular notion. M.A. Mohar, a contemporary Islamic writer, is convinced that the confusion arising from whether *jahiliya* connotes a timeframe or specific practices arose from early attempts by Orientalists to translate the word. In his view, its sense is discernible through usage in the Quran and Hadith. Scrutiny of the evidence Mohar uses to support his conclusion—"*Jahiliya* denotes a state of belief, habits and practices, and as such, it may not be confined to any specific period of time, or to any given people"[3]—reveals that he is obviously keen to advance the *"jahiliya* as practice" side of the argument. The time factor is not something that can simply be ignored, however, for this connotation features in Quranic verses such as 5:50 and 33:33 and is supported by numerous references in the Hadith. The Prophet is reported to have told one of the companions who boasted to another of a superior tribal lineage, "You still have in your blood some traces of the *jahiliya.*" Still, it can be argued that the issue between "*jahiliya* as practice" and "*jahiliya* as a period" stems from the fact that it is exceedingly difficult to dissociate events from the space and time in which they transpire. While *jahiliya* as a practice virtually belongs to the period in which it occurred, if the need arises for usage of the term to describe a contemporary situation, nothing prevents that, just as the Prophet reprimanded his companion.

What is *takfir?* The closest equivalent perhaps would be "excommunication," which, strictly speaking, does not connote the actual sense of the word. Often, one is tempted to use *takfir* and *ridda* (apostasy) interchangeably. Linguistically, the two terms share close affinity, but they are two different things altogether. Both *ridda* and *takfir* are related to the concept of *kufr,* meaning "disbelief." They differ in the sense that the former refers to the act of making utterances or embarking on deeds that are tantamount to disbelief, and the latter, *takfir,* is the act of passing the verdict of *kufr* on anyone whose utterances or deeds openly manifest disbelief. Technically, there are complex and rigorous ethical, theological, and legal considerations underpinning *takfir,* which need not be discussed in detail here. Suffice it to say for our purposes that *takfir* is the act of pronouncing an individual or group of people who have professed their faith in Islam to be non-Muslims. This is the sense in which *takfir* shall be used throughout this chapter, and the emphasis will dwell on its implications rather than its technicalities, which reputable scholars have found a good cause to address.[4] No one needs to be reminded that of all the terrible experiences that Islam has passed through, *takfir* has proven to be the most dreadful. The fact that the International Islamic Conference held in Jordan in 2005, on the theme "True Islam and its Role in Modern Society," was committed mainly to denouncing *takfir* is enough of an indication of how this cancer has permeated the fabric of Islam. *Takfir* has been largely responsible for most of the violent actions that many individuals have committed against Muslims and non-Muslims alike, often in the name of jihad.

The word "jihad" is well known. It basically means "to strive in the course of Allah." The injunctions on jihad (and *qital,* or armed jihad) were revealed following the migration of the Prophet and the Muslim *umma* to Medina. Anyone who reads between the lines of the verses relating to jihad will realize that it was meant to serve two major purposes: first, as a tool for self-defense in the event of attack by the Meccan infidels; and, second, to clear away the obstacles that hindered Muslims from practicing their faith or propagating it appropriately.[5] Of its several possible connotations, jihad is used in this chapter to refer to the use of force to change or correct what is considered a wrong practice. This has been described by Abu Bakr al-Jazairi as *jihad al-fusaq.*[6] It is worth acknowledging that in recent times there has been a growing tendency for adventurous groups to label and justify their violent attacks on innocent persons as jihad. In other words, the term jihad has been abused so much that it is fast losing its religious sanctity.

IBN TAYMIYYA'S FAMOUS *FATWA*

The relationship between *jahiliya, takfir,* and jihad is demonstrated in the infamous *fatwa* issued by the Muslim scholar Ibn Taymiyya in the year 1303 regarding whether jihad could be waged by the Egyptian Mamluks against the Mongols, who had openly embraced Islam. Ibn Taymiyya's position on this question was quite militant. He held that the Mongols were heretics or apostates (*kafir*), and jihad against them was not only legitimate but mandatory. His contention was that the Mongols, despite embracing Islam, continued to live in a state of *jahiliya* since they had adhered to the use of "man-made laws." In the words of Emmanuel Sevan, "Ibn Taymiyya's novel reinterpretation of *jahiliya* was a double-edged sword. By predicating absolute condemnation of governments on inexactly defined proscriptions, it set a precedent which would haunt Muslim regimes into the modern era."[7] The legitimate question one may pose here is: "Did Ibn Taymiyya deliberately set out to reinterpret *jahiliya* and predetermine future events, or was he genuinely reacting to a threat against the *umma*?"

The moral decay that had earlier wrecked the Umayyad reign had gripped the Abbasids as well. Muslims continued to pursue material gains and to indulge in the pleasures of the world until the Mongols overthrew the Abbasid dynasty in 1258. It was in the wake of these developments that Ibn Taymiyya took a hard-line stance and began advocating for a close association between society, state, and religion. He viewed the world as starkly divided between *Dar al-Islam* and *Dar al-Harb*. John L. Esposito acknowledges the situation facing Taymiyya, who "lived during the one of the most disruptive periods of Islamic history, which had seen the fall of Baghdad and the conquest of the Abbasid Empire in 1258 by the Mongols."[8] Later, it was the writings of Ibn Taymiyya and those of his student, Ibn al-Qaim al-Jawzi, that principally inspired religious revivalists such as Muhammad bin Abdul Wahab, as well as figures such as Sayyid Qutb, Abul A'ala Mawdudi, and Shukri Mustapha, who today are considered the primary theoreticians of radical Islam.

In sum, at the core of what has come to be known as radical Islam, or political Islam, are the concepts of *jahiliya, takfir, kufr,* and jihad.[9] Whereas in the Middle East and North Africa the term "political Islam" is well known, it may be less so in parts of West Africa. The West African region, by its sheer geographical size, cultural history, socio-political dispensation, religious orientation, and multi-ethnic nature, may be somewhat inimical to the full-scale growth of political Islam, notwithstanding the ripple effects of its penetration into the region for several decades. Still, the overall experience varies from one country to another, from Nigeria, Niger, Mali, Senegal, Gambia, and Burkina Faso to Togo and Abidjan.[10] Let us take a closer look at its manifestation in Ghana.

TAKFIR AS A TOOL FOR THE INSTIGATION OF JIHAD IN GHANA

This chapter asks the question, "What makes it impossible for Muslims in Ghana to cohere as a community, to speak with one voice?" The argument here is that the issue of *takfir* has tended to threaten unity among Muslims and has engendered unnecessary suspicion and animosity. This chapter further makes the claim that anytime Muslims have had to engage each other in a contest, the concept of *takfir* is often at play. This may be explicitly stated or implied through other means. Both hidden and manifest traces of *takfir* usually characterized Muslim-on-Muslim clashes throughout the Ghanaian past. In West Africa as well, the great Islamic revivalists who championed jihad, such as Uthman Dan Fodio, Ahmed Lobbo, and Umar Tall, were found taking cover under the banner of *takfir* whenever they were called upon to justify raising arms against those they considered nominal Muslims. The Ghanaian case of *takfir*, it must be admitted, is a mild one and is best detected by discerning minds. Hence, it is not surprising that those writers who have discussed the subject of Muslim unrest in Ghana have not paid due consideration to its influence.

HISTORICAL BACKGROUND TO THE AHLUS SUNNAH—TIJANIYYA CONFLICT

It is worth pointing out that the years before the 1970s marked a period of relative calm among Muslims in Ghana. This all changed with the outburst of conflict between the Ahlus Sunnah wal Jama'h and the Tijaniyya in that decade. Ahlus Sunnah (The People of Sunnah) is a revivalist Sunni group that assumed responsibility for ensuring that the practice of Islam in Ghana was rendered free of syncretism and acculturation. The Tijaniyyas, on the other hand, subscribe to the Sufi (mystic) tradition of Ahmad Tijani, an eighteenth-century scholar from Mauritania.

Sheikh Abdul Wadud Harun, a leading member of the Tijaniyya in Kumasi, recounts that the problems started when a group of Ghanaian Muslim scholars who had studied in Sudan, Egypt, and Saudi Arabia began returning home in the 1970s. It was mainly the violent preaching of the students from Saudi Arabia that set ablaze dissension among Muslims. Akin to the movement started by Abdul Wahab in Saudi Arabia, it was obvious that these Ahlus Sunnah scholars intended to pronounce as non-Muslims, or *takfir*, many of their Sufi counterparts, who not only had consolidated Islam in Ghana and Africa, but who also left behind ineffaceable legacies. Fortunately, the majority of the *umma* were affiliated to the Tijaniyya sect and therefore resisted this move as strongly as they could, hence the beginning of a conflict lasting several decades.[11]

The accounts of Sheikh Muhammad A. Sualah, the supervisor of the Supreme Council for Islamic Affairs in the Ashanti region and a member of the Ahlus Sunnah community in Kumasi, and Sheikh Ismail S. Adam, deputy imam of Ahlus Sunnah in the same area, seem to agree in many respects. They believe that those who introduced Islam into Ghana were mostly traders who barely resided long enough to propagate Islam properly. More so, given that Islam travelled to West Africa via North Africa before reaching Ghana, somewhere along the line it was suffused with certain Sufi practices, which the pioneering Muslims accepted wholesale, believing that the adulterated Sufi practices were genuinely part of Islam. Such was the case until some Ghanaian scholars made a pilgrimage to Mecca and acquainted themselves with true Islam in the late 1950s. Upon their return they shouldered the responsibility of reviving Islam, but they made little impact until they were joined by a group of scholars who had studied in Saudi Arabia. The movement realized major growth in the 1970s under the leadership of Sheikh Abdul Samad Habibbullah, who had lived with the Tijaniyya for thirty years before denouncing them and joining Ahlus Sunnah. His effort was complemented by the likes of Adam Baba from Saudi Arabia. The Tijaniyyas, for their part, were not prepared to let go of their doctrines, believing them to be part and parcel of Islam, and hence a struggle commenced in the late 1970s.[12]

The explanations provided by both Sheikh Muhammad A. Sualah and Sheikh S. Adam Ismail substantively conform to the observations by Alexander Knysh with respect to the evolution of religious revivalism within the main body of religious belief. He notes that there is always the tendency of creating "dramatic cleavages" between the orthodox and heterodox, between genuine religious tradition and its "corrupted surrogates."[13]

AHLUS SUNNAH-TIJANIYYA CLASHES

The first major clash between the Ahlus Sunnah and the Tijaniyya took place in Tamale, the capital of the northern region, in 1977. In this incident nine people were killed and numerous properties destroyed. The story, as narrated by an eyewitness, is that while the Tijaniyyas were holding a meeting to discuss the impending festival of *maulid nabi* (commemorating the birth of Muhammad, which is popular in West Africa), they successfully fended off a surprise attack by Alfa Yusef Ajura, the founder of Ahlus Sunnah in Tamale, and some of his followers.[14] Ajura dubbed the clash a "jihad against *bid'a* [condemned innovations] in Islam," while the Tijaniyyas termed it "the Victory of Badr." This event eclipsed an earlier encounter in 1973 that led to the temporary closure of the central mosque of Takoradi, the capital of the western region.

The series of military coups that took place in Ghana from 1977 to 1981, and the stringent rule of Jerry John Rawlings from 1982 to 1992, temporarily spared Muslims further brutal exchanges. Nathan Samwini has referred to the Rawlings period as a violence-free decade, while noting that as Ghana became more democratic in subsequent years, with a greater degree of freedom of association and freedom of speech, the clashes escalated.[15] A quick review of the newspaper headlines confirms this. Examples include "Two Muslim Sects on Rampage at Wenchi";[16] "Otumfuo warns on Religious Extremism in Kumasi";[17] "Atebubu Refugees Asked to Return";[18] "Atebubu Muslims Clash, Probe Takes Off";[19] "Security Alert at Gumani, As Clash Between Muslim Sects Results in Fatality";[20] "Property Worth Millions Destroyed";[21] "Ahlus Sunnah Muslim Leaders on Bail";[22] "The Clash of Muslim Sects at Wenchi: 57 Now Under Arrest";[23] and, after twenty-five years of religious hostilities from 1973 to 1998, "Takoradi Muslims Resolve Dispute."[24]

The above are but some highlights of the damage. In most cases, not only were human lives ended, but properties burned to ashes, with hundreds of people rendered refugees in their own country. The Atebubu case, for instance, resulted in the displacement of about 320 Muslims who had to seek refuge in nearby safe havens such as Ajura, Mampong, and Kumasi. One of the groups that called for the intervention of the government following the Wenchi clashes lamented bitterly, "Islam is a religion of peace and we should not, through our religious differences, create a bad name for it. Let us agree and disagree, but to pick up arms and kill in the name of religion is very regrettable."[25]

CLASHES IN KUMASI

Most of these clashes initially took place in the cities of Tamale and Kumasi, and later spread to the hinterlands, to Wenchi, Atebubu, Takoradi, and Sunyani. Indeed, Kumasi became one of the principal stages where both intellectual and physical battles were acted out. Perhaps the larger Muslim populace in Tamale was preoccupied with the delicate Abudu-Andani chieftaincy disputes to which both the Ahlus Sunnah and Tijaniyya sects were connected. Another factor that made Kumasi a battleground was the fact that most of the scholars who had championed the cause of Tijaniyya, as well as the Ahlus Sunnah scholars who had graduated from the Islamic University of Saudi Arabia, were concentrated there.

The first time the issue of *takfir* was verbalized was in 1989 when, at the Rex Mosque, Sheikh Hasan Shuaib, a member of the Ahlus Sunnah community, was asked whether it was legal to follow a Tijaniyya imam in prayers. The sheikh gave a very concise and clever answer, to the effect that it was permissible to follow an innovator (i.e., a Tijani) in prayers, but not recommended when there was another option. Another eminent scholar, Sheikh Tawfiq, whose opinion was revered by young men and women in the area, later asserted that it was totally forbidden to follow an innovator in prayers. The imminent danger was that this question was raised at a time when most of the regional and district mosques were being led by scholars who belonged to the Tijaniyya *tariqa* (path). Given the confusion that followed this *fatwa*, the elders of the Ahlus Sunnah agreed that the matter should be settled once and for all, and that no one should revisit it again. Surprisingly, one Friday, Sheikh Tawfiq made this contentious issue the subject of his *khutbah* (sermon), much to the annoyance of the leading founders of the group. Dr. Ahmad Umar, a founding member, immediately condemned in no uncertain terms Tawfiq's militant position and reiterated that a great deal of caution and diligence should be exercised when passing such judgments, considering the serious repercussions they had not only for the Tijaniyyas but for the Ahlus Sunnah members as well. The young men, who were not comfortable with Dr. Ahmed's rebuttal, almost pounced on him.

It was in the midst of these escalating tensions that Sheikh Tawfiq seceded from the group and formed a more activist base at Aboabo Number 2, one of the most popular districts in Kumasi. He represented a new vision of leadership for the younger students; he likewise had a clear insight into their psychological makeup. He managed to galvanize and rally them around a cause. Aboabo Number 2 also happened to be a stronghold of the Tijaniyya, and with the sheikh's uncompromising stand against them, the conflict entered one of its worst periods, recounted in the media headlines discussed above.

TIJANIYYA ACTS ATTRIBUTED TO *TAKFIR*

Naturally, any time a clash has happened in Ghana, leaders from both sides of the Muslim divide have been quick to point accusing fingers as to who started the jihad, with each trying to occupy the comfortable zone of "defensive jihad." While several attempts have been made to explain this conflict, few have addressed the one doctrinal issue that motivates Muslims to raise arms against other Muslims—that is, *takfir*. I have already suggested that the notion of *takfir* in Ghana was less intense and in most cases implied rather than direct. Of course, no one expects such a verdict to be openly declared by any worthy scholar. The implications of pronouncing *takfir* are so serious that no one would do so merely for enjoyment. The Prophet once said that if a Muslim calls another a *kafir* (unbeliever), certainly one of them is worth the title.

The idea of *takfir* in the doctrine of Ahlus Sunnah across West Africa started from an intellectual point of view. In Nigeria, the late Sheikh Abubakar Gumi, in his book *al-Aqeeda al-sahiha bi-muwafaqat al-shariah (The Correct Creed in Accordance with Shari'a)* raised serious concerns about the validity of the creeds of Tijaniyya adherents. In Ghana, Sheikh Abdul Samad Habibullah equally cast doubt on the Tijaniyyas in two of his books, *Maa da'a ilaihi deenullah (What Allah's Deen is All About)* and *Risalat da'i ilas sunnah, azzagir anil bid'a (An Epistle Which Calls for Upholding Sunna and Warns Against Bid'a)*. In the second book, Samad minced no words when he said, "I have completely absolved myself from the Tijaniyya *tariqa* which I held onto for thirty years, unaware of the dirty polytheistic creeds, which are far from Islam, which this *tariqa* contained. . ."[26]

One may wonder what these "polytheistic creeds" and their related practices are that warrant such a description. The major activities for which Ahlus Sunnah scholars have taken Tijaniyyas to task can be placed into two categories: those that relate to Tijaniyya spiritual rituals, such as the recitation of *salatul fati'h* (seeking blessings for the Prophet), and those that fall outside the spiritual realm, such as the celebration of *maulid nabi* and the observation of funeral rites. The first constitute the grounds on which the creeds of the Tijaniyyas are held to ransom, and the latter are those that are referred to as "condemned innovations." The late Baba al-Wahiz, a leading Tijani scholar, comprehensively outlines some of the issues at stake in his book *Saiful haqqi ala nuhurul wahabiyeen (The Sword of Truth on the Throat of the Wahabis)*. The volume addresses eighteen of them; however, the most relevant in connection to this chapter include "intercession," "healing and seeking protection with written verses from the Quran," "offering excessive respect to elders by bowing to them and removing footwear in their presence," "offering charity [*sadaqa*] on behalf of the deceased and saying prayers for them in groups," "the legal basis of Tijaniyya supplications [*awrad*]," and "attribution of lesser miracles [*karama*] to saints [*awliya*]."[27]

Without dwelling on the finer details of the issues raised by Baba al-Waiz, the essential question worth considering here is, "Do these activities really offer adequate grounds for passing *takfir* on others?" Emphatically, the answer is no. On the question of creeds, these are matters of the heart, and the general legal rule is that individuals should be held responsible for what they say they mean, rather than what we think they mean to say. The story of how the Prophet strongly rebuked Usama bin Zayd for killing a person who had declared his faith in battle lends credence to this. The Prophet also said, in what stands out as one of the most important quotes in the domain of *takfir*, "We only judge by that which is manifest. For that which is hidden, Allah will take care of it." On the question of the innovations, one may condemn them in the strongest terms possible, but that certainly would not constitute the grounds for passing a judgment of *takfir*.

TECHNIQUES FOR EMBARKING ON *DA'WAH*

More often than not, the immediate pretext for igniting a clash has occurred at preaching grounds, informal outdoor settings where scholars set up platforms and microphones. The latest incident in Asakore-Effiduase in 2000, which resulted in many members of the Ahlus Sunnah escaping to Kumasi, is a case in point. It is no wonder that the first major step the government takes when intervening in such incidents is to impose a temporary ban on public preaching. One may therefore ask again whether the Ahlus Sunnah has adopted the right technique regarding *da'wah* (preaching), as recommended by Quran 16:125: "Call unto the way of thy Lord with wisdom and fair exhortation, and reason with them in the better way. Lo! Thy Lord is Best Aware of him who strayeth from His way, and He is Best Aware of those who go aright." This writer asked Sheikh Ismail S. Adam if his movement had blundered in its confrontational style. He argued that it is usually the setting, the time, and the target audience that dictate the approach to be employed. He reiterated, "It was the method that we used which guaranteed the survival of the movement and consolidated its achievements thus far."[28]

Yet this writer is inclined to believe that whatever success Ahlus Sunnah has recorded could have been achieved at a much smaller cost and without causing such a deep divide among the Muslim *umma* in Ghana. One wonders what would have happened to the fate of Islam if the Prophet and his followers, at the initial stage of Islamic *da'wah*, risked demolishing the 360 in the Ka'bah. Ahlus Sunnah could have addressed whatever differences they had with the Tijaniyya by appealing to human intellect rather than by outright condemnation. Such an approach is of extreme importance, particularly in confronting condemned innovations. For in discussing *bid'a* in Islam, a *da'iya* must not pretend to be living fourteen centuries ago. The compilation of the Quran, for example, is often cited as a recommended innovation. The initial opposition by Abu Bakr and Zayd Thabit, who could not understand why they had to do something the Prophet did not do, is worthy of notice. Another good example is the case of multiple imams in the Ahlus Sunnah mosques in Ghana. This is a recent development worth emulating, for it may help break the monopoly that some individuals have gained over observation of the Imamat. Again, a *da'iya* must never lose sight of the socio-cultural realities of his environment. The total condemnation of the Tijaniyya and, for that matter, Sufism, clearly does not reflect the reality of the history of Islam in West Africa. Early scholars such as Uthman Dan Fodio, Ahmed Lobbo, and Umar Tall, who championed the cause of Islamic revivalism in a stronger sense and sought to preserve Islam against cultural corruptions in the West African region, were strong pivots around which Sufism thrived.

RETROGRADE EFFECTS AND THE END OF THE STRUGGLE

The long-standing feud between the Ahlus Sunnah and the Tijaniyya has had a devastating impact on the Muslim community in Ghana. It has given Islam a negative image in the country. Islam prides itself as a religion that promotes peace and a sense of universal brotherhood, but the rapid rate at which the clashes occurred painted a different picture altogether. By way of contrast, the many Christian denominations in the country, ranging from the highly orthodox to the highly charismatic, have managed to coexist peacefully despite their sharp ideological and theological differences. Until the suppression of the struggle in 2000, the two Muslim sects, alas, had not done the same.

The source of funding for the activities of Ahlus Sunnah has been shrouded in mystery from the very beginning and continues to generate speculation. Given the relative peace and stability that Ghana has experienced in recent years as a result of the cessation of violence in 2000, there is a strong feeling among the Tijaniyyas that it has something to do with the economic embargo the United States and its allies imposed on Islamic terrorist networks following the horrible events of 9/11. While there is no proof of this, one cannot deny the fact that this move has decreased the inflow of capital into the system and has caused some organizations, such as al-Muntada, a Saudi-linked NGO based in the United Kingdom, to become quiescent.

Other factors have also facilitated peaceful coexistence. First has been the realization among the Ahlus Sunnah and the Tijaniyyas that the conflict has been partly responsible for their backwardness and their diminished contribution to the country's socio-economic development. This awareness did not actually materialize in a vacuum; it has much to do with comparisons of their achievements with the Ahmaddis, another Muslim sect in Ghana since 1921, whose socio-economic contribution to the country in the pre- and post-independence eras has been phenomenal.

Second, most graduates in Islamic and Arabic studies from Arab countries like Saudi Arabia and Egypt seem to have found a better way to integrate themselves into the Ghanaian economy. Usually their credentials are now translated into English, they are required to do national service, and they are subsequently employed through the Voluntary Services Agency. Even though this integration has not yet been formalized, it has cooled off the economic factor that triggered clashes in the past.

Third, the American Embassy, through its outreach program to the Muslim community in Ghana, has played a laudable role in promoting peace. Under the auspices of this program, many of the leaders of both sects travelled to the United States to learn what religious tolerance within a diverse community is all about. Since 2003, the Embassy has continuously organised *iftar* (group supper during Ramadan), where leaders of all religious sects are invited to talks on the essence of religious toleration.[29]

Fourth, the separation of the mosques, with the Ahlus Sunnah acquiring their own and no longer being dependent on the Tijaniyya sites, despite initially being deemed a disuniting factor, has proved helpful. Aside from facilitating easy access to prayer grounds, it has minimized the tendency of the sects to be constantly at each other's throats. Gone are the days, in

Kumasi or Accra, for example, when the faithful could observe Friday Jumu'ah only at military camp mosques or central mosques.

Last, internal divisions among both the Ahlus Sunnah and Tijaniyya have diluted the aggressiveness of both sects. The major split among the Ahlus Sunnah is between the more militant wal Jama'h wing and the Majlis. The latter, for instance, do not see any urgency in creating the office of National Imam of Ahlus Sunnah, an idea proposed by the former group. The Tijaniyya have also encountered divisions among themselves, starting in the late 1980s, when it became known that the late Malam Abudullah Maikano, a well-known scholar and leader of the Tijaniyya brotherhood, had married more than four wives. The tension between the supporters of Malam Maikano and the other Tijaniyyas, who condemned the former for dragging the name of the movement into disrepute, has over the years become rife as well.

DERIVING LESSONS, PROMOTING PEACE

It is essential that the Muslim *umma* in Ghana derives the appropriate lessons from the events described in this chapter. The question we must ask is, "In what innovative ways can we deepen and consolidate further the tolerance and peace that has existed for the past five years?" What specific roles can Muslim elders and preachers play to reinforce the peace so that we can gear our energies and resources toward contributing to the socio-economic progress of the country and giving Islam the image it richly deserves?

My primary concern is directed to the Islamic *du'at* (preachers), due to the unique influence they wield in terms of molding and reforming societies. Preachers may be described as politicians of the human soul. In today's multifaceted world, there are some basic facts that an Islamic *da'iya* must not lose sight of. The first is that division is a natural phenomenon among humans and that diversity of thoughts, views, or even creeds does not necessarily amount to enmity. In fact, anyone who seeks to have the *umma* agree on everything must be living in a utopian realm. Such a demand may even be deemed a direct challenge to the message inherent in Quran 11:118–119, namely, that disagreement among humans is natural: "And if your Lord had so willed, he could surely have made mankind one *umma*, but mankind will never cease to disagree, except him on whom your Lord has bestowed His mercy, and so did he create them ..."

This point granted, the primary focus of a preacher must be to promote those ideals that unite us as Muslims rather than the few that divide us. We must avoid passing judgment in our preaching, for when we do so we are indirectly arrogating to ourselves a divine function. Indeed, the worst form of judgment is *takfir*. By pronouncing this verdict we incite Muslims to attack one another, making ourselves victims of the Prophetic quote: "Any time two Muslims raise up arms against each other, both the killer and the killed will end up in hell. The companions asked: 'Oh Prophet, the position of the killer is well established, what about the killed?' The Prophet said: 'Yes, when he took up the arms, his intention as well was to kill his fellow Muslim brother.'"

While speaking on the subject of unity in Islam, Yasin Rushdi, a celebrated Egyptian scholar, expressed his strong wish that Muslims abandon the innovative nomenclatures with which they have branded Islam. For example, he stressed that by calling oneself a Sufi, which means someone whose heart has been purified, the implication is that the rest of the *umma* bears an unclean heart. As well, when a person calls him- or herself "Ahlu Sunnah," i.e., "followers of Sunnah," he or she is presupposing that others are followers of *bid'a*. Rushdi reiterated that the greatest pride of the Prophet and the Companions had been to proclaim, "I am a Muslim." What other name could be more welcome?[30]

CONCLUSION

This chapter opened by establishing the relationship between *jahiliya, takfir,* and jihad in the light of Ibn Taymiyya's *fatwa* authorizing jihad against the Mongols. It was argued thereafter that the concept of radical political Islam, which was conceived and nurtured by Sayyid Qutb, Abul A'ala Mawdudi, Shukri Mustapha, and others, was built upon the basis of these terms as well as on the perceived legitimacy that Ibn Taymiyya bestowed upon them.

Subsequently, this chapter asserted that when Muslims in Ghana engaged in conflict, *takfir* must have been at work, albeit in an implicit manner. It proceeded to critique the propensity of Ahlus Sunnah scholars to adjudge the beliefs and rituals of the Tijaniyyas as *kufr,* and concluded that they do not, from an Islamic jurisprudence point of view, have grounds for passing *takfir* on others. It was noted that the causes of the conflict demonstrate an apparent failure to adopt the appropriate technique of *da'wah.*

This chapter also examined the factors that led to the spread of tolerance between the two Muslim sects and affirmed that there are concrete factors underpinning the peace and stability enjoyed in recent years. Last, the lessons that must be learned from the clashes as a whole have been highlighted, with emphasis placed on the role that Islamic scholars and preachers should play to ensure that such events remain in the past.

NOTES

1. Ghana Statistical Services (GSS), *2000 Population and Housing Census, Summary Report of Final Results* (Accra: Ghana Statistical Report Press, 2002).

2. Nathan Samwini, *The Muslim Resurgence in Ghana Since 1950: Its Effects Upon Muslims and Muslim-Christian Relations* (New Brunswick: Transaction Publishers, 2003), 80; Mbillah Johnson, "The Causes of Present Day Muslim Unrest in Ghana" (unpublished Ph.D. thesis, University of Birmingham, 1998), passim.

3. See M.A. Mohar, *The History of the Prophet and the Orientalists* (Riyadh: King Fahd Complex, 1997), 1: 68.

4. See Yusuf al-Qardawi, "Islamic Awakening: Between Rejection and Extremism," in *Liberal Islam: A Sourcebook*, ed. Charles Kurzman (Oxford: Oxford University Press, 1988).

5. Some of the verses that discuss jihad and *qital* in the Quran include, but are not limited to, 22:39–41, 2:190–94, 2:246–51, 8:39–40, 8:61–62, 8:65, 47:20, 48:17.

6. For detail on this, see Abubakar J. al-Jazairi, *The Muslim's Path: The Book of Creed, Manners, Morals, and Social Dealings* (Riyadh: King Fahd Complex, n.d), 282.

7. Emmanuel Sivan, *Radical Islam: Medieval Theology and Modern Politics*, enlarged ed. (New Haven: Yale University Press, 1990), 96.

8. John L. Esposito, *Unholy War: Terror in the Name of Islam* (New York: Oxford University Press, 2002), 45.

9. For details on how these terms relate to one another, refer to David Zeidan, "The Islamic Fundamentalist View of Life as a Perennial Battle," *Middle East Review of International Affairs* 5, no. 4 (December 2001).

10. See Ricardo Laremont and Hrach Gregorian, "Political Islam in West Africa and the Sahel," *Military Review* 86, no. 1 (January/February 2006): 27–36; and William F.S. Miles, ed., *Political Islam in West Africa: State-Society Relations Transformed* (Boulder: Lynne Rienner Publishers, 2007).

11. Interview with Sheikh Abdul Wadud, a leading figure of the Tijaniyya during the clashes, February 27, 2008.

12. Interviews with Sheikh Muhammad A. Sualah, the Supervisor of Supreme Council for Islamic Affairs, Ashanti Region, and Sheikh S. Adam Ismail, Deputy Imam of Ahlus Sunnah wal Jama'h, Ashanti Region, February 27, 2008.

13. Alexander Knysh, "Orthodoxy and Heresy in Medieval Islam: An Essay in Reassessment," *The Muslim World* 63, no. 1 (January 1999), 49.

14. See Johnson, "The Causes of Present Day Muslim Unrest in Ghana," 284.

15. Samwini, *The Muslim Resurgence in Ghana*, 193–94.

16. *Daily Graphic*, June 16, 1995, 1/3.

17. Ibid., December 5, 1995, 1.

18. *Ghanaian Times*, June 4, 1996, 1.

19. Ibid., June 24, 1996, 3; January 5, 1998, 1.

20. *Daily Graphic*, December 6, 1997, 1/3.

21. Ibid., December 12, 1997, 1.

22. Ibid., December 12, 1997, 1/3.

23. Ibid., January 20, 1998, 1.

24. *Ghanaian Times*, July 3, 1998, 3.

25. *Daily Graphic*, January 20, 1998, 1.

26. Abdul Samad Habibullah, *Risalat dahi ilas sunnah, azzagir anil bid'a* (Beirut: Darul Arabia Press, 1978), 31.

27. Baba Ahmed al-Waiz, *Saiful haqq ala nūrul wahabiyeen* (unpublished, unclassified, IAS archive, 1973), 5–6.

28. Interview with Sheikh Ismael Saeed Adam, February 27, 2008.

29. See http://www.state.gov/g/drl/rls/irf/2006/71304.htm.

30. Yasin Rushdi, *We are Muslims* (undated audio cassette).

PART V

Political Islam in Iran, Iraq, and Palestine

CHAPTER 10

Reading Tehran in Washington: The Problems of Defining the Fundamentalist Regime in Iran and Assessing the Prospects for Political Change

Ofira Seliktar

From its inception, the fundamentalist regime in Iran has defied classification, triggering a fierce debate among observers. This lack of consensus stems from the difficulty of Western analysts to comprehend key features of the Islamic Republic, aggravated by the limits of Western political vocabulary. One popular theory holds that the fundamentalists created an Islamic version of a fascist state, often labeled as "Islamofascism." Academic discourse has yielded such definitions as Islamic theocracy, Islamic police state, a barrack regime, garrison state, Islamic neopatrimonialism, clerical oligarchy, or theodemocracy.

The quest to understand the Islamic Republic has vital policy applications. Iran, a major geopolitical player in the Middle East, has used terrorism to destabilize neighboring states, derailed the Arab-Israeli peace process, and created a nuclear energy program that is suspected to be preparatory to constructing a nuclear bomb. Taking a page from Ronald Reagan's playbook on communism, the Clinton administration tried to effect regime change in Tehran. Indeed, many leading Iran experts claimed the reformist victory in the "Tehran Spring" of 1997 was a harbinger of the coming democracy, only to be taken aback by the election of the hard-line Mahmoud Ahmadinejad in 2005.

Such prognostications are a testimony to the intellectual convention that treats Iran as a unitary actor in the Western mode and expects it to follow a Western-style trajectory of change. Using Max Weber's analysis of political authority, this work argues that the Iranian clerics have evolved a unique hybrid political system that reflects Islamist and European elements. The sheer intricacy, confusion, and unpredictability of this system have repeatedly confounded Iran watchers and have made assessment of political change difficult. The 2009 presidential election made this task even more complicated, as its unexpected outcome may signal a break with the foundational character of the Islamic Republic.

LEGITIMACY AND POLITICAL REGIMES: ORIGIN, MAINTENANCE, AND CHANGE

Max Weber, in his well-known study *On Charisma and Institution Building*, postulated that individuals are persuaded to obey political authority and to comply with its coercive power due to compliance with legitimacy principles underlying the political order; these are expressed as normative validity claims, "reasoned elaborations" embedded in the collective discourse of a society.[1]

Weber identified three pure validity claims—rational, traditional, and charismatic—that have often been conflated into two categories: the rational-legal and the numinous-traditional. The former is said to be derived from the consent of the members of a collective and is contractual in nature; the latter is based on claims of a divine right that is conferred on a designated representative of the super-rational authority. Procedural rules required to establish and maintain rational-legal legitimacy obviously include those employed by democracies (i.e., periodic elections), but rules pertaining to numinous-traditional authority are vague. Complicating dependence upon simplistic constructs, regimes have historically used a bewildering combination of validity claims to legitimize their rule; various mixes of traditional, charismatic, and rational-legal claims have been bolstered by either restricted or "ritualistic" elections.

Weber's analysis indicates that change is generated when certain validity claims are delegitimized in the discursive process and replaced by others, followed by a change in political institutions and processes. Scholars have struggled to identify the ways in which individuals delegitimize established norms. At the core of the problem is the difficulty in deducing how norms of legitimacy operate as a mental construct. One view holds that legitimacy is sentimental and diffuse, a "strong inner conviction of the moral validity of the authority system."[2] A competing view asserts that legitimacy is functional, that is, related to the performance of the system, particularly in terms of material benefits.[3] Rational choice theory suggests that when considering a challenge to validity norms, individuals engage in a complex calculus of costs and benefits. On the positive side, there are psychic and material rewards that stimulate feelings of legitimacy; on the negative side lie fear of opprobrium, punishment, and coercion that may dissuade an individual from rejecting established norms. The latter may trigger learned helplessness or preference falsification, defined as a decision to conceal true beliefs and adopt behavior expected by the regime.[4]

Given the lack of consensus, students of legitimacy argued that individuals are guided by a mix of three modes: an integrative mode based on a diffuse sense of support for the authority system, an exchange mode based on benefits that it provides to individuals, and a threat system based on its coercive power.[5] In democracies, the integrative mode is dominant, followed by the exchange mode. In totalitarian regimes, the threat mode plays a large role in creating the appearance of legitimacy, with exchange considerations substituting for intrinsic support.

Weber's treatment offers an insight into the complex nature of the fundamentalist regime in Iran and its remarkable ability to survive challenges to its legitimacy.

THE ISLAMIC REPUBLIC: RELIGIOUS DESPOTISM AND DEMOCRATIC IMPOTENCE

In the wake of the fundamentalist revolution in 1979, Ayatollah Ruhollah Khomeini laid the foundation for a numinous authority system based on the novel doctrine of Islamic governance of *velayat-e-faqih*, the divine rule by a religious guardian. Khomeini saw such rule as indispensable for the creation of a "republic of virtue," an Islamic polity and society based on the Quranic principles where people, considered to be deficient by nature, could be perfected (thereby assuring their salvation). Khomeini and his followers justified such religious despotism by claiming it would block the emergence of "flawed and non-divine perspectives and ideas that are aimed at enhancing the power of the individual to dictate its social and political lives." As one Khomeini loyalist put it, "The legitimacy of our Islamist establishment is derived from God. The legitimacy will not wash away, even if people stop supporting it."[6]

While the concept of divinely guided guardianship required a religious theocracy, Khomeini could not ignore the democratic ferment that had toppled the shah. Mindful of his broad-based coalition of secularists and Western-style liberals, the Ayatollah had to flavor the numinous validity claims with rational-legal legitimacy vested in the "people." Though dissonant with the assertion that ordinary people "lack the perspicacity to distinguish between good and evil," Khomeini was compelled to add a contractual component to the Islamist Republic, paving the way to an elected assembly, the Majlis, and an elected presidency.[7]

By compromising on the issue of numinous legitimacy, Khomeini avoided the crippling costs of imposing and maintaining a religious totalitarianism. Still, the constitution of 1979 clearly safeguarded the dominance of the *velayat-e-faqih*, turned into a Supreme Spiritual Leader. An Assembly of Experts of Leadership, a deliberative body of 86 *mujtahids* (learned clerics), elects the Supreme Leader and supervises his actions. Members of the Assembly are elected from a government list of candidates by direct vote for eight year terms. The charismatic Ayatollah Khomeini, who became the Supreme Leader before the Assembly of Experts was established, controlled all aspects of governance, including the armed forces and the judiciary. The Council of Guardians, whose 12 members are not popularly elected, extends the reach of Islamic governance; it approves the credentials of candidates for the Majlis and the presidency and judges the compatibility of Majlis legislation with Islamic principles. In a unique arrangement, the Supreme Leader serves as the commander-in-chief and the head of the Supreme National Security Council. A 1989 amendment extended the powers of the Supreme Leader to include control over all national media.

By design and default, clashing imperatives of such bifurcated legitimacy created an extremely complex power arrangement in which a large number of elites compete in statist forums as well as parallel channels that duplicate state functions. The parallel structure of coercion is a case in point. Article 151 of the constitution obligates the government to provide military training to all citizens who have the ability to take up arms to defend the state. In 1979, Khomeini created the Iranian Revolutionary Guards Corps (IRGC) and its Basji militia that unleashed the "Reign of Terror," the bloody suppression of leftists, liberals, and labor. The Ministry of Intelligence and Security (MOIS) is another enigmatic organization with complex links to the Supreme Leader, the Guards, and their al Quds unit that runs terrorist operations abroad.

Unlike the dual state-party structure in Nazi Germany and the Soviet Union, the Iranian system is polycentric, creating a negotiated political order. In addition to clashes between the clerical establishment and the legislative body, there are ongoing tensions between the state bureaucracy and the parallel, non-statist centers of powers. To confuse matters, each of these elites has fragmented internally along ideological and/or personal lines. The chaotic, fluid, and opaque nature of Iranian politics stems from the fact that power is negotiated among the various groups, sometimes in highly dramatic ways, but more often through subtle, barely detectable symbolic exchanges. The constant give-and-take of such a process has prevented the reemergence of the kind of legitimacy crisis that toppled the shah.

If the negotiated political order accounts for the durability of the Islamic Republic, the Islamist economic system helps to nourish its exchange-based legitimacy. Historical observations and rational choice theory indicate that the economic well-being of individuals has a universal impact on their evaluation of political authority. Nevertheless, the actual mechanism by which individuals judge the economic output of their government is filtered by notions of distributive justice. Validity claims that underlie modern market economies derive from the principles of merit and efficiency, but do not address the large social gaps that capitalism creates. Influenced by egalitarian notions of distributive justice, Ali Shariati, a neo-Marxist intellectual, developed a novel synthesis between Islam and socialism. Shariati condemned the budding market economy of the shah and called for a return to an egalitarian system based on the Quran. While still in exile, Khomeini adopted Shariati's precepts, peppering his messages with references to the Islamic justice concept of *adalah*, which prohibits gross disparities in wealth, and the plight of the *mustazafin*, the poor and dispossessed.

Once in power, the anti-shah coalition split over the particulars of an Islamic economy. Socialists like Abdolhasan Bani Sadr, Sadiq Gobzadeh, and radical clergy such as Ayatollah Mahmud Talaqani pressed for large-scale nationalization and redistribution of wealth. However, wealthy clerics and merchants were strongly opposed to state-run socialism. Reflecting these various imperatives, the constitution provides for an enormous state sector comprised of all large-scale industry (including oil, banking, aviation, shipping, and communications). A small cooperative sector calls for companies "concerned with production and distribution" to be run in accordance with "Islamic criteria"; the even smaller private sector is confined to agriculture, husbandry, trade, and services.

Nationalization and confiscation of royal assets and upper-class property concentrated up to 80 percent of the economy in the hands of the state and public sector, either through direct ownership or through a number of large revolutionary and religious foundations, the *bonyads*. Clerics and other regime loyalists have used the foundations, which operate outside the regulatory sphere of the state, as their power bases. The Iranian Revolutionary Guards Corps is the largest beneficiary of the *bonyad* system, presiding over a vast economic empire that includes both ownership of oil, telecommunication, and transportation companies and command over the nuclear and military industries, including missile production. Over the years, the IRGC, which has an extensive network of contacts in the government bureaucracy, has profited from lucrative no-bid contracts, including the $1.2 billion tender to develop the huge South Pars oil field. Because of its murky character, the real worth of the IRGC's enterprises is virtually impossible to estimate.

During the 1980s, inefficiencies of a state-run economy, mismanagement, massive corruption, and the burden of the Iraq-Iran war caused a negative Gross Domestic Product in all but the oil sector. To prevent the resulting economic hardship from undermining popular support, the regime resorted to subsidizing basic foods, fuel, and an array of services, resulting in the establishment of subsidies as a key instrument of the Islamist pledge of social justice. Inflationary pressures created by this remedy were addressed through a combination of loans from the Central Bank and foreign borrowing. Unlike other socialist states that were forced to adopt market principles in the 1980s, Iran's oil revenues prevented an economic collapse and alleviated pressure to privatize the economy. Nevertheless, the resulting budgetary imbalance created stagflation: high rates of inflation that reached 70 percent in the 1990s and high rates of unemployment in a country where natural growth—50 percent of the population is under the age of twenty—has required rapid job creation.[8]

To tackle these problems, the state's Plan and Budget Organization (PBO) produced the First Five-Year Development Plan (1989–1994) and a Second Five-Year Development Plan (1995–2000). Among its key goals was privatizing and liberalizing the economy, modernizing the financial sector, introducing a single exchange rate for currency, and developing mechanisms for transparency and accountability. The PBO planners also recommended a sharp reduction in subsidies. However, key sections of the PBO plans were either ignored by the *bonyads* or sabotaged by a coalition of the Revolutionary Guards, conservative merchants, and mullahs. With the authorities increasingly forced to use brutal methods to suppress the mass protest against unemployment and deteriorating standards of living in the 1990s, there was little appetite for abolishing the subsidies. The vision of a market economy was, in the words of one observer, "abhorrent" to these elites.[9]

If the exchange system has protected the regime from delegitimizing impulses, the control and coercion system has created the necessary threat perception that generated learned helplessness and preference falsification, which, as noted, minimizes demands for change. The introduction of Shari'a law shocked liberals and many women in the anti-shah coalition who resisted the Islamist agenda of creating a "regime woman," who was preferably a "housewife and mother, modest of dress and demeanor, pious, dutiful and committed to raising children . . . under the wise guidance of men."[10] Particularly unpopular were mandatory dress codes and public and workplace segregation and discrimination. In addition, the regime abolished Pahlavi-era legislation that enabled women to petition courts regarding divorce and child custody.

The incompatibility of the political order in the Islamic Republic with Western-style human and political rights has fomented protest among a broad swath of the population. In addition to women, the intellectual elites—writers, university professors, journalists—have fought for free speech, and labor unions have demanded the right to use labor disputes and strikes to fight for better working conditions. The teacher unions—a sector dominated by women—have demonstrated for better pay and government investment in the crumbling educational infrastructure.

Although there was no repeat of Khomeini's "Reign of Terror," the regime has relied on considerable coercion to quell protest since the 1990s. Human Rights Watch and Amnesty International, among others, have documented a wide array of coercive measures, including murder, abductions, arbitrary incarceration, torture, prolonged solitary confinement, show trials, use of vigilantes, and threats against family members. They have concluded that such steps have been highly successful in eliminating opposition leaders. Threat of dismissal has proven effective in intimidating rank-and-file workers. Special vice squads have broken down the widespread resistance to Shari'a lifestyle laws by meting out stiff punishments to offenders.

The parallel power structure of the Islamic Republic facilitates the management of the control and coercion system. Many of the detention centers are run by the Revolutionary Guards and are virtually autonomous from state controls. Under General Qassam Kagar, a former IRGC commander, the Ashura Brigades enforce the Islamic dress code and patrol the universities. Groups of self-professed vigilantes, the Hezbollahis (who have murky connections to the Revolutionary Guards and the Basji), monitor the workplace, harass dissidents, firebomb bookstores, disrupt meetings, and physically and verbally assault "enemies of the state." The Revolutionary Guards run many of the detention centers— including the notorious Evin prison, the secretive Prison 59 in Tehran, and underground centers around the country—where brutal torture has been administered. The Islamic Revolutionary Courts (which preside over a wide array of security, economic, and lifestyle crimes) are part of the parallel system of governance; the mullah judges have been known to legitimize torture and other abusive practices against political detainees.

The above analysis provides a schematic view of the working of the system. The following discussion offers a look at a case study of its dynamics.

RAFSANJANI, KHATAMI, AND AHMADINEJAD: A CASE STUDY IN REGIME MAINTENANCE

From its inception, the Islamic Republic has struggled with challenges to its legitimacy. The issue of reconciling the principles of Islamic justice with economic performance has proved to be particularly vexing. Khomeini's limited economic understanding aggravated the problem; as Bani Sadr related, "We were asking, how can we increase production and Khomeini was asking, how can we increase our faith."[11] After the Ayatollah's death in 1989, the simmering struggle between the Islamist literalists and the more pragmatic clergy and their secular allies intensified. Ayatollah Ali-Akbar Hashemi Rafsanjani, one of the architects of the revolution, was elected president in the same year and led the pragmatists.

Mindful of the need to improve economic performance to bolster exchange-based legitimacy, Rafsanjani and his party, the Servants of Construction, set out to replace the revolutionary commitment to the *mustazafin* with a market-oriented approach modeled after China's. Signaling Iran's willingness to conform to international norms, his Foreign Minister, Ali Akbar Velayati, claimed, "Economic considerations overshadow political priorities." In what resembled a classic market argument, Rafsanjani took to claiming that a modern economy would not only address the issue of inequality, but would also generate the sense of well-being necessary for the Islamic Republic to survive.[12]

Rafsanjani, an astute observer of the public discourse, was also perturbed by the amount of coercion needed to limit rebellion by the younger generation against Islamist values and by others who were critical of clerical corruption fed by the *bonyads*. Worried that the resulting disaffection would create a legitimacy crisis, Rafsanjani wanted to relax moral strictures and provide more personal and political freedoms. Although Rafsanjani and his circle of pragmatic clerics and economic technocrats were loyal to the numinous principles enunciated by Khomeini, the proposed reforms threatened to alter the missionary goals of the state. By elevating the exchange component in the legitimacy equation, if successful, the reform would have diminished the role of the state as a provider of personal salvation.

For the ideological purists, such a change was anathema. The head of the Guardian Council, Ayatollah Ahmad Jannati, averred that the role of the state was to support "[t]rue Islamic culture by reinforcing the religious bedrock of the people and fighting all those who are anti-Islamic and Western-stricken," a reference to "Westoxication," a term coined by Jalal Al-e Ahmad, an iconoclastic intellectual who accused his countrymen of developing a false identity based on Western values. Ali Khamenei, the new hard-line Supreme Leader, affirmed that religion rather than economy was the constitutive domain of the state, stating that "[i]f we spend billions on development projects and ignore moral issues, all achievements amount to nothing."[13]

By manipulating the lists of eligible candidates in the 1992 election, Rafsanjani's hard-line opponents captured 150 out of the 270 seats in the Majlis. The Second Five-Year Plan scheduled for March 1994 was delayed for a year by fierce parliamentary opposition. Even so, many of its targets went unfulfilled because so much of the economy was outside the purview of the state. The government's lifestyle reforms and efforts to relax coercion met with an equally determined opposition from the Revolutionary Guards, the MOIS, the Basji, and the Ashura Brigades.

With little to show for his efforts, Rafsanjani ended his second term in 1997 presiding over a status quo economy with negative growth rates, a shrinking per capita GDP, a recession, and a record foreign debt of $30 billion, aggravated by a decline in oil prices. Although the president could count on popular support and the pragmatist-technocratic elite in the state bureaucracy, he became defensive and increasingly deferred to Islamist sensibilities; unable or unwilling to challenge his rivals, Rafsanjani often retreated from his own principles or defended them in the approved religious rhetoric.

If the mixture of obstructionisms and coercions was able to cow the pragmatic-technocratic elite, it proved less successful in staving off an ideological rebellion fomented by a loose alliance of religious leaders and lay activists in the Khomeini revolution. Not unlike Mikhail Gorbachev and his allies in the Politburo who decided to reform communism, the Iranian counter-elite asserted that the Islamic Republic was facing a major crisis of legitimacy. Ayatollah Hussein Ali Montazeri, once a designated successor to Khomeini, Ayatollah Jalaleddin Taheri, Hojjatolislam Mohsen Kadivar, and others accused Khomeini and his successors of misinterpreting the Quran to establish a temporal authority. The philosopher Abdol Karim Soroush went so far as to argue that the legitimacy of the authority system should rest on a "collective rationality" reaffirmed through democratic elections. In what some observers described as the "Islamic Reformation," Soroush and his colleagues adopted the Protestant notion of personal voluntaristic piety. In this view, the state should limit its role to providing a framework for the free exercise of religion rather than force salvation-appropriate behavior.[14]

Another insider, Hojjatolislam Seyyed Muhammad Khatami, the Minister of Culture who was fired in 1992 for relaxing censorship, shared this reformist impulse. Khatami, seen as an inoffensive intellectual, was approved by the Guardian Council to run as a nominal candidate for president against the hard-line Speaker of the Parliament, Ali Akbar Nateq-Nuri, in 1997. Much to the surprise of the conservatives, Khatami garnered 69 percent of the vote; he topped this success in 2001 when he won 77.8 percent of the vote. This resounding victory for a relatively unknown cleric was widely seen as a popular mandate to limit, if not abolish, the Islamic Republic.

The reformist agenda was two-fold. Like Rafsanjani, Khatami and his cabinet of economic technocrats understood that the stagnant economy, hobbled by years of corruption and mismanagement, needed to be restructured and privatized. In August 1998, he presented an Economic Recovery Plan designed to stimulate employment, break the monopolies, curb the foundations, and increase badly needed foreign investment. To broaden the economy, the plan advocated industrialization and development of non-oil exports. The Third Five-Year Plan (2000–2005) reflected these priorities. In an effort to fight the sanctions policy and end Iran's international isolation, Khatami declared that his country was ready to abandon terrorism and embrace the Oslo peace process. In a 2000 CNN interview, Khatami called for a "dialogue of civilizations" to counteract the then-current concern with the "clash of civilizations."

Khatami's civil and political reforms were even more ambitious. The government lifted some of the more onerous lifestyle restrictions and ignored others, notably the strict dress code for women. In the first wave of what became known as the "Tehran Spring," there was a dramatic increase in freedom of speech and the press, epitomized by a loosening of the censorship guidelines. Dozens of newspapers and journals appeared, along with hundreds of publications. Western books, banned since the revolution, were translated, adding to the growing body of ideas that challenged the Islamic Republic. The government granted permits for scores of new associations, professional groups, and free trade unions. So much so, that both Iranian observers and Western watchers heralded the advent of a vibrant civil society. The reformers' victories in the 1998 municipal elections and the 2000 parliamentary contest seemed to bear out this assumption.

Following the complex rules of the negotiated political order, the hardliners, faced with massive support for Khatami, refrained from a public assault on the president. Instead, they relied on the power of the foundations, state managers, and conservative merchants to sabotage the economic reforms and used the Revolutionary Guards and MOIS to persecute reformers and dissidents. For his part, Khatami, a cautious and low-key leader, was highly reluctant to take on the Supreme Leader or the Guardian Council, let alone the revolutionary security forces. Commenting on his reelection in 2001, the *New York Times* presciently noted that "the other government" made up of hard-line conservative clerics and their foot soldiers was likely to run Iran, "while the state that Khatami purports to represent remains on the sidelines."[15]

Ironically, by defusing the legitimacy crisis, Khatami's "Tehran Spring" helped the Iranian Republic to survive. Yet it also galvanized a new generation of hard-line opponents described as Iranian neoconservatives. At its core was the Alliance of Builders of Islamic Iran (Abadgaran), a coalition of younger politicians (with roots in the IRGC, revolutionary foundations, and religious seminaries) that urged the revival of Khomeini's orthodoxy. In 1999, General Muhammad Ali Jafari and other Guards leaders wrote a letter threatening to take "necessary measures to establish Islamic values." Circumventing the state, the Guards and the Basji increasingly murdered reformers and imprisoned and tortured others. The popular reformist mayor of Tehran was accused of corruption in a show trial, and more than a hundred publications were closed and their editors jailed.[16]

Khatami's inability to protect his followers was matched by his embarrassment over an increasingly belligerent Iranian foreign policy, driven by the Revolutionary Guards and al Quds. Using their control of Bank

Melli and Bank Saderat, and ties to the Central Bank, the Guards funneled large sums of money to Hezbollah, Hamas, and Islamic Jihad in order to destabilize Lebanon and undermine the Oslo peace process.[17] A year after Khatami's plea for a "dialogue of civilizations," the Israeli navy seized the Karine A, a boat loaded with Iranian weapons destined for the Palestinian Intifada. The resulting publicity highlighted the role played by Imad Mughniyeh, the arch-terrorist and co-founder of Hezbollah and its chief liaison to MOIS and al Quds. Worse for a president who tried to dispel Iran's image as a rogue state, in 2002 the American intelligence community obtained evidence—subsequently confirmed by the International Atomic Energy Agency (IAEA)—of a secret nuclear program in Nantaz and Arak. Following Operation Iraqi Freedom in 2003, the Revolutionary Guards cooperated with the Mahdi Army of the radical cleric Muqtada al Sader to mount a serious challenge to American troops.

Khatami's increasingly lame duck presidency, coupled with an economic slump, did little to revive the political fortunes of the reformers. They were even less prepared for a well-organized campaign led by Mahmoud Ahmadinejad, then a little-known Abadgaran leader with previous service in the Guards. In 2003, Ahmadinejad was named mayor of Tehran and, in 2005, he handily defeated the reformist candidate Mustafa Moeen (of the Iran Participation Front) in the first round of balloting in the presidential election. Much to the surprise of everyone, Ahmadinejad garnered 61.7 percent of the vote in the second round, defeating his main rival, Hashemi Rafsanjani. Promising to put "the oil money on people's tables," Ahmadinejad and his colleagues criticized clerical corruption and the growing gap between the poor and rich.

In contrast to the pragmatic Rafsanjani and the market-oriented Khatami, Ahmadinejad pushed to reinstate the Islamist economy of Shariati in order to remedy the persistent inequality gap. The Abadgaran parliamentary faction introduced legislation that effectively undercut the market reforms of the prior decade; it rolled back privatization, hampered foreign investment, and made it difficult for the government to negotiate deals with foreign companies. Ahmadinejad moved even more quickly to eliminate the civil liberties of the Khatami era, triggering an unprecedented spike in coercive measures against lifestyle violators and regime opponents. Suppression of the independent labor movement has been especially harsh; in a highly symbolic showdown, the leader of the bus drivers union of the IRGC-owned Vahed Company, Mansour Osanlou, was imprisoned and Mahmoud Salehi, the head of the Bakery Workers Association in a provincial town, has been held in prison in spite of a serious health condition.

To compensate for the legitimacy deficit, Ahmadinejad adopted a confrontational foreign policy that, among other goals, called for "wiping out" Israel and questioned the Holocaust. In 2007, the authorities arrested a number of American-Iranians on charges of conspiring against the Islamic Republic, and the Guards seized British sailors outside Iran's territorial waters. More to the point, Ahmadinejad refused to abandon the nuclear enrichment program in spite of considerable pressure from the international community.

While appeals to traditional Iranian nationalism earned Ahmadinejad the name "dark genius" of public relations, his foreign policy was more than an exercise in public mobilization. Ahmadinejad and the Abadgaran elites have embraced the Khomeini dictate of a permanent revolution in the Middle East and beyond. Some analysts suggest that Ahmadinejad may have a mystical belief in his own mission, as part of the mahdaviat movement that has been preparing for the coming of the Mahdi. Ayatollah Mohammad Taqi Mesbah Yazdi, the spiritual leader of the Abadgaran, has been a prominent figure in mahdaviat circles.[18]

Whatever the divine inspiration for Ahmadinejad's policy, his performance has earned mixed reviews. The continuous economic crisis has been a major source of contention. Critics, including many among Rafsanjani's pragmatic-technocratic elite, have argued that reliance on oil revenues to finance subsidies and buy cheap imports for the poor has kept the inflation level at 30 percent and has forestalled job creation in local industries. Ahmadinejad further weakened fiscal reasonability by lowering interest rates to 10 percent, much to the chagrin of the Central Bank. The new regulations against foreign investment starved the crucial oil sector of funding for much-needed modernization. Shortages in natural gas and electricity led to rolling blackouts and kept many without heat during the severe winter of 2008. Shortages of gasoline and staples have triggered periodic riots that the Revolutionary Guards have had to put down.

In addition to the Rafsanjani pragmatists, the Supreme Leader Khamenei was reported to be critical of his protégé. Khamenei and traditional conservatives apparently have been worried that the economic hardship would unleash a major legitimacy crisis and undermine the regime. Khamenei was also said to be upset by the forced resignation in 2007 of Ali Larijani, Iran's top nuclear negotiator, because he implied that Iran was more open to negotiations with the international community than the official hard-line had suggested. Although both Rafsanjani and Khamenei have been staunch supporters of the nuclear program, they and traditional conservatives have preferred the strategy of obfuscation and deception rather than the open confrontation favored by Ahmadinejad.

The subtle but fierce jostling among the various elites culminated in the March 2008 Majlis election, billed as a referendum on Ahmadinejad's tenure. Some 70 percent of the reformist Islamic Participation Front candidates were disqualified, but, significantly, the recommendation came from the local Executive Councils controlled by Abadgaran loyalists rather than from the Guardian Council, a stronghold of Khamenei. Using the local boards was seen as a clever maneuver to get the Supreme Leader and the Guardian Council to share the blame for what was, even by the standards of the Islamic Republic, a blatant disregard for the civic-contractual element of its authority system. For his part, Khamenei was eager to dispel his differences with Ahmadinejad; describing the nuclear program as "a great success" of the revolution, he praised the president and "the people who have stood up all over the country over the nuclear issue." Still, Khamenei's new protégé, Larijani, won the post of the speaker in the Majlis in a 232–31 vote against Gholam ali Hadda Adel, an Ahmadinejad ally.[19]

Before the election, some observers had suggested that the neoconservatives not only had eclipsed the reformists but also the Old Guard clerics, and that they were in the process of recasting the Islamic Republic into a European-style fascist state. In this view, the Revolutionary Guards and the Basij have provided the "storm troopers" to intimidate opponents and to force the government to change its policies. In the words of one insider, the Guards are a "unique organization in the world: a political body, a military force, and a big complex company." Ahmadinejad has cultivated a dedicated mass following among the pious poor, the Iranian equivalent of the supporters of the Fascist and Nazi parties. As the historian Kaveh Bayat noted: "Like Europe in the 1920s, we have a disaffected proletariat looking for radical and extreme solutions. Ahmadinejad is not imposed on us."[20]

THE 2009 PRESIDENTIAL ELECTION: THE END OF THE NEGOTIATED POLITICAL ORDER?

The presidential election of June 12, 2009 was the most fiercely contested in the history of the Islamic Republic. Confronting the incumbent were the Independent Reformist Mir Hussein Mousavi, a former hard-line prime minster and the leader of the National Confidence Party, and former Majlis speaker Mehdi Karroubi, another hard-liner turned reformist. Mohsen Rezai, a former head of the Revolutionary Guards, described as a conservative with a pragmatic turn, ran as an independent. Like President Khatami, Mousavi became the unexpected focal point of youthful democracy advocates. At the same time, Mousavi had the support of an impressive array of Old Guard clerics such as the former President and the head of the Expediency Council, Ali Akbar Rafsanjani, and the former Interior Minister, Ali Akbar Mohtashemi-Pur, whose conversion from an extreme hardliner to a reformist was most astounding.

The election campaign was conducted in a vibrant democratic spirit, but was also highly acrimonious. Mousavi charged that Ahmadinejad lied about the state of the economy, which is plagued by high inflation and high unemployment rates. He advocated further privatization and other free market measures, as opposed to Ahmadinejad's deficit-creating populist policy of subsidies for the poor. The Reformist candidate accused Ahmadinejad of isolating Iran by espousing Holocaust denial and engaging in frequent diatribes against the West. Emulating Khatami, Mousavi promised a relaxation in lifestyle regulations and the disbanding of the unpopular "vice police." Ahmadinejad compared Mousavi to Hitler. Still, on the crucial issue of the nuclear program there was little difference between the two main contenders, though Mousavi promised a less confrontational style of negotiations.

There was a major shift toward Mousavi in the last two weeks before the elections, and some surveys predicted that he would win a considerable majority. However, just hours after the polls closed, Ahmadinejad claimed an overwhelming victory, a result that Mousavi and his supporters rejected as fraudulent. Millions marched to protest the rigged elections, chanting "death to the dictator" and "give us our votes back." Taken aback, Supreme Leader Ayatollah Ali Khamenei urged Iranians to get behind Ahmadinejad, calling the elections a "divine assessment." In face of continuous protest, however, on June 15 Khamenei ordered the Guardian Council to investigate the fraud allegations. More large scale protests, which demanded the annulment of the elections, compelled Khamenei to announce a recount of a random sample of 10 percent of the ballot. Upon its completion on June 24, the Guardian Council certified the election in favor of Ahmadinejad: the Abadgaran leader received 24,527,516 votes (62.63 percent of the total) and the Independent Reformer won 13,216, 411 votes (33.75 percent).

Outside analysts and some regime insiders pointed out numerous irregularities. For instance, the breakdown of votes was not listed by province. The city of Tabriz, where Mousavi was a "favorite son," gave Ahmadinejad a plurality of votes, and the incumbent did surprising well in ethnic regions where he had been known to be particularly unpopular. Ali Akbar Mohtashemi-Pur, who monitored the election on behalf of Mousavi, noted that in seventy municipalities the number of ballots exceeded the number of eligible voters; in all them Ahmadinejad did very well.

With little electoral credibility, the regime faced crowds that defied Ayatollah Khamenei's calls for calm. Indeed, chants of "death to the dictator," a reference to the Spiritual Leader, became a signature event of the protest movement along with nightly shouting of 'Allah Akbar" from the rooftops, a technique adopted from the 1979 revolution. After a few days of hesitation, the Revolutionary Guards and the Basji militia decided to suppress all demonstrations. The highly brutal crackdowns resulted, according to an official estimate, in more than twenty dead and hundreds injured. Unofficial estimates indicated a much higher casualty count. The regime arrested some 5,000 protestors, opposition figures, journalists, and even foreigners; imposed a strict censorship; and interfered with cell phone and Twitter communications. In spite of intense international condemnation, there were few signs of a letup in the brutal clampdown that many compared to the "Reign of Terror" in the early years of the Islamic Republic.

Driven underground, the protest movement found new ways of challenging the regime. For instance, the junior but influential Assembly of Qom Scholars and Researchers issued a statement urging the cancellation of the election results. Some senior clerics, including Hussein Ali Montazeri and Ali Akbar Nateq-Nuri, condemned the regime for falsifying the outcome and the harsh treatment of the protesters. Most significantly, on July 17, during the important Friday prayer in Tehran, Ayatollah Rafsanjani urged the government to restore its legitimacy in the eyes of the people. Rafsanjani's contention that the regime had lost its legitimacy was the most serious challenge to the Supreme Leader to date.

That a regime normally careful to preserve an appearance of legitimacy would blatantly rig the ballot and brutally suppress the resulting protest raises important questions about the future political order of the Islamic Republic. The decision to falsify the results was apparently taken after a secret poll indicated a huge victory margin for Mousavi. This should not have come as a surprise because of the demographic changes that had favored reformists for some time. Rather than repeat the Khatami experiment, the Abadgaran leaders decided to disregard popular opinion and rely on coercion. As noted, the coercion system and its attendant preference falsification and learned helplessness are effective in preserving authority, but require an ever-increasing measure of totalitarian centralism. This, in turn, threatens to undermine the negotiated political order that has granted the regime the necessary flexibility to maneuver through the badly fractured political landscape.

The behavior of Ayatollah Khamenei may actually point in this direction. As recently as the 2008 Majlis election, the Supreme Leader was careful to preserve the appearance of staying above the fray. This time around, and in spite of fierce pressure from Rafsanjani and many of the Old Guard, Khamenei cast his lot with the Abadgaran cohort. It is virtually impossible to determine whether the Supreme Leader was strong-armed by the Abadgaran-dominated Revolutionary Guard, a backbone of his power for more than two decades, or simply decided that, given the popular trends, a dictatorial posture was needed to preserve the hard-line Islamist vision of the Republic. Either way, the future of the negotiated political order may be in question. Indeed, some observers have already concluded that the Islamic Republic has transformed into a military dictatorship, albeit with a thin theocratic veneer. For those who envision a fascist future, the Revolutionary Guard and its brutal Basji foot soldiers have provided a compelling analogy.

As of this writing, one month after the election, it is difficult to predict whether Iran is on the way to becoming a military dictatorship or worse. In this sense, the current upheaval only adds to the problem of Iran watchers in the United States who have been confounded by its political system for the past three decades.

READING TEHRAN IN WASHINGTON: CONTAINMENT, REGIME CHANGE, OR ACCOMMODATION?

Well before Ayatollah Khomeini landed in Tehran on February 1, 1979, the Carter administration assumed that the successor regime in Iran would be democratic and Western-oriented. Virtually the entire academic community, the State Department, and the CIA predicted that moderate politicians would assume power following the collapse of the Pahlavi dynasty.[21] The unprecedented taking of American diplomats as hostages and Tehran's support for terrorist organizations landed it on the State Department's list of state sponsors of terrorism. As evidence of Iran's nuclear ambition accumulated in the early 1990s, Congress enacted the Iran-Libya Sanctions Act (ILSA), later changed to the Iran Sanctions Act (ISA). In the wake of 9/11, the Bush administration tightened the sanctions regime in response to evidence uncovered by the 9/11 Commission that Iran had aided al-Qaeda. In a move that acknowledged the parallel nature of Iranian politics, the State Department added the IRGC and al Quds to its terrorist list in 2007, unprecedented because it specifically identified organizations within a sovereign state. To curb Iran's nuclear program, the United States pressed the United Nations Security Council to institute international sanctions against Iran. Challenging also has been Iran's continuous support of Hezbollah (which reached new operational heights during the Second Lebanon War), its help for Hamas and Islamic Jihad, and its vehement opposition to the Israeli-Palestinian peace process. Although the 2007 National Intelligence Estimate concluded that Iran had suspended its uranium enrichment program, which could yield a nuclear bomb, the administration has intensified its efforts to broaden its sanctions regimen.

Over the years, an array of critics has questioned the sanctions policy and, indeed, the assumptions underlying American relations with Islamist Iran. Trita Parsi, a former president of the National Iranian-American Council (NIAC), an Iran lobbying group, claimed that in 2003 Khamenei offered to stop Iran's sponsorships of terrorism and switch to a strictly peaceful nuclear program in exchange for an end to American sanctions and the return of Iran to the family of nations. In his view, this so-called "grand bargain" was sabotaged by the Jewish lobby, working as an agent of Israel, a charge repeated by two respected political scientists in a book about the Israel lobby. Without accusing American Jews, the 2006 Iraq

Study Group (ISG), co-chaired by James Baker and Lee Hamilton, urged the Bush administration to abandon containment and to "engage constructively" with Iran in order to stabilize Iraq.[22]

Democratic regime change enthusiasts have argued that Washington's hard-line policies are detrimental to Iranian moderates and have suggested that "greater economic and cultural contacts with the outside world" and "continued international insistence on political reform and human rights" would strengthen civil society and "dilute the conservatives' hold on power." These and other likeminded observers have pointed out that Larijani's victory in the Majlis in 2008 portends a possible moderation of the regime in a direction first chartered by Rafsanjani. To this end, some have suggested the so-called "small bargain," which would allow for a "delayed limited enrichment scheme" under an "intrusive inspection regime."[23]

While the impact of containment on the Islamic Republic can be debated, these suggestions fail to take into account its complex negotiated political order. Some observers have been ignorant of the power of the Revolutionary Guards and are equally unaware of the emergence of the neo-conservative Abadgaran movement. Others have been naïve to expect that popular opinion alone would prevail against a regime that has used coercion to manufacture preference falsification and learned helplessness. Still others have nursed overly optimistic hopes that support for terrorism, a singularly effective tool in spreading the Islamist revolution, can be successfully negotiated away. Perhaps most puzzling has been the persistent reference to Iran as a rational unified actor.

Indeed, during his presidential campaign, Barack Obama announced that in contrast to the Bush administration, he would "talk to Iran," and he has favored this policy of engagement while in office. Many of Obama's advisors were close to the Baker-Hamilton group and shared its belief in a universe populated by rational state actors and the redeeming virtues of traditional diplomacy. Not incidentally, Obama's pronouncements, like the ISG report, were replete with references to "Iran" and "Iranians."

Ironically, if the assumption that Iran is on its way to becoming a military dictatorship comes true, the notion of a unified actor may be closer to reality. However, the Obama administration should not draw much comfort from a more unified regime. Lacking domestic legitimacy, the Khamenei-Ahmadinejad Abadgaran government would be quite reluctant to compromise on the nuclear program, its signature foreign policy achievement, or give up its widespread support for terrorism, a *raison d'être* of the Islamic revolution.

The failure to comprehend the Islamist challenge was at the root of Jimmy Carter's disastrous policy in Iran. Given its consequences, a more serious effort to relate policy options to the political realities of the Islamic Republic is in order today.

NOTES

1. Max Weber, *On Charisma and Institution Building—Selected Papers* (Chicago: University of Chicago Press, 1968).

2. David Easton, *A Systems Analysis of Political Life* (Chicago: University of Chicago Press, 1979), 273.

3. E. J. Hollander and J. W. Jullien, "Studies in Leader Legitimacy, Influence and Innovation," in *Advances in Experimental Social Psychology*, ed. Leonard Berkowitz (New York: Academic Press, 1970), 5: 33–69.

4. Timor Kuran, *Private Truth, Public Lies: The Social Consequences of Preference Falsification* (Cambridge: Harvard University Press, 1995), 110, 123, 125.

5. Kenneth E. Boulding, *Conflict and Defense: A General Theory* (New York: Harper, 1962); Ofira Seliktar, "Identifying a Societal Belief System," in *Political Psychology*, ed. Margaret G. Hermann (San Francisco: Jossey-Bass Publishers, 1986), 320–354.

6. Ray Takeyh, *Hidden Iran: Paradox and Power in the Islamic Republic* (New York: Times Books/Henry Holt, 2006), 36.

7. Mohsen M. Milani, "Reform and Resistance in the Islamic Republic of Iran," in *Iran at the Crossroads*, eds. John L. Esposito and R. K Ramazani (New York: Palgrave, 2001), 31.

8. Bijan Khajehpour, "Economy: Twenty Years after the Islamic Revolution," in Esposito and Ramazani, *Iran at the Crossroads*, 94.

9. Quoted in Khajehpour, "Economy," 96.

10. Takeyh, *Hidden Iran,* 42; Haleh Esfandiari, "The Politics of the 'Women's Question' in the Islamic Republic, 1979–1999," in Esposito and Ramazani, *Iran at the Crossroads*, 75.

11. Abdolhassan Bani Sadr, *My Turn to Speak: Iran, the Revolution and Secret Deals with the U.S.* (Washington: Brassy's, 1991), 56.

12. Takeyh, *Hidden Iran,* 41, 42.

13. Anoush Ehteshami and Mahjoob Zweiri, *Iran and the Rise of its Neoconservatives* (London: I. B. Taurus, 2007), 54.

14. Abdol-Karim Soroush, *Reason, Freedom and Democracy in Islam* (New York: Oxford University Press, 2000), 80–131.

15. *New York Times*, June 12, 2001.

16. Ehteshami and Zweiri, 83–84; Abba Milani, "Testimony Before the Foreign Relations Committee of the House of Representatives," January 31, 2007, http://www.stanford.edu/~amilani/downloads/Foreign%20Affairs%20Committee%20Hearing%20testimony-FINAL.pdf.

17. Shimon Shapira, "The Nexus between Iranian National Banks and International Terrorist Financing," *Jerusalem Issues Brief*, February 14, 2008; Andrew Higgins, "A Feared Force Roils Business in Iran," *Wall Street Journal*, October 14, 2006.

18. Daniel Pipes, "The Mystical Menace of Mahmoud Ahmadinejad," *New York Sun*, January 10, 2006.

19. Stuart Williams, "Iran Leader Hails Ahmadinejad for Nuclear Success," *Yahoo! News*, February 26, 2008.

20. Quoted in Michael Slackman, "A Frail Economy Raises Pressure on Iran's Rulers," *New York Times*, February 3, 2008; see also Abbas Milani, "Testimony

Before the Foreign Relations Committee of the House of Representatives,"
January 31, 2007, http://www.stanford.edu/~amilani/downloads/Foreign%
20Affairs%20Committee%20Hearing%20testimony-FINAL.pdf.

21. Ofira Seliktar, *Failing the Crystal Ball Test: The Carter Administration and the Fundamentalist Revolution in Iran* (Westport: Praeger, 2000), 126–27

22. Trita Parsi, *Treacherous Alliance: The Secret Dealings of Israel, Iran and the United States* (New Haven: Yale University Press, 2007), 243–341; John J. Measheimer and Stephen M. Walt, *The Israel Lobby and U.S. Foreign Policy* (New York: Farrar, Straus and Giroux, 2007), 286; Ofira Seliktar, "Ignorance is Not Realistic: A Critique of the Mearsheimer and Walt Thesis," *Middle East Review of International Relations* 12, no. 1 (2008), http//meria.idc.ac.il/news/2008/February.html.

23. "Engaging Iran? Contrasting Views on U.S. Diplomacy," Washington Institute of Near East Studies, Policy Watch, no. 1250, June 22, 2007; Karim Sadjadpour, "Testimony Before the Senate Foreign Relations Committee," May 18, 2006, http://www.crisisgroup.org/home/index.cfm?id=4143; Karim Sadjadpour, "Testimony Before the House Committee on Oversight and Government Reform," October 30, 2007, http://carnegieeurope.eu/publications/?fa=19677.

CHAPTER 11

The Modern Impact of Mahdism and the Case of Iraq

Timothy R. Furnish

In my first book, I examined the history of eight Mahdist claimants in the Sunni world over the last millennium.[1] I focused on Sunni Islam for several reasons: to poke a hole in the conventional wisdom that Mahdism was, and is, strictly a Shi'a phenomenon; such Mahdist fervor as could be discerned seemed to be emanating, via books and Web sites, from the Sunni Arab world; the last openly declared Mahdist movement had been that of Juhayman al-'Utaybi in the name of the Mahdi Muhammad al-Qahtani in Saudi Arabia in 1979; Twelver Shi'a Mahdism seemed to be so institutionalized, even in the Islamic Republic of Iran, that official channels in Tehran and Qom would never, or so I thought, allow for overt Mahdism in that brand of Shi'ism; Saddam Hussein kept such a tight Sunni Baathist lid on Twelver Shi'ism that Mahdism would never boil forth in Iraq.

Then three things happened in the opening decade of the twenty-first century: a fervent Mahdist was elected president of Iran; Sunni jihadists carried out the 9/11 attacks on the United States; and the latter led to President George W. Bush's war on terror, with overt fronts in both Afghanistan and Iraq. These momentous changes have revivified Twelver Shi'a Mahdism in Iraq and Iran (although Mahdism's status in Shi'a Lebanon is less clear), while at the same time heightening Sunni Mahdist fervor around the globe.

GENERAL BACKGROUND

Mahdism is the belief in *al-Mahdi*—"the Rightly Guided One"—in both Sunni and Shi'a Islam. While not appearing, per se, in the Quran, the Mahdi is attested to in Hadith collections from both branches of Islam. He is one of two positive eschatological figures in the world's second-largest religion, along with Jesus. To make a long eschatological story short: the forces of unbelief and evil will come to predominate toward the end of history, led by the *al-Dajjal*, the "Deceiver," assisted by not only his human followers, but by *Yajuj wa-Majuj*, "Gog and Magog"—ravening hordes who will escape their incarceration (accomplished long ago at the order of none other than Alexander the Great) somewhere in Central Asia—and *al-Dabbah*, "the Beast," who will brand unbelievers with the scarlet letters *k-f-r*. The world will divide into believers (Muslims) and *kafirun* (non-Muslims) and, in a series of battles and wars, the Mahdi and Jesus (who kills the *al-Dajjal*) will eventually triumph, creating a global Islamic state, a divine caliphate, before the actual end of time and the Judgment.

This belief system is extant in both Sunnism and Shi'ism, with a number of differences, the most important of which goes back to the situation at the death of the fourth caliph (or prophetic "successor"), Ali, in the year 661. His *shi'ah*, or faction, thought he should have been the first caliph at Muhammad's death in 632. At Ali's death, his supporters said one of his sons, Hasan or Hussein, who were also Muhammad's grandsons (Ali having married Muhammad's daughter Fatimah), should be the caliph. Instead, control of the new Islamic empire was seized by the Sunni Umayyad dynasty of Damascus. Hasan renounced his caliphal claims, but Hussein decided to lead a counterrevolution against the Umayyads in 680, only to be killed, or martyred, in Shi'a thought, along with many of his followers at Karbala in southern Iraq. Thereafter, the minority Shi'as took solace in the line of Imams descended from Ali through Hussein, until 874, when the Twelfth Imam, Muhammad, went into *ghaybah*, hiding or occultation, where he remained in contact with his followers via certain proxies. By 941 this communication had ceased, ending the lesser *ghaybah* and launching the greater one, which continues to this day, according to most Twelver Shi'a (but not according to all, especially in Iraq today).

SHI'A MAHDISM AND JIHAD

Shi'a movements thereafter tended to follow one of several patterns:[2] activist (jihad-wielding), centered around a quasi-messianic leader who, even if he did not claim the Mahdiyah, might claim to be the Mahdi's representative or precursor;[3] or passive, awaiting the coming of the

Mahdi to do the eschatological heavy lifting and establish Allah's king-dom on earth. However, even among the latter, "his hiding was only a temporary measure adopted until the time would come for him to rise up with the sword."[4]

As a minority within Islam, most of the time and in most locales, Shi'as were normally quietist, content to wait for the return of the Twelfth Imam as the Mahdi in the eschatological future. These "Twelvers," also called "Imamis," eventually became the largest group of the Shi'as, espe-cially after the forced conversion of Iran to the branch by the Safavids be-ginning in the early sixteenth century. (Other branches of the Shi'a, most notably the Seveners, or Isma'ilis, sometimes seized power, as with the Fatimids, who ruled Egypt and much of the Red Sea region from 909 to 1171.) But Shi'ism, like Sunnism, included a belief in jihad, albeit with two distinctions: 1) only one of the twelve Imams, or their official repre-sentative(s), could wage it; and 2) only those opposed to the Imams, the *ahl al-baghy/bughat* (family of dissension), could be legitimate targets of such jihad.[5] For about a millennium the Twelvers retained these reserva-tions about jihad, positing a *hudnah* (truce) between them and their ene-mies until the Mahdi should come,[6] even when Shah Isma'il and the Safavid state invoked the Mahdi to fight the arch-enemy Sunni Ottomans. But this reluctance to set loose fully the dogs of jihad finally eroded, ironically, not under the Safavids but under their successors, the less-legitimate (at least to the Shi'a *'ulama*) Qajars. Under that nineteenth-century dynasty in Iran (and parts of Iraq), and during its ongoing wars with the expansionist Orthodox Christian Russian Empire, Twelver cler-ics began declaring jihad in the Mahdi's absence, even going so far as to deem jihad *sans* the Mahdi as ordained by Allah.[7]

Mahdi-less jihad was defined as acceptable in a defensive posture under four categories: to preserve Muslim territory while under attack; to prevent unbelievers from "gaining control over the person of Muslims"; "to repel a particular group of unbelievers" trying to "gain control over a particular group of Muslims"; and to eject unbelievers from Muslim terri-tory.[8] The nineteenth-century Twelver clerics also differentiated this *jihad-i difa'i* from offensive jihad on many levels. Defensive jihad can be waged in the Mahdi's absence; in fact, it doesn't even require a *mujtahid* (or judge) for sanction, simply "whoever is best equipped to win the war." Muslims normally exempt from offensive jihad must fight in the defensive kind. Defensive jihad is not limited only to the traditional sa-cred months; taxes or levies can be set at any level to support defensive jihad; "booty" is to be reinvested in defensive jihad, not distributed; and coercion to obtain resources to fight this kind of jihad is allowable by rul-ers. In the defensive jihad realm of agreements and diplomatic relations with non-Muslims, treaties with *dhimmi*s may be broken at will; Muslims who aid and abet unbelievers "by divulging military secrets and spreading sedition" are considered *ipso facto* outside the pale of the *umma* and, as such, can be killed. Furthermore, in defensive jihad there is no need to invite the enemy to convert to Islam before (counter) attacking; the 2:1 ratio of Muslims to unbelievers required in offensive jihad can be exceeded; *hudnah*s ("cease-fires" or "treaties") with non-Muslims can be violated at will; and—most ominously—killing modes normally off limits ("surprise attack, attack at night . . . muskets, pistols, carbines and grenades, uprooting trees, releasing water to flood the unbelievers or preventing water from reaching them so they die of thirst") are sanctioned.

IRAQI SHI'A MAHDISM: FROM THE NINETEENTH
TO THE TWENTY-FIRST CENTURIES

This Shi'a jihad concept was aimed originally at the Christian Russians, but it could also be applied to other Muslims, as happened in the nineteenth century in Karbala, Iraq, in response to Sunni Ottoman occupation.[9] Iraq in Safavid and Qajar times was a border zone, alternating between Ottoman and Persian control: for the former "because of its prevailing Shiism [sic] and the large Iranian ethnic element, Ottoman officials saw Karbala as a potential fifth column"; while for the latter, Shi'as "execrated the Ottoman ruler as a heretic and a usurper of an office that should by right belong only to the Twelfth Imam."[10]

Karbala's status as something of a "frontier" town, often lacking strong state authority, meant that gangs, akin to mafias, proliferated there. But "they were united by a religious consciousness of being [Shi'a]," as well as by a shared anti-Ottoman fervor.[11] Eschatological expectations were also heightened by the fact that the year 1844 was a millennium since the last Imam had gone into occultation.[12] By the early 1840s the Ottomans had had enough of this criminal anarchy and sent troops in to reassert control, which they finally achieved in 1842 after a months-long bloody siege. Ironically, Sunni Ottoman (re)conquest of Shi'a Karbala may have contributed to the outbreak of the Babi/Baha'i movement in 1844, wherein Sayyid Ali Muhammad of Shiraz claimed to be the *bab*, "door" or "gate," of the Twelfth Imam.[13]

Quietist Twelver Shi'ism was largely reasserted in Iran and Iraq with the crushing of the Babi/Baha'i movement in the latter nineteenth and early twentieth centuries.[14] But in the latter part of the twentieth century, two Twelver thinkers changed the equation: Ali Shariati, influenced by France's violent repression of Algerian independence movements, reenvisioned Ali as not simply a Christ-like martyr and intercessor, but also as a something of a Muslim Che Guevara. Ayatollah Salehi Najafbadi, in his 1970 book *The Eternal Martyr*, downplayed Hussein's supernatural suffering in favor of his militant defense of Muslim (that is, Shi'a) political rights.[15] Taken together, these ideas reinfused Twelver Shi'ism with, if not quite jihadism, at least a political activism that would bear fruit with the Ayatollah Khomeini's revolution of 1979—that is, the *vilayet-i faqih*, "rule of the jurisprudent," a system of clerical supervision of the state that is to remain in effect until the return of the Hidden Imam Mahdi.

Despite some claims that the Ayatollah Khomeini was in contact with the Mahdi, Mahdism was at best given lip service by most in the Islamic Republic during his decade of power, 1979 to 1989. After his death, the clerical leadership, exemplified by the likes of Ali-Akbar Hashemi Rafsanjani and Sayyid Muhammad Khatami, seems to have been rather lukewarm about the Twelfth Imam's return. But Mahmoud Ahmadinejad's elevation to the presidency once again put Mahdism on the front burner of Iranian, Twelver, and, indeed, regional Middle Eastern politics. Not only does he speak of it frequently—in Iran and in international venues like the well of the United Nations—but Tehran's incessant efforts at pan-Islamic unity are probably best seen as a resurrection of the concept of "spiritualized jihad" (*jihad-i 'ilm-i wa-tablighi*) until such time as the Islamic Republic of Iran deems it prudent to declare "holy war aimed at victory" (*jihad-i ghalaba*) against its foes.[16] An entire arm of the Iranian government, the "World Forum for Proximity of Islamic Thought," or *Majmu'ah Jihan-i Taqrib-i Madhdhahib Islami*, is dedicated to fostering pan-Islamic unity, to bridging the Sunni-Shi'a divide. Every year for four years, the Ahmadinejad administration has sponsored the Bright Future Institute's Conference on Imam Mahdi in Tehran. Iran is championing its Twelver co-religionists of Hezbollah in Lebanon; it is building Islamic centers and mosques as far away as West Africa; and, of course, it is supporting the Twelvers of Iraq on many levels. As the United States has learned since its occupation began five years ago, the relationship between Iranian and Iraqi clerics does not stop at the national border.[17]

IRAQI MAHDISM TODAY

Three prominent Mahdist movements have arisen in Iraq since the American invasion in 2003: Muqtada al-Sadr's Jaysh al-Mahdi; Ahmad al-Hassan al-Yamani's Ansar al-Mahdi; and the Jund al-Sama'. Al-Sadr is said to have founded his Jaysh, or "army," in order to provide the Mahdi with a ready-made vanguard upon his arrival. He is also reported to have said that the U.S. invaded in order to stymie the Mahdi's emergence. (Al-Sadr has kept silent on how a Methodist American President and his intelligence community would have known this.) While there is no doubt an element of the mafioso in al-Sadr's behavior, it would be wise to keep two points in mind: first, "when the modern state asserts itself"—as al-Maliki's government recently has done in southern Iraq— "the status of the mafioso changes from sub-cultural folk-hero to criminal";[18] and, second, thug that he might be, there is little denying the Mahdist element of al-Sadr's movement.

Jund al-Sama', or "Soldiers of Heaven," is one of two groups, along with Ansar al-Mahdi, accused by the media and the Iraqi government of sparking the violent clashes of January 2007.[19] Baghdad claimed that "hundreds of gunmen of the SoH [Soldiers of Heaven] were about to implement a plan to assassinate the top [Shi'a] clerics" in order to "pave the way for the return of al-Imam al-Mahdi . . ." Over 250 members of Soldiers of Heaven were claimed to have been killed, including the putative leader, Abd al-Zahra al-Ghar'awi, and 500 captured.[20] This analysis is part of the "hot wiring the apocalypse" thesis, most fully articulated by Reuven Paz of the Project for the Research of Islamist Movements (PRISM), in which Sunni, and now Shi'a, "eschatologists" are imputed the motive of fostering conditions for conflagration in order to summon the Mahdi. I am not convinced that this theory is accurate. More about this below.

Violence again erupted in southern Iraq in January 2008, and this time the Iraqi central government blamed another Mahdist group, Ansar al-Mahdi. Its leader goes by the name Ahmad al-Hassan al-Yamani. This is what has been reported about him:

> [His] real name is Ahmad Isma'il Gat'a . . . he was sent to jail in the 1990s for unknown reasons . . . In 2004 he participated in the Najaf battle between Coalition forces and . . . [the] al-Mahdi Army. Eventually al-Yamani led his followers to his home town of Basra and the adjacent Nairiya and Emara areas, where they established their own mosques and offices . . . In 2006 Ansar al-Mahdi started to increase their propaganda efforts in Basra and Baghdad with slogans like "Every Solution Has Failed but the Solution of al-Mahdi." On August 28, 2007, the first issue of the group's newspaper (al-Sirat al-Mostakeem [sic]) was published . . . the editorials had a clear anti-American position . . . In the January 25 [2008] issue, there was a statement by al-Yamani . . . declaring that America would fall by Imam al-Mahdi's hands. The United States is customarily referred [to] as al-Masih al-Dajjal . . .[21]

The Iraqi government claims not only that Ansar al-Mahdi is a violent "cult," but that it is supported, funded, and armed by Iran.

However, I have been in e-mail contact with individuals claiming to belong to Ansar al-Mahdi and to be in contact with al-Yamani. Here is some of what they have told me over the past several months. Al-Yamani is the son of the Twelfth Imam, the "promised Yamani" (one of five signs preceding the Mahdi's arrival is the appearance of al-Yamani).[22] The group is totally unrelated to Jund al-Sama', as well as to the Jaysh al-Mahdi. Neither the government of Iraq nor that of Iran is legitimate, since both deny the authority of the Twelfth Iman and his son, al-Yamani. Imam al-Mahdi and Sayyid al-Yamani "expect followers from all sects and religions," including Sunnis and Christians and even Jews, to join them. They are peaceful, but "what happened last January [2008] was that the Iraqi government forced us to defend ourselves. They burned our homes with our families and children inside, they destroyed our holy places and arrested many followers. . ." Sayyid Ahmad al-Hassan al-Yamani's first public role was in 1999 and 2000, when he opposed Saddam Hussein's "crime" of desecrating the Quran by having it written in his own blood, after which al-Yamani "and his followers were exposed . . . to the hunt of the Saddam regime's security forces and intelligence services." In December 2007, "Najaf Authorities held a conference . . . that was viewed on satellite and TV channels . . . but their words in that conference explicitly urged the government to totally get rid of us in any way, and . . . once the conference ended . . . government security forces began to attack our homes . . . and the series of arrest and pursuit continues to this moment . . ." They indeed "fought with the government last January," but only defensively, because "the Iraqi Government and the religious leaders . . . decided . . . to eliminate us completely." "Different political parties are fighting each other for power in Basra"—not Ansar al-Mahdi, they claim. Finally, as for when the Mahdi—who walks the Earth even now—will reveal himself to others beside al-Yamani, "this is the will of God alone and basically no one knows."

SO WHAT?

Ansar al-Mahdi claims to be at root a quietist Mahdist movement forced, if you will, to take up arms and resort to defensive jihad only as a last resort. Two major pressing questions should concern us now: will the Mahdism of the Ansar al-Mahdi, Jund al-Sama' and—yes—Jaysh al-Mahdi switch from defensive to offensive jihad? And, will Mahdism spread from Shi'a Iraq to the larger Sunni world? Each of these groups can appeal to an earlier Twelver delineation of the circumstances allowing for jihad when the Mahdi has not yet come. *Mutatis mutandis,* these include: preserving Muslim territory under attack (Iraq); preventing non-Muslims (Americans, some members of the Iraqi government forces) from controlling individual Muslims or particular groups of Muslims (members of the three Mahdist organizations); and ejecting unbelievers (Americans, the British) from Muslim lands.

Now that the Mahdi's proxy is here and the occultation has reverted to merely a lesser from a greater one—since, for example, Muqtada al-Sadr and/or Sayyid al-Yamani is/are in contact with the Twelfth Imam—it might be permissible soon to move from defensive to offensive jihad. However, even if that official step is not taken, several aspects of Twelver defensive jihad (as defined in the nineteenth century against the Russians) should give us pause. Most notably, the lives of Muslims who "aid the unbelievers"—in Iraq or elsewhere—are forfeit. In addition, treaties or truces with not only "domestic" *dhimmis*—protected Christians or (much fewer in number) Jews under Islamic rule—but also with "foreign" non-Muslim belligerents, can be discarded at will by Muslims. This makes enforcing international law rather problematic. Iraqi Shi'as had a hard time with the Muslim (albeit Sunni) Ottomans ruling them—no wonder Christian infidels from across the sea have found it tough going. The twenty-first-century version of the "muskets, pistols, carbines, and grenades," as well as the "flood[ing]" of non-Muslims, could easily be analogized to weapons of mass destruction ranging from exploding chlorine tankers to nuclear weapons and everything in between. Defensive jihad is bad enough. God preserve us (and "apostate" Muslims) from the offensive kind!

As for the second major question: there are disturbing hints that Mahdism may be about to spread beyond its current Shi'a nexus in Iraq and Iran. Recent reports indicate that increasingly large numbers of Sunnis in places like Egypt and the Palestinian territories are "converting" to Shi'ism.[23] Perhaps this will lead to a greater willingness to embrace Mahdism, although I am not convinced of that. More worrying, actually, are the reports that certain Sufi orders (or at least some members thereof) in Iraq have taken up arms against Baghdad.[24] While Sufis are often, historically, quietist and reflective, it is nonetheless an unpleasant fact that many (if not most) of the Sunni Mahdist movements that have erupted in history have been led by charismatic Sufi sheikhs. In fact, six of the eight Mahdist revolutions analyzed in my book were Sufi in origin, including the nineteenth-century ones of Muhammad Ahmad in Sudan, Muhammad Amzian in Algeria, and Ahmad Barelwi in India.[25] And Sufism not only exists around the world, it is a strain of devotional Islam that often serves as a halfway house between the Sunni and Shi'a branches. For several centuries, one of the main criticisms of Sufism among its detractors, most notably the Salafi/Wahhabi movement, has been that it allows questionable practices and doctrines to seep into the Sunni world from the Shi'a one.

In the eighteenth and nineteenth centuries (and even into the twentieth), the Sufi orders, with their extant organizational structures and obedience to a charismatic leader, often proved a ready vehicle for a Mahdist hijacking. Could something similar happen in Iraq, with the Naqshabandi Sufi order accepting the leadership of an al-Yamani (or another representative of the Mahdi, in the near future), whether out of shared utilitarian opposition to Baghdad, mystical sympathy, or a combination thereof? As I have argued before,[26] it is all too possible. And if Mahdism infects the Sufi world, it would not only hinder (if not undermine and destroy) the progress made to date in Iraq post-surge, it may even spread beyond Iraqi Shi'a circles to a significant slice of the Sunni world. The perfect Mahdist storm would be for the Shi'a and Sunni worlds—or at least large, strategic portions of each—to actually agree that someone is the Mahdi. This has never happened before in history, but then the

Internet did not exist until recently, and never before has the *umma* felt itself to be under determined global attack by its ancient historical foe, the Christian West. But even localized or regional Mahdism(s), as we are seeing in Iraq (but curiously, not in Lebanon—yet), will complicate enormously American interests in the Middle East and the Muslim world

CONCLUSIONS

Mahdists like al-Sadr may be thugs (or "mafioso"), but they are ardently messianic thugs, and so not really amenable to the utilitarian approach of, say, the Iraq Study Group. However unlikely it may seem that the Sunni world would accept a Mahdist claimant from the Shi'a ranks, the fact remains that even Sunni jihadists are not above grabbing onto such a one's robe to advance their own political agenda. This happened with Juhayman al-'Utaybi's movement in the Kingdom of Saudi Arabia in 1979, where "even among al-'Utaybi's supporters, which included Egyptians as well as Saudis, there were skeptics; but *'Mahdi or not, for them this was an uprising against a puppet regime of American infidels, and Juhayman sounded charismatic and well-intentioned enough to succeed.'"[27] If the remnants of al-Qaeda in Iraq start linking up with Mahdist movements, they could be revivified and transmogrified. While it may be true that "even jihad and suicide bombing can be interpreted through a tribal lens,"[28] I am not sure if Mahdism (always) can. Tribal cleavages in Arab Muslim society are clearly part of the equation in Iraq, but let us not fall off the horse on the other side and reduce the Islamic religious element to a mere sideshow. What was true of Shi'a Islam during uprisings against the Ottomans, that "the cleavages among the rebellious groups in Karbala were bridged" by it,[29] holds exponentially true for Mahdism throughout history, as it was used many times by charismatic leaders to unite disparate elements, even tribal ones, under the Mahdi's banner.

Mahdist movements almost always begin violently, waging jihad, but sometimes transform into quietist, pacific movements (the Isma'ils, the Baha'is, the Mahdavis of fifteenth-century Gujarat). This may already be the case with the Ansar al-Mahdi in Iraq. More study needs to be undertaken on the reasons for such peaceful evolutions. Two of the three parts of the Twelver world, Iran and Iraq, have evidenced overt Mahdism. But the third, Lebanon, has not. Why is that so? Is Hezbollah less eschatological or simply more reticent about openly expressing it? I am currently doing research on this topic, but much more needs to be done.

Finally, perhaps most importantly, what is going on in southern Iraq represents the return of overt Shi'a jihad under the guise of Mahdism. In the minds of these aforementioned groups in Iraq, jihad is now being waged in the name of, and under the guidance of, the Imam Mahdi, who, while not openly proclaimed, has at the very least reverted from the

greater (incommunicado) to the lesser (hidden, but accessible) occultation. It matters not whether the Iraq Study Group, the intelligence community, or the media believes this, so long as a growing number of Iraqis
(or other Muslims) do.

NOTES

1. Timothy R. Furnish, *Holiest Wars: Islamic Mahdis, their Jihads and Osama bin
Laden* (Westport: Greenwood, 2005).
2. Denis McEoin, "Aspects of Militancy and Quietism in Imami Shi'ism,"
British Journal of Middle Eastern Studies 11, no. 1 (1984): 18–27.
3. Such movements were cropping up in al-Iraq within less than a century
after the Prophet Muhammad's death, according to William Tucker, *Mahdis and
Millenarians: Shi'ite Extremists in Early Muslim Iraq* (Cambridge: Cambridge University Press, 2008).
4. McEoin, "Militancy and Quietism in Imami Shi'ism," 21.
5. Etan Kohlberg, "The Development of the Imami Shi'i Doctrine of Jihad,"
Zeitschrift der Deutschen Morgenländer Gesellschaft 126, no. 1 (1976), 68ff.
6. Ibid., 80.
7. Ibid., 82.
8. Ibid., 83ff.
9. See Juan Cole and Moojan Moomen, "Mafia, Mob and Shi'ism in Iraq: The
Rebellion of Ottoman Karbala, 1824–42," *Past and Present* 112 (August 1986):
112–43.
10. Ibid., 113.
11. Ibid., 120.
12. McEoin, "Militancy and Quietism in Imami Shi'ism," 23.
13. Cole and Moomen, "Mafia, Mob and Shi'ism in Iraq," 140.
14. Although research needs to be done on whether Mahdism was ever
declared under British occupation or under Saddam's rule, or anytime in
between.
15. Yann Richard, "Les debats sur le martyre dan le chiisme," *Maghreb-Mashrek*
186 (Winter 2005–06): 79.
16. See McEoin, "Militancy and Quietism in Imami Shi'ism," 22.
17. This is clearly demonstrated by 'Ali Haydar Khalil, *al-Imamah wa-al-
Khawaja: al-Murji'ah al-Shi'iyah fi Iran wa-al-Iraq* (Kuwait: Dar Quras lil-Nashr, 1997).
18. Cole and Moomen, "Mafia, Mob and Shi'ism in Iraq," 118.
19. See the independent, online Iraqi news agency *Aswat al-Iraq*, as well as
Fadhil Ali, "The Ansar al-Mahdi and the Continuing Threat of the Doomsday
Cults in Iraq," *Jamestown Terrorism Monitor* 6, no. 4 (February 22, 2008).
20. Ali, "The Ansar al-Mahdi and the Continuing Threat."
21. Ibid.
22. The others are: the Shout (al-sayha); the eclipse of the moon; the appearance of al-Sufyani (an evil eschatological figure in Shi'a, but not Sunni, tradition); the killing of al-Nafs al-Zakiyya (a prominent early eschatological leader).
McEoin, "Militancy and Quietism in Imami Shi'ism," 22.

23. L. Azuri, "Debate over the Status of Shi'ites in Egypt," Middle East Media Research Institute [MEMRI], Inquiry and Analysis, no. 311, December 27, 2006, http://www.memri.org/bin/articles.cgi?Page=archives&Area=ia&ID=IA31106.

24. Fadhil Ali, "Sufi Insurgent Groups in Iraq," *Jamestown Terrorism Monitor* 6, no. 2 (January 24, 2008).

25. Furnish, *Holiest Wars*.

26. Timothy R. Furnish, "Will Iraq Stoke Flames of Islamic Messianism?" *PajamasMedia*, April 7, 2008.

27. Sergei Trofimov, *The Siege of Mecca: The Forgotten Uprising in Islam's Holiest Shrine and the Birth of al-Qaeda* (New York: Doubleday, 2007), 65 (emphasis added).

28. Stanley Kurtz, "I and My Brother Against My Cousin," review of Philip Carl Salzman's *Culture and Conflict in the Middle East* (Amherst: Humanity Books, 2008), *Weekly Standard*, April 14, 2008, 32.

29. Cole and Moomen, "Mafia, Mob and Shi'ism in Iraq," 113.

CHAPTER 12

Palestinian Precedents: The Origins of Al-Qaeda's Use of Suicide Terrorism and *Istishhad*

Benjamin T. Acosta

Over the last decade, the suicide-terror phenomenon has spread from the Middle East and South Asia to the West and Eurasia, establishing itself as a global epidemic. Recently, the gravity of suicide terrorism has been most apparent in Iraq, where al-Qaeda has thoroughly demonstrated the incorporation of *istishhad* (deliberate martyrdom) into its grand strategy. From March 2003 to April 2007, al-Qaeda and affiliated groups carried out over 600 suicide-terror attacks in Iraq, nearly surpassing all other similar campaigns combined.[1] Though the frequency of such attacks has since declined substantially, one terrorism expert has recognized al-Qaeda's guiding role: "suicide bombing in Iraq is largely an imported phenomenon."[2] Furthermore, coming from Sunni Arab countries like Saudi Arabia, Libya, and Morocco, the foreign fighters who predominately use this tactic did not develop it firsthand.[3] With its operational roots in Shi'a Iran and southern Lebanon, the suicide-homicide attack went through a lengthy evolution before finding widespread legitimacy in the Sunni Muslim world. More than eleven years passed between the first Shi'a suicide-homicide attack and the first Sunni act of suicide terrorism.[4] This tactic thus required significant preparation before its exportation to Iraq and elsewhere by Sunni jihadis.

Indeed, the Palestinian *shahid* (martyr) has paved the way.[5] Between April 1993 and December 2005, Palestinians successfully carried out 191 suicide-homicide attacks in which bombers reached a target and detonated their explosives, and prepared at least another 450.[6] Alas, the excessive amount of international media coverage of the Arab-Israeli conflict has provided Palestinian terror organizations with a high-profile platform for their operations. With such exposure, strategic "victories" associated with suicide terrorism have earned Palestinian terror groups even more respect among international terror networks than the high level of prestige they have enjoyed for decades.[7] The efforts of Hamas and Palestinian Islamic Jihad (PIJ) to derail the Oslo peace process, the daily suicide-homicide bombers of the Fatah-instigated *al-Aqsa intifada* (or second *intifada*) of 2000 to 2005, and Israel's subsequent retreat from Gaza all brought renewed praise and admiration from Islamists across the *umma* (global Islamic community). This prestige has translated into imitation of the Palestinian *shahid* (usually in the form of a suicide-homicide bomber) and its supplementary culture of martyrdom. Palestinian terror organizations refined the *modus operandi* of suicide-homicide bombers in two concurrent yet specific ways, setting important precedents that precipitated waves of Sunni suicide terrorists such as those employed in al-Qaeda's post-9/11 strategy.

First, Palestinians legitimized suicide-homicide attacks as "martyrdom operations" in the Sunni Muslim world. The Palestinian cause has always functioned as a galvanizing Islamic issue, particularly for Sunni Arab countries. Consequently, the Palestinian use of suicide terrorism before and during the second *intifada* had a direct effect on the general population of the Sunni Arab world concerning how it viewed martyrdom operations. As support in Palestinian society increased, they accordingly found wide support across the Sunni Arab world (as well as in the Islamic world in general). By 2002, as one analyst recognized, "Martyrdom [had] replaced Palestinian independence as the main focus of the Arab media."[8] Palestinian terror organizations effectively used the media to spread acceptance of a *modus operandi* that previously only Shi'a groups had used in the Islamic world. The Sunni community's acceptance of the Palestinian twist of semantics that presents suicide-homicide attacks as "martyrdom operations" led to the use of similar attacks by other militant Sunni organizations.

Second, by turning the suicide-homicide bomber into a weapon of terror,[9] Palestinian organizations demonstrated the strategic advantages of attacking soft targets and garnered Islamic legitimacy for doing so. Suicide-terror attacks on Israeli civilians raised this *modus operandi* to a new level. Outdoing the suicide-homicide attack campaigns of Hezbollah and the Liberation Tigers of Tamil Eelam, which regularly attacked military targets, Palestinian organizations made it overt policy to target Israeli civilians *en masse*. Due to the religious undertones of their conflict with Israel, Palestinians received approval from Islamic authorities not only for launching "martyrdom operations," but also for targeting civilians.

The support for suicide terrorism from important Islamic authorities across the Sunni Arab world served to solidify the legitimacy of such acts in the eyes of millions of people. Notably, the *fatwa* issued in 2001 by

influential Sunni cleric Sheikh Yousef al-Qaradawi backing the use of suicide-homicide attacks against civilians buttressed Palestinian employment of suicide-homicide bombers against Israeli civilians and closed
somewhat the debate over their general validity within the greater Sunni
world.[10] Referring to the importance of al-Qaradawi's role in legitimizing
suicide terrorism, Hamas' current leader, Khaled Mashal, states: "[al-
Qaradawi's] unequivocal fatwa . . . considered martyrdom operations to
be the most noble level of jihad. That was unparalleled support for the
people of Palestine, because . . . you cannot imagine how difficult it is
psychologically for a young Palestinian man or woman to sacrifice themselves or what is most dear to them . . ."[11] At a conference honoring him
in 2007, al-Qaradawi recalled his role in providing Islamic legitimacy for
suicide terrorism:

> I support the Palestinian cause. I support the resistance and the jihad. I support
> Hamas, the Islamic Jihad, and Hizbullah [sic] . . . I support martyrdom operations,
> and this was the straw that broke the camel's back . . . Our brothers in Palestine
> were forced to resort to martyrdom operations. The divine destiny is just, and so it
> gave these brothers something the enemy lacks . . . Their enemy is bombing them
> from above and below . . . and all they want is [to sacrifice] their own lives. The
> Palestinian man or woman booby-trap themselves—they turn themselves into
> human bombs—and sacrifice themselves for the sake of Allah, in order to strike
> fear in the hearts of their enemies.[12]

The endorsement of suicide-homicide attacks by other prestigious Islamic authorities,[13] and the subsequent widespread acceptance of
suicide-homicide bombers as *shuhada* (martyrs), effectively precluded
other Sunni figures from offering any serious rebuttals.[14] As a result,
those organizations that promote global Islamist ideologies, specifically
al-Qaeda, have taken note of the Palestinians' successes in employing
suicide-homicide bombers—regarding both political victories and their
greater propaganda value within the *umma*. Consequently, al-Qaeda has
sought to adapt both the suicide-terror tactic and *istishhad* strategy to the
pursuit of its own goals.

AL-QAEDA'S PALESTINIAN AURA

Contrary to popular belief, al-Qaeda's connection to the Palestinian cause
is nothing new. The organization's founder, Sheik Abdallah Azzam al-
Filastini, hailed from a village outside Jenin in the disputed territories. Its
pre-9/11 chief of operations, Abu Zubaydah, who at this writing sits in
U.S. custody at Guantanamo Bay for his role in the 9/11 attacks, is Palestinian. Abu Musab al-Zarqawi pulled many of his original lieutenants for
Tawhid wal-Jihad, the precursor to al-Qaeda in Iraq, from Palestinian
groups operating in the Levant.[15] Even al-Zarqawi, a Jordanian-born
Bedouin killed by a U.S. airstrike in 2006, claimed his *hamula* (clan)

originated in the Jerusalem area.[16] Predating al-Qaeda's founding, the first known PIJ suicide-homicide bomber plot in 1986 called for using a device built by an "Afghan-Alum" *mujahid*.[17] Many suspect that al-Qaeda and Hamas cosponsored the April 30, 2003 suicide-terror attack that targeted a popular Israeli pub in Tel Aviv, which killed three and wounded more than fifty.[18] The Palestinian-al-Qaeda connection, however, extends beyond links between individual members and network-affiliated groups. The Palestinian precedent has influenced, in part, al-Qaeda's strategy and tactics, while having an effect on the international jihadi-Salafi movement via the popularization of the *istishhad* concept.

Al-Qaeda recognizes that making *istishhad* a key part of its strategy can set the stage for consolidating a durable global movement. Before 9/11, al-Qaeda saw its main purpose as training and financing like-minded Islamists to wage jihad.[19] Since 9/11, Osama bin Laden and Ayman al-Zawahiri have sought to motivate as many of the faithful within the *umma* as possible to participate in terrorism, if not "martyrdom operations." Al-Qaeda expert Rohan Gunaratna summarizes this goal: "Bin Laden directed the attack on America's most outstanding landmarks to inspire and incite the wider Muslim community and to show the way to the other Islamist movements."[20] With its ability to strike on a spectacular scale now greatly reduced, al-Qaeda's post-9/11 attacks have increasingly resembled more the *modus operandi* of the Palestinian suicide-homicide bomber than the Hezbollah-inspired simultaneous large-scale attack that characterized its style from August 1998 to early 2003. The July 2005 attacks in London bore a resemblance to both methods, as they included four concurrent suicide-homicide bomber attacks yet targeted common transportation systems. In Iraq, al-Qaeda's campaign has looked almost entirely Palestinian in mode: numerous individual bombers attacking average civilians on a seemingly daily basis.

The shift in method goes to the top. Bin Laden has sought to reboot his approach, as well as to return al-Qaeda to its rhetorical roots. In May 2008, he released a tape stating: "To Western nations . . . this speech is to understand the core reason of the war between our civilization and your civilians. I mean the Palestinian cause . . . [which] is the major issue for my (Islamic) [sic] nation. It was an important element in fueling me from the beginning and the nineteen with a great motive to fight for those subjected to injustice and the oppressed."[21] Bin Laden's statement demonstrates a refocusing of al-Qaeda's attention; moreover, it echoes the distant words of Abdallah Azzam, who once stated: "Our presence in Afghanistan today, which is the accomplishment of the imperative of jihad and our devotion to the struggle, does not mean that we have forgotten Palestine. Palestine is our beating heart, it comes even before Afghanistan in our minds, our hearts, our feelings and our faith."[22] Marking the sixth anniversary of the 9/11 attacks, bin Laden called on righteous Muslims to participate in the "caravan" of martyrs.[23] Playing off Azzam's pamphlet, *Join the Caravan*, which called on Muslims to join the *mujahideen* against the Soviets in Afghanistan, bin Laden's call displays al-Qaeda's commitment to a new *istishhad*-driven strategy to replace Azzam's jihad-based strategy. It exhibits al-Qaeda's evolution from promoting *shahada*, or "incidental martyrdom" obtained during jihad, to *istishhad*, or "deliberate martyrdom" attained by intentional self-inflicted death during jihad. The latter concept emphasizes personal choice, thus further empowering the individual and thereby increasing al-Qaeda's magnetism to disaffected Muslims across the Islamic world.

THE "OCCUPATION" OF *DAR AL-ISLAM*: DEFENSIVE JIHAD AND *FARD AYN*

Today al-Qaeda's ideology and strategy revolve around the individual.[24] Since its founding, it has presented jihad through the ideological tenet of *fard ayn* (individual obligation). Lacking a real-world method that truly lived up to its abstract ideation, *istishhad*, as expressed through a suicide-homicide attack, offers the paramount outlet to express the fulfillment of one's individual obligation to an Islamic calling to jihad. Remote and mostly disconnected from the wide variety of affiliated organizations and groups within its global "network of networks,"[25] al-Qaeda maintains a small core leadership hierarchy. Bin Laden and al-Zawahiri understand that they lead a war of patience, resolve, and, ultimately, one that pits the will of the individual Muslim against that of various nation-states and the world's remaining superpower, the United States.

Incorporating *istishhad* into its grand strategy allows al-Qaeda to wage a *laissez-faire* war against its enemies, claiming responsibility anytime an ideologically linked jihadi-Salafi group decides to launch an attack. As Yoram Schweitzer and Sari Goldstein Ferber note, "The concept of sacrificing one's life in the name of Allah (*istishhad*) became a supreme organizational ideal within al-Qaeda and then spread to its operatives and affiliates in what might be described as a self-reproducing, self-disseminating virus."[26] *Istishhad* optimizes al-Qaeda's strategy by maximizing its ideological attraction. With suicide-terror attacks, al-Qaeda and groups affiliated with the international jihadi-Salafi movement collectively benefit from the advancement of shared goals, while individual bombers earn the highest status of Islamic martyrdom and supposedly enjoy eternal glory.

For individuals to receive social support for waging jihad, the establishment of a congruent interpretation of Islam is necessary. Al-Qaeda has thus promoted the position that its war with the West represents a defensive jihad, which makes participation in it, whether physically or financially, a *fard ayn* of each and every Muslim. Going back to the teachings of Abdallah Azzam, *fard ayn* has played a central role in al-Qaeda's policy concerning "occupied" Islamic lands; as Azzam argued, "jihad will remain an individual obligation until all other lands which formerly were Muslim come back to us and Islam reigns within them once again. Before us lie Palestine, Bukhara, Lebanon, Chad, Eritrea, Somalia, the Philippines, Burma, South Yemen, Tashkent, Andalusia."[27] Localized social reinforcement of these interpretations has therefore become essential to al-Qaeda's execution of its global strategy.

Like al-Qaeda, the Islamist Palestinian organizations view jihad as *fard ayn*.[28] While Abdallah Azzam, and before him Muslim Brotherhood ideologue Sayyid Qutb, articulated the notion of *fard ayn*, Hamas and PIJ put the doctrine into practice beginning in 1993, a strategy that perhaps reached its apex during the second *intifada*. Serving as the utmost examples of individuals fulfilling their obligation to free the land of *Dar al-Islam*, Palestinian suicide-homicide bombers opened the door to al-Qaeda's own *shuhada*. Indeed, al-Qaeda did not begin employing suicide-homicide bombings until its August 1998 attacks on the U.S. embassies in Kenya and Tanzania. Its first operations inside the United States, the assassination of popular Rabbi and former Israeli Knesset member Meir Kahane in November 1990 and the first attempt to destroy the World Trade Center in February 1993, did not involve suicide terrorists. The Palestinian introduction of the *shahid* as a suicide-homicide bomber to the Sunni world in April 1993 likely had an impact on Egyptian Islamic Jihad's decision to launch its own suicide-homicide attack later that year, and the Palestinian refinement of suicide terrorism throughout the mid-1990s surely influenced al-Qaeda's decision to start using the tactic in 1998. At this time most of al-Qaeda's top leadership had been in the jihad business either before or since the Afghan-Soviet war, yet suicide-homicide attacks did not occur during that conflict or directly after it when al-Qaeda first began operating as an international terror organization. Al-Qaeda designed its attacks in the late 1990s and early 2000s to shock, yet they did not occur relentlessly until the mass production of *shuhada* in Iraq.

AL-QAEDA'S ADAPTATION OF THE PALESTINIAN CULTURE OF MARTYRDOM

Uniting organizational strategy with the motivations of individuals requires coordinating social forces and securing cultural accommodation. To launch suicide-terror attacks on a large scale, an organization must maintain exceptional support from its constituency.[29] A complementary culture of martyrdom rests as the sole variable distinguishing organizations that employ suicide-homicide attacks from those that do not.[30] Palestinian Media Watch director Itamar Marcus identifies three socio-cultural components imperative to motivating suicide terrorism: (1) create an enemy; (2) legitimize killing the enemy; (3) engender a willingness to die while killing the enemy.[31] The Palestinian culture of martyrdom perpetuates and ensures the function of these three components.[32] First, the culture of martyrdom alters the defined "other" to represent an explicit "enemy." Second, the culture of martyrdom legitimizes the killing of this enemy by framing its intentions as specifically threatening to Palestinian collective identity and generally sinister in its dealings with the world. Third, the culture of martyrdom motivates and sanctions the willingness of individuals to die in the process of killing the enemy.

Installed in various mosques and Islamic centers in urban areas of European cities, embedded within underground political organizations in Middle Eastern capitals, and implanted in South Asian madrassas, the culture of martyrdom has been decentralized by Islamists, just as al-Qaeda has done to its organizational structure. In contrast to the original Palestinian version, al-Qaeda's international jihadi-Salafi culture of martyrdom remains less overt. Rather, it operates in the shadows of Western and Islamic societies and flourishes more as a satellite culture of martyrdom and a virtual culture of martyrdom, wherein adherents can turn on an Arabic-language news outlet or enter an online Islamist chat room to get a dose of a jihadi worldview. Indeed, global communications and media have redrawn the boundaries of cultural enclaves. No longer society specific, cultures in a post-modern world often function as transnational forces in their own right. The jihadi-Salafi milieu of martyrdom exemplifies such a culture.

FRAMING CONFLICT

As noted above, generating a willingness to die while killing entails defining the enemy and then explaining why it needs to die. Thus, while political value provided by suicide-homicide attacks ultimately works as the greatest catalyst to an organization's continued use of the *modus operandi*, motivating individuals to carry out such operations necessitates continuous framing of "social ills." Commenting on the necessary preparation for launching effective campaigns, scholar Mohammed M. Hafez maintains: "Mobilizing collective action consists of more than calling on people to rise up or take to the streets; it involves framing social ills as threats and opportunities for action, networking among activists and their constituencies, building formal and informal organizations, forging collective identities and alliances, making claims against opponents and states, and motivating individuals to assume personal costs when the benefits of success are not readily apparent."[33] In this regard, step one is subsuming the individual within the collective identity. Step two entails merging the individual obligation with the need to fix social ills.

Most Islamist denominations commonly frame the world as though it teeters on the brink of an apocalyptic struggle between the forces of Islam and a sinister "Zionist-Crusader" alliance. Al-Qaeda's rhetoric has shaped up no differently, often warning that Muslims must defend their religion against Zionist-Crusader aggression. In 1998, the World Islamic Front for Jihad against Jews and Crusaders, an umbrella network headed by al-Qaeda, stated:

> The ruling to kill the Americans and their allies—civilians and military—is an obligation incumbent upon every Muslim who can do it and in any country—this until the Aqsa Mosque [in Jerusalem] and Holy Mosque [in Mecca] are liberated from their grip, and until their armies withdraw from all the lands of Islam, defeated, shattered, and unable to threaten any Muslim. This is in accordance with the Word of the Most High—"fight the pagans all together as they fight you all together" [Quran 9:36] and . . . "Fight them until there is no more tumult or oppression, and [all] religion belongs to Allah" [Quran 8:39].[34]

Such statements from al-Qaeda's leadership, commonplace since 9/11, clearly articulate who their enemy is, why they are an enemy, when victory against this enemy will be apparent, and why it is divine obligation for all Muslims to participate in bringing about such a victory. Simply put, al-Qaeda seeks to energize as many individual Muslims as possible to fight the Christian, Jewish, and other non-Muslim peoples that threaten Islam. Regarding the occupation of *Dar al-Islam*, Israel, the United States, Spain, Russia, India, Christian Lebanon, the Philippines, and other non-Muslim states controlling occupied Muslim land become the obvious targets. At the forefront, however, sit America and Israel. Al-Qaeda suggests that the United States designs its foreign policy to "serve the Jews' petty state, [and divert] attention from its occupation of Jerusalem and the murder of Muslims there."[35] Islamists have elevated the supposed Jewish threat to a more severe level. The Israeli-Palestinian conflict, coupled with various Quran *suras* and Hadith sayings that promote anti-Jewish beliefs, has allowed Islamists to frame the Islamic world's problems within the context of an international Jewish conspiracy, in which the U.S. plays a key supporting role.[36]

Islamist entities like al-Qaeda understand the important part the "other" plays in solidifying a collective identity—in this case, an Islamic identity as represented by the *umma*. Judaism, one of Islam's earliest foes, additionally fills this role today for Islamists. In March 2003, bin Laden warned his fellow Muslims:

> One of the most important objectives of the new Crusader attack is to pave the way and prepare the region, after its fragmentation, for the establishment of . . . the Greater State of Israel, whose border will include extensive areas of Iraq and Egypt, through Syria, Lebanon, Jordan, all of Palestine, and large parts of the Land of the Two Holy Places . . . What is happening to our people in Palestine is merely a model that the Zionist-American alliance wishes to impose upon the rest of the region: the killing of men, women and children . . . People [there] live in perpetual fear and

paralyzing terror, awaiting death at any moment from a missile or shell that will destroy their homes, kill their sisters, and bury their babies alive . . . The founding of "Greater Israel" means the surrender of the countries of the region to the Jews . . .[37]

Sheikh al-Qaradawi has lent his authority to confirming the Islamist viewpoint. On the conflict with Judaism he argues:

We do not disassociate Islam with war . . . We are fighting in the name of Islam . . . They fight us with Judaism, so we should fight them with Islam. They fight us with the Torah, so we should fight them with the Koran. If they say "the Temple," we should say "[the] Aqsa Mosque." If they say: "We glorify the Sabbath," we should say: "We glorify the Friday." This is how it should be. Religion must lead the war. This is the only way we can win.[38]

Referring to Islamic suicide terrorism, Reuven Paz, an expert on Islamist movements, contends:

The perception of the struggle between Islam and Judaism is actually the main justification for the general use of terrorism, and particularly for suicide bombing . . . The core perception of the Islamist Arab groups is that they face a global conspiracy against the Islamic world . . . [A]fter the establishment of Israel and the renaissance of the Islamist groups since the [1960s] and [1970s] this conspiracy came to be viewed as a constant and perhaps eternal struggle between Judaism and Islam.[39]

Giving credence to his conspiratorial rhetoric, bin Laden employs Quran *suras* to bolster his evidence against Judaism. For example, he states: "The Jews have lied about the Creator, and even more so about His creations. The Jews are murderers of the prophets, the violators of agreements . . . These are the Jews: usurers and whoremongers . . . Allah said of them: 'Have they a share in [Allah's] dominion? If they have, they will not give up so much [of it] as would equal a spot on the stone of a date [Quran 4:53].'"[40] By designating an incorrigible enemy, whom even Allah condemns, and by consistently articulating this enemy's sinister goals, al-Qaeda intends to create a sense of dire urgency among Muslims to defend Islam, so that they seriously contemplate the prospects of participating in jihad, if not pursuing *istishhad*.

Similar to their roles in the operational advancement and legitimization of suicide terrorism, Palestinian organizations have helped to construct the commonly accepted anti-Jewish narrative that currently exists in the Islamic world. For example, Hamas reinvigorates the traditional anti-Semitic line in its 1988 Charter, stating that:

[The Jews] stood behind the French Revolution, the Communist Revolution, and most of the revolutions we have heard and hear about, here and there . . . [I]t has become common knowledge that [they caused] World War I . . . [and] World War II . . . [They also] inspired the formation of the United Nations and the Security Council instead of the League of Nations, in order to rule the world through them. No war broke out anywhere without [Jews'] fingerprints on it.[41]

Predating al-Qaeda's practice by a decade, Hamas goes on to quote the Quran, citing *sura* 5:64: "So often as they shall kindle a fire for war, Allah shall extinguish it; and they shall set their minds to act corruptly in the earth, but Allah loveth not the corrupt doers."[42] To connect the Quranic passages to the present day, Hamas makes statements such as: "The Nazism of the Jews includes [even] women and children; it terrorizes everyone. These Jews ruin people's livelihoods, steal their money, and their honor."[43] Hamas, like al-Qaeda, seeks to awaken a sense of duty among average Muslims. It declares, "jihad [in Palestine is] an individual obligation for every Muslim. In the confrontation with the usurpation of Palestine by the Jews, we must raise the banner of jihad."[44] With the massive media exposure that the Israeli-Palestinian conflict receives across the Islamic world, the rhetoric of Hamas and Fatah is commonly broadcast along with breaking news. Their views of Israel, Jews, and Zionism accordingly reach countless households across the greater Arab and Islamic worlds.

Establishing a nexus between the potential jihadi and the larger-than-life struggle of the *umma* provides an opportune way to increase the number of new jihadis, especially within communities already disaffected by one of the defined enemies of Islam. Contrasting Western society with an idealized Islamic one gives those Muslims who might find the West disillusioning, immoral, or corrupt an additional impetus for participating in something that aims at "correcting" these ills. However, Israel's "occupation" of the *al-Aqsa* mosque in Jerusalem, the third holiest site in Islam, and the U.S. "occupation" of the Grand Mosque in Mecca, the holiest site in Islam, stand as the two foremost Islamist grievances that have motivated nascent jihadis. Accordingly, an overwhelming majority of al-Qaeda's attacks have targeted either U.S. or Jewish/Israeli interests. Ultimately, al-Qaeda has learned from Palestinian Islamists how to shape arguments to best direct the individual to the decision that one must personally defend Islam at all costs, even if it means paying the price with one's own life.

SOCIAL NETWORKS

In both the Palestinian and jihadi-Salafi cases, social networks have played increasingly prominent roles in facilitating suicide terrorism, largely because they provide a social space for immersing individuals in the concepts of jihad and *istishhad*. For Palestinians, the culture of martyrdom has influenced society to the extent that since the late 1990s organizations no longer have to seek out potential *shuhada*, but instead select them from a long line of willing and eager candidates. Ami Pedahzur notes: "[today] suicide bombers are not recruited, nor do they undergo a training process. They are peripheral figures in the network who join the ranks ad hoc from the environment close to the network, for the purpose of carrying out a suicide attack."[45] Al-Qaeda *shuhada* are usually not recruited, per se. Instead, a future *shahid* joins a social network,[46] a web of contacts that immerses the individual in the jihadi lifestyle, transmits its values, and puts him or her in contact with a dispatcher. Initially lured by tribal ties or identity-based religious, political, or social issues, the individual accepts over time the ideological framing, solutions, and prescriptions of those around him or her. Eventually, if an opportunity presents itself, the person volunteers for a "martyrdom operation." The culture of martyrdom, often within the confines of a social network, succeeds in awakening the individual's duty to take matters into his or her own hands.

THE PALESTINIAN LEGACY TODAY: SUICIDE TERRORISM AS A GLOBAL PHENOMENON

Since the onslaught of the second *intifada* in September 2000 and the 9/11 attacks a year later, suicide-terror attacks have increased dramatically. Palestinians launched more suicide-terror attacks than any other movement until surpassed by al-Qaeda in Iraq in late 2005.[47] Today, organizations affiliated with al-Qaeda's global jihad continue to comprise the majority of those launching such attacks. Yet without the precedents set by Palestinians, al-Qaeda's *istishhad*-fueled jihad would have required much more preparation. Palestinian organizations perfected the process of deploying suicide-homicide bombers, as they went from recruiting to selecting *shahid* candidates within a decade. Palestinian organizations convinced not only Palestinian society, but also large portions of the greater Sunni world, that suicide-homicide attackers truly are "martyrs," and thus that suicide-homicide attacks are really "martyrdom operations." Palestinians garnered international support from prestigious Islamic authorities, leading to the Sunni legitimization of suicide-homicide attacks against civilians, i.e., suicide terrorism. Furthermore, by demonizing Israelis and Jews, Palestinian society has helped to perpetuate conspiracy theories and other forms of conflict framing that encourage a violent response from Muslims.

In formulating a unique *modus operandi*, al-Qaeda synthesized Hezbollah's symbolic and simultaneous targeting with the Palestinians' mass targeting of civilians. Characterized by suicide-homicide bombers attacking Israeli civilian buses, cafés, malls, and other pedestrian targets, the Palestinian *shahid* became a premier icon in the Sunni world. The Palestinian *shahid*, ingrained in the mind of anyone who viewed Arabic-language satellite television, particularly during the second *intifada*, surely offered an important inspiration on its own. In addition, the 9/11 attacks exemplify the grandiose jihadi terror attack. But for the smaller, localized groups that have carried out most of al-Qaeda's post-9/11 operations, the Palestinian *shahid* has offered a more tenable model.

Ultimately, the Palestinian suicide-homicide bomber, as the icon of the second *intifada*, symbolized the Palestinian cause, and in so doing produced a prototype for terrorist organizations such as those within al-Qaeda's international network. Palestinian suicide-homicide bombers, then, have had anything but an isolated effect. Terrorism, and particularly suicide-homicide attacks, is a continuous learning process for the global terror community. Since the early Palestinian suicide-terror campaigns in the mid-1990s, popular Islamic concepts of martyrdom and jihadi suicide terrorism have steadily merged. Already, al-Qaeda has adopted the socio-cultural and religious lessons put into practice by Palestinians (e.g., *fard ayn*, conflict framing, etc.) and combined them with bin Laden's universal message, which has rapidly disseminated across the *umma* via satellite television, the Internet, and other means of contemporary mass communication. Al-Qaeda's shift in focus from jihad to *istishhad* represents a Palestinianization of the international jihadi-Salafi movement. Moreover, it signals that the advancements in suicide terrorism made by the Palestinian *shahid* and its complementary culture of martyrdom will likely continue to inspire imitation and, therefore, have reverberating effects for years to come.

NOTES

1. See Assaf Moghadam, *The Globalization of Martyrdom: Al Qaeda, Salafi Jihad, and the Diffusion of Suicide Attacks* (Baltimore: The Johns Hopkins University Press, 2008), 41, 222–24, 251, 304, note 1; Mohammed M. Hafez, *Suicide Bombers in Iraq: The Strategy and Ideology of Martyrdom* (Washington, DC: United States Institute for Peace Press, 2007), 3, 26, note 1.

2. Martha Crenshaw, "Foreword," in Hafez, *Suicide Bombers in Iraq*, ix.

3. Joseph Felter and Brian Fishman, *Al-Qa'ida's Foreign Fighters in Iraq: A First Look at the Sinjar Records* (West Point: Combating Terrorism Center, 2007), 19; Richard A. Oppel Jr., "Foreign Fighters in Iraq Are Tied to Allies of U.S.," *New York Times*, November 22, 2007; Susan B. Glasser, "'Martyrs' in Iraq Mostly Saudi," *Washington Post*, May 15, 2005.

4. Ami Pedahzur, *Suicide Terrorism* (Malden: Polity Press, 2005), 241–42.

5. See Benjamin T. Acosta, "The Palestinian Shahid and the Development of the Model 21st Century Islamic Terrorist" (unpublished M.A. thesis, California State University-San Bernardino, 2008), 1–13, 173–209.

6. See the comprehensive list of Palestinian suicide-homicide attacks (1993–2008) in Acosta, 225–233; and Intelligence and Terrorism Information Center, *Anti-Israeli Terrorism, 2006: Data, Analysis and Trends* (2007): 51–55, http://www.terrorism-info.org.il.

7. See Bruce Hoffman, *Inside Terrorism*, revised and expanded ed. (New York: Columbia University Press, 2006), 64, 71–79.

8. David Brooks, "The Culture of Martyrdom: How Suicide Bombing Became not Just a Means but an End," *The Atlantic Monthly* 289, no 6 (June, 2002), 19.

9. Recognized by Robert Baer in *The Cult of the Suicide Bomber*, prod. and dir. David Betty and Kevin Toolis, 1 hr. 35 min., Many Rivers Films, 2006.

10. See Mohammed M. Hafez, "Dying to Be Martyrs: The Symbolic Dimension of Suicide Terrorism," in *Root Causes of Suicide Terrorism: The Globalization of Martyrdom*, ed. Ami Pedahzur (New York: Routledge, 2005), 76, note 2 and 77, notes 4–5; also Hafez, *Suicide Bombers in Iraq*, 168, 185, note 7.

11. Khaled Mashal, Al-Jazeera TV, July 16, 2007, trans. in "Hamas Leader Khaled Mash'al Praises Sheikh Yousef Al-Qaradhawi," Middle East Media Research Institute [hereafter MEMRI], Special Dispatch, no. 1672, August 2, 2001, 2007, http://www.memri.org.

12. Ibid.

13. See Hafez, "Dying to Be Martyrs," 77, note 4.

14. See Moghadam, *The Globalization of Martyrdom*, 104.

15. Alexis Debat, "Osama bin Laden's Heir," *National Interest* 80 (2005): 155–57; Hafez, *Suicide Bombers in Iraq*, 171–73, 178–83.

16. Ely Karmon, "Who Bombed Northern Israel? Al-Qaida and Palestine," *International Institute for Counter-Terrorism (ICT): Articles* (2006), http://www.instituteforcounterterrorism.org.

17. Notes from ICT seminar on "The Global Jihad," given by Reuven Paz, in Herzliya, Israel, on June 21, 2005.

18. Prime Minister's Office, Israel. "The two British Muslims who were involved in the bombing at Mike's Place were dispatched to perpetrate the attack by the Hamas military command in the Gaza Strip," June 15, 2003, http://www.pmo.gov.il/PMOEng/Archive/Press+Releases/2003/06/Spokes man7306.htm.

19. Rohan K. Gunaratna, "The New al-Qaida: Developments in the Post-9/11 Evolution of al-Qaida," in *Post-Modern Terrorism: Trends, Scenarios and Future Threats*, ed. Boaz Ganor (Herzliya: Publishing House, 2005), 47.

20. Gunaratna, "The New al-Qaida," 43.

21. "Usama bin Laden: Al Qaeda Will Continue Holy War Until Liberation of Palestine," *Associated Press*, May 16, 2008.

22. Quoted in Gilles Kepel, *Jihad: The Trail of Political Islam,* trans. Anthony F. Roberts (Cambridge, MA: Harvard University Press, 2002), 147.

23. Lee Keath, "Bin Laden Wants 'Caravan' of Martyrs," *Associated Press*, September 11, 2007.

24. Yoram Schweitzer and Sari Goldstein Ferber, "Al-Qaeda and the Internationalization of Suicide Terrorism," *Memorandum no. 78* (Tel Aviv: Jaffe Center for Strategic Studies, 2005), 11 and 40.

25. Gunaratna, "The New al-Qaida," 48.

26. Schweitzer and Goldstein Ferber, "Al-Qaeda and the Internationalization of Suicide Terrorism," 9.

27. Quoted in Kepel, *Jihad*, 147.

28. Mohammed M. Hafez, *Manufacturing Human Bombs: The Making of Palestinian Suicide Bombers* (Washington, DC: United States Institute for Peace Press, 2006), 36.

29. Pedahzur, *Suicide Terrorism*, 163.

30. Assaf Moghadam, "The Roots of Suicide Terrorism: A Multi-Causal Approach," in *Root Causes of Suicide Terrorism: The Globalization of Martyrdom*, ed. Ami Pedahzur (New York: Routledge, 2005), 98.

31. Notes from ICT seminar on "Modern and Post-Modern Terrorism Strategies," given by Boaz Ganor and Itamar Marcus, in Herzliya, Israel on June 9, 2005.

32. See Acosta, "The Palestinian Shahid," 50–172.

33. Hafez, *Suicide Bombers in Iraq*, 16.

34. *The World Islamic Front's Declaration to Wage Jihad against the Jews and Crusaders* in Raymond Ibrahim, ed. and trans., *The Al-Qaeda Reader* (New York: Broadway Books, 2007), 13.

35. In Ibrahim, *The Al-Qaeda Reader*, 12.

36. See statements by Osama bin Laden in Ibrahim, *The Al-Qaeda Reader*, 211.

37. In Ibrahim, *The Al-Qaeda Reader*, 276–77.

38. Sheikh Yousef al-Qaradhawi, Qatar TV, on February 25, 2006, trans. in "Leading Islamist Yousef Al-Qaradhawi: We Are Fighting in the Name of Islam," MEMRI, Special Dispatch, no. 1102, February 28, 2006, http://www.memri.org.

39. Reuven Paz, "The Islamic Legitimacy of Palestinian Suicide Terrorism," in *Countering Suicide Terrorism*, updated ed., ed. Boaz Ganor (Herzliya: ICT, 2007), 61–62.

40. Osama bin Laden, "Sermon for the Feast of the Sacrifice," Al-Jazeera TV, February 16, 2003, trans. in "Bin Laden's Sermon for the Feast of the Sacrifice," MEMRI, Special Dispatch, no. 476, March 6, 2003, http://www.memri.org. I would like to thank Dr. Richard Saccone for identifying this *sura* as Quran 4:53.

41. Hamas charter in Shaul Mishal and Avraham Sela, *The Palestinian Hamas: Vision, Violence, and Coexistence* (New York: Columbia University Press, 2000), 189–90.

42. Hamas charter in Ibid., 190.

43. Hamas charter in Ibid., 188.

44. Hamas charter in Ibid., 184–85.

45. See Ami Pedahzur and Arie Perliger, "The Changing Nature of Suicide Attacks: A Social Network Perspective," *Social Forces* 84, no. 4 (2006): 2000.

46. Marc Sageman, *Understanding Terror Networks* (Philadelphia: University of Pennsylvania Press, 2004), 121–24.

47. According to data compiled by the National Security Studies Center at the University of Haifa, al-Qaeda in Iraq and affiliated groups passed Palestinian organizations sometime shortly after June 2005. See Pedahzur, *Suicide Terrorism*, 247–53; Moghadam, *The Globalization of Martyrdom*, 222–24, 304, note 1; compare with Palestinian suicide-homicide attacks, in Acosta, 225–33; and Intelligence and Terrorism Information Center, 51–55. Regarding Liberation Tigers of Tamil Eelam (LTTE) suicide-homicide attacks, Hoffman notes: "No precise widely accepted total is easily accessible. Dr. Rohan Gunaratna claims that the total was 168 as of the year 2000 . . . A *New York Times* article, however, puts the total number at 220 attacks . . . The Tigers themselves claim that as of 1999 the LTTE had conducted 147 suicide attacks." See Hoffman, 327, note 33.

PART VI

Economic Reform and Reforming Islam

CHAPTER 13

Economic Justice in the Middle East: A Bad Idea, Badly Done

Patrick Clawson

Middle Easterners have good reason to complain about their econo-mies—not only about the mediocre growth but also about the injustice of corruption, inequities, and bad government services for the poor. That said, Islamists offer no credible argument that "Islam is the solution." Their economic proposals are simply repackaging of the old socialist ways that captured the region's imagination when so charismatically articulated by Egyptian President Gamal Abdul Nasser. The Middle East's experience with these policies has been disappointing, whether implemented by Third World socialists, pan-Arabists, or Islamists. By contrast, international development experts have articulated a clearer indictment of the region's economic injustices and a more convincing program for achieving a more just economy.

BACKGROUND: THE CAUSE FOR COMPLAINT

How one evaluates the Middle East's economies depends in no small part on what time period one considers and what expectations one has. Over the last few decades, the region's performance has been middling in comparison to other developing regions. But the longer the time frame adopted, the more consideration given to the region's inherent advan-tages, and the more the point of comparison is the absolute gap with the industrial West rather than the growth rate relative to other developing countries, the more disappointing has been the Middle East's perform-ance. The region was well placed for rapid growth in the last 50 years, being close—physically, historically, and often culturally—to the

booming European market, having many countries well endowed in natural resources or human capital (though seldom in both), and in many
cases having powerful friends prepared to extend significant assistance.
Despite these advantages, only a few Middle Eastern countries have nar-
rowed the gap between themselves and the advanced industrial economies in the last fifty years, while many other Middle Eastern countries
have fallen further and further behind the West. And fifty years is only a
blink of an eye for the history-conscious people of the Middle East,
whose point of reference for how their societies should be faring is often
the days of glory in centuries past, when the Middle East was more
advanced and more powerful than Europe—by which standard the
region is sadly lacking.

Middle Easterners are harsh judges of their region's economic performance. The first *Arab Human Development Report* in 2002, written by leading
Arab thinkers, had harsh criticism of the region's performance, especially
the failure to turn higher income into broader development, leading to
deficits in freedom, women's empowerment, and human capabilities and
knowledge.[1] The sense of profound disappointment in that report comes
in no small part from the Arab peoples' self-conception that the Middle
East should have great and powerful societies; the Iranian self-conception
is even higher, namely, that they are a great and powerful society, under-
valued by the rest of the world. After all, the Middle East was a world
power center in a time that seems to Middle Easterners like only yester-
day. A mere 300 years ago, the Ottoman Empire, which at the time
included the Arab Middle East all the way to North Africa, stood at the
gates of Vienna; it was defeated only by the combined armies of Europe.
Only 200 years ago, with Napoleon's invasion of Egypt, was the Arab
world rudely awakened to its backwardness relative to Europe. About
the same time, Iran began to lose half of its territory in a disastrous series
of wars against Russian and British Indian forces.

Even closer to the present day, the gap with Europe was nothing like
what it has become. Consider how the Mediterranean looked on the eve
of World War II. With fascist rule in Spain and Italy, its European shores
were arguably less democratic than the imperfect parliamentary democracies in Egypt and Iraq. Alexandria, if not Cairo, was arguably more liberal socially, freer intellectually, and generally more cosmopolitan than
southern Europe; Islam had less of a deadening role in Egypt than did
the Catholic Church in Italy and Spain or the Orthodox Churches in
southeast Europe. It is depressing to read in *Egypt at Mid-Century*,
Charles Issawi's description of the relative income of various Mediterranean economies in 1950, that Egypt's income per person was 80 percent
that of Greece and 45 percent that of Italy. And French Algeria was much
richer than Egypt.[2] The best estimate is that on the eve of World War II,
the gap in income between the Mediterranean's northern and southern

shores—between southern Europe and North Africa and the Levant—was no more than the two-to-one gap existing then between the northern and southern parts of the United States. By contrast, World Bank data show that in 2005 Egypt's income was a mere 11 percent that of Greece and 6 percent that of Italy.

Indeed, as recently as twenty years ago, the Middle East looked like an economic success story. In the period 1960–85, its growth was well above the world average, at 3.7 percent per person per year in real terms. The region was blessed by an international environment favorable for growth. Vigorous world economic growth in the 1960s raised demand for Middle East products, especially oil. The Middle East kept growing in the 1970s when the rest of the world economy went into the doldrums; the Middle East was uniquely insulated because of the oil price boom (the exception was Israel, where the economy fell into deep trouble).

The 1960–85 boom years were misused by Middle East governments to lay the foundations for later problems. The public sector's weight in the economy expanded massively; private investment was only a modest share of national income, while massive sums were poured into public investments. Much of those public investments went either into overbuilt infrastructure well in excess of needs or into inward-oriented industries that were uncompetitive and intensive users of expensive imported inputs and non-renewable natural resources, as well as being highly polluting. At least as damaging was the steering of the benefits of the sustained economic growth to key constituencies, especially civil servants and workers in state-owned enterprises. This was at the root of the "authoritarian bargain" in which the public acquiesced to autocrats controlling politics in return for jobs and generous public services for the privileged middle classes. Furthermore, the "redistributive state" entrenched and empowered bureaucrats who extended and deepened their control over the economy.

From 1985 to 2005, most of the Middle East economies outside Israel fell badly behind the rest of the world, growing at a slower rate than even sub-Saharan Africa. The region did not fall backward in an absolute sense; it just stopped moving forward. For the Middle East and North Africa overall (excluding Israel), the International Monetary Fund (IMF) calculated that 2002 per capita income was no higher than it had been at its peak in 1977, twenty-five years earlier. The region largely missed the global 1990s boom; only Israel grew rapidly in that decade, although some of the modestly reforming non-oil economies, especially Tunisia and Egypt, grew at respectable rates. The inward-oriented, uncompetitive Middle East industries were not able to take advantage of the explosion in world trade in manufactured goods; in 2003, the entire Arab Middle East exported fewer manufactured goods than did the Philippines. Particularly disappointing has been the extent to which productivity has stagnated and private investment lagged. Overall investment levels have stayed relatively high only because Middle East governments, especially in the oil-rich states, kept up their high spending on public investment. But all too often, they were pouring good money after bad. More and more investment has been needed to produce each additional unit of output; in economic jargon, the incremental capital output ratio, or ICOR, has risen sharply.

One encouraging development, however, is that on some important social indicators like longer life expectancy and better female education, the Middle East in recent decades has done quite well compared to other regions. Even more hopeful, the improvements in education and health came primarily from greater efficiency, such as better targeting to underserved groups, rather than from greater spending.

POLITICS OVER ECONOMICS

Those who have done best in the Middle East over the last fifty years have been Israel and the Gulf oil monarchies. Israel has transformed itself from a poor country into an advanced industrial economy, much like those in the middle of the European pack. The Gulf oil kingdoms have gone from being some of the most backward and isolated countries on earth—well behind sub-Saharan African countries such as Ghana, Kenya, or Ivory Coast—to being both well-to-do and modern. It is striking that these high performers have been the countries excoriated by the region's radicals—leftists in the past, Islamists now—for their close relations with the United States. Other Middle East countries that have done relatively better than most, such as Tunisia and Jordan, have also been more friendly to the United States than most. By contrast, the region's worst economic performers have been Iraq and Algeria, both with per capita incomes barely above the levels of forty years ago—and both are countries that had radical governments sharply hostile to the United States for most of the last few decades.

It would be quite wrong to say that the reason for Israeli or Gulf monarchical prosperity has been good relations with the United States, or that the cause of Iraqi and Algerian stagnation has been bad relations with the United States. Instead, both the economic performance and the state of relations with the United States have flowed from the same cause: the absolute priority placed on radical political ideology at the expense of all else. Placing priority on politics has been a major problem for economic development across the region, whether that ideology was Zionism, Palestinian nationalism, Arab unity, Islamic revolution, or anything else. Most obviously, those ideologies have been at the root of the region's many wars, some of which have devastated economies—witness the state of the Iraqi economy after more than twenty-five years of war.

In addition, ideology has often impeded sensible economic policymaking; leaders have been unwilling to challenge long-held shibboleths, afraid that the short-term political risks would outweigh the long-term economic advantage. The priority on politics over economics has become a self-reinforcing cycle in which poor economic performance creates discontent off which radical ideologues can feed. Prosperity could facilitate solutions to the region's political problems: people who are more satisfied are more likely to consider difficult political compromises.

For decades, the region's various political ideologies converged on much the same economic approach, which can best be described as Third World socialism. The most charismatic articulator of this approach was Egyptian president Gamal Abdul Nasser, whose eloquent rhetoric about Arab socialism captured the imagination of a whole generation of Arabs and Iranians in the early 1960s. Ironically, many of the elements of "Nasserism" were similar to the economic policies long applied by the Labor socialists in Israel, both of which were openly inspired by Marxism. The Third World socialist economic policies were much like the left wing of European social democracy: the leading role of state-owned firms in all aspects of the economy, be it finance, industry, services, or even agriculture; strict government regulation of private enterprise; large government bureaucracies that provided employment for the politically well connected; redistributive policies that taxed the wealthy heavily and provided extensive subsidies. The Middle East's experience with these policies has not been that different from Europe's: at first, good growth and improved well-being, but increasing problems as bureaucracy becomes entrenched, until the spreading of inflexible regulation impedes growth and drags down efficiency. Unfortunately for the Middle East outside Israel, the problems of Third World socialism were masked for a decade by the post-1973 oil boom. While politically influential Egypt spoke loudly about opening the economy as early as the mid-1970s, in practice, little happened until the late 1980s. And in Egypt, as throughout most of the region, Third World socialism still retains significant support among intellectuals, despite its dismal track record.

In recent times, the ideology sweeping the Middle East has been political Islam. Despite the political Islamists' slogan "Islam is the solution," they have in fact had few economic ideas except the old socialist ways. When the Islamist revolutionaries came to power in Iran in 1979, they proceeded to implement much the same economic program that Nasser had developed in the early 1960s, with much the same result: modest results at first, followed by steadily worse problems. The Iranian revolutionaries made few attempts to introduce clearly Islamic elements in their economic policy. For instance, faced with the problem of how to ban interest, as required by most interpretations of Islamic law, they decided on blatant hypocrisy, simply renaming interest as profit-sharing while in fact doing nothing to change the underlying economic reality. This is particularly striking, given that some eminent Western economists have long advocated that banks share profits rather than pay fixed interest, on the grounds that this is a better way to ensure banking stability than government-guaranteed deposit insurance. In any case, twenty-first-century political Islamists barely refer to economic issues and rarely argue that Islam will solve the region's economic problems. Perhaps they agree with Ayatollah Ruhollah Khomeini's comment: "A wise man cannot imagine that we sacrificed in order to get cheaper watermelons."[3]

In contrast to the region's fascination with politics, Arabs in particular have been much less interested in economic development. In *The Arab Economies in a Changing World*, Howard Pack and Marcus Noland document the relative absence of Arab voices in contemporary debates about development strategy and how little Arabs discuss the development experiences of other countries, such as East Asia's success.[4] This is less true of Israel and Iran; for instance, Iranian intellectuals have much debated what lessons to learn from Asia's rapid development, arguing about which country's model would be most appropriate for Iran to emulate. Yet even in Israel and Iran, the national focus is on politics rather than economics. It would be simply unthinkable for Iranian president Mahmoud Ahmadinejad or supreme religious leader Ali Khamenei to emulate the attempts of Chinese Communist Party leader Deng Hsiao Ping "to make some people rich first, so as to lead all the people to wealth" (this is commonly translated into the slogan "To get rich is glorious").[5] China came through its Cultural Revolution determined to put economic development above ideological purity. Many in the Middle East would disagree with that ordering of priorities.

Even those who care about economics frequently have a zero-sum mentality. In the Middle East, mutual benefit is not necessarily seen as a good thing. Locals may view the other side as an enemy that they do not want strengthened—a trait often evident in Israeli-Palestinian dealings on economic matters. Or they may be sure that if the foreigner benefits, that means they are being cheated and exploited—an attitude heard often in Arab and Iranian objection to dealings with international oil companies and other foreign investors. Such an atmosphere, where politics matters more than prosperity, where mutual benefit is regarded with suspicion, is far removed from the "rational economic man" assumed in economic theory. It is hard to achieve a more just economy when important social groups are most dedicated to preventing the advancement of others. Islamists are among the leading adherents to such a view, as illustrated by their dedication to attacking ordinary Israelis, in striking contrast to their general indifference to improving the situation of Palestinians. The focus is on tearing down the perceived enemy, not on building up one's friends.

THE MIDDLE EAST FREEDOM AND DEMOCRACY DEFICIT

To Western ears, justice seems closely related to democracy and freedom. However Westerners define a "just economy"—whether as free markets reigning supreme or as social welfare plus regulation—they generally see that just economy as closely linked to political freedom and democratic governance. Perhaps counter-intuitively, democracy and freedom are not, in fact, the most important governance issues for economic development.

The Middle East Freedom Deficit

The most obvious characteristic of Middle Eastern political systems is the "freedom deficit," in the words of the first *Arab Human Development Report* in 2002.[6] That report, prepared by leading Arab intellectuals for the United Nations Development Programme (UNDP) and the Arab Fund for Economic and Social Development, bluntly identified the lack of freedom as the first of three key deficits plaguing the region; the others were the women's empowerment deficit and the human capabilities/ knowledge deficit. That report pointed out that on the "freedom scores" prepared annually by the UNDP as a component of its "human development index," the Arab world's score was less than half that of any other part of the world, and less than a fifth that of North America. An equally bleak picture emerges from the detailed Freedom House annual reports, *Freedom in the World*.[7] In 2006, the Middle East had exactly one of the world's eighty-nine "free" countries, namely, Israel. By contrast, the Middle East's twenty countries included twelve of the world's forty-five "not free" countries, including three of the eight countries that were at the absolute bottom of the freedom scale. Seen another way, whereas 46 percent of the world's peoples lived in free countries, only 2 percent of Middle Easterners lived in free lands. While 36 percent of the global population lived in states that were not free, 80 percent of Middle Easterners were in lands that were not free. The only bright spot was that the Middle East's record was improving slightly; over the preceding few years, some countries had graduated from "not free" to "partly free."

The Freedom House index is based on a checklist of ten political rights and fifteen civil liberties, such as the right to organize political parties, realistic possibility for the opposition to gain power, a political process free of domination by the military or other unelected group (e.g., religious hierarchies), freedom from pervasive corruption, full political rights for minority groups, freedom of the press, freedom of assembly, free trade unions, independence of the judiciary, an open government operating with full transparency, rule of law, equal treatment for the various segments of the population, the right to own property, and personal social freedoms. As these criteria illustrate, the concept "freedom" is much broader than the question of whether a country has elections. Many Middle Eastern states have elections, but subject to significant limitations, such as pre-vetting of candidates for acceptability to the authorities (e.g., Iran), regime scrutiny of ballots as they are cast by the voter (e.g., Syria), or severely limited powers of the elected officials (e.g., the advisory character of the partially elected, partially appointed Bahraini Majlis). The only one of the twenty Middle Eastern states that Freedom House rates as an electoral democracy is Israel. By contrast, it rates 122 of the 172 states outside the Middle East as electoral democracies. Put another way, 5 percent of Middle Eastern states are electoral democracies, whereas 71 percent of non-Middle Eastern states are electoral democracies.

Scholars have vigorously debated the reasons for the "Middle East democracy exception." The most common factor cited is that many Middle East countries are "rentier states," to use Vladimir Lenin's evocative expression; the government gets its revenue without having to tax the people, either from oil income or foreign aid (much of it from oil-rich Middle East states).[8] Lisa Anderson coined the phrase "no representation without taxation," arguing that "the taxed devise ways to be represented."[9] This thesis is hard to evaluate by looking at the Middle East's experience, since both rentier and non-rentier states in the Middle East are generally undemocratic; however, statistical studies of the global experience offer support for the theory.

Other factors cited for the absence of democracy in the Middle East outside Israel include cultural and ideological factors. The particular cultural factors cited by authors to make this case have varied over time; the current favorite seems to be "neo-patriarchy," that is, traditional patterns of gender relations and authority within the family. As for ideological impediments to democracy, perhaps the broadest formulation of the phenomenon was John Waterbury, who argued, "I can think of no other region in the world where the rhetoric of governance has been more ends-oriented, moralizing and patronizing. Because the mission is sacred—anti-imperialism, liberation, socialism, Islamic justice—debate over ends and means is immediately seen and characterized as subversive or blasphemous."[10]

A particularly sensitive issue has been whether and to what extent Islam explains the Middle East's poor record of freedom and democracy. Certainly the historical record offers little reason to think that is the case. When Europe was deep in the Dark Ages, Muslim societies were much more tolerant, offering greater freedoms for intellectuals and minorities. Nor do the Muslim sacred books and the teachings of the major Muslim religious leaders show attitudes to freedom and democracy that contrast with those of Christianity or Judaism. Indeed, the fairest interpretation of the texts and traditions of all three monotheistic traditions is that they are neither particularly enthusiastic about nor particularly hostile to political freedom. All that said, it is a disturbing fact that empirical studies of what holds back democracy have found that the proportion of the population that is Muslim is a statistically significant factor.[11] Of course, it is only one of several such factors, none of which by itself explains in full the absence of democracy in any society. Still, the effect is there. And there can be no denying that the loudest and most extreme opposition to political freedoms in the contemporary world come from the radical Islamist fringe that resonates with some Middle Eastern youth.

Freedom, Democracy, and Growth

While disturbing, the poor Middle Eastern record on freedom and democracy is not necessarily a major factor in the region's weak record of economic development. The link between economic growth and freedom, much less democracy, seems weak. As Nobel Prize-winning economist Amartya Sen presented in *Development as Freedom*—a book dedicated to arguing the merits of freedom—"the hypothesis that there is no relation between them in either direction is hard to reject."[12] Intense study of the East Asian growth miracle, in contrast to the poor growth record in Africa, has resulted in a fairly agreed-upon list of policies that promote growth. Political freedom and democracy is not one of these policies. On the other hand, there is no empirical evidence for the thesis, much promoted by authoritarian rulers, that freedom hampers economic growth. The example long cited for that proposition—China's rapid growth under authoritarianism, contrasted with India's slow growth under democracy—looks less convincing today, given that India's growth rate has risen to about the same level as China. In any case, it is only one anecdotal data point, no more convincing than the opposite anecdote that the best growth record in Africa by far is Botswana, an oasis of democracy in that continent.

While they may not affect economic growth as such, political and civil rights do seem connected to some other aspects of economic well-being. In particular, in freer societies, popular pressure forces governments to be more responsive to natural disasters, such as famines and earthquakes. There is good reason to think that democratic societies are less likely to engage in war; as the people of the Middle East know all too well from the many wars that have ravaged the region, there are fewer aspects of well-being more important than peace. Finally, the case can be made that freer societies are more stable politically and less prone to be torn apart by ethnic and religious tensions. Even there, the evidence is not completely firm; consider the contrast between Lebanon, with its relatively free politics and its raging religious tensions—including a fifteen-year civil war—and Syria, with its strict authoritarian politics that has kept a cap on ethno-religious tensions in a deeply divided society (the

Syrian government is controlled by a minority group, the Alawites, who are despised by many in the majority Sunni Arab community).

The economic argument for freedom and democracy was ably summarized by World Bank economist Mustapha Kamel Nabli: "Democratization yields benefits in the form of individual freedom and empowerment that are valued independently of their consequences in terms of growth and material wealth. But democratization is also good because democracies can (a) yield long-run growth rates that are more predictable; (b) produce greater short-term stability; (c) handle adverse shocks much better; and (d) deliver better distributional outcomes."[13]

More problematic for Middle East economic development than the lack of democracy and freedom has been the misguided search for economic justice through government intervention. The Middle East has been plagued by governments that try to do too much, and do it poorly. The region's two great economic problems have been (1) the heavy hand of the state intervening in areas where the free market would do better and (2) governments that do not deliver effective basic services and rule of law. The second problem—poor governance—deserves some explanation.

In the 1980s, the term "poor governance" was often used as a euphemism for corruption. Since then, research on the role of political institutions and arrangements in economic development has advanced considerably. Armed with a clearer understanding of what constitutes good governance, researchers can say with considerable confidence that compared to other regions of the world, the Middle East and North Africa, in the words of the World Bank, "ranks at the bottom on the index of overall governance quality."[14] That is true in each of the two major categories of governance that matter for economic development: accountability and inclusiveness—that is, nondiscrimination in access to services and equality before the law. Furthermore, the Middle East ranks at the bottom of global indices of freedom and democracy, which affects quality of life even if the impact on economic growth is less clear.

One of the basic economic problems caused by poor governance is poor public services. Inadequate basic infrastructure drives up costs. Yemen averages 75 days a year without electrical power, while Algeria averages sixteen outages a year, 70 percent of them lasting up to five days. Businesses are forced to rely on high-cost generators or to make do without electricity for days at a time. Meanwhile, poor public education deprives the region of adequate human capital.[15] In Morocco, nearly 35 percent of adult men and 60 percent of adult women are illiterate, about the same level as much poorer countries such as the Central African Republic.[16]

Poor governance also leads to burdensome regulation and inadequate rules enforcement. A 2003 World Bank study of its Middle East and

North Africa region found that registering a new business on average took 60 days and cost 62 percent of per capita income, compared to 11 percent in developed Western countries. Dispute resolution is cumbersome and protracted: the average time to complete a commercial court case is more than two years in Jordan and Lebanon, which have among the most efficient court systems among non-democratic Middle Eastern states, while the average time in Egypt exceeds six years.[17]

A state that is unable to deliver public services and unable to enforce its rules can hardly be seen as a just state. The complaints of Islamists that Middle Eastern states are unjust have much merit. What is much less clear is whether there is anything uniquely Islamic about the character of justice that Middle Eastern peoples want, and whether Islamists' rule would be any better at delivering good governance. One way to get at the question is to examine the record in one country long under self-described Islamic rule, namely the Islamic Republic of Iran. Let us therefore examine how governance, and the economy in general, has fared under the Iranian Islamic Republic.

ISLAMIST IRAN: A JUST ECONOMY?

Economics was not at the center of the Iranian Islamist revolutionaries' vision of a just society, and they have had great difficulty articulating and implementing a specifically Islamic economic justice. Their poor record at achieving a more just economy suggests the shortcoming of an Islamist approach to economics.[18]

While disappointment about the economy contributed to the shah's unpopularity, the revolution was about politics, not economics. While a minority of his followers—bazaar merchants and traditionalist clerics—opposed almost any state intervention as incompatible with traditional Islamic jurisprudence, and another minority consisted of Western-oriented technocrats, within two years after the 1979 revolution, the levers of power were firmly controlled by a Third Worldist group seeking comprehensive state control in the name of social justice. Faced immediately after the revolution with chaos in the factories and a banking system close to collapse, the new government nationalized much of the economy. At the same time, extensive assets of the former shah and his supporters were confiscated and transferred to new revolutionary foundations (*bonyads*) that were controlled by revolutionaries. Only smaller industries remained in private hands.

Over time, the state's control of the economy grew even further. After war with Iraq started in 1980, the state controlled prices, parceled out foreign exchange only to the politically favored, effectively banned foreign investment, and strictly regulated all economic activity through an unwieldy permit system. Rationing was introduced for staples, with ration coupons distributed at mosques. Since the prices of rationed goods were well below market prices, the producers of such goods—primarily farmers—had little incentive to increase output and felt cheated because their income suffered. The manufacturing sector suffered from a stranglehold of price controls and severe shortages of tightly rationed foreign inputs; profits depended on manipulating the complicated regulations. In this atmosphere of legal confusion and bureaucratic restriction, the companies that did best were those owned by the state or by the various revolutionary foundations (*bonyads*). Despite soaring prices, the official exchange rate was not adjusted; as a result, the price of the dollar on the black market rose to more than ten times its official rate, and anyone who received permission to buy dollars at the official rate (in order to import goods) was then able to sell the dollars (or, more often, the goods imported with those dollars) at a huge markup. To make matters worse, the government went through bouts of overspending that exhausted the available foreign exchange, followed by excessive restrictions, including periodic bans on "luxury" imports, that largely served to enrich those who were able to import such items.

The economy performed as badly as would be expected given the extensive state meddling. Adjusted for inflation, national income fell more than 20 percent between 1977 and 1989. The population rose at a brisk clip, with the result that per capita income fell by nearly half. This occurred at a time when the economy was benefitting from considerable investment and the labor force was increasingly better educated. By the IMF's calculation, these factors should have led to economic growth of 7.2 percent a year, whereas the economy actually shrank 2.4 percent a year.[19] The government's surveys on household budgets confirm the dramatic decline in living standards; adjusted for inflation, the average urban household's income fell in 1988–89 to less than half its 1977–78 level.[20] To be sure, some were hurt much more than others; the modern middle classes (i.e., professionals) were hit particularly hard, while those with good political connections did well.

During the 1980s, the Iranian leadership repeatedly blamed the country's economic problems on the war with Iraq, but there is little evidence that was the case: without the war, the inappropriate revolutionary policies would probably have led to much the same result as was actually observed. A more accurate assessment of the country's economic problems is that oil income allowed the revolutionaries to persist in their economic folly. Having criticized the shah for excessive dependence on oil exports, the revolutionaries did worse: oil's share in government revenue and exports rose, as non-oil revenues and exports fell.

After a decade of poor results, the Iranian revolutionaries shifted economic policy in 1989, adopting many of the same structural adjustment reforms recommended by the World Bank and International Monetary Fund for other developing countries (though revolutionary sensitivities kept Iran from working closely with either of the Bretton Woods institutions). The results were not particularly good, both because of low oil prices in the 1990s and because of the half-hearted nature of the reforms. As the 1990s unfolded, Iran's economic policies and the structure of its economy looked more and more like those of much of the Middle East: dominated by inefficient and corrupt bureaucrats claiming to make modest reforms. In the last decade, it would be hard to see anything uniquely Islamic about the economic policies of the Islamic Republic of Iran. From the widespread popular complaints about corruption, poor government services, and the plight of the poor, it would be hard to say that Iranians view the Islamic Republic's economy as just.

WHAT COULD WORK

While neither Third World socialism nor Islam have brought economic justice or growth, globalization and Western-style economic reform have delivered improved standards of living for ordinary Middle Easterners. Outside observers have often dismissed the Gulf kingdoms' prosperity as artificial and temporary because they are dependent on oil exports, but in fact their export-based approach has done better than the region's inward-looking economies. Algeria and Iran have wasted vast sums—as did Iraq when it had the money—on the vain pursuit of import-substituting industrialization, only to end up with uncompetitive factories that are able to survive only if competing imports are blocked and inputs are subsidized. Iran's automotive industry produces a million vehicles a year, but the cost of imported inputs exceeds what Iran would pay for importing those vehicles; that is, the net value added by Iran's automotive industry is negative. To be sure, world markets are uncertain, but they have proved a better engine for growth than trying to make do on one's own. Consider how Israel's economy bounced back by 2005 after suffering from the 2000 collapse of the high-tech industry in which it was so concentrated. Indeed, the problems encountered by the region's high performers resulted primarily when they resisted globalization, as during the 1990s when the Gulf monarchies dragged their heels against allowing investment by international oil companies. Those Gulf monarchies that have been most open have been the most successful economically. As everyone in the Gulf knows, embracing globalization has been at the heart of Dubai's spectacular prosperity, in spite of its limited oil revenue.

If one important part of the answer has been globalization, another has been Western-style economic reform. The Middle East has been bedeviled by well-entrenched elites that resist needed change. Economic policies and institutions need to evolve to fit changing times. Resistance in the Middle East to pro-growth reforms is deep, in no small part because the bureaucracies that employ most of the region's middle class are suspicious that easing their control over the economy will undercut their political and economic power.

For all their talk of economic reform, bureaucracies prove highly resistant to change. Consider that for all the proclaimed enthusiasm for more openness to trade, less than half of the population of the region lives in a country belonging to the World Trade Organization, the lowest share by far of any developing region. The bureaucrats' corrosive impact held back productivity, which had already stopped growing after 1973 in the few Arab countries for which data are available. In *Trade, Investment, and Development in the Middle East and North Africa*, the World Bank summarizes the problem:

> The underlying reason for poor performance is the lack of commitment by the leadership in governments of the region to new policy directions. . . And a large and influential civil society—comprising large sections of public sector employees, unions, media opinion leaders, and private enterprises—remains deeply wedded to the security and benefits of the old order. Unlike the transition in Eastern Europe, there is no deep commitment to reforming trade and investment—or to fostering markets more generally—within or outside the government. This situation has severely limited the credibility and extent of critical reforms.[21]

Perhaps as damaging has been the bureaucrats' refusal to keep up with the times. For instance, the region's education systems are largely geared toward producing bureaucrats rather than entrepreneurs or technicians, which may have been appropriate when government bureaucracies were expanding rapidly—but that was decades ago.

The single most important reform needed in most countries of the region is greater openness to the world economy by reducing administrative barriers to trade and investment. In *Reducing Vulnerability and Increasing Opportunity*, the World Bank provides an excellent checklist of the other top reform agenda items:

- Sounder macroeconomic management, especially counter-cyclical rather than pro-cyclical fiscal policy; that is, saving the windfalls when oil prices are high to use when prices drop;
- Better governance, with more transparency, respect for law and liberties, and more efficient bureaucracies;
- Reformed labor markets, including trade union rights and bans on ethno-religious discrimination;
- Smaller price distortions, especially lower tariffs, more realistic exchange rates, and smaller subsidies for water, gasoline, and food;
- Strengthened regulatory institutions, especially enforcing property rights and competition;
- More efficient education and health expenditures targeted toward the poor, while providing a framework to encourage private providers; and
- Mitigation of and relief for the risks faced by the most vulnerable, with government social expenditures focused where they can be most efficient rather than tackling too many problems at once.[22]

The prospects look modest for the Middle East economies in coming decades. The great barriers of the past—priority of political ideology over prosperity, suspicions about the outside world and resistance to change—remain largely in place in too many countries for one to be able to predict a bright future for the region. The more likely prospect is that many countries will be unable to create enough meaningful jobs to take advantage of the many young people joining the labor market in the next few years, nor will they prepare adequately for the exploding elderly populations in coming decades. The "demographic transition" the Middle East is undergoing—with birth rates falling dramatically—could be the basis for rapid economic growth, but most countries seem likely to miss the opportunity. The second oil boom, which began in 2005, will provide many countries a substantial windfall, but that may remove the sense of urgency about reforms rather than fueling a transition to sustainable rapid growth. In the next few decades, as in the last few, the region is likely to have a modest economic performance when it could have an excellent one.

NOTES

1. United Nations Development Programme and Regional Bureau for Arab States, *The Arab Human Development Report 2002: Creating Opportunities for Future Generations* (New York: United Nations Development Programme, Regional Bureau for Arab States, 2002).

2. Charles Issawi, *Egypt at Mid-Century: An Economic Survey* (Oxford: Oxford University Press and The Royal Institute for International Affairs, 1954).

3. Ruhollah Khomeini, *Sahifeh-ye Noor* (Tehran: Vezarat-e Ershad-e Eslami, 1999 [AHS 1378]), 5: 409.

4. Marcus Noland and Howard Pack, *The Arab Economies in a Changing World* (Washington, DC: Peterson Institute for International Economics, 2007).

5. Orville Schell, *To Get Rich Is Glorious: China in the Eighties* (New York: Pantheon Books, 1984), 13.

6. *The Arab Human Development Report 2002.*

7. Freedom House, *Freedom in the World Annual Report,* (Washington, DC: Freedom House, 2006).

8. Vladimir Lenin, *Imperialism, the Highest Stage of Capitalism* (New York: International Publishers, 1939), 100.

9. Lisa Anderson, "The State in the Middle East and North Africa," *Comparative Politics* 20 (October 1987): 1–18. See also Michael Ross, "Does Taxation Lead to Representation?" *British Journal of Political Science* 34 (2004): 229–49.

10. John Waterbury, "Democracy without Democrats: The Potential for Linearization in the Middle East," in *Democracy without Democrats? The Renewal of Politics in the Muslim World*, ed. Ghassan Salame (New York: I.B. Tauris, 1994), 26.

11. Michael Ross, "Does Oil Hinder Democracy?" *World Politics* 53 (April 2001): 325–61.

12. Amartya Sen, *Development as Freedom* (New York: Knopf, 1999), 150.

13. Mustapha Kamel Nabli, *Breaking the Barriers to Higher Economic Growth: Better Governance and Deeper Reforms in the Middle East and North Africa* (Washington, DC: World Bank, 2006), 128.

14. Mustapha Kamel Nabli and Charles Humphreys, *Better Governance for Development in the Middle East and North Africa* (Washington, DC: World Bank, 2003), 6.

15. World Bank, *Better Governance for Development in the Middle East and North Africa: Enhancing Inclusiveness and Accountability* (Washington, DC: World Bank, 2003), 98–101.

16. World Bank, *2007 World Development Indicators* (Washington, DC: World Bank, 2007), 87.

17. World Bank, *Better Governance for Development in the Middle East and North Africa: Enhancing Inclusiveness and Accountability* (Washington, DC: World Bank, 2003), 93–96.

18. Patrick Clawson, "The Islamic Republic's Economic Failure," *Middle East Quarterly* 15, no. 4 (Fall 2008): 15–26.

19. International Monetary Fund, *Islamic Republic of Iran—Selected Issues*, IMF Country Report 04/308, September 2004, 13.

20. Patrick Clawson and Michael Rubin, *Eternal Iran: Continuity and Chaos* (New York: Palgrave, 2005), 119.

21. Dipak Das Gupta and Mustapha K. Nabli, *Trade, Investment, and Development in the Middle East and North Africa* (Washington, DC: World Bank, 2003), 22–23.

22. World Bank, *Reducing Vulnerability and Increasing Opportunity: Social Protection in the Middle East and North Africa* (Washington, DC: World Bank, 2002), 83–90.

CHAPTER 14

"For Truth Does Not Oppose Truth": The Agreement of Divine Law and Philosophy in Averroës' *The Book of the Decisive Treatise (Kitab Fasl al-Maqal)*

Terence J. Kleven

In 2004 Fauzi M. Najjar published an essay titled "Ibn Rushd (Averroes) and the Egyptian Enlightenment Movement."[1] In the essay, Najjar provides a useful summary as well as a preliminary evaluation of the Enlightenment Association (*Jam'iyyat al-Tanwir*), which was founded in Egypt in 1992. As the title of Najjar's article suggests, he is interested in the examination of the Association's advocacy of Ibn Rushd as a precursor of the modern scientific outlook, as a defender of the freedom of rational investigation, and as a harbinger of the liberal ideals of freedom, democracy, and equality. Najjar notes that the *Tanwir* Association promotes Averroës as a model of enlightenment, which is evident, for example, in the reprinting in 1993 of Farah Antun's book *Falsafat Ibn Rushd*. Furthermore, several of the leaders in the Association, Mona Abousenna, Mourad Wahba, and 'Atif al-'Iraqi, have published books in support of a modern enlightenment derived from the rationality of Averroës. The *Tanwir* Association positions itself against the Islamists, who reject both democracy and the separation of religion and the state. In opposition to the Association's account of enlightenment, the Islamists claim that Averroës is the founder of the European Enlightenment, with its attendant secularism, and thus they argue that he will lead to the rejection of Islam as the Enlightenment led to the rejection of Christianity in Europe. Najjar's evaluation of the arguments of the *Tanwir* Association is equivocal; he notes the inevitable limitations of an intellectual movement in the midst of masses who are too poor, too busy, or too illiterate to study their writings, but he also affirms that the *Tanwir* Association continues to keep alive cultural discourse by sponsoring conferences and publications. Najjar's judgment would have been more definite and more useful if he had determined whether the Association's advocacy of Averroës is derived from an accurate account of Averroës' philosophy, and also whether the Islamists' rejection of this philosopher is as well founded as they suppose.

Averroës may well provide a more serious source for intellectual revival in the Islamic world than, for example, Mawdudi's defense of Islam in the 1930s through his imitation of fascist attacks on democracy, or Sayyid Qutb's defense of Islam with an action-oriented European existentialism, or Ayatollah Khomeini's advocacy in 1979 of a mixture of Islamic and Western forms in the Constitution of Iran.[2] But has either side in this debate, the advocates of *Tanwir* or the Islamists, adequately understood this medieval Andalusian philosopher? To be sure, if Ernst Renan's account of Averroës is accurate in concluding that Averroës intends philosophy to be the "hidden poison"[3] against religion, Muslims have good reason to reject one of their own illustrious philosophers. Renan's account of the incompatibility and even hostility between science and religion in the writings of Averroës is stated in the first paragraph of his book *Averroès et l'averroïsme*. He writes: "When Averroës died, in 1198, Arab philosophy lost in him its last representative, and the triumph of the Quran over liberal thought was assured for at least six hundred years."[4] Later in the book, in a section on religion, he continues: "Philosophy is the most elevated aim of human nature, but few men are able to attain it. Prophetic revelation is supplied for the commoners. The philosophic debates are not necessary for the people because they only result in weakening faith. These debates are defended with reason, since it is sufficient for the happiness of the simple that they comprehend what they are able to understand."[5] Near the conclusion of this section he writes: "Arab philosophy was therefore in the context of their coreligionists in nearly the same situation as the *libertines* of the seventeenth century."[6] Renan draws a significant parallel between the thought of Averroës and the criticism of religion of the European Enlightenment.

This version of Averroës has been repeated more recently. In 1994 the Afro-Asian Philosophy Association held its fifth international conference in Cairo, with the theme of "Ibn Rushd and the Enlightenment," and the essays presented at the conference were collected and published in 1996 in a volume called *Averroës and the Enlightenment*. The collection was edited by Mourad Wahba and Mona Abousenna; numerous authors in the volume maintain the view that Averroës contributed significantly to the European Enlightenment.[7] Furthermore, many express agreement with Renan's evaluation of Averroës' criticism of religion. The following are the quotations from two authors in the collection. Oliver Leaman writes: "It is important to realize that the sort of thinking which emerged in the Enlightenment did not come from nowhere, but arose as a result of extended and extensive discussions taking place over many centuries in the West, and there can be little doubt that Averroism played a large part in establishing a tradition in which it became possible to question the status of religion by comparison with reason."[8]

In the last paragraph of his essay, Leaman makes a decisive judgment regarding Averroës' account of religion: "It [the argument of Averroës] does not explicitly disparage religion, it does not even implicitly disparage religion, but it provides religion with a role which is essentially secondary and demeaning."[9]

Another writer in the collection, Stefan Wild, says in specific reference to Renan:

> Renan was the loudest voice to proclaim that in Arabic philosophy as shown by Ibn Rushd the Aristotelian tradition had eliminated Islam and put itself at [sic] its place: "What is Arabic in this so-called Arab science? The language, nothing but the language . . . Is it at least Muhammadan? Has Muhammadanism been in any way a support for those rational studies? In no way." This quotation comes from the well-known lecture published in the Parisian *Journal des Débats* of March 29, 1883.[10]

Although Wild expresses some reservation regarding the accuracy of Renan's account, he and many of the authors in the collection suggest that Islamic *Tanwir* should be modeled after the European Enlightenment. Furthermore, they argue that since Averroës has been part of the European Enlightenment, he should be a foundational thinker for a Muslim Enlightenment.[11] Yet is it not necessary to evaluate whether Renan's appropriation of Averroës for his secularizing purposes is a proper understanding of Averroës' thought? It would seem reasonable to ask whether some European scholars, such as Renan, and, more recently, some of the advocates of an Averroist *Tanwir* have misunderstood the complexity and depth of Averroës' thought on the relation between reason and revelation and, if so, to ask whether they settled for a more limited form of enlightenment than Averroës actually advocated.[12]

The purpose of this essay is to make a case that this formulation of Averroës' criticism of religion is inaccurate. Although my essay is not a complete account of Averroës' treatise or his work as a whole, there is enough evidence in his renowned dissertation, *The Book of the Decisive Treatise (Kitab Fasl al-Maqal)*, to indicate that divine Law[13] and philosophy are not the rivals that Renan and others have proposed. As Averroës says in the treatise in reference to this topic of faith and reason: "Truth does not oppose truth; rather it agrees with it and bears witness to it" (§12, 9:1–2).[14] In the conclusion to the book, he also makes the following beautiful statements: "I mean that wisdom is the companion of the Law and its milk sister" (§59, 32:19) and "These two [that is, wisdom and Law] are companions by nature and lovers by essence and instinct"

(§59, 32:21–33:1). Through a careful exposition of the central inquiries of the *Decisive Treatise*, it is possible to see that Averroës can and should be read as a powerful source for enlightenment, for both the East and the West, precisely because he did not settle the question of the relation between divine Law and philosophy as facilely as Renan. A proper account of Averroës' enlightenment, and, we might add, an account recognized and appropriated by his contemporary, Moses Maimonides, may still offer modern states, whether they be Eastern, Middle Eastern, or Western, a true enlightenment that will lead to an ennobling of the political order and of the place of religion in that order.

DIVINE LAW COMMANDS THE STUDY OF PHILOSOPHY

Charles Butterworth's publication in 2001 of the Arabic text and English translation of the *Decisive Treatise & Epistle Dedicatory* has made available two key treatises necessary for the examination of the relation between religion and philosophy in the thought of Averroës.[15] Butterworth's Arabic text is based on a revised edition of the Arabic text, prepared at least in part by Muhsin Mahdi and edited and published by George F. Hourani as *Kitab Fasl al-Maqal*.[16] Hourani published an English translation in 1961.[17] Thus, with this edition, a reasonably accurate version of the Arabic text is now established. Furthermore, Mahdi wrote two essays on the treatise, one titled "Averroës on Divine Law and Human Wisdom,"[18] published in 1964, and a second essay, "Remarks on Averroës' *Decisive Treatise*,"[19] published in 1984. These essays prepared the groundwork for an appreciation of the organization and understanding of the book. Butterworth followed Mahdi's delineation of the book as consisting of two parts. The first part proceeds with his inquiry according to what Law-based reflection requires, that is, Averroës proceeds in his own inquiry in deference to Islamic Law. The topic of investigation is stated from the beginning: "Now, the goal of this statement is for us to investigate, from the perspective of Law-based reflection, whether reflection upon philosophy and the sciences of logic is permitted, prohibited, or commanded—and this as a recommendation or an obligation—by the Law." (§1, 1:3–6). The answer that Averroës gives, although with a certain moderation at one point, is that the study of philosophy and logic are commanded as an obligation according to the divine Law. The second part emphasizes this argument of the first part by stating what the intention of the Law is and the methods used in it for speaking to all people. Butterworth uses this two-part division in his exposition of the book, although he further subdivides each of the two parts into two divisions. Thus, through the scholarship of Mahdi and Butterworth, our exploration of the book's purpose can proceed with considerable confidence in the Arabic text, the translation, and the explanatory divisions in this recent publication.

Following a brief introduction in which Averroës presents the goal of his statement (§1, 1:3–6), Averroës articulates his argument. He begins with a definition of philosophy:

> So we say: If the activity of philosophy is nothing more than reflection upon existing things and consideration of them insofar as they are an indication of the Artisan—I mean insofar as they are artifacts, for existing things indicate the Artisan only through cognizance of the art in them, and the more complete cognizance of the art in them is, the more complete is cognizance of the Artisan—and if the Law has recommended and urged consideration of existing things, then it is evident that what this name indicates is either obligatory or recommended by the Law. (§2, 1:7–2:3)

What follows immediately after this statement is the reference to five Quranic passages, all of which call for the reflection on existing things by means of the intellect. As Averroës said from the outset, he proceeds from the perspective of Law-based reflection. In so doing, he discovers Quranic justification for the study of philosophy. Averroës' inquiry begins by way of exegesis, that is, by way of a believer.

Several elements in this statement we have quoted may cause us to reflect further on Averroës' formulation. First, it is introduced by "we say" (*naqul*), in contradistinction with his use of "I say" (*qala*) as the first word of section one. Averroës begins section two with a statement of opinions that are held by many people—that is, he proceeds with dialectical statements. Second, the two "if" ('*in*) clauses in this sentence leave the statements that follow indefinite. The first "if" encourages us to ask whether philosophy is the investigation of "existing things" (*mawjudat*) in the plural rather than the investigation of being (*mawjud*). The strength of his definition of philosophy is that it relies upon the particular instances of beings rather than universal being and, as Butterworth judges, is consistent with the traditional definition of philosophy that the general entity can only be known through its particular instances.[20] In this definition of philosophy, Averroës avoids the question of being or Being, and in doing so he avoids deliberate metaphysical or theological implications. Thus, there is no reason that this definition could not be accepted by either the philosopher or the advocate of religious Law. The second "if" clause encourages us to ask whether knowledge of the art in the artifacts is an indication of the Artisan and whether a more complete knowledge of the art in them leads to a more complete knowledge of the Artisan. Averroës does not answer these questions; their conditional nature means that they are introduced dialectically rather than demonstratively. As dialectical premises, they are not necessarily incapable of being demonstrated, but they are not introduced here as demonstrative premises. They are hypothetical rather than categorical propositions. In order to make a case for the dialectical premises, Averroës proceeds to cite five references in the Quran that indicate that God commands the consideration of existing things. He proceeds by way of exegesis of prophetic texts.

Averroës' carefully written introductory statements are a harmonization of the philosophic and the religious, even if each side will have to redefine itself, albeit only moderately. As we have already noted, the definition of philosophy as the study of existing things is not particularly problematic for philosophy, but philosophy may not accept as easily the second conditional statement that the greater knowledge of the artwork leads to a greater knowledge of the Artisan. Still, the most fundamental premise of philosophy or science is that it is possible to understand causes by an examination of effects. Concomitantly, the lover of the words of prophecy is reminded or taught that the meanings of Quranic terms such as "consider" (*'a'tabiru*), "sight" (*al-absari*), "reflect" (*yanzuru*), "see" (*nuri*), and "ponder" (*yatafakkaruna*), which are quoted from Quranic verses in section two, are admonitions to reflect on existing things. Divine Law-based inquiry studies existing things rather than that which is imaginary. Thus the aim of philosophy and the aim of the divine Law are the same.

Did we not observe, however, that Averroës begins his treatise with dialectical premises? Therefore, does he not enact the harmonization through a compromise in what is philosophically demonstrative? In regard to the teachings concerning religion in the *Decisive Treatise* and *The Incoherence of the Incoherence*, Richard Taylor says that both these writings are addressed to those who are capable of a dialectical grasp of the truth. He writes: "But what group is Averroës addressing in these works? In each it is the people only capable of the dialectical grasp of the truth. The *Decisive Treatise* is a monograph on religious law and as such presupposes the truth of certain starting points of discussion and argument on the basis of revelation, tradition, and faith."[21] Taylor argues the same for the *Incoherence*. Because both treatises are dialectical, and therefore are for "people *only capable* of the dialectical grasp of truth" (italics mine), he turns to another treatise that contains Averroës' demonstrative philosophical statements on religious matters. Taylor argues that he discovers demonstrative statements in the *Long Commentary on the De Anima of Aristotle*. He thus makes a distinction between the genres of treatises according to the type of proof found in each. Although Taylor recognizes that the *Decisive Treatise* is dialectical, this identification is too general. The grammatical formulation of section two, as we have argued already, alerts us to the unproven nature of the dialectical premises. Yet dialectical premises are not necessarily false premises and may even be demonstrative, but what makes them dialectical is that they are presented as generally accepted and in need of validation or refutation. Averroës' definition of philosophy as the study of existing things may not be a sufficient definition, but it is not necessarily untrue. Thus, the measure of agreement Averroës presents between religion and philosophy is not false simply because it uses dialectical premises.

The next part (§§3–10) of the book makes the case that such reflection must be carried out by "intellectual syllogistic reasoning" (al-qiyas al-'aqli) in Butterworth's translation. Syllogistic reasoning is "inferring and drawing out the unknown from the known." (§3, 2:12). Syllogistic reasoning consists in analogies: if this or since this, then that, or something is like something else. Analogy (qiyas) is familiar to Muslim readers because in Sunni legal discussions it is one of the roots of the Law and is an approved method of legal argumentation. What the Muslim jurists had discovered was necessary for legal argument had also been discovered by philosophical inquiry.

Next, Averroës distinguishes between different types of intellectual reasoning. The most perfect kind of syllogistic reasoning is demonstrative. The three other types are dialectical, rhetorical, and sophistical syllogistic reasoning. Dialectical reasoning starts from premises that are generally accepted, though not yet demonstrative; rhetorical reasoning starts from premises that are true but proceeds by way of forceful rhetoric rather than proof; sophistical reasoning starts from a premise that is false and through legerdemain makes the argument strong. At this point Averroës introduces the reader to "unqualified syllogistic reasoning" (al-qiyas al-matlaq,§4, 3:8), by which he means logic, and to the matter of the types of premises that are used in logic. All of these types of reasoning the Law commands us to identify and to use appropriately.

Averroës draws an analogy between juristic syllogistic reasoning and intellectual syllogistic reasoning. The Islamic jurists already adhere to a legal obligation to practice juristic reasoning, and, thus, Averroës says that intellectual syllogistic reasoning is like juristic reasoning and is justified even as juristic reasoning is justified. Moreover, he says that intellectual reasoning is higher in rank than juristic reasoning because it pertains to the knowledge of existing things. Furthermore, even as juristic reasoning was not present in the early days of Islam and had to be discovered, yet was not considered a heretical innovation, so too intellectual reasoning, which also had to be discovered even if by non-Muslims, is not a heretical innovation. Averroës says there is a "reason" (sabab) that intellectual syllogistic reasoning had to be discovered, although he says this is not the place to mention the reason, and he explains that its usefulness must simply be believed (yu'taqad,§4, 4:4–5). Nevertheless, belief and reason are not in disagreement with one another. Averroës concludes this section by saying that only a small group of religious adherents who are "strict literalists" reject intellectual syllogistic reasoning, and they are refuted by Quranic texts.

Averroës reassures his readers three times in the next series of sections, sections four, six and eight, that syllogistic reasoning is like a tool in relation to work. The parallel is first used in section four (§4, 3:13). In section six he extends his explanation of the useful and benign nature of the tool because he says that even in sacrifice the knife that is used may belong to someone of another religion, but as long as it fulfills the conditions of validity it can be used and the sacrifice is valid (§6, 4:17–20). In section eight he says that once we have acquired the tools it is possible to see the artfulness of the Artisan in existing things (§8, 5:5–8). Thus, he argues, if the Ancients who lived before us discovered and perfected a tool, we should not as Muslims be afraid to use the tool. The tool even assists in the understanding of the Artisan.

It is necessary to retrace our steps in the argument because Averroës has at several points introduced a softening of the obligatory nature of the injunctions in the Quran to study existing things. The softening was first noted by Mahdi,[22] and is further explicated by Butterworth.[23] In section four, Averroës says, "the one who has faith in the Law and follows its command to reflect upon existing things *perhaps* comes under the obligation to set out, before reflecting, to become cognizant of these things . . ." (§4, 3:10–13, italics mine). The softening is introduced with the word "perhaps" (*faqad*). That this softening is not accidental is confirmed because it is used in several adjacent sections: in section seven, he writes, "therefore, we ought perhaps to seize (*faqad yanbaghi 'an nadrabu*) their [the Ancients'] books in our hands" (§7, 5:2–3); in section eight, he says, "therefore, it is perhaps obligatory (*faqad yajib*) that we start investigating existing things according to the order and manner we have gained from the art of becoming cognizant about demonstrative syllogisms" (§8, 5:8–10); in section nine, he says, "it is perhaps obligatory (*faqad yajib*) for us to reflect upon what they [our predecessors from foreign nations] say about that and upon what they establish in their books" (§9, 6:10–13).

The purpose of this softening, as Butterworth astutely judges, is to prepare the reader for the subsequent argument that emphasizes that most people need to read the Law in its apparent sense, without the elaborate tools of logic. Thus, the obligatory nature of the study of philosophy is moderated because it is only obligatory for some but not obligatory for all. In section ten, Averroës explains this point more fully. He states that since "their [the Ancients'] aim and intention in their books is the very intention to which the Law urges us . . . whoever forbids reflection upon them by anyone suited to reflect upon them . . . surely bars people from the door through which the Law calls them to cognizance of God" (§10, 6:11–7:2). Lest we underestimate the significance of this distinction for Averroës, the rest of section ten explains the differences in the innate dispositions of people in their capacities for reflection, and in sections eleven through thirty-six Averroës explains that people come to know the truth of the Law because the Law teaches different innate dispositions differently. There is nothing in this argument that entails an opposition between the truths of religion and the truths of philosophy.

THE VARIOUS MEANS OF ASSENT TO THE TRUTH FOUND IN THE LAW

The distinction between the innate dispositions of individuals leads Averroës to an extensive delineation of the three means of assent which are found in the Law. In sections eleven through thirty-six, Averroës explains these means of assent. They are 1) demonstrative, 2) dialectical, and 3) rhetorical. The demonstrative is the most excellent way, but assent to the truth is offered by the Law to every human being, and many need to arrive at assent through dialectical and rhetorical means. Although Averroës holds up a standard of demonstrative argumentation, we have already noted in the examination of the first premises of the treatise that dialectical premises may be quite useful in the determination of what is true. Immediately following the introduction of these three means of assent, Averroës makes yet another forceful statement of the agreement between the different means of assent. He says: "Since this Law is true and calls to the reflection leading to cognizance of the truth, we, the Muslim community, know firmly that demonstrative reflection does not lead to differing with what is set down in the Law. For truth does not oppose truth; rather it agrees with and bears witness to it" (§12, 9:1–2).[24] The title of this chapter is taken from this passage.

Yet the three means of assent lead to serious study of the words of prophecy in order to determine whether a phrase of the Quran should be understood in a demonstrative, dialectical, or rhetorical sense. Thus, what Averroës establishes in this middle section of the book, and what is also continued through to the end, is a carefully articulated set of what he calls "statutes for interpreting the Law" (§37, 23:2). Some texts of Scripture ought to be understood in their apparent sense, while other texts need to be understood in a figurative way. In section fourteen, Averroës reminds his readers that this distinction between the literal and the figurative is nothing new because the jurists recognize that they need to make such distinctions. In keeping with the legal types of argumentation of Islamic jurisprudence, he says that Muslims have formed a consensus that it is not obligatory for all the utterances of the law to be taken in their literal sense. Thus, figurative interpretation is consistent with the Law and is even promulgated by the nature of the Law itself.

The challenge is, however, to discern which verses ought to be taken in the literal sense and which ought to be taken in the figurative sense. To take a verse that ought to be understood in a literal sense and give it a figurative meaning is to lead to or cause unbelief. Conversely, to take a verse in a literal sense that should be understood in a figurative way will lead to unbelief as well. Thus, Averroës guides the reader of Scripture in the proper exegesis of verses. In the course of doing so, he reintroduces the distinction he made between those with excellent innate dispositions and who are adept in science and philosophy and those who are not. Those adept in science read a certain verse in a figurative sense, while those who use dialectical and rhetorical arguments read the same verse in a literal sense. The one adept in science may not disclose the figurative reading to the one who arrives by assent through dialectical or rhetorical means because the figurative meaning may actually confuse the one who assents by dialectical and rhetorical means, and this confusion may lead to unbelief. At the same time, the literal meaning of the passage contains a contradiction that the one adept in science cannot accept. If he does not have the wisdom to recognize a figurative meaning, that is, if he was not truly one of the adept in science and philosophy, it would lead him to unbelief. The proper emphases and elements of faith are being sorted out and refined in Averroës' procedures, but he is not rejecting religion.

Thus, the exposition of the meaning of the Quran conforms to the means of assent that accompany the variety of innate dispositions of men. That the Quran addresses each reader according to his natural disposition and leads to belief in each case is not a criticism of the Quran but actually an indication of its excellence and inimitability (§58). Averroës does not go into elaborate studies of the verses or *suras* of the Quran in this book. In the conclusion of the entire book, he explains that he would love to devote himself to the explanation of the teachings of the Law and of examination and criticisms of false teachings of the Quran that have been made because the various groups of Islamic jurisprudence and *kalam* have not understood the various means of assent and therefore have not understood the verses of the Quran. Averroës says that instead of harmony being established in the Islamic community, the failure to appreciate the various means of assent—demonstrative, dialectical, and rhetorical—leads to the promulgation of innovative heresies, and these heresies divide people and cause unbelief. Averroës is aware that what he has produced in the *Decisive Treatise* is only the prolegomenon, only the programmatic document, that is needed to guide further exposition of the Quran. If God grants him long life, he says, he hopes to continue his study.

CONCLUSIONS

The force of Averroës' argument for the harmonization of religion and philosophy continues throughout the entire document. Those who suggest that Averroës can be commandeered into the service of secularism do not seem to have absorbed the import of his argument in the *Decisive Treatise*. The Islamists who argue that he is too secular seem to have accepted a reading of the book that denies its endeavor to show that the truth of philosophy, rightly understood, confirms and elucidates the truth of religion, rightly understood. No one can deny the powerful defense of the intellect in the *Decisive Treatise*, and this rationality, according to Averroës, does not deny the truth taught in religion. Averroës also suggests in this treatise that dialectical premises and the investigation they foster are useful to both philosophy and religious inquiry. It is the subtle, vigorous, and simultaneous defense of both religion and philosophy and the correction of the dogmatisms that are possible in both that are missing in the accounts of this treatise of Averroës by the epigones of Renan and in the irrational defenses of religion. Both the *Tanwir* and the Islamists, who are in public disagreement in the political sphere, seem to be shaped by the same erroneous reading of this classical text. Averroës offers a way through the morass of this debate and of the political options that ensue, and in doing so he offers direction and wisdom on the relation between politics and religion both in the Middle East and elsewhere. Since a proper reading of Averroës offers much-needed resources for the future, I will let the last word be his. I repeat a statement of his that I quoted in the introduction to this essay and that I have not found repeated in Renan. Averroës says: "These two [that is, Wisdom and the Law] are companions by nature and lovers by essence and instinct."

NOTES

1. Fauzi M. Najjar, "Ibn Rushd (Averroes) and the Egyptian Enlightenment Movement," *British Journal of Middle Eastern Studies* 31, no. 2 (2004): 195–213.

2. Malise Ruthven, *Islam: A Very Short Introduction* (Oxford: Oxford University Press, 1997), 5–6.

3. The phrase "hidden poison" (*al-samm al-kamin*) is Najjar's summary of Farah Antun's account of the effect Renan says philosophy has on religion. Najjar, "Ibn Rushd (Averroes) and the Egyptian Enlightenment Movement," 203.

4. Renan's original says: "Quand Averroès mourut, en 1198, la philosophie arabe perdit en lui son dernier représentant, et le triomphe du Coran sur la libre pensée fut assuré pour au moins six cents ans." Ernest Renan, *Averroès et l'averroïsme. Essai historique*, Troisième ed. (New York: Georg Olms Verlag, 1986), 2. The third edition was originally published in Paris in 1866 by Michel Lévy Frères Libraires. The English translation is mine. I wish to thank Nicole Kaplan for checking my French translations.

5. Ibid., 167. Renan's original says: "La philosophie est le but le plus élevé de la nature humaine; mais peu d'hommes peuvent y atteindre. La révélation prophétique y supplée pour le vulgaire. Les disputes philosophiques ne sont pas faites pour le peuple, car elles n'aboutissent qu'à affaiblir la foi. Ces disputes sont avec raison défendues, puisqu'il suffit au bonheur des simples qu'ils comprennent ce qu'ils peuvent comprendre."

6. Ibid., 172. Renan's original says: "Les philosophes arabes étaient donc au milieu de leurs coreligionnaires à peu près ce qu'étaient les *libertins* au XVIIe siècle."

7. Mourad Wahba and Mona Abousenna, eds., *Averroës and the Enlightenment*, Foreword by Boutros Boutros-Ghali (Amherst: Prometheus Books, 1996).

8. Oliver Leaman, "Averroës and the West," in Wahba and Abousenna, *Averroës and the Enlightenment*, 65.

9. Ibid., 66.

10. Stefan Wild, "Between Ernest Renan and Ernest Bloch: Averroës Remembered, Discovered, and Invented: The European Reception Since the Nineteenth Century," in Wahba and Abousenna, *Averroës and the Enlightenment*, 157.

11. It is unfortunate that 'Atif al-'Iraqi, who is one of Egypt's finest scholars of Averroës and also part of the *Tanwir* movement, did not have an essay in the collection edited by Wahba and Abouseena.

12. See Charles Butterworth, "Averroës, Precursor of the Enlightenment?" *Alif: Journal of Comparative Poetics* 16 (1996): 6–18. This issue of the journal is dedicated to the theme of "Averroës and the Rational Legacy in the East and the West." Butterworth's essay is the finest critical judgment on the relation between religion and philosophy in Averroës that I have found.

13. In consistency with Butterworth's usage in his edition (see note 16 below), the word "Law" is capitalized to indicate Shari'a or divine Law. In this essay, Law refers to Islamic Law. The adjectival form of Shari'a is Shar'i, and, when it is used in Averroës' treatise, I translate it as "Law-based," again in consistency with Butterworth's usage.

14. The sections, indicated by the symbol §, are those delineated in Butterworth's edition (as cited in the following note), and they are followed by the Arabic page and line numbers. The English section divisions are the same in this edition and the English line numbers are almost identical.

15. Averroës, *Decisive Treatise & Epistle Dedicatory*, trans., with introduction and notes, Charles E. Butterworth (Provo: Brigham Young University, 2001).

16. Averroës, *Ibn Rushd (Averroës): Kitab Fasl al-Maqal*, ed. George F. Hourani (Leiden: E. J. Brill, 1959).

17. Averroës, *Averroës on the Harmony of Religion and Philosophy*, translation, with introduction and notes, of Ibn Rushd's *Kitab fasl al-maqal*, with its appendix (*Damima*) and an extract from *Kitab al-kashf 'an manahij al-adilla*, by George F. Hourani, E. J. W. Gibb Memorial Trust: New Series 21 (Cambridge: The University Press, 1961).

18. Muhsin Mahdi, "Averroës on Divine Law and Human Wisdom," in *Ancients and Moderns: Essays on the Tradition of Political Philosophy in Honor of Leo Strauss*, ed. Joseph Cropsey (New York: Basic Books, 1964), 114–31.

19. Muhsin Mahdi, "Remarks on Averroës' *Decisive Treatise*," in *Islamic Theology and Philosophy: Studies in Honor of George F. Hourani*, ed. Michael E. Marmura (Albany: State University of New York Press, 1984), 188–202.

20. Butterworth, *Decisive Treatise*, xxii.

21. Richard C. Taylor, "'The Future Life' and Averroës's *Long Commentary on the De Anima of Aristotle*," in Wahba and Abousenna, *Averroës and the Enlightenment*, 264.

22. Mahdi, "Remarks," 199–200.

23. Butterworth, *Decisive Treatise*, xxiv.

24. Ibid., 8–9.

CHAPTER 15

Hermeneutics and Human Rights: Liberal Democracy, Catholicism, and Islam

Edward T. Barrett

While the material aspect of a strategy to defeat militant Salafism has received due consideration, the ideological component requires more attention. In response to the Salafist goal of delegitimizing, controlling, and purifying "near enemy" regimes through insurgency and terrorism against enemies both near and far, the United States has implemented a global counterinsurgency strategy in order to rollback Salafists combined with conventional warfare in order to rollback supporting rogue regimes. Given the importance of indigenous state effectiveness and justice to countering insurgencies, included are interagency measures to improve state capabilities, especially those related to security and economic vitality and fairness.

Despite ongoing debates over certain conceptual issues, such as the efficacies of punishment and denial to deter Salafists and rogue states, the material variables of our counter-Salafism strategy are relatively well established. On the other hand, the strategy's ideological dimensions are marred by numerous conceptual confusions. First, some analysts refuse to take religion seriously, adhering to Marx's dictum that ideas are merely epiphenomenal and thus merely focusing on improved economic conditions. Second, confusion reigns over which ideas are important, i.e., Islamic public opinion, tolerance of terrorism, or elements of Islamic culture that may support Salafist ideology. While Defense Department leaders have emphasized the delegitimization of terrorism and promotion of ill-defined "moderation," the State Department has emphasized an improved American "brand" through media-based public diplomacy. Third, inasmuch as a broader, culturally oriented agenda is crucial,

238 Political Islam from Muhammad to Ahmadinejad

what are "moderation" and its causes? More pointedly, assuming that liberalism—a human rights-oriented social system—is the goal, democracy may actually undermine liberalism if certain cultural preconditions are absent. Finally, what are these ideological preconditions?

This work will attempt to clarify the ends and means of an effective ideological strategy against militant Salafism in three parts. The first will discuss the nature and foundations of liberal democracy in order to establish the descriptive and normative assumptions necessary for any religious tradition to reconcile itself to liberalism, which should be our strategic goal. Intended as an instructive case study, the second part will outline the three stages of Catholicism's gradual and nuanced pro-liberal shift: first, pragmatism in the face of post-Reformational religious pluralism, democratization, secularism, and totalitarianism; second, nineteenth-century concern for the working class and post-Enlightenment culture; and third, an embrace of liberalism for noncircumstantial, principled reasons. Based on these latter anthropological and ethical assumptions, the Catholic Church now endorses a panoply of negative and positive human rights and, as governed by the principle of subsidiarity, a situationally dependent combination of democratic state and civil society initiatives to moderate the economic and cultural effects of the market and thus secure these rights.

With this Catholic ideological evolution in the background, the third section will argue that an Islamic theory of rights capable of supporting gender equality and full religious freedom has been impeded by a voluntaristic doctrine of divine omnipotence that limits human freedom, reason, and subsequent interpretive possibilities. I outline the origins and effects of this doctrine in the course of evaluating the attempts of four Islamic liberals to challenge competing revivalist and secularist responses to modernity: (1) Soroush's postmodern contextualization and reinterpretation the existing revealed corpus; (2) An-Na'im's hermeneutic of Meccan primacy; (3) Rahman's combination of historical criticism and hermeneutics that narrows and then reinterprets Islamic revelation; and (4) Hourani's reevaluation of Islamic limitations on ethical reasoning. I ultimately argue that Soroush's postmodern hermeneutic lapses into a relativism unacceptable to human rights and Islamic sensibilities; that An-Na'im's attempt to circumscribe a liberal Meccan period is beset by practical difficulties; that Rahman's combination of historical criticism and hermeneutics effectively delimits many apparently anti-liberal aspects of Islamic revelation but retains a Maturidite distrust of independent ethical reasoning; and that Hourani's reinterpretation of reason's efficacy permits philosophical ethics to independently evaluate interpretive claims, augment revelation, and thus serve as a source of liberal political philosophy.

LIBERAL DEMOCRACY: NATURE AND FOUNDATIONS

Liberalism is a political theory asserting that certain human rights exist, and that these rights should be directly or indirectly secured through the state. Democracy is the direct or indirect participation of all citizens in politics. I will define human rights as the due preconditions necessary for human fulfillment. In order to limit our discussion, I will not address three important issues: who qualifies as a person (i.e., whether the unborn possess rights), the conditions under which persons might mitigate or even forfeit some or all of their rights (i.e., philosophically based just war and domestic punishment theories), and whether non-persons or future generations possess these rights.

Given this definition, the central normative question becomes, "What would we have to know and believe in order to affirm that all persons are due these preconditions?" The descriptive fact imbuing these preconditions with normativity is "dignity," otherwise referred to as "non-relative value" or "sanctity." This foundation comports with Article One of the Universal Declaration of Human Rights and the two 1966 International Covenants. Contrary to the compelling thought of Perry, dignity alone renders these preconditions inviolable; no other quality, such as "inviolability," is necessary.[1]

Three important issues concerning a theory of human rights remain: the ontological ground of this dignity, the source of one's consciousness of dignity (rationalism versus theism), and the question of liberty versus welfare rights that addresses which preconditions are necessary to the flourishing of a social being. On these first two issues, there are many possible combinations. Many natural law adherents, and especially Kantians, attribute dignity to capabilities, such as reason and freedom. Other natural law theorists argue that the first principle of the natural law presupposes direct apprehension of human dignity. Certain phenomenological realists, intuitionists, and emotivists also emphasize our direct apprehension of value. Others, like Kant, argue that consciousness of duties implies dignity.[2] On the other hand, theistically minded rights theorists employ similar claims: God-like capabilities impart dignity—the *imago Dei* argument; God's love for persons reveals that persons possess dignity; and revealed duties imply dignity. For some theorists, the reality of human dignity is overdetermined by the validity of several of these claims. For the purposes of this chapter, I will not closely evaluate the relative merits of these claims, but will merely suggest two concerns. First, capability-based claims, whether rationalistic or theistic, are more tenuous than those based on the apprehension of dignity itself or on duties. Second, reason-derived claims are at least potentially universalizable.

The issue of liberty versus welfare rights also distinguishes rights theorists. Classically, liberties or negative rights were the hallmarks of

liberalism. Non-interference allows one to use one's metaphysical freedom in fulfilling ways and, through these acts, also allows one to constitute oneself, which is a core insight of virtue ethics. These rights logically
coincide with the notion of the person as not-to-be-violated by others.
But the practical tension between opportunities and results, created by
human nature and liberty, also generated the notion of preconditions that
ought to be received from others, such as a just wage. Again, I will not
adjudicate between these competing claims about which preconditions to
flourishing are due because of known or revealed human dignity. I
will merely assert that liberal democracies, perhaps because of an
overlapping consensus, affirm the existence of a dignity that is not
merely constructed and contractualized, and cannot be overridden by
consequence-derived utilitarian calculations.

Prudence, however, dictates that three consequence-related issues
should not be entirely removed from an ethical analysis of human rights.
First, is democracy a right—a precondition to human flourishing—in
itself, or is it justified by its ability to support liberalism and promote
human rights? Second, if the latter is true and democracy is derivatively
legitimate, does it ultimately deliver the goods; or does the "illiberal democracy" phenomenon require casuistic evaluation of institutional and
even cultural prerequisites? Third, assuming that democracy sometimes
supports rights, what are the international and domestic effects of liberal
democracy? Internationally, does the much debated dyadic "liberal democratic peace" supply an additional legitimization? And if so, which does
the work: liberalism or democracy? The foreign policy implications are
obvious: if democracy is derivatively and conditionally legitimate, and if
dyadic international stability issues not from democracy but from human
rights, then our emphasis should be on promotion of liberalism and its
material and cultural preconditions, not democracy.

The debated domestic effects of liberal democracy are even more
numerous and complex. Democracy, in addition to the danger of an illiberal "tyranny of the majority," is accused of promoting cultural problems
definitively described by Tocqueville in *Democracy in America*, including
moral relativism, materialism, secularism, and individualism.[3] In such a
cultural milieu, democracy becomes merely procedural and antithetical
to liberalism properly understood: the outcome of democratic procedures
becomes individualism and the "soft despotism" of those most capable of
influencing politics and forming opinions.

Other critics, such as nineteenth-century anti-liberal Catholics, have
argued that liberalism itself encourages secularization (the erosion of religious belief and practice) in at least two ways. The first argument asserts
the likelihood of rights-bearing monads who, misunderstanding the
bases of the freedoms to think and express, will lapse into subjectivism,
relativism, and the related loss of faith that accompanies the denigration

of reason. The second and more common concern associates state-protected religious freedom with indifferentism. These two arguments have been resurrected and reworked by, respectively, contemporary communitarians and Catholic "theoconservatives."[4]

My positions on these three consequence-related normative issues are as follows. First, democracy is a derivative right, justified by its ability to promote rights more fundamental to human flourishing. Second, there are many cases in which institutional and cultural realities indeed favor democracy as the most effective political form for securing human rights. Particularly crucial is a shared apprehension—reason- or faith-based—of the dignity of all persons. Third, the effects of liberal democracy on international relations and domestic culture are, respectively, positive and indeterminate. Regarding the former, the liberal democratic peace phenomenon seems empirically robust, theoretically cogent, and to favor human rights as the key variable. In other words, liberal democracies tend not to fight each other not because majorities reject war as a solution to conflicts of interest, but because human rights-based regimes ameliorate the problem of unknown intentions highlighted by neorealists.

As for the effects on domestic culture, I would argue that liberalism and democracy are neither grounded in, nor necessarily conducive to, the cultural maladies of which they are accused—materialism, relativism, secularism, individualism, and consumerism. Democracy, like the market, is a permissive cause allowing choices that may either undermine or strengthen culture and liberalism. Similarly, liberal states permit one to be an immoralist or atheist. However, liberal states also assert that all persons possess an inviolable dignity and thus protect a host of preconditions to authentic human fulfillment, including the abilities to freely enter into a relationship with God, describe this relationship to others, and share the fruits of such a relationship with others.[5]

CATHOLICISM AND LIBERAL DEMOCRACY: INITIAL EXPLANATIONS

The trajectory of Catholic thought on the foundations and effects of liberalism is rather surprising. While official Church proclamations throughout most of the 1800s excoriated liberalism, Pope John Paul II's 1991 social encyclical, *Centesimus Annus*, was a qualified but unmistakable endorsement of liberal economic and political thought. Much to the consternation of many Catholics and secular observers, the Church now champions a "free economy," a host of other human rights, including religious freedom, and a limited and democratic state through which these rights must be secured.

How does one explain this puzzling shift from critique to endorsement of liberalism? One theory cites purely pragmatic reasons. In the face of post-Reformation religious pluralism, waning support for monarchy, secularism, and the hostility of totalitarian regimes, the Church endorsed liberalism in order to promote its independence and even survival. However, while such a theory is logical and describes the motives of some Church actors, a second explanation more accurately reflects the prevailing intellectual forces. Within this "cultural conversion" explanation, one can distinguish two groups of adherents: social Catholics and liberal Catholics.

On the one hand were social Catholics of the late 1800s, such as the German Bishop Wilhelm Ketteler and Pope Leo XIII. Their primary concern was economic, specifically, the abject poverty of the new and growing industrial working class. According to their simple but insightful analysis, three factors combined to cause the intolerable conditions. The first was the private but centralized ownership of the new industrial means of production—in other words, "capitalism." Second was these owners' callous disregard for the workers' humanity. The third factor was the predominance of *laissez-faire* policies toward the market, including the market for labor, on the part of the ruling class due to either self-interest or their belief that the free market best served society. The increasingly popular Marxist response to such injustice was to alter the first factor, the private ownership of the means of production, by abolishing it. Social Catholics considered this Marxist response problematic not only because it would abnegate the benefits of ownership and the market, but also because its atheism and recommended "class struggle" threatened to draw the working class away from the Church and into violent conflict. The economic, moral, and spiritual well-being of the worker thus demanded that the Church offer not only an immediate and practical response, but also a more far-reaching analysis with public policy ramifications.

According to historical accounts, a relatively small number of social Catholics prescribed two other possible solutions. The first was joint, and therefore decentralized, ownership and management of firms (sometimes called "corporatism"). This solution was generally rejected because it was considered unlikely given the new production methods. Second, some recommended legalized labor unionization, through which workers themselves would force owner fairness. This solution was generally rejected at the time as conducive to social conflict. Instead, the two most popular and competing solutions were direct labor legislation on the part of the ruling class, and the moral formation of the owning class, specifically, the promotion of Christian charity with an attendant social role for the Church. In other words, the two dominant factions within social Catholicism disagreed over whether the solution to the plight of the working class was political or cultural, the purview of justice or charity.

On the other hand were the "liberal Catholics," such as Lamennais, Acton, Döllinger, and Newman. For them, the central problem was not economic, and culture was not one of the possible means to solving it. For liberal Catholics, the central problem facing European society was spiritual. The problem was not the material conditions of one class, but the state of the souls of all, and the cause was cultural. More precisely, the West was increasingly skeptical about the metaphysical and ethical claims of theology and philosophy that had comprised the core of Western culture since Constantine. Since liberal Catholics regarded these claims—about the essence of God and the human soul, about authentic human fulfillment and its contributing virtues and moral precepts, and about our need for God—as necessary for happiness in this life and the next, the crisis had both temporal and eternal ramifications.

However, while modern culture was beset with great errors, some argued that it was also graced with new insights, including the scientific method, philosophical schools sensitive to the subjective dimension of consciousness and acts, new approaches to interpreting texts, and new historical data. Liberals such as Dollinger argued that these insights might even be appropriated in order to better understand and explain the faith. Such an appropriation would, in turn, require new independence for philosophers, theologians, and historians within the Church. Given concerns with the compatibility of new intellectual currents with timeless truths, and with the motives of such scholars, this call for internal Church freedom was controversial. It is this context of concern that partially explains several Church events of the late 1800s and early 1900s: ultramontanism (a heavy reliance on Papal authority), the neo-Scholastics of Mainz, the ultra-reactionary *Syllabus of Errors*, Vatican I, Leo XIII's call for a Thomistic revival, and the harsh reaction to the modernists.

But the breach between moderate liberals and conservatives was not that wide. The former merely wanted adjustments and more effective arguments, not accommodation. These liberals shared with conservatives the conviction that the cause of the spiritual crisis was cultural, and that the Church was the solution. At issue were the ideas and social arrangements that would best encourage this transformation.

It was on this issue of the optimal social conditions within which the Church could best transform modern culture that agreement occurred between liberals calling for freedom within the Church, certain conservatives, and social Catholics who emphasized the cultural solution to the problem of the working class. Common to each group was the conviction that only an unhindered, engaged, and convincing Church could solve the developing cultural problems. And in their analysis of how to promote such an institution in the midst of increased state power and religious pluralism, they began to question the Church's thought on the political and economic aspects of liberalism. While state-protected religious freedom, which denied the Church its guaranteed influence over education, the press, and marriage, had been associated with indifferentism and immorality (and Church poverty), they pointed out that religious establishment also held the potential for state interference and even suppression, as well as for Church corruption. They argued that religious freedom would make the Church more effective, and supported this conclusion by pointing to the American experience. And in order to protect the mission of a disestablished and unfettered Church, other liberal freedoms, such as private property, association, and speech, would also be necessary. Finally, as Lamennais argued in the early 1800s, these freedoms would be best secured through universal suffrage, an argument that eventually encouraged the formation of Christian democratic parties.

Social Catholics interested in promoting economic justice through state action added other arguments that pointed in the direction of a more favorable posture towards liberalism. Rights language could be appropriated not only to protect private property and the free market, but also to criticize their misuse by capitalists. All persons, in other words, possessed rights to a just wage adequate for themselves and their family, and to humane working conditions. As the ultimate guarantor of rights, the state had the duty to exercise concern for the poor and family life and to act appropriately, to include limiting both market freedom and ownership when necessary. And perhaps a democratic state, albeit a representative and well-constituted one, would be more likely to act appropriately. These arguments were also responsible for the emergence of early Christian Democratic parties in Belgium and Germany.

The Church's assessment of liberalism that began with these nineteenth-century social and liberal Catholics continued throughout the next century, adding new rationales and nuances. Prudential considerations regarding the Church's independence and survival were, of course, not absent from the process. But ultimately more important than expedience for the evaluation process were the conclusions of social and liberal Catholics: liberalism possessed analytically distinct spheres of activity—economic, political, and cultural—and under the reigning circumstances, the Church would more effectively address the main problems of modern culture, namely secularism and moral relativism, and of modern economies within liberal democratic societies that secured a host of human rights, including religious freedom. This logic nicely summarizes that of the Second Vatican Council: religious liberty (*Dignitatis Humanae*) will allow the communion that is the Church (*Lumen Gentium*) to encounter and thus transform the modern world (*Gaudium et Spes*).

ANTHROPOLOGICAL EXPLANATION

Since the Second Vatican Council, however, the non-circumstantial, anthropological justifications for human rights and a limited liberal democratic state have also been emphasized and more deeply developed. Setting the stage for this anthropological turn were two related doctrinal foundations. First, Christian doctrinal development affirmed the efficacies and teleological significance of the human will and reason. Consistent with this tradition, John Paul II's encyclical letter on faith and reason asserts, on the one hand, that reason has natural limitations that are exacerbated by human sinfulness, and thus benefits from guidance by the faith. On the other hand, he insists that reason assists faith in important ways, allowing us to interpret the data of revelation and more readily assent to its content. As we will discuss, this confidence in reason led him to employ a realist phenomenology in defense of a philosophical anthropology that included human freedom, the self-constitutive dimension of action, human dignity, duties, rights, and a self-donative teleology. Second and related, the venerable notion of natural law set the theoretical stage for the appropriation of human rights as a central ethical and political principle. As historian Brian Tierney has argued, the twelfth century commentaries on Gratian's *Decretum* were not only a catalyst of Aquinas' reflections on natural law, but also, through canon law, were the impetus behind the Spanish Scholastics' derivation of natural rights from natural law.[6]

Since the thought of John Paul II represents the culmination of this anthropological turn, our remaining treatment of a Catholic theory of liberal democracy will first examine his philosophically and theologically derived anthropology, and then highlight the related pillars of his social thought.

PHILOSOPHICAL ANTHROPOLOGY AND ETHICS

John Paul's faith in Christian revelation, life experiences during World War II, and formal education convinced him that modern philosophy had followed paths that were potentially both false and harmful. One of these paths is referred to as a "turn toward the subject" or "subjectivism." This aspect of modern philosophy, which has its roots in Descartes, concluded that we are certain about our thinking or "consciousness," but uncertain of the correspondence between our thinking about things and the things in themselves, including human persons. Undermined in the process were reason's confidence in previously mentioned anthropological and ethical notions, such as human fulfillment and the human dignity that makes this fulfillment and its preconditions normative.

However, John Paul also considered a turn toward the subject and interiority to be a potentially positive development, one that could fruitfully supplement the older, objective, and Thomistic philosophical approach. While this traditional approach supported ideas that John Paul endorsed, he was convinced that there were alternate methods capable of both supporting these aspects of experience and arriving at others. For example, he regarded Boethius' definition of a person as "an individual subsisting in a rational nature" as incapable of capturing important anthropological aspects such as human uniqueness and value, and the personal significance of freedom.

Accordingly, at the suggestion of a former theology professor, John Paul decided to investigate a methodological alternative known as phenomenology. The phenomenological movement was founded by German philosopher Edmund Husserl (1859–1938). Influenced by his mentor Franz Brentano's theories of intentionality and value, Husserl sought to counter the prevailing climate of post-Kantian idealism. Kant's epistemology resulted in the assertion of a radical divide between consciousness and reality, between things as they appear to us (*phenomena*) and things in themselves (*noumena*). Husserl, at least in his earlier works such as *Logical Investigations* (1900–01), posited that such a radical divide could be bridged through a suspension of the convictions that comprise one's "natural attitude" toward things and a precise description of consciousness' phenomena or appearances. The first step in such a description was the recognition that one's conscious experiences are always "intentional." In other words, conscious acts are always of or about something, focused on independently existing things given to one's consciousness. The next descriptive step was "imaginative variation," through which one removes various features from the objects of consciousness. While the removal of some features leaves the object intact, the removal of other features is experienced as eliminating the object and thus an aspect that is essential to the thing. Husserl deemed this latter experience to be an "eidetic intuition," an insight that such features belonged to the *eidos* or essence of the object. Max Scheler, a student of Husserl, took his mentor's thought in a new direction. Like many social critics of his time and the present, Scheler lamented the rise of individualism in modern societies. Influenced by moral philosopher Rudolph Eucken, who argued that human flourishing and unity were realized by ascribing to timeless spiritual values (i.e., virtues), Scheler sought to employ phenomenology ethically in order to more precisely describe these values and how they were apprehended. Scheler asserted that our experience of the essential features of an object of consciousness is always accompanied by affectivity, by an attraction or repulsion indicative of value or disvalue. Kant was thus wrong in insisting that our moral life was properly divorced from all inclinations. The phenomenological method disclosed that ethical mandates emerged from one's experience of things in themselves, including other persons.

Interested in both phenomenology and ethics, John Paul decided to do his post-dissertation thesis on Scheler. His review was mixed. While a few aspects of Scheler's ethical thought made it attractive to Catholics, John Paul concluded that Scheler's account of the moral life suffered from two problems. First, it put too much weight on discernment through emotions. More precisely, John Paul argued that affective responses were not always an accurate reflection of the value of values, and that one's valuation is not limited to such responses. On this latter point, he felt that reason, specifically one's conscience, plays a complementary and more definitive role than emotions in grasping the value of an object and act. A second problem with Scheler's account was its depiction of us as passive subjects of emotions rather than free and acting persons. Ultimately, John Paul concluded that these two errors—inattention to the phenomena of conscience and the will—were not the fault of phenomenology. They were the result of inattention to certain aspects of experience.

This critique of Scheler sparked John Paul's subsequent phenomenological reflections on human action and conscience. The aspects of these reflections germane to his social thought are the following, and there are seven of them. First, we are conscious of ourselves as free. While some phenomena, such as emotions and psychosomatic functions, happen to us, others—"acts"—are caused by us. Second, this experience of freedom implies that purely materialistic conceptions of the human person are incorrect. Third, the structure of acting is such that we are not only its cause, but also its effect. Actions inhere in the actor and affect one's ontological status and subsequent orientation vis-à-vis human fulfillment. For example, acts that involve physical and emotional phenomena happening in us (i.e., one's sexual urges) can result in a lack of fulfillment in oneself and others, and a limitation of one's freedom, or in the fruitful "integration" of these phenomena into one's being and subsequent choices so that the body and emotions positively reinforce the will's movement toward the right and the good. Fourth, as this reference to normative realities—the right and the good—indicates, some formative choices are experienced as better than others. Prior to the moment of willing, one experiences the cognitive and normative dimensions of conscience. After an act that conforms to the dictates of a well-formed conscience, one experiences a sense of well-being. Fifth, the nature of the truths that, when freely acted upon, result in this sense of well-being indicates that persons are fulfilled through the "free gift of self" that is oriented toward the good of others. Describing human sociality merely in terms of being affected by our human environment or needing the contributions of others is thus incomplete. Sixth, these normative truths point to goods that contribute to human fulfillment. Finally, one's experience of these normative realities reveals the metaphysical basis of the duty to secure human fulfillment and human goods. This basis is the value or dignity of all persons, a fact embodied in what John Paul calls in *Love and Responsibility* the "personalistic norm."

In addition to using phenomenology, John Paul insisted that his philosophical ethics was heavily indebted to various Thomists, including

Aquinas. Since John Paul's endorsement of two "opposing" schools is controversial and too complex to detail here, I will merely suggest that he considers Thomistic philosophy to be both enduringly important and fruitfully augmented and reinforced by alternative philosophical approaches. Ultimately, the best way of viewing this relationship is to see Aquinas as the guiding background to a phenomenologically informed description and analysis of human experience.

THEOLOGICAL ANTHROPOLOGY AND ETHICS

This notion of one set of ideas guiding another also applies to John Paul's theological anthropology and ethics. As mentioned earlier, in *Fides et Ratio*, his letter on faith and reason, he asserted that revelation and reason are both harmonious and complementary. On the one hand, reason assists faith in important ways, allowing us to interpret the data of revelation and verify its content. On the other hand, reason has natural limitations that are exacerbated by human sinfulness, and thus needs to be guided by the faith.

John Paul employed several theologically derived anthropological and ethical notions in order to guide his philosophizing and social thinking. First, the ethical precepts revealed through the Decalogue and Jesus' life confirm and radicalize what is given through one's conscience and direct experience. Second, Jesus' elevation of the virtue of charity further clarifies the nature of human fulfillment as self-donation. Third, this conception of human fulfillment and the dignity that makes it normative are revealed through the fact that we are made in the image of, and loved by, a God who is three distinct Persons nevertheless united through self-giving love. Fourth, Jesus' dual nature allays any doubt that we are persons in the same sense as the Persons of the Trinity. Finally, John Paul emphasized, particularly in his papal thought, a fifth revealed anthropological issue in order to explain both our difficulty with conforming our wills to normative realities and the subsequent need for grace, including revelation: original sin or human sinfulness.

SOCIAL THOUGHT

How do these philosophically and theologically derived ethical and anthropological notions undergird and thus explain John Paul's social thought? This section highlights relationships between these notions and three issues central to his social thought: the existence of human rights; the purpose and optimal form of the state; and the relationship between the state and non-state institutions.

John Paul's championing of human rights makes perfect sense in light of his philosophical and theological assertions. Because of their value, all persons are due the goods necessary to their fulfillment—rights. Because of the human propensity to disregard these goods, they must be circumscribed as such. Rights exist in two forms: negative and positive. Because of the formative effects of human acts, persons are due certain freedoms—the rights to life, to assent to and practice one's faith, to form and follow one's conscience, to associate, to marry and beget a family, to express oneself, and to possess and exchange material goods. Because of their relationships to the social nature of persons, associational and family rights were especially important to John Paul.

However, John Paul was not a libertarian. Freedoms ought to be exercised in ways that are fulfilling to others. Formulated differently, what is received from others conditions the use of freedom in either helpful or harmful ways. Persons thus possess positive rights that may require the curtailment of negative rights. Specifically, a just wage, an authentic culture, and the right to a united family may require the limitation of economic, expressive, and family-related choices.

These tensions bring us to the second issue: the role of the state. Simply put, John Paul asserted that the state exists in order to secure rights. He was thus a liberal. Because rule by the many is more likely to encourage both respect for the rights of the many and participation, John Paul endorsed democracy as the political form "most consonant with the dignity and nature of the person." However, he caveated this endorsement by saying that authentic democracies will possess certain cultural and institutional qualities, and that democracies must not misinterpret their reason for existence and embrace moral relativism.

But what kind of a liberal democrat was John Paul? In other words, which rights-securing state limitations on human freedom did he deem legitimate? I think the short answer is: it depends on the situation. His relationship to political liberalism was complex. As Catholic neoconservatives such as Michael Novak and George Weigel have highlighted, his defenses of religious freedom, expression, private property, and the market appear to solidly align him with classical liberals such as Locke, Mill, and Smith. But John Paul took positive rights seriously: he not only insisted that they exist, but also asserted that they fall under the purview of the state no less than negative rights. Thus, when necessary, he insisted that the state has the duty to: (1) protect culture from certain products and forms of expression; (2) impose legal constraints on employers; (3) offer unemployment assistance; and (4) even socialize the means of production. This would all point to the possibility that he was a welfare liberal—and a rather radical one at that.

His credentials as a welfare liberal, however, were compromised by his compunctions about using direct state action in order to secure positive economic and cultural rights. For example, he preferred non-state solutions to the problem of wages and working conditions, i.e., unions and joint ownership schemes. He emphasized indirect state action to prevent unemployment (i.e., pro-growth fiscal and monetary policies) and to help non-state institutions such as the family and charities help the unemployed. And he recommended that cultural transformation be effected through state policies supportive of families, churches, and schools, the primary culture-forming institutions.

This preference for "civil society" autonomy and support issues from the anthropologically informed logic undergirding the venerable "principle of subsidiarity"—the idea that lower and non-state institutions should be preferenced in solving social problems. A functionally limited state is likely to be both less corrupt and more capable. State intervention in the economy risks losing the benefits of private property and the free market. Non-state institutions, given their higher degrees of knowledge and concern, are often more capable performing necessary social functions. In fact, some non-state institutions, especially the family and the Church, are uniquely capable of encouraging and allowing the free self-donation that makes us fully human, and of thus promoting what he called a "culture of love."

ISLAM AND LIBERAL DEMOCRACY: FOUR ANALYSES

As the evolution of Catholic ethics and social theory indicates, a religious tradition can, with the help of scientific, historical, hermeneutical, and philosophical reason, reinterpret and augment its revealed corpus. In under a century, Catholicism radically but convincingly revised its conceptualizations of the preconditions to fulfillment and of the roles of the state and civil society in effecting human flourishing. We now turn to four influential Islamic thinkers who, using similar assumptions and strategies, have attempted to reconsider the relationship of their tradition to liberal democracy.

Abdul-Karim Soroush

Iranian pharmacologist and philosopher Abdul-Karim Soroush became famous, and infamous, in the 1990s for his defenses of scientific freedom and the "rational" study of religion. Founder of *Kiyan*, a monthly magazine dedicated to cultural reform, he was subsequently censored in 1998 and has spent much of the past decade as visiting professor at various universities in the United States and Germany.

The hermeneutic key to Soroush's thought is his post-positivist, postmodern view of reason.[7] While raised in a Shi'a culture that, compared to Sunni Islam, harbors fewer suspicions about the efficacy of reason, his thought is more indebted to Kuhn, Foucault, and perhaps Sufism than to the Mutazilites. Kuhn's philosophy of science, influenced by Kant's epistemology, posited that empirical observation is "theory laden"—preceded by received and unrecognized assumptions that structure what is subsequently "known." Since many of these assumptions are received from one's social environment, which includes language and conventions, "reality" is largely socially constructed and evolves as theoretical difficulties emerge and social determinants change.

Soroush applies postmodern epistemological assumptions to the interpretation of religious texts with stunning results. Religion, using his word, is "silent." The texts of the Quran and Hadith were colored by their worldview, and our interpretation of their worldview is irremediably colored by ours. The issue at hand, therefore, is not whether the intended meaning can be recovered from knowledge of context, but is, instead, which meaning we will ascribe to it. The assumptions we bring to the texts will be the philosophical, historical, theological, linguistic, and sociological constructions that comprise the "worldview of the age." Revelation itself may be divine. But inasmuch as these assumptions are socially determined and the interpretive process is socially adjudicated, religion is a social construct. And because these assumptions and their worldview are in continuous flux, the "voice of revelation" is actually multiple interpretations.

As a means of reconciling Islam and liberal democracy, I am inclined to judge Soroush's project as flawed—hermeneutically, ethically, and prudentially. First, while possessing the postmodern virtue of "rational modesty," his anti-reason hermeneutic may be erroneous. As we will discuss in our treatment of Rahman's dialogue with Gadamer (below), the recognition and transcendence of socially derived pretext may be possible, and thus allow a derivation of intended meaning.

Second, ethical relativism is an unacceptable posture for defending human rights, leaving no basis for even the relativist's call for a tolerant respect of difference. Aware of his theory's relativistic implications, Soroush responds to the Quranic warning against imposing one's views on texts by rejecting the use of "unsubstantiated theories" during our theory-laden interpretive process. But his epistemology rejects the possibility of substantiation in the first place. Ultimately, we are left without philosophically derived moorings and with a text interpreted according to changing conventions that may—or may not—allow one to derive human dignity and rights from revelation.

Finally, given the Islamic cultural climate, Soroush's project is imprudent. Current reaction to the West is anchored not only in perceived political and economic injustices, but also in the rejection of moral relativism, a rejection shared by many in the West, especially conservative Catholics and evangelical Protestants. Given this animus against the potential globalization of a postmodern sensibility, Soroush's arguments promise to generate scarce Muslim support and aggravate an already tense relationship with Western culture.

Abdullahai Ahmed An-Na'im

Like Soroush, Sudanese-born Emory Law School professor Abdullahai Ahmed An-Na'im takes context seriously. But unlike Soroush, he is somewhat sanguine about the effect of context on reason, and about the subsequent ability to apprehend authentic textual meaning through knowledge of context—present and past—and its effects.

The distinctive aspect of An-Na'im's thought is how his understanding of Quranic context leads him to emphasize certain parts of the text. Deeply influenced by Sudanese religious thinker Taha (executed in 1985 for his views), his argument has two major pillars. First, An-Na'im defends Taha's claim that the early Meccan period constituted the definitive "First Message" of Islam that should now be considered normative. This early period "recognized the inherent dignity of all human beings, regardless of gender, religious belief, race and so forth. That message was characterized by equality between men and women and complete freedom of choice in matters of religion and faith."[8] Regarding non-Muslims, the Meccan period's desired religious tolerance was only temporarily suspended until the imposition of law rendered defensive jihad unnecessary.

Second, since reason can be affected by social context, since slavery and religion/gender-based discrimination were conventional, and since the temporary needs of the later Medinan period were more closely aligned with these dominant values, the countercultural Meccan values were unrecognized as definitive, and could only improve the treatment of slaves, women, and non-Muslims. Shari'a subsequently developed from the Medinan period, supported by the principle of abrogation that preferenced later revelation. Accordingly, An-Na'im recommends "reverse abrogation" and the primacy of Meccan norms, which happen to be consistent with modern human rights.

An-Na'im's argument has several weaknesses, however. First, Muhammad's prudential reasons for instituting slavery and gender discrimination in the Meccan period are unspecified. Second, as several critics have highlighted, it is impossible to accurately distinguish earlier and later verses of the Quran. Although Meccan period pronouncements generally correspond to the concluding and shorter Quranic chapters, exegetes argue that Meccan verses are contained in the early chapters and vice versa. Third, and perhaps related to this problem, and as Sachedina has argued, many of the so-called Medinan verses are liberal, and many of the purported Meccan verses are anti-liberal.[9] Fourth, and most problematic, one can argue, as contemporary jihadists do, that conditions legitimizing anti-liberal norms are present now. In other words, an Islamic hermeneutic capable of supporting liberal democracy must consider the entire text, in addition to more carefully stipulating any prudential reasons for Muhammad's acceptance of anti-liberal practices.

Unfortunately, An-Na'im's recent effort is herculean, but wrought with even deeper problems.[10] Instead of offering an interpretive methodology and subsequent Islamic theory of human rights, he defends a secular state—one in which Shari'a is freely interpreted and lived—on historical and theoretical grounds. As others have commented, his historical account of religious freedom in Islam is strained. Most problematically, An-Na'im's theory merely assumes the truth of what needs to be proven: that, because of human fallibility and psychological and political dynamics, religious freedom is a precondition of the fulfillment to which all persons are entitled; that Muslims can somehow substantiate and develop this assertion through "hermeneutical or exegetical arguments"; and that other religiously inspired values can nevertheless be demonstrated and legislated in pluralistic societies if adequately supported by "civic reason." Regarding the latter, he is unclear about the nature of such ethical reasoning—natural law, overlapping consensus, or another framework—and its compatibility with Islam.

Fazlur Rahman

A more promising avenue to reconciling Islam and liberal democracy is the thought of the late Fazlur Rahman. Initially a professor of Islamic philosophy in England and Canada, Rahman returned to his native Pakistan in 1961 at the invitation of President Ayub Khan to staff and eventually lead the state-sponsored Central Institute of Islamic Research in Karachi. Enlisted by the President to promote the modernization of Islamic political theory and jurisprudence, Rahman was forced to leave Pakistan in 1969 due to conservative reactions to both his thought and Khan's governance. He arrived at the University of Chicago in late 1969 and remained there until his death in 1988.

While subtle and complex, Rahman's evaluation of Islamic theology is ultimately grounded in two assertions.[11] First, the historicity of some of the Hadith is dubious; and second, Islamic revelation has never been correctly interpreted and thus applied. As a Muslim and a serious scholar, Rahman councils moderation on this first point. On the one hand, he strongly opposes wholesale "anti-Hadith" skepticism, an extreme modernist position he believes is refuted by the Quran itself.[12] On the other hand, Rahman argues that Quranic textual evidence frequently militates against the normativity of certain Hadith. For example, citing Hasan al-Basri's early treatise on the issue of human free will, he argues that later tradition or orthodoxy attributing a doctrine of divine determinism to the words of the Prophet is an innovation, incompatible with both the Quran and the behavior of the Prophet and his Companions.[13] More broadly, and in agreement with Schlacht, Rahman asserts that new or expanded Traditions in later Hadith versions should be considered forgeries.[14] As a general but not inflexible rule, for the period after Hadiths were gathered he recommends the assignation of greater authenticity to earlier Hadith versions, especially since canonization resulted from problematic trans- missional evaluations and ideological concerns.[15] In addition to employ- ing historical criticism, he also recommends assessing historicity based on consistency with the "general spirit of the Quran"—an issue to be dis- cussed later.

Although Rahman does not dwell on the causes of Hadith innovations, he mentions the desires to sway public opinion, cultivate social stability, and address new moral and legal situations through a consensus of the experts' personal opinion (ra'y) or, slightly later, analogical reasoning (qiyas).[16] This latter point is particularly unique: Rahman is asserting that methods later used to compensate for the lack of clear revealed text were, earlier and with the endorsement of many scholars, used to create text.[17] Overall, Rahman argues that while the Quran itself attests to the possible validity of verbal and performative behavior of the Prophet outside of the Quran, the Prophetic Sunna, "outside of the fundamental matters touching the religious and the social and moral life of the Community, could not have been very large, let alone being of such titanic inclusive- ness of all the details of daily life as medieval law and Hadith literature make out to be the case."[18]

The second major pillar of his evaluation of Islamic theology involves the interpretation of what remains as normative, namely, the Prophetic Sunna and especially the Quran. Rahman's critiques of classical herme- neutics, of subsequent Shari'a and legislative developments, and of reviv- alists attempting to prescind to the classical period are sixfold. First, based on a Hadith according to which the Prophet purportedly affirmed that "[m]y Community shall never agree in error," the statuses of ijma' (the consensus of the religious scholars) and its conclusions were ele- vated from authoritative to infallible.[19]

Second, this consensus dictated interpreting the sources not holisti- cally, but in parts, an approach that Rahman deems "atomistic."[20] Although these parts often provided conflicting guidance that might have otherwise encouraged a holistic hermeneutic, the dominant doc- trines of the primacy of God's will and the subsequent inefficacy of human reason rendered these conflicts theoretically possible and accepta- ble, and required the principle of abrogation. These doctrines had their roots in the Kharajite opposition to the legitimacy of Umayyad rulers, coincided with the period's popular moral laxity, and reached their frui- tion in the debate over human free will between the Mutazilite and Asharite theological schools.[21] The Mutazilites insisted that the revealed fact of an afterlife compensation for earthly acts logically meant that a just God imparted human beings with responsibility and freedom.[22] To this argument they added direct human consciousness of choice. The

Asharites, on the other hand, countered that absolute divine omnipotence required divine determinism, thus nullifying the efficacy of both the will and reason. The remaining problems of human responsibility, our consciousness of freedom, and God's justice were, respectively, rationalized by al-Ashari's theory of "acquisition" (acts are produced by God but somehow attach themselves to the human will); by al-Ashari's speculation that our consciousness of owning acts is itself created by God; and by his insistence that God's justice could not be defined in human terms. Once this formulation of theological voluntarism was in place, the apparent inconstancy and incomprehensibility of God's commands only reinforced the argument for the inefficacy of human reason.

Rahman's third critique of classical theology deepens the effects of the second: while scholars could have agreed to interpret revealed texts allegorically, preference was given to interpreting these abrogated parts according to a "direct and commonsense meaning."[23] Fourth and related, this commonsense meaning was, consistent with the "custom-bound" Arab society of the time, heavily indebted to particularities of time and place.[24] Fifth, in the absence of clear textual guidance, dogmatic and normative judgments were gradually limited to consensus-approved cases of analogical reasoning from abrogated parts, particularly the reasoning of seventh-century Medinese jurists.[25] And sixth, largely in order to promote social stability, both dogma and law were fixed in the late ninth and early tenth centuries. More specifically, the consensus (*ijma'*) of scholars was employed to fix not only Prophetic revelation itself, but also interpretations (*ijtihad*) of the texts, including those derived via analogical reasoning (*qiyas*), thereby abolishing *ijma'* itself.[26]

Given this sketch of Rahman's two-pronged critique of the classical period, his constructive project—methodological, dogmatic, metaphysical, and ethical—is fairly apparent. First, he recommends renewed efforts to evaluate the historicity of the Hadith through historical criticism and even consistency with Quranic dictates, similar to the recent project at Ankara University.[27] Since much of Islamic ethics and legislation emerges from Hadith-derived Sunna, such a reassessment would deeply impact an Islamic theory of human rights and politics. Second (and relevant to this Hadith historicity project), Rahman argues for "a correct method of interpreting the Quran."[28] While endorsing the value of scholar consensus, he rejects the notion of the infallibility of *ijma'*, particularly the consensus of the late ninth and early tenth centuries. In place of this classical interpretation, he insists upon one derived from contemporary hermeneutical methods that consult linguistic and historical context, the entire text, and scientific data.

He establishes the importance of context based on two related assumptions grounded in historical data and the Quran itself. First, Muhammad's desire to address particular problems in seventh-century Arabia forms the backdrop of Islamic revelation, what Rahman calls the "occa-sions of revelation." Second, he maintains that while the Quran was indeed God's word, this word "flowed through the Prophet's heart," thereby linking these occasions of revelation with revelation itself.[29] Since the Quran is thus God's response, through Muhammad, to a historic sit-uation, Rahman insists that its authentic interpretation requires an under-standing of both the situation and Muhammad's consciousness of it.[30]

In opposition to Gadamer, Rahman argues that such an understanding is possible.[31] Gadamer asserted that all attempts to "objectively" under-stand a situation and author are doomed by an interpreter's predetermin-ing "effective history" that allows merely a "historical consciousness." Even an "effective-historical consciousness," possessed of an awareness of such predetermination, is merely capable of perspective, not knowl-edge. Rahman disagrees. Citing Christian and Islamic reformers, he points out that critique and modification of an effective history or tradi-tion "involves a consciousness of what is being criticized or rejected."[32] In other words, pretext presents an epistemological and interpretive chal-lenge, but not a barrier.

Rahman thus argues that the meaning of Islamic revelation is context dependent and comprehensible. He also insists that the Quran possesses an inner unity and consistency, and not only because the Quran explicitly states so.[33] Attention to historical context and the text as a whole also dis-closes that the issues of concern to Muhammad to which God responded were limited in scope. This unity undergirds Rahman's overall interpre-tive process, which consists of two "movements."[34] In the first, one derives "statements of general moral-social objectives that can be 'dis-tilled' from specific texts in light of the sociohistorical background and often-stated *rationes legis* [rationales]."[35] The second movement applies these general principles to the "present concrete sociohistorical context" in order to "implement the Quranic values afresh."[36] While the first movement is primarily the purview of the historian, the second is the work of the ethicist and social scientist.[37]

What, then, are the general principles emerging from such a hermeneu-tic? Ultimately, Rahman finds that all of them are related to the "central concern of the Quran," which is "the conduct of man."[38] Accordingly, in the crucial realm of metaphysics, which is the "ground of values," he argues for a revision of the orthodox doctrines of God and human free-dom. Within the context of the early Umayyad's politically motivated ad-vocacy of determinism, Rahman deems the al-Basri and Mutazilite defenses of free will both necessary and legitimate. But based on the Quran, he also critiques excessive Mutazilite humanism, especially the negation of God's attributes, the limitation of God's power to the natural world, and the denial of God's forgiveness. However, he ultimately laments the harmful and anti-Quranic overreach of the subsequent Asharite response:

> And, even more so, who could claim that the Asharite reaction in terms of the doc-
> trine of the omnipotence of God at the expense of all human power and will, of the
> purposelessness of divine commands and moral prohibitions, of making works
> essentially irrelevant to faith, of the denial of cause and effect, and, consequently,
> the elevation of atomism to the position of a cardinal principle . . . was representa-
> tive of the Quranic teaching on God, man, and nature?[39]

Given this understanding of both the context-driven function of the deterministic tradition and the overall Quranic spirit, he recommends revisions to the Islamic worldview that include two elements: a doctrine of God that reconciles divine omnipotence with human freedom, with the stability and goodness of divine commands, and with the laws of na-ture; and an affirmation of human freedom, both metaphysically and normatively.[40]

The stability and goodness of divine commands imply, respectively, two things. First, since only a fixed ethical realm is amenable to human reason, these commands are knowable, at least in theory. Second, since these commands are a function of the human good, human fulfillment and its preconditions are imbued with normativity. In other words, Islam possesses a theistically based conception of human duties, dignity, and corresponding negative and positive rights in addition to one's duties to, and the rights of, God.

According to Rahman, the duty-based ethics of the Quran is, specifi-cally, a reformist "divine response, through the Prophet's mind, to the moral-social situation of the Prophet's Arabia, particularly to the prob-lems of the commercial society of his day."[41] At its core, this response is egalitarian, and accordingly focused on one's socioeconomic duties to, and the subsequent rights of, all others.[42] But since man is free but also an "obdurate rebel," the Quran provided the necessary moral motivation: respect for, and fear of, God.[43] In his words, "no real morality is possible without the regulative ideas of God and the Last Judgment."[44] For Rah-man, then, the Quran's central moral goal is to induce a state of *taqwa*, or "God-fearingness" or consciousness, in order to orient the free will to-ward human fulfillment and rights.

Given this ethical and moral motivational centrality, Rahman argues that Muhammad's primary mission was moral reform, not legislation.[45] In Thomistic terms, the emphasis was on divine law, not human law. He notes that "the strictly legislative portion of the Quran is actually quite small."[46] Regarding legal injunctions about relationships with non-Muslims, he deems these too situational to award any one with overarch-ing legal status. Other enactments, such as those concerning women and slavery, need to be understood in context. He argues "whereas the spirit of Quranic legislation exhibits an obvious direction towards the progressive embodiment of the fundamental human values of freedom and responsibility in fresh legislation, nevertheless the actual legislation of the Quran had partly to accept the then existing society as a term of reference. This clearly means that the actual legislation of the Quran cannot have been meant to be literally eternal by the Quran itself."[47] Dominant norms imparted practical constraints to be transcended later, a strategy found in Aquinas' discussion of the relationship between natural law and human law.[48] Accordingly, Rahman calls for legal reforms that better differentiate the ethical and legal, and then link them "organically" with regard for social particularities.[49]

Rahman's resulting political theology is, however, somewhat unclear. He argues that Islamic ethics supports human rights, including religious freedom. As social situations permit, therefore, legislation should embody the liberal values of human dignity and freedom. But his emphases on both the fallibility of ethical cognition and the necessity of God-consciousness for moral motivation incline against secularism. Ultimately, he seems to recommend a form of "soft establishment" for Islamic societies, with a focus on state support for reformed educational institutions.[50]

However, while Rahman's position on moral motivation, and even some forms of establishment, are not necessarily problematic for liberalism, his position on moral cognition presents a greater challenge for Islamic liberalism. His anti-reason stance is consistent with a broader "epistemological crisis" within Sunni Islam described by Sachedina.[51] While liberal strands of Sunni Islam allow the use of reason for logical and some interpretive tasks, reason is still deemed ineffectual for independently formulating a philosophical ethics that could guide interpretation and augment revelation. Rahman seems to hold a similar, Maturidite position: reason can apprehend the truth of revealed norms and thus motivate adherence to faith, but not independently access a natural law.[52] Wedded to such a position, Sunni ethics and political theory will likely remain primarily theological, divine command-centric, and anchored to contentious debates over historical contexts and Muhammad's disposition toward them.[53]

George Hourani

Although not a practicing Muslim, George Hourani was an esteemed philosopher and sympathetic scholar of Islam. Born in England to nationalized Lebanese Christian parents, he studied classics and modern philosophy at Oxford, completed graduate studies in Princeton's Department of Oriental Studies, and taught classics and philosophy at the Government Arab College in Jerusalem until the British mandate ended in 1948. He taught in the Department of Near Eastern Studies at the University of Michigan from 1950 until 1967, focusing his research on philosophical ethics and Islamic philosophy, and then moved to the SUNY Buffalo Department of Philosophy, where he taught until retiring in 1983.

While also a defender of the Mutazilite position on human freedom, Hourani focuses on the possibility and efficacy of human reason. Specifically, his primary goal is to validate, on Islamic theological grounds, the ontological and epistemological preconditions for an Islamic theory of natural law. Considering Islamic ontology as it impacts ethics, Hourani challenges the orthodox view that ethically relevant facts are necessarily linked to God's will in a way that precludes their immutability and thus intelligibility. According to Hourani's historical reconstruction, Shafii's dismissal of independent reasoning, and insistence that ethics and jurisprudence be anchored to revelation or its extensions derived through analogical reasoning, developed into the theologically grounded Asharite position of "ethical voluntarism."[54] An assumption of absolute divine omnipotence, which logically precluded a fixed ethical realm accessible to human reason, reigned supreme after the eleventh century suppression of Mutazilism.[55]

While acknowledging the Quranic emphases on the strength and primacy of God's will, and on human fallibility, Hourani's critique of what he, echoing Ibn Rushd, deems "theological subjectivism" is threefold. First, echoing Mutazilites, he insists that nothing in the Quran precludes a more moderate view of divine power consistent with human freedom and ethical "objectivism."[56] Second and more directly, "the Quran frequently refers to objective values, which cannot be analyzed completely in terms of commands and obedience." Third, Hourani notes that human fallibility neither implies nor requires a metaphysics marked by teleological instability or shifting degrees of human dignity. In other words, it is entirely possible that a fixed ethical realm is nevertheless inaccessible to human reason, and accessible solely through revelation.[57]

This epistemological issue is Hourani's second major consideration, and his conclusions are more nuanced. On the possibility that all people (an "extreme" position), or an elite ("modified" view), can *always* apprehend ethical truths via reason, he finds the Quran, with its emphasis on passion-induced error, decisively critical.[58] However, for several reasons, including appeals to pagan moral responsibility and the lack of explicit refutation of rationalism, he deems it "quite probable" that the Quran affirms the possibility of ethical reasoning independent of revelation.[59] Belief and ethical acts are tightly affiliated, but inasmuch as their affiliation is attributable to difficulties with moral cognition and not moral motivation, belief is neither a necessary nor sufficient cause of ethical acts.

RECOMMENDATIONS

In this chapter I have attempted to refine the ideological component of an adequate strategy to counter Salafism, arguing that the primary goal should be neither public diplomacy nor secularization, but instead theological and philosophical reform in support of an Islamic theory of human rights. While Islamic liberals have been hindered by interpretation-limiting theological notions, Rahman's and Hourani's sympathetic critiques of the tradition suggest four areas for future theoretical inquiry.

First, a doctrine of God's omnipotence compatible with human freedom and ethical objectivism must be more fully elaborated. Second, the normativity of metaphysical freedom must be defended, perhaps using Quranic appeals to virtue ethics.[60] Third, perhaps assisted by the venerable notions of equity and public welfare, Islamic theology must develop the ability to employ natural law precepts and natural rights as hermeneutic tools. Fourth, Islamic theology must develop a more constrained conception of the necessary relationship between ethics and legislation.

While further analysis is also needed to refine the practical means to promote such reform, two guidelines bear consideration. First, given Islamic post-colonial sensitivities, Western reform efforts should be discreet. For example, using Cold War counter-ideology strategy as template, a recent RAND analysis recommends channeling assistance through U.S. and foreign NGOs in order to help liberal culture-forming actors and institutions, i.e., academics, scholars, writers, schools, madrassas, and universities.[61] Deemphasized is the State Department penchant for public diplomacy through television and radio. Second, executing these measures will require not only additional resources, but also cultural reform of the State Department. Concern for open communication channels with elites and foreign public opinion must be matched with serious interest in religious matters, and with the moral clarity and courage to engage in that most delicate human endeavor: respectful disagreement.

NOTES

1. Michael J. Perry, *Toward a Theory of Human Rights: Religion, Law, Courts* (New York: Cambridge University Press

2. The relationship of duties to rights is complicated and contested. While some duties may not correspond to rights, I will merely assert that some duties do imply rights.

3. The argument is based on two related premises. The first is that laws, including laws legitimizing forms of legal decision-making (i.e., constitutions), have a pedagogical effect and function. Consciences are formed not only through culture-forming institutions that affect law, but by law itself. Second, constitutionally sanctioned democracies can affect consciences, and thus inform lawmaking and legal interpretation, in ways perhaps inimical to even

constitutionally articulated rights. An egalitarian political decision-making system may be misinterpreted as implying the equal validity of all opinions, or may exaggerate intellectual self-reliance and confidence, resulting in a culture permeated by moral relativism, materialism, and secularism. The majority may gradually believe that such notions are the foundational principles of democracy and guarantors of its social peace and that less skeptical viewpoints lead to intolerance and authoritarianism. In such a cultural milieu, freedom is individualistically deployed in service of one's autonomously defined conceptions of morality and the good life.

4. For communitarians such as MacIntyre, liberalism is a political philosophy that, for a variety of reasons, extols individual autonomy or separation from others, and circumscribes this autonomy through state-protected individual rights. Such an atomistic anthropology, imparted and/or reinforced through pedagogically significant laws, is obviously antithetical to the various ways in which persons are social. A political emphasis on rights—in contradistinction to an emphasis on the good and one's duties to contribute to the provision of certain goods—will promote a notion of an "unencumbered" self who constructs his own identity and moral universe, has minimal obligations to others, and is fulfilled through self-promotion. Attendant to this anthropology is not only a negative conception of rights, but a negative conception of freedom, i.e., freedom *from* versus freedom *for*.

For theoconservatives such as Schindler, laws protecting religious liberty constitute an "initial moment of silence" about the veracity and importance of religious ideas and practices. A well-intentioned Catholic such as Murray, who nevertheless defends the First Amendment, "fails to build positive relation to God into the first meaning he accords the human act in his proposals for the public (constitutional) order." This failure stems from a previous, ontological error: an inadequate understanding of our "creatureliness." Liberalism understands the "basic act" of the human being to be "'creativity' or 'self-determination,'" while "creatureliness properly understood implies that our being is *constitutively related to God* . . . not by virtue of what the *self* first *does* but by virtue of what is first *done to* the self by *God* (the divine *Other*)." The effects of this ontology extend beyond those associated with the capitalist market, which derives from an anthropology extolling creativity and initiative and thus encourages selfishness and domination. The resulting "initial silence" about religion means that "worldviews that favor silence about God in the affairs of the earthly or temporal order therefore always retain a theoretical advantage over worldviews that favor speech about God." Since God's grace is necessary for the perfection of nature (specifically, for the guidance of reason and proper orientation of the will), this political silence about religion concretizes a deadly "nature-grace dualism." Shorn of grace, the human condition degrades into skepticism about all but the material, consumerism, moral relativism, self-centeredness, unhappiness, and social conflict that preference the strong. The "ontological self-centeredness and hence implicit a-theism" at the core of "even the most benign forms of Anglo-American liberalism" are thus "the source of what John Paul II describes as the 'culture of death' and Balthasar as the culture that results from the abstraction of nature (human being) from its original creaturely context." See David

Schindler, *Heart of the World, Center of the Church: Communio Ecclesiology, Liberalism, and Liberation* (Grand Rapids: Eerdmans, 1996); and his *"Communio* Ecclesiology and Liberalism," *Review of Politics* 60, no. 4 (Fall 1998): 743–64 (emphasis in original). A well-intentioned Catholic such as Murray, who nevertheless defends the First Amendment, "fails to build positive relation to God into the first meaning he accords the human act in his proposals for the public (constitutional) order." This failure stems from a previous, ontological error: an inadequate understanding of our "creatureliness." Liberalism understands the "basic act" of the human being to be "'creativity' or 'self-determination,'" while "creatureliness properly understood implies that our being is constitutively related to God . . . not by virtue of what the self first does but by virtue of what is first done to the self by God (the divine Other)." The effects of this ontology extend beyond those associated with the capitalist market, which derives from an anthropology extolling creativity and initiative and thus encourages selfishness and domination. The resulting "initial silence" about religion means that "worldviews that favor silence about God in the affairs of the earthly or temporal order therefore always retain a theoretical advantage over worldviews that favor speech about God." Since God's grace is necessary for the perfection of nature (specifically, for the guidance of reason and proper orientation of the will), this political silence about religion concretizes a deadly "nature-grace dualism." Shorn of grace, the human condition degrades into skepticism about all but the material, consumerism, moral relativism, self-centeredness, unhappiness, and social conflict that preference the strong. The "ontological self-centeredness and hence implicit a-theism" at the core of "even the most benign forms of Anglo-American liberalism" are thus "the source of what John Paul II describes as the 'culture of death' and Balthasar as the culture that results from the abstraction of nature (human being) from its original creaturely context." See David Schindler, Heart of the World, Center of the Church: Communio Ecclesiology, Liberalism, and Liberation (Grand Rapids: Eerdmans, 1996); and his "Communio Ecclesiology and Liberalism," *Review of Politics* 60, no. 4 (Fall 1998): 743–64 (emphasis in original).

5. Thus, contrary to communitarian characterizations, a rights-based polity is not the product or cause of theological/philosophical skepticism and a resulting odious self-conception. On the contrary, a commitment to protecting certain rights is necessarily the product of prior theological and philosophical commitments, i.e., the validity of certain normative precepts and the dignity of all persons. The anthropological conception undergirding and suggested by this analysis of human rights is thus far different from that attributed to liberalism by MacIntyre or Schindler. Liberal societies put theoretical and practical limits on self-legislation and the use of one's freedom. Positive rights mean that one has the duty to do more than just leave others alone; citizens, acting individually or through non-state and political associations, also have responsibilities to the "common good." Finally, associational rights imply that human beings are not merely conflictual monads.

And contrary to theoconservative assertions, the legal protection of religious freedom is neither grounded in nor implies "a-theism." One can maintain that a relationship to God is the most important of the preconditions to human fulfillment, but insist that the formative effect of human action means that one is due the freedom to enter into such a relationship. Additionally, since this relationship with God is enhanced by entering into an ecclesial relationship with others, one is also due the freedom to associate within a church that, in turn, is itself due freedom from interference by others, including the state. While this arrangement may deny the state a pedagogical moment officially affirming the validity of a religious worldview, it also affords individuals and churches the perpetual possibility of publicly proposing their worldviews, even in political contexts.

6. See Brian Tierney, *The Idea of Natural Rights: Studies on Natural Rights, Natural Law, and Church Law, 1150–1625* (Grand Rapids: William B. Eerdmans, 2001), especially Chapters 2, 11, and 12.

7. In English, Soroush's thought can be accessed in Abdul-Karin Soroush, *Reason, Freedom, and Democracy in Islam: Essential Writings of Abdul-Karim Soroush*, trans. M. Sadri and A. Sadri (Oxford: Oxford University Press, 2000).

8. Abdullahai Ahmed An-Na'im, *Toward an Islamic Reformation: Civil Liberties, Human Rights, and International Law* (Syracuse: Syracuse University Press, 1990).

9. See Abdulaziz Sachedina, *The Islamic Roots of Democratic Pluralism* (New York: Oxford University Press, 2001).

10. Abdullahai Ahmed An-Na'im, *Islam and the Secular State: Negotiating the Future of Shari'a* (Cambridge: Harvard University Press, 2008).

11. The subtlety of Rahman's thought sometimes borders on ambiguity. He occasionally seems to support two contradictory positions or weakly support one position. However, I would interpret his approach as one of "caution," and attribute it to both his uncomfortable experience in Pakistan and his association with the University of Chicago's Committee on Social Thought when Leo Strauss' thought was regnant. But while his approach may be "Straussian," I see no evidence of a "two truths" philosophical-theological position associated with Ibn Sina and Strauss. See Leo Strauss, *Persecution and the Art of Writing* (Chicago: University of Chicago Press, 1988).

12. Fazlur Rahman, *Islam* (Chicago: University of Chicago Press, 2002), 48, 50–51.

13. Rahman, *Islam*, 48, 243. See also Fazlur Rahman, "The Living Sunna and al-Sunnah wal Jamah," in *Hadith and Sunnah: Ideals and Realities*, ed. P. K. Koya (Kuala Lampur: Islamic Book Trust, 2003), 171–73.

14. Rahman, *Islam*, 47.

15. Ibid., 49, 64–65.

16. Ibid., 49, 56–57, 74–77. Determinism, for example, lent legitimacy to Umayyad rule. See Ibid., 57. Note that the assertion is analogical reasoning was used not only to interpret the canon, but to construct it.

17. Fazlur Rahman, *Islamic Methodology in History* (Karachi: Central Institute of Islamic Research, 1965).

18. Rahman, *Islam*, 50–52.

19. Ibid., 74.

20. Fazlur Rahman, *Islam & Modernity: Transformation of an Intellectual Tradition* (Chicago: University of Chicago Press, 1982), 2, 101. See also Fazlur Rahman, *Major Themes of the Quran* (Minneapolis: Bibliotheca Islamica, 1989), xi.

21. Rahman, *Islam*, 85–99.

22. The Mutazilite appeal to God's justice in defense of human freedom seems odd given their critique of divine attributes/qualities in defense of God's unity, a critique that logically led to their position that the Quran was not the eternal word of God but was instead created.

23. Rahman, *Islam*, 73.

24. Rahman, *Islam & Modernity*, 17.

25. Rahman, *Islam*, 72–74 and *Islam & Modernity*, 2.

26. Rahman, *Islam*, 77.

27. Ibid., 250.

28. Rahman, *Islam & Modernity*, 1.

29. Rahman, *Islam*, 16, 31–33.

30. This notion of inspiration and the subsequent necessity of interpretation resembles that of the Second Vatican Council document *Dei Verbum*: "The divinely revealed realities, which are contained and presented in the text of sacred Scripture, have been written down under the inspiration of the Holy Spirit. To compose the sacred books, God chose certain men who, all the while he employed them in this task, made full use of their own powers and faculties so that, though he acted in them and by them, it was as true authors that they consigned to writing whatever he wanted written, and no more" (para. 11). I am indebted to George Weigel for this insight.

31. Hans George Gadamer, *Truth and Method* (New York: Seabury Press, 1975).

32. Rahman, *Islam & Modernity*, 10.

33. Ibid., 6, 143.

34. Ibid., 5–9, 139

35. Ibid., 6. See also 20.

36. Ibid., 7. See also 20.

37. Ibid., 7.

38. Ibid., 14. See also Rahman, *Islam*, 98–99.

39. Rahman, *Islam & Modernity*, 152. See also Rahman, "The Living Sunna," 182–83 and *Islam*, 85, 242.

40. On the explanatory power of considering context-driven functions as a source of doctrine, see Rahman, *Islam & Modernity*, 182–83. Rahman's concept of the nature of God's omnipotence resembles Mutazilism and later Maturidism. See Rahman, *Islam*, 93 and *Islam & Modernity*, 152.

41. Rahman, *Islam & Modernity*, 5.

42. See Rahman, *Islam*, 12–13, 15, 25, 32.

43. Ibid., 15, 85, 241 and *Islam & Modernity*, 5, 14, 155.

44. Rahman, *Islam & Modernity*, 14.

45. Ibid., 37, 83.

46. Ibid., 16.

47. Ibid., 39.

48. Ibid., 38–39, 232.

49. Rahman, *Islam*, 256 and *Islam & Modernity*, 154–55.

50. Rahman's educational reforms recommend the integration of religious studies with modern historical, philosophical, and scientific disciplines, versus the dominant approach that simply supplements traditional religious studies with modern ones. See Rahman, *Islam and Modernity*, chapters 3 and 4.

51. Sachedina, *The Islamic Roots of Democratic Pluralism*, 57–62.

52. Rahman, *Islam & Modernity*, 134–35, 155–56. I am indebted to John Kelsay for this insight.

53. On the other hand, while Shi'as are less suspicious of independent reason, they labor under controversy over who is allowed to accomplish theological interpretation.

54. George Hourani, *Reason and Tradition in Islamic Ethics* (Cambridge: Cambridge University Press, 1985), 8, 16–17.

55. Ibid., 57, 273.

56. Ibid., 18, 28.

57. Ibid., 28, 44, 64.

58. Ibid., 37–43.

59. Ibid., 43–45.

60. Ibid., 15, 21, 45, 270.

61. Angel Rabasa, Cheryl Benard, Lowell H. Schwartz, Peter Sickle, *Building Moderate Muslim Networks* (Santa Monica: RAND Corporation, 2007).

Index

About the Contributors

Benjamin T. Acosta is currently working on a Ph.D. in political science at Claremont Graduate University. He holds Master of Arts degrees in Middle East studies from Ben-Gurion University of the Negev and in national security studies from California State University-San Bernardino. He has conducted research in Israel and the Disputed Territories, Lebanon, Syria, Morocco, and Dearborn and Detroit, Michigan. His primary research interests include Middle East security, political Islam, suicide terrorism, and Palestinian politics and society.

Robert P. Barnidge, Jr., a lecturer in the School of Law at the University of Reading, received his Ph.D. from Queen's University Belfast in 2007. He recently published the book *Non-State Actors and Terrorism: Applying the Law of State Responsibility and the Due Diligence Principle* (The Hague: T.M.C. Asser Press, distributed by Cambridge University Press, 2008), and has published in such journals as *Israel Yearbook on Human Rights, Critical Studies on Terrorism, International Journal of Refugee Law, International Community Law Review, Irish Studies in International Affairs*, and *African Human Rights Law Journal*. His research interests include international law and terrorism, the law of state responsibility, and the relationship between international law and politics.

Edward T. Barrett is director of research at the U.S. Naval Academy's Stockdale Center for Ethical Leadership, and an ethics professor in the Academy's Department of Leadership, Ethics, and Law. A graduate of the University of Notre Dame, he completed a Ph.D. in political theory at the University of Chicago. He is the author of *Personalistic Liberalism: The Ethical and Political Thought of Karol Wojtyla/John Paul II* (forthcoming, Lexington). While in graduate school, he served for two years as a speechwriter to the Catholic Archbishop of Chicago and was an adjunct professor at the University of Chicago. He served for nine years with the U.S. Air Force on active duty as a C-130 instructor and examiner pilot, and is currently serving in the U.S. Air Force Reserve. He has completed four deployments as an operations officer and aircraft commander in Operation Enduring Freedom and Operation Iraqi Freedom, and is now at the Pentagon in the Air Force's Division of Long Range Plans.

Patrick Clawson is deputy director for research at the Washington Institute for Near East Policy. He is the author or editor of twenty-four books and monographs, as well as more than seventy articles about the Middle East and international economics and op-ed articles in major newspapers. His books include, with Michael Rubin, *Eternal Iran: Continuity and Chaos* (New York: Palgrave Macmillan, 2005) and, edited with Henry Sokolski, *Getting Ready for a Nuclear- Ready Iran* (Carlisle, PA: Strategic Studies Institute of the U.S. Army War College, 2005). He has testified before congressional committees more than twenty times and has been an expert witness in more than a dozen federal cases. Dr. Clawson holds a Ph.D. in economics from the New School for Social Research.

David Cook is associate professor of religious studies at Rice University, specializing in Islam. He received his Ph.D. from the University of Chicago in 2001. His areas of specialization include early Islamic history and development, Muslim apocalyptic literature and movements, radical Islam, historical astronomy, and Judeo-Arabic literature. His first book, *Studies in Muslim Apocalyptic* (2003), was published by Darwin Press. Two volumes, *Understanding Jihad* (Berkeley: University of California Press) and *Contemporary Muslim Apocalyptic Literature* (Syracuse: Syracuse University Press), were published in 2005. Recent books include *Martyrdom in Islam* (Cambridge: Cambridge University Press, 2007) and, with Olivia Allison, *Understanding and Addressing Suicide Attacks* (Westport: Praeger Security International, 2007).

Timothy R. Furnish earned his Ph.D. in Islamic history from Ohio State University and taught college history for seven years. He served in the U.S. Army as an Arabic interrogator and a commissioned chaplain. His research interests are Islamic eschatology, especially Mahdism, Islamic sects, the caliphate, pan-Islamic ideologies, African Islam, and jihadism. He is the author of *Holiest Wars: Islamic Mahdis, Their Jihads and Osama bin Laden* (Westport: Greenwood, 2005) and is currently writing a book on the caliphate, particularly competing modern plans for resurrecting it.

He operates a Web site dedicated to tracking Mahdist claims and movements: www.mahdiwatch.org.

Mohammed Hafiz is a Ph.D. candidate at the Asia Institute of the University of Melbourne. He is a recipient of the Melbourne International Fee Remission Scholarship and the Melbourne International Research Scholarship. He previously worked as a senior research assistant at the Institute of African Studies at the University of Ghana. His current research focuses on the teaching of the Arabic language and its development in the Kumasi region of Ghana.

Sherko Kirmanj is a Ph.D. candidate in the School of International Studies at the University of South Australia in Adelaide, Australia. His areas of interest are Islamism, nationalism, and ethnic conflict. He is the author of *Politicisation of Islam: The Phenomenon of Islamism* (Suleimaniya: Sardam House for Publishing and Printing, 2005). His recent publications include "Islam, Politics, and Government" in the journal *Totalitarian Movements and Political Religions*, "The Relationship Between Traditional and Contemporary Islamist Political Thought" in *Middle East Review of International Affairs*, and "The Clash of Identities in Iraq" in A. Baram and R. Zeidel, eds., *Iraq: Past and Present* (New York: Routledge, 2009).

Terence J. Kleven teaches in the Department of Religion and Philosophy at Central College, Pella, Iowa, and is chair of the Division of the Humanities. He graduated from McMaster University, Hamilton, Ontario, Canada with a Ph.D. in religious studies. He was a Bradley Fellow at Boston College, a Yad Hanadiv/Barecha Fellow at the Hebrew University of Jerusalem, a National Endowment for the Humanities Fellow at the American Research Center in Egypt, and was selected as the Carnegie Foundation's 2001 U.S. Professor of the Year for Iowa. He has published articles on Arabic Political Philosophy, in particular on Alfarabi, Maimonides, and Ibn Daud, in *Interpretation: A Journal of Political Philosophy* and *American Research Center in Egypt Bulletin*, and has published book reviews on Greek and Arabic Philosophy for *Mind* and *Journal of the History of Philosophy*. He has also published on philosophy and liturgy in the recent volume in honor of Reverend Dr. Robert D. Crouse. He has presented papers at the international congresses of the Société Internationale d'Histoire des Sciences et la Philosophie Arabes et Islamic and the Société Internationale pour l'Étude de la Philosophie Médiévale. He is currently editing and translating a number of Alfarabi's logical writings.

Daniel J. Lav is a graduate student in Islamic and Middle Eastern studies at the Hebrew University of Jerusalem, and is director of the Jihad and Terrorism Threat Monitor, a division of the Middle East Media Research

Institute (MEMRI). His research focuses on contemporary Salafi jihadist movements and ideology. He is co-author, with Pessah Shinar, of "Three Stages in Algerian Islamism: From Reformist Salafism to Al-Qaeda by Way of the Islamic Salvation Front (FIS)," forthcoming in Aharon Layish, ed., *Conversion, Sufism, Revival, and Reform in Islam: Essays in Memory of Nehemia Levtzion* (in Hebrew).

Joseph C. Myers is a career infantry and Latin America foreign area officer in the United States Army. Previous duties include chief of the South America Division and senior military analyst for Colombia at the Defense Intelligence Agency; 2004 senior Army fellowship at the George C. Marshall European Center for Security Studies; Air Command and Staff College Joint Forces instructor; and instructor, Joint Special Operations University's Combating Terrorism and Irregular Warfare programs. He holds a Bachelor of Science from West Point and a Master of Arts from Tulane University. He is completing his Ph.D. dissertation in public policy at Auburn University and the Certificate Program in Homeland Security at Texas A&M. Currently, he is serving as a political-military officer deployed with U.S. Forces–Afghanistan. His publications and commentary have appeared in *Parameters: The Journal of the Army War College, DefenseNews, Congressional Quarterly, American Thinker,* and *Frontpage Magazine,* among others.

Philip Carl Salzman is a socio-cultural anthropologist and professor of anthropology at McGill University in Canada. Dr. Salzman has authored and edited numerous scholarly articles and books, including the recently released *Culture and Conflict in the Middle East* (Amherst, NY: Humanity Books, 2008) and *Black Tents of Baluchistan* (Washington, DC: Smithsonian Press, 2000). He has contributed to a more general treatment of pastoral nomads and tribes, discussed in *Pastoralists: Equality, Hierarchy, and the State* (Boulder: Westview Press, 2004). His interests in nomadic peoples led him to organize the Commission on Nomadic Peoples of the International Union of Anthropological and Ethnological Sciences, and to found the international journal *Nomadic Peoples.* Dr. Salzman's current research on the compatibility of ultimate value objectives focuses on freedom and equality, and the ways in which these are reconciled or balanced in societies around the world, such as among nomadic tribes in the Middle East and Africa.

Ofira Seliktar is professor of political science at Gratz College and adjunct professor at Temple University. She was previously associated with the Middle East Research Institute at the University of Pennsylvania and served as a visiting professor in the National Security Studies Program at Tel Aviv University. Dr. Seliktar specializes in Middle East and intelligence studies. She is the author of scores of articles and chapters as well as seven books, including *Failing the Crystal Ball Test: The Carter Administration and the Fundamentalist Revolution in Iran* (Westport: Praeger, 2000), *Politics, Paradigms and Intelligence: Why So Few Predicted the Collapse of the Soviet Union* (Armonk, NY: M.E. Sharpe, 2004), *The Politics of Intelligence and American Wars with Iraq* (New York: Palgrave Macmillan, 2008), and *Doomed to Failure: The Politics and Intelligence of the Oslo Peace Process* (Westport: Praeger, 2009). She is currently completing a book entitled *The Politics of Intelligence and American Encounters with Islamist Iran, 1979–2009.*

George L. Simpson, Jr. is professor of history and chair of the History Department at High Point University in High Point, North Carolina, where he teaches undergraduate and graduate classes in African and Middle East history. He was a Fulbright-Hayes scholar in Kenya. He has published articles on African and Middle East history in academic journals such as *International Journal of African Historical Studies* and *Journal of Imperial and Commonwealth History, Northeast African Studies*. Currently, Dr. Simpson and the Kenyan historian Peter Waweru are in the final stages of editing a manuscript for the monograph *Fathers and Sons: A History of the Samburu through 1963.*

Joseph Morrison Skelly is treasurer of the Association for the Study of the Middle East and Africa. An associate professor of history at the College of Mount Saint Vincent in New York City, he specializes in diplomatic history, international terrorism, and military affairs. His books include, with Richard English, *Ideas Matter: Essays in Honour of Conor Cruise O'Brien* (Dublin: Poolbeg Press, 1998) and, with Michael Kennedy, *Irish Foreign Policy, 1919–1966: From Independence to Internationalism* (Dublin: Four Courts Press, 2000). He has published articles and reviews in scholarly journals such as *International Journal of Intelligence and Counterintelligence, Middle East Quarterly*, and *Israel Journal of Foreign Affairs*, and essays for the *Washington Times, National Review Online*, and *United Press International*. An officer in the United States Army Reserve, he has completed a tour of duty in Operation Iraqi Freedom.